THINKING FOR YOURSELF

W9-ADX-500

Developing Critical Thinking Skills Through Reading and Writing

Fifth Edition

Marlys Mayfield

College of Alameda

Harcourt College Publishers

Fort Worth   Philadelphia   San Diego   New York   Orlando   Austin
San Antonio   Toronto   Montreal   London   Sydney   Tokyo

Publisher	Earl McPeek
Acquisitions Editor	Stephen Dalphin
Market Strategist	John Meyers
Developmental Editor	Jill Johnson
Project Manager	Andrea Archer

Cover credit: Candice Carta, York Production Services

ISBN: 0-15-506256-5
Library of Congress Catalog Card Number: 00-106316

Address for Domestic Orders
Harcourt College Publishers, 6277 Sea Harbor Drive,
Orlando, FL 32887-6777
800-782-4479

Address for International Orders
International Customer Service
Harcourt College Publishers, 6277 Sea Harbor Drive,
Orlando, FL 32887-6777
407-345-3800
(fax) 407-345-4060
(e-mail) hbintl@harcourtbrace.com

Address for Editorial Correspondence
Harcourt College Publishers, 301 Commerce Street, Suite 3700,
Fort Worth, TX 76102

Web Site Address
http://www.harcourtcollege.com

Printed in the United States of America

0 1 2 3 4 5 6 7 8 9   023   9 8 7 6 5 4 3 2 1

Harcourt College Publishers

Brief Contents

Contents

PART II
PROBLEMS OF CRITICAL THINKING

PART III
FORMS AND STANDARDS OF
CRITICAL THINKING

Preface

"Wait! Wait! Listen to me! . . . We don't HAVE to be just sheep!"

Used with permission of Universal Press Syndicate.

HISTORY OF THE TEXT

Critical thinking has no agreed-upon definition. Nevertheless its awakening is an unmistakable experience. Sometimes the jolt appears in the momentous, sometimes in the ordinary, but invariably, it's a reminder that we don't have to be just sheep! This book originated through some acts of waking up in 1980. I began to focus on the nagging dissatisfaction I had felt over fifteen years about teaching English composition. I could help my students improve their writing, but I could not help them improve what generated their writing: their thinking and perceiving. Over time, by applying principles derived from my own art education, I was able to help make my students more aware of how to use their perceptions and thus improve their descriptions of photographs. However, I did not know how to help them work more consciously with their thinking, nor, for that matter, did I know how to do that for myself.

When I finally decided to take the time to study this problem, I discovered that there were a number of educators who were already beginning to talk about the possibility of teaching thinking; some were even saying that thinking was a trainable skill, just like reading and writing. In the fall of 1981 I found my teacher: Arthur Costa, then a Professor of Education at Sacramento State University. I entered into an internship program under his supervision for one year, a program for teaching thinking skills that was developed for junior high and high school students by Professor Reuven Feuerstein of Israel. By 1982 I was teaching a college course in basic thinking skills based on the Feuerstein method. In 1983 the California state universities instituted new general education requirements which included a course in critical thinking. Aside from the fact that this requirement was a national innovation, what was even more remarkable was the chancellors' suggestion that critical thinking instruction need not be limited to philosophy courses alone. With this encouragement, I developed an English 1C Critical Thinking/ English composition course at the College of Alameda. By 1989, the advantages of combining critical thinking with composition was validated in a uniform agreement made by the University of California system, the California state universities, and the community colleges which recommended that critical thinking be offered in conjunction with composition writing.

This book is based on the material I developed for use in that first critical thinking composition course. I wrote it chapter by chapter based on my students' questions. Inevitably their needs surprised me: they could not write argumentation because they did not know the differences between facts and inferences, between facts and opinions, facts and evaluations, reasons and conclusions. I discovered, moreover, they had real difficulties in understanding assumptions and viewpoints. It took three years of writing and revision for me to produce the first edition which was released in 1986. The text was unique in that it served two purposes:

- To teach English composition through a focus on the perceiving-thinking process.
- To teach critical thinking through exercises in writing.

Today, eighteen years later, this book is still continuing to flourish and respond to the needs of the changing times as well as to feedback received from students, colleagues, and reviewers. This present fifth edition, published by Harcourt College Publishing, represents the most complete and thorough revision of this book to date. Every paragraph in the book has been newly revised to improve clarity and comprehensibility. This text also includes twelve new readings, seventeen new cartoons, six new photographs, new charts, diagrams, discussion questions, and boxed definitions of every central term and concept. As usual, in this edition all social, economic, and political examples have been updated. I enjoy making each new edition truly new.

The guiding purpose in each edition has been to provide more flexibility and teaching options. This text is intended chiefly for use in either first or second semester English university transfer courses. It contains enough materials for two semesters of work, yet, with omissions, can serve for either course alone. Philosophy instructors can use the text with or without the composition writing assignments. Instructors who wish to emphasize critical reading have numerous selections to choose from. Those who wish to assign a research paper will find detailed guidance for students in the new Appendix: Writing the Research Paper. Instructors who wish to use collaborative learning will find that each chapter includes that option. Finally, while the text contains material sufficient for a two-quarter or two-semester English or philosophy course, instructors can tailor the material to fit the requirements of a one-quarter or one-semester course.

From all those who contributed to this new edition as it grew from 1996 to 1999, I wish primarily to thank my students at Contra Costa College, the College of Marin, Dominican College, and Golden Gate University. Each edition has been dedicated to my students whose questions have always given me the direction I needed. My most special thanks go to Elana Dolberg, of Wadsworth Publishing, who first helped me plan this edition, as well as to Stephen Dalphin, English editor at Harcourt Publishing, who brought the book into production and publication. I also want to thank those many friends and colleagues who gave me so much active support during these years, in particular Maureen Girard, Jim Wallace, Dan Clurman, Dianne Romain, and Walter C. Frey. This book continues to draw from a new collaboration of minds.

APPROACH AND COVERAGE

1. This text teaches both critical thinking and composition by emphasizing awareness of the personal thinking process. From the training of personal awareness, it moves to the more advanced stages of analyzing the thinking of others.

2. This book begins on a more fundamental level than most other critical thinking books, yet proceeds to a more advanced level than most, leading students to develop and some highly sophisticated analytical skills applied to reading and writing.

3. The first half of the text works extensively with critical thinking in *nonverbal* problems, using photographs, cartoons, descriptive assignments, and report assignments. The second half moves into the more

traditional application of critical thinking through *verbal* problems, analyses, and arguments.

4. The text constantly provokes its readers to think; indeed, they are obliged to think in order to work their way through the materials. Its problem and writing assignments require personal confrontations with thinking habits that might otherwise be elusive.

5. In its style and pedagogy, the text shows consistent concern for the interaction of the cognitive and affective domains of learning. It also addresses directly the problems of distinguishing between feelings that clarify thinking and those that hinder thinking.

6. The text uses practical, everyday examples, connecting the concepts learned about thinking to everyday problems. Direct quotations concerning current political and social issues are used extensively to illustrate the ubiquity and influence of arguments in our lives. They also show our need for standards by which to judge them.

7. The text builds self-confidence in students by validating the skills they already own as well as by encouraging them to discover key principles for themselves through the Discovery Exercises. Students also learn and remember more readily because they are required to apply every principle that they learn. In addition, the text offers the simplicity of an organization based on concepts, concepts which are familiar, yet often misunderstood, concepts which, when correctly understood, make critical thinking simple.

SPECIAL FEATURES AND FURTHER REVISIONS

1. A study of the table of contents shows that Parts I and II cover basic material not usually presented in such depth in critical thinking texts, whereas Part III offers extensive treatment of the more traditional topics of critical thinking, such as argument, fallacies, inductive reasoning, and deductive reasoning.

2. Multiple tools for evaluating student progress appear in this fifth edition. Each chapter ends with a summary and true-false chapter quiz. These quizzes can be used to provoke further learning through oral review as well as for written exams. Reviews of Learning Objectives appear at the end of each major section and scoring boxes provide an opportunity for peer scoring of most composition assignments. The Instructor's Manual contains tests for Parts I and II; it also includes

content questions and essay questions for each chapter; tests on dictionary skills; additional tests on fallacies, reasons, and conclusions; a model research take-home final; and additional in-class final exams.

3. *Two* types of writing applications appear in the text. The Composition Writing Applications follow a progression of rhetorical complexity from description and narration through the longer research papers. This edition also introduces new advanced optional writing assignments for this series. The Core Discovery Writing Applications offer experiential understanding of the concepts and skills taught through the text. Each core application is designed to mirror thinking through the writing process, heighten self-awareness, and bring skill deficiencies to the surface. Instructors using this text for an English course can choose from the composition assignments as well as use the core discovery applications, whereas those using this text for a critical thinking course may want to use only the core discovery applications.

4. Multicultural viewpoints and themes predominate in this edition in essays, short stories, and the boxed series on argument. Twelve new readings appear in this edition, which illustrate the concept theme of each chapter. They are all designed to stimulate thinking, whether in the form of fiction or essays concerning issues of current interest and controversy.

5. For the sake of greater unity and consolidation, some chapters have been expanded in this edition, while two have been omitted: the chapters on research skills and problem solving. References are provided to other texts which can provide the fuller and more adequate treatment than these evolving subjects deserve. A new appendix has been added to this edition called Appendix: Writing the Research Paper, which has been prepared to guide students through the two research assignments made in the text. It also includes a model student assignment.

6. Argument building and analysis are the most complex skills taught in the text. They are therefore introduced through the Building Arguments series in each chapter, leading and following Chapter 9—Arguments. The first assignment requiring the writing of a short argument appears in Chapter 6—Opinions.

7. The Induction chapter has been expanded to provide more illustrations. In the Deduction chapter, the Euler diagrams from each have also been reintroduced in order to offer better clarification of the concept of validity.

8. The presentation of fallacies in this edition has again been revised, updated, and expanded for faster comprehension, memory, and assimilation; it includes new charts and new examples.

ACKNOWLEDGMENTS

The twenty years I have spent writing these five editions have brought me many devoted helpers and illuminating advisors. First, I would like to thank the reviewers of the first three editions, who let me know the needs of their students. They include Gary Christensen, Macomb County Community College; Robert Dees, Orange Coast College; Yvonne Frye, Community College of Denver; Helen Gordon, Bakersfield College; Patricia Grignon, Saddleback College; Elizabeth Hanson-Smith, California State University, Sacramento; Ralph Jenkins, Temple University; Shelby Kipplen, Michael J. Owens Technical College; Eileen Lundy, University of Texas, San Antonio; Daniel Lynch, La Guardia Community College; L. J. McDoniel, St. Louis Community College, Meramec; Paul Olubas, Southern Ohio College; Sue Sixberry, Mesabi Community College; Patricia Smittle, Santa Fe Community College; Fran Bahr, North Idaho College; Charlene Doyon, University of Lowell; Carol Enns, College of the Sequoias; Jon Ford, College of Alameda; Nancy Glock, California Community Colleges; James Haule, University of Texas, Pan American; Jerry Herman, Laney College; Becky Patterson, University of Alaska; Suzette Schlapkohl, Scottsdale Community College; Pamela Spoto, Shasta College; and Mark Weinstein, Montclair State College.

Reviewers I wish to thank for the fourth edition included C. George Fry, Lutheran College of Health Professions; Adrienne Gosselin, Cleveland State University; Marilyn Hill, American River College; Susan A. Injejikian, Glendale Community College; Henry Nardone, King's College; Ronn Talbot Pelley, City University; and Edith Wollin, North Seattle Community College.

Reviewers for the fifth edition included Sandra G. Brown, Ocean County College, Tom's River, New Jersey; Dan Clurman, Golden Gate University, San Francisco; Maureen Girard, Monterey Peninsula College, Monterey; Elizabeth Nelson, Tidewater Community College, Chesapeake; Alice K. Perrey, St. Charles County Community College, St. Peters, Missouri; Jim Wallace, King's College, Northeastern Pennsylvania.

Finally, I extend my greatest gratitude goes to those Harcourt Publishing staff members who produced and published this fifth edition. They include Jill Johnson, administrative assistant to Stephen Dalphin, and Gretchen Miller of York Graphic Services.

I

Introduction

Introduction to Critical Thinking

"How do people plead insanity? Who's gonna believe a crazy person?"
Used with permission of Richard Guindon.

LEARNING HOW YOU THINK

This is a book about thinking that will constantly require you to think.

Sometimes you will be asked to think out problems for yourself before they are discussed either in the text or in class. In addition, you will always be asked *to observe the way you think* as you go. Each chapter in this text starts with Discovery Exercises that will show you *how* you think. They will also help you discover some principles about thinking on your own.

Even this introduction will begin with a Discovery Exercise. All students should complete it at the same time together in class before

Photo by Rick Fanthorpe-White. Used with permission of the photographer.

continuing to read in this book. After the whole class shares and discusses this exercise, you might each better appreciate the remainder of this introduction, which discusses the attitudes needed to study critical thinking, a definition of critical thinking, and the habits of a critical thinker.

Discovery Exercise

Experiencing How We Actually Think: An Exercise for the Whole Class to Complete Together

This is an exercise designed for thinking in two stages: first quietly alone and then only afterwards with others. Look at the photograph. Based on what you see there, rate each of the following statements as either *true, false, or can't answer.* Write your answers without discussing either the questions or your replies with anyone else.

_____ 1.   This is graduation day for the Thomas family.

_____ 2.   The father is proud of his son.

_____ 3.   The sister looks up to her brother.

_____ 4.   This is a prosperous family.

_____ 5.   The son has just graduated from law school.

When you have finished this quiz, wait, without talking to anyone else about your choices. Sharing too soon could spoil the results of this experiment. When all have finished, the instructor will poll your answers to each statement. Then you will be asked to break up into two or more groups to defend your answers. Each group will try to arrive at a consensus, functioning somewhat like a *jury.*

After the Discussion

Review the following questions through discussion or writing. You will notice that some of these questions will already have been raised in your *groups.*

1.   What are your definitions of the following terms?

    True   False   Can't Answer

2.   Can a statement be rated *true* if it contains an assumption?

3.   Is it possible to determine whether a written statement is *true* if it contains ambiguous words or phrases?

4.   Should a statement be rated *true* if it is highly probable?

5.   What makes a statement true or false?

6.   Did you find yourself reluctant to choose the option of *can't answer?* Why or why not?

7.   How can we know whether or not something is true?

8.   What did this exercise teach you?

LEARNING FROM SHARING HOW WE THINK

A surprise can be an opportunity for learning.

Your work on this last assignment took you from thinking alone to thinking with others. You may have been surprised to discover that there were such different perceptions of a simple photograph.

If your discussion moved your thinking from certainty into uncertainty, you may feel somewhat confused or unsettled at this time. The term we will use for this unsettled state is *disequilibrium*. We feel this kind of discomfort when we need more time to integrate something unfamiliar. Moreover, we feel vulnerable when our thinking is exposed. Even in school, where we are committed to learning, it is not always easy to say "I don't know," "I am confused," or "I was wrong." We have to ascertain first if it is safe to be so honest.

Yet if we want to learn new skills, we have to be willing to feel awkward at times. We have to expose our thinking before we can review it. Such a process requires humility, sensitivity, kindness, and humor from everyone involved—from instructors as well as students. Indeed, if we are not feeling awkward, we may not be really learning.

In review, this assignment was meant to remind you

- what occurs when you think on your own;
- how we can further our thinking together in groups;
- how such a process can teach us more about thinking.

WHAT IS CRITICAL THINKING?

When we look up the word *thinking* in a dictionary, we find it covers nineteen different mental operations. These range from reasoning to solving problems, to conceiving and discovering ideas, to remembering, to daydreaming. Some of these forms are conscious and directed, while others seem to operate on their own without control or awareness. When we need to solve a math problem, we focus and concentrate. When we relax, thoughts and fantasies can come and go without direction. In this book, we will be using the word *thinking* in the sense of *purposeful mental activity*.

What then is critical thinking? Most of us associate the word *critical* with negativity or habitual fault-finding. Yet if we look at the history of the word, we can see that connotation was not in its original meaning. The root of *critical* comes from *skeri*, which means to cut, separate, or sift; thus its original idea was to take something apart or to analyze it. Moreover, *critical* is also related to the Greek word *kriterion*, which means a standard for judging. Putting together these two original ideas, we see that the word *critical* means *analyzing on the basis of a standard*. When we are negative and fault-finding, our standards are not clear, and our purpose is not that of developing reliable knowledge.

Dictionaries do not, as yet, define critical thinking, nor is there one definition that all teachers in this field can agree upon; today there are as many definitions of critical thinking as there are writers on the subject.

Critical thinking brings conscious awareness, skills, and standards to the process of observing, analyzing, reasoning, evaluating, reading, and communicating.

Thinking is purposeful mental *activity*. **Critical** means to take something apart and analyze it on the basis of a standard.

Critical comes from *skeri* (Anglo Saxon) = to cut, separate, sift and *kriterion* (Greek) = a standard for judging.

Standards of Critical Thinking

Clarity	Completeness
Accuracy	Reliability
Precision	Soundness
Relevance	Fairness

But all would agree that critical thinking is a purposeful form of mental activity; many would agree that it involves learning conscious awareness of the thinking process itself. Finally, all agree that it is one guided by clear **standards.**

Now what are the standards of critical thinking? They are the same intellectual standards scientists and scholars have used for centuries to evaluate the reliability of reasoning and information. They include clarity, accuracy, precision, consistency, relevance, reliability, soundness, completeness, and fairness. All these standards help us to aim for truth or to come as close to truth as we can.

When we study critical thinking, we gain **knowledge** of norms and rules for clear and effective thinking. While the norms embody the standards, the rules help us measure them. Each chapter of this text explains norms through rules and examples that compare skilled with unskilled forms of thinking.

What is most difficult about learning critical thinking, however, is that it cannot be mastered through knowledge of norms and rules alone. Critical thinking is an active skill-building process, not a subject for passive academic study. We need to learn how to apply these standards to our own thinking and help others do the same. And when we accept the challenge of such learning, we go through a process of *unlearning* old habits while also acquiring better ones. Then gradually as we develop these new skills and habits, our knowledge of critical thinking becomes integrated into our lives.

As we work our way through this text, we will be learning both knowledge and skills in spirals of repetition and expansion. What we learn about knowledge and standards will better help us understand the skills required. And developing these skills will help us better appreciate the knowledge and standards required. Thus we will progress through this text not like mountain-climbers, but like the surfer on the cover of this book. We will move forward by sometimes rising with the waves, sometimes falling, and sometimes balancing in wondrous new spirals.

> **Critical thinking** brings conscious awareness, skills, and standards to the process of observing, analyzing, reasoning, evaluating, reading, and *communicating*.

COMPARISONS TO CREATIVE THINKING

Critical thinking analyzes, while creative thinking invents.

It is beyond the scope of this book to teach creative thinking, but a brief comparison can help us understand critical thinking better. In brief, while critical thinking analyzes and evaluates ideas, creative thinking invents

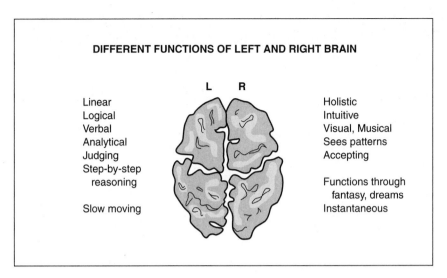

Figure I.1 Different Functions of Left and Right Brain

new ideas. To engage in critical thinking, we rely more on the "left brain" for its verbal, linear, logical, and analytical functions. Creative thinking uses both hemispheres of the brain, but relies more on the right because of its intuitive-holistic-visual way of knowing. Our right brains help us recognize faces and images, to generate new ideas, to sing, and to dance. Even if we do not use our right hemispheres to create in the arts, we all know the pleasant right brain "trance" that comes when we feel relaxed and suspended in a timeless continuum.

We shift automatically back and forth between both brain hemispheres when we are doing a math problem, drawing a picture, reading a newspaper, or writing an essay. However, those who want to work more consciously with our thinking can make the shifts purposefully. In writing, for instance, we can use such techniques as free writing or clustering to get the help of our right brains in generating topics for discussion. Then, when we begin to outline and organize our thinking, we shift over into our left brain. We think critically to revise, edit, and evaluate our final product. However, if we criticize our writing too soon, our creative flow will falter. Creativity needs to play like a child without the threat of premature interruptions. Critical thinking is more like a practical parent who can be too interfering at times. Ideally, when our brains are in balance, the parent can relate wisely to the child's holistic-artistic inner way of knowing, and the child can learn from the parents' practical knowledge of the world.

We learn to make more conscious use of our critical or creative thinking abilities as we respect their different ways of functioning. If we need to analyze a situation, we sit down in the posture of Rodin's statue of "The Thinker" in order to remain still and concentrate. Creative thinking requires concentration as well, but its spirit allows for more movement and playfulness. In addition, our minds can continue to work creatively on a problem when we have stopped concentrating, proceeding even when we are in dream sleep or taking a walk. Moreover, once the process is complete, a fresh solution to a complex problem can occur in a sudden flash of insight; it can surprise us while we are doing something entirely mundane and unrelated, such as washing the car, patting a dog, or opening the refrigerator door.

In addition to working with our creative and critical abilities, we need to also remember that their standards differ. Critical thinking is concerned mainly with truth, while creative thinking also loves beauty; it wants its designs, ideas, or solutions to be not just adequate: it wants them to be elegant. Albert Einstein was the model of a scientist who worked quite consciously with his capacities for both creative and critical thinking. He conceived theorems with a simplicity that proved to be both practical and beautiful. Einstein himself valued the creative process so highly that he once said, "Imagination is more important than knowledge."

A familiar assumption is that one must be born to be either a scientist or an artist. The good news—and most recent news—in education is that both critical and creative thinking are both based on skills that can be taught. If you are interested in learning more about the skills of creative thinking, many good books are available such as *A Whack on the Side of the Head* by Roger Van Oech, *Creating Minds* by Howard Gardner, and any of the dozens of books by Edward de Bono.

WHY LEARN CRITICAL THINKING?

We already know how to do many complex kinds of thinking, for many purposes. All of us have developed our own way of solving problems, using "street smarts" and common sense or even trial and error. Yet what we already know can be substantially strengthened by conscious attention, just as those who already know how to walk or fight can greatly improve their abilities by studying dance or karate. This improvement comes from paying closer attention to what we already do, finding the right labels, and finding ways to do it better.

Critical thinking isn't the only form of clear thinking, nor is it always appropriate. If you are just hanging out, swapping stories, sharing feelings, speculating, the killjoy who demands that every term be defined, every fact be supported, every speculation be qualified is completely out of place. You don't use an electric saw to slice a roast, but when you do need an electric saw, it is invaluable.

Critical thinking skills are powerful skills. They can empower those who use them more so than anything else you can learn in college. They can't be picked up on the run; they require careful, disciplined, systematic study. But such study will also pay off not only in the short run by improving performance in every other single course, and in the long run by

- providing protection from manipulation and propaganda;
- helping you exercise more awareness and self-control;
- lessening the likelihood of making serious mistakes;
- helping you make better decisions;
- contributing to better decision making in groups.

Thus although the study of critical thinking leads to mental independence, it is also a path to more productive work with others. It helps people to openly share the workings of their minds: to recognize and direct inner processes for understanding issues, to express ideas and beliefs, to make decisions, and to analyze and solve problems. Critical thinking allows us to welcome life's problems as challenges to be solved. And it gives us the confidence that we can make sense and harmony out of a confusing world.

THE HABITS OF CRITICAL THINKING

Many of these habits may already be part of your life; others may be unfamiliar to you. Some will be seen with freshness and clarity as you learn to monitor and direct your own thinking habits. Once you have finished studying this book, return to the habits listed here to see how far you have come. The goal is clear, and the time has come to start down the path toward it.

HABITS OF A CRITICAL THINKER

AWARENESS OBSERVES	SELF-CONTROL Restrains Impulses to	SKILLS
• self and others in process of thinking • feelings • level of concentration • confusion and clarity	Stereotype Jump to conclusions Jump to judgments Glance instead of observe Hurry to finish Take things for granted Not ask questions Not verify information Cover up mistakes Avoid what is difficult **Stands by Values** To discover and express what is true To be fair, reliable, respectful, and responsible to self and others To seek truth before rightness; to be willing to admit mistakes and concede to a better argument	Suspends judgments when appropriate Listens and observes Persists to gather and understand information, get across communications, and complete problems Methodically separates facts from inferences, from opinions, and evaluations Checks for evidence and valid reasoning Recognizes assumptions Views content in terms of frame of reference Looks for a viewpoint's frame of reference Uses words with precision and sensitivity to word definition, connotations, slant, ambiguity Reads critically Uses writing to improve thinking and get ideas across Can prepare a persuasive argument based on evidence and valid reasoning Recognizes fallacies of reasoning Recognizes unfair persuasion and propaganda

Figure I.2 Chart: Habits of a Critical Thinker

PART I
Basics of Critical Thinking

CHAPTER 1

Observation Skills: What's Out There?

"Billy, sweetums, please think
carefully!...where did you bury Daddy?"

Used with permission of Vier/Whelan. Copyright 1998.

O bservation skills help us keep one another alive, but to use them we have to stay alert and attentive. Let's hope the mother in this cartoon will return to her own observing instead of relying on her son's memory.

Observation skills form an essential foundation for critical thinking. If we base our thinking on poor observations, then no matter how many strategies we devise, or how well we reason, that thinking will be faulty. A wise saying puts it more simply: "You don't have to stay awake at night to get ahead. All you have to do is stay awake in the daytime." This chapter consists mainly of exercises that require you to observe. The opening Discovery Exercises are meant to show you how *you* observe and how that may be different from the way others observe. Additional exercises are intended to help you make your own discoveries about how to observe better and how to guide your own progress.

Discovery Exercises

Comparing Our Perceptions

In class, write a one-paragraph description of the photograph on page 14. Try to describe what you see in such a way that your readers will be able to visualize it even without the picture before them. Do not discuss your work with anyone else in class while you observe and write.

When you have finished, form small groups to read your descriptions aloud to one another. As you listen, notice in what details your descriptions are similar or different. When your group has finished, signal to the instructor that you are ready for a full class discussion of the following questions.

1.   How can our differences be explained?
2.   How can we know what is correct and what is not?

In completing this exercise, you may have discovered that what we see is what is familiar, that the unfamiliar is harder to see, and that sometimes we distort unfamiliar situations to make them familiar. Moreover, some details that are irrelevant to some are relevant to others.

What Is Observing?

The word *observe* is one that we hear and use every day, like other words which are the subjects of future chapters. Therefore you might wonder why it needs defining at all. Let's hold that question until the following exercises are completed.

To **observe** means to hold something in front of us.
ob (Latin prefix) = in front of
servare (Latin) = to keep, hold, watch, pay attention

To **watch** is to stay awake.
waeccan (Old English derived from Indo-European *weg*, meaning to stay strong) When we watch, therefore, we stay strong and awake.

Photo by John Pearson. Used with permission of the photographer.

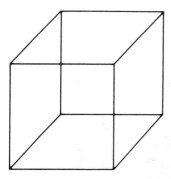

Figure 1.1 Observing a Cube

Observing a Cube

In this exercise, look at Figure 1.1. Observe the cube by watching it, looking at it intently, and staying "strong and awake" in your concentration. Then write down your answers to the two questions given beneath the figure.

1. What happens to the cube as you observe it?
2. How does observing feel as you do it?

Observation and Insight

Study the cartoons on pages 16–17 carefully. Notice and write down (1) how you go about trying to decode their meaning; (2) how you feel when you experience an insight or revelation; and (3) how you feel when you can't understand them.

USING OBSERVATION SKILLS TO DEVELOP NEW KNOWLEDGE

The beginning of science is the ability to be amazed by apparently simple things. (Noam Chomsky)

It is more convenient to assume that reality is similar to our preconceived ideas than to freshly observe what we have before our eyes. (Robert Fritz)

Those of you studying this text, who learned something new from these exercises, learned because you observed in its true sense of staying awake and closely attentive. Therefore you became aware of details in your subjects that a sweeping glance would have missed, details that revealed significance about the whole. The following reading illustrates this process

Used with permission of Mark Stivers.

"Have you seen a Frisbee?"
Used with permission of Richard Guindon.

Used with permission of John Heine.

of learning. It is the story of a kind of trial a student went through that tested his capacity to do graduate research in science. Samuel H. Scudder (1837–1911) was an American naturalist who attended Lawrence Scientific School at Harvard, where he studied under the great biologist (then called a naturalist) professor Jean Louis R. Agassiz. Read carefully, for at the end you will be asked some questions followed by a writing exercise.

READING

LOOK AT YOUR FISH
Samuel H. Scudder

It was more than fifteen years ago that I entered the laboratory of Professor Agassiz,   1
and told him I had enrolled my name in the Scientific School as a student of natural

history. He asked me a few questions about my object in coming, my antecedents generally, the mode in which I afterwards proposed to use the knowledge I might acquire, and, finally, whether I wished to study any special branch. To the latter I replied that, while I wished to be well grounded in all departments of zoology, I purposed to devote myself specially to insects.

"When do you wish to begin?" he asked. 2

"Now," I replied. 3

This seemed to please him, and with an energetic "Very well!" he reached from 4
a shelf a huge jar of specimens in yellow alcohol. "Take this fish," he said, "and look at it; we call it a haemulon; by and by I will ask what you have seen."

With that he left me, but in a moment returned with explicit instructions as to the 5
care of the object entrusted to me.

"No man is fit to be a naturalist," he said, "who does not know how to take care 6
of specimens."

I was to keep the fish before me in a tin tray, and occasionally moisten the surface 7
with alcohol from the jar, always taking care to replace the stopper tightly. These were not the days of ground-glass stoppers and elegantly shaped exhibition jars; all the old students will recall the huge neckless glass bottles with their leaky, wax-besmeared corks, half eaten by insects, and begrimed with cellar dust. Entomology was a cleaner science than ichthyology, but the example of the Professor, who had unhesitatingly plunged to the bottom of the jar to produce the fish, was infectious, and though this alcohol had a "very ancient and fishlike smell," I really dared not to show any aversion within these sacred precincts, and treated the alcohol as though it were pure water. Still I was conscious of a passing feeling of disappointment, for gazing at a fish did not commend itself to an ardent entomologist. My friends at home, too, were annoyed when they discovered that no amount of eau-de-Cologne would drown the perfume which haunted me like a shadow.

In ten minutes I had seen all that could be seen in that fish, and started in search 8
of the Professor—who had, however, left the Museum; and when I returned, after lingering over some of the odd animals stored in the upper apartment, my specimen was dry all over. I dashed the fluid over the fish as if to resuscitate the beast from a fainting fit, and looked with anxiety for a return of the normal sloppy appearance. This little excitement over, nothing was to be done but to return to a steadfast gaze at my mute companion. Half an hour passed—an hour—another hour; the fish began to look loathsome. I turned it over and around; looked it in the face—ghastly; from behind, beneath, above, sideways, at a three-quarters' view—just as ghastly. I was in despair; at an early hour I concluded that lunch was necessary; so, with infinite relief, the fish was carefully replaced in the jar, and for an hour I was free.

On my return, I learned that Professor Agassiz had been at the Museum, but had 9
gone, and would not return for several hours. My fellow students were too busy to be disturbed by continued conversation. Slowly I drew forth that hideous fish, and with a feeling of desperation again looked at it. I might not use a magnifying glass; instruments of all kinds were interdicted. My two hands, my two eyes, and the fish: it seemed a most limited field. I pushed my finger down its throat to feel how sharp the

teeth were. I began to count the scales in the different rows, until I was convinced that that was nonsense. At last a happy thought struck me—I would draw the fish; and now with surprise I began to discover new features in the creature. Just then the Professor returned.

"That is right," said he; "a pencil is one of the best of eyes. I am glad to notice, **10** too, that you keep your specimen wet, and your bottle corked."

With these encouraging words, he added: **11**

"Well, what is it like?" **12**

He listened attentively to my brief rehearsal of the structure of parts whose names **13** were still unknown to me; the fringed gill-arches and movable operculum; the pores of the head, fleshy lips and lidless eyes; the lateral line, the spinous fins and forked tail; the compressed and arched body. When I finished, he waited as if expecting more, and then, with an air of disappointment:

"You have not looked very carefully; why," he continued more earnestly, "you **14** haven't even seen one of the most conspicuous features of the animal, which is as plainly before your eyes as the fish itself; look again, look again!" and he left me to my misery.

I was piqued; I was mortified. Still more of that wretched fish! But now I set myself **15** to my task with a will, and discovered one new thing after another, until I saw how just the Professor's criticism had been. The afternoon passed quickly; and when, toward its close, the Professor inquired:

"Do you see it yet?" **16**

"No," I replied, "I am certain I do not, but I see how little I saw before." **17**

"That is next best," said he, earnestly, "but I won't hear you now; put away your **18** fish and go home; perhaps you will be ready with a better answer in the morning. I will examine you before you look at the fish."

This was disconcerting. Not only must I think of my fish all night, studying, with- **19** out the object before me, what this unknown but most visible feature might be; but also, without reviewing my discoveries, I must give an exact account of them the next day. I had a bad memory; so I walked home by the Charles River in a distracted state, with my two perplexities.

The cordial greeting from the Professor the next morning was reassuring; here was **20** a man who seemed to be quite as anxious as I that I should see for myself what he saw.

"Do you perhaps mean," I asked, "that the fish has symmetrical sides with paired **21** organs?"

His thoroughly pleased "Of course! of course!" repaid the wakeful hours of the **22** previous night. After he had discoursed most happily and enthusiastically—as he always did—upon the importance of this point, I ventured to ask what I should do next.

"Oh, look at your fish!" he said, and left me again to my own devices. In a little **23** more than an hour he returned, and heard my new catalogue.

"That is good, that is good," he repeated; "but that is not all; go on"; and so for **24** three long days he placed that fish before my eyes, forbidding me to look at anything else, or to use any artificial aid. "Look, look, look," was his repeated injunction.

This was the best entomological lesson I ever had—a lesson whose influence has **25**
extended to the details of every subsequent study; a legacy the Professor had left to
me, as he has left it to many others, of inestimable value, which we could not buy,
with which we cannot part.

A year afterward, some of us were amusing ourselves with chalking outlandish **26**
beasts on the Museum blackboard. We drew prancing starfishes; frogs in mortal com-
bat; hydra-headed worms; stately crawfishes, standing on their tails, bearing aloft um-
brellas; and grotesque fishes with gaping mouths and staring eyes. The Professor came
in shortly after, and was as amused as any at our experiments. He looked at the fishes.

"Haemulons, every one of them," he said; "Mr. _____ drew them." **27**

True; and to this day, if I attempt a fish, I can draw nothing but haemulons. **28**

The fourth day, a second fish of the same group was placed beside the first, and **29**
I was bidden to point out the resemblances and differences between the two; another
and another followed, until the entire family lay before me, and a whole legion of jars
covered the table and surrounding shelves; the odor had become a pleasant perfume;
and even now, the sight of an old, six-inch, worm-eaten cork brings fragrant memories.

The whole group of haemulons was thus brought in review; and whether en- **30**
gaged upon the dissection of the internal organs, the preparation and examination of
the bony framework, or the description of the various parts, Agassiz's training in the
method of observing facts and their orderly arrangement was ever accompanied by
the urgent exhortation not to be content with them.

"Facts are stupid things," he would say, "until brought into connection with some **31**
general law."

At the end of eight months, it was almost with reluctance that I left these friends **32**
and turned to insects; but what I had gained by this outside experience has been of
greater value than years of later investigation in my favorite groups.

Study Questions

1. Why did Agassiz keep saying "Look at your fish!"? What was he trying to teach
   Scudder?
2. How would you describe the stages in Scudder's process of looking? What
   happened at each stage?
3. How did Scudder change personally in the course of his "trial"?
4. Explain why you think Agassiz's method of teaching was either effective or
   wasteful.

CORE DISCOVERY WRITING APPLICATION

Observing the Familiar: Vegetables and Fruit

1. This exercise may be done either at home alone or in class. First of
   all, prepare a report sheet of two columns with these two headings:

Physical Details (what I observe and discover about the object)	**Inner Process Details** (what I observe and discover happening within myself as I work: my moods, reactions, associations, and thoughts.)

2. Bring to class one vegetable or fruit of any kind in a brown paper bag. It does not have to be of any exotic variety—an ordinary orange or potato will do. (If you are working at home alone, ask a family member or a roommate to give you a fruit when you are seated at a table with your eyes closed.)

3. If you are at school when you begin this exercise, give your sack to someone who does not know what is inside. The first part of the exercise involves exploring and describing the object without seeing it. Place the sack in your lap under the desk; then, still with your eyes closed, take the object out and hold it. (Since this exercise is done in silence, the sack should be discarded because its rattling will be annoying.) Open your eyes. With your other hand, take notes in the left-hand column about your investigation of the object while jotting down in the second column notes about your personal process as you become aware of it. Explore this unknown object for twenty minutes, using all senses except sight. This will mean really slowing down sufficiently to experience your senses of touch, smell, temperature, and even, if you dare, taste. Record your findings carefully.

4. At the end of twenty minutes, the instructor will call the time and you can look at your object. But remain quiet. Carefully note your reaction, and write that down and continue to work silently, completing your visual description. If you are at school, you can take your object home to dissect and describe every detail you see inside. Strive to make an exhaustive study of your fruit or vegetable with the attitude of a child or scientist. Make drawings if you wish.

5. If you are working at home, prepare to spend an hour with this first part of the exercise.

6. Finally, taking your notes, write up a two-page typed paper describing your fruit or vegetable. Include at least one paragraph about your inner process.

Student Writing Example

This example is not offered as a model for you to imitate like a recipe. Rather, it is meant to demonstrate how one student became absorbed in her work and solved the problem of staying sensitive to her subject and herself at the same time. Read it as a reminder of what the assignment is asking you to do, then forget it, and create your own paper by being true to your own experience. Remember that one purpose of this exercise is to help you discover your own observation style and biases.

KIWI

Yvette Padilla

The girl in the row behind me just gave me a bag with some unknown fruit or vegetable inside. I reached inside with my eyes closed and touched a fuzzy and prickly surface. I clasped my fingers and palm against it and drew out of the bag a shape almost like a Wilson tennis ball. As I held it on my lap, I tried to guess what type of fruit it was. By its shape and weight, I knew it could not have been an apple, orange, or banana. My first guess was that it was a potato. It made me feel anxious to not be sure. I had to explore more in order to know. My attention went back to the fuzz. There were hairs, each about 1/8 inch long. They felt like the stubby nubs of fine hair on a man's beard. There was also a gritty feel, almost like the sensation of grit on an unwashed leaf of spinach. It was then that I realized it must be a kiwi fruit.

Its temperature was cool, like the weather on a crisp spring day. I explored the whole surface, still with my eyes closed. There were no warm spots; the cool temperature was consistent. I reasoned that this even coolness must mean that it was not handled much by the person who gave it to me. Its gritty feel gave me a sudden urge to wash my hands. I brought my attention back to its shape. I wondered how it could feel so like a tennis ball, although I knew it must not be a perfect sphere. I stroked its hairs some more; it reminded me of the peach fuzz that grows down the nape of your neck.

Now it was time to look at my kiwi. I was expecting an intense green color. But that was only the stereotype in my mind. I realized the color, as usual with kiwis, was more light brown or ashen, like the color of coffee with cream. Underneath the coffee color was only a hint of green in the shade of oak tree leaves. Then I noticed the surface shed brown flakes resembling the splinters from a piece of cherry wood with a size no greater than flea dander off a cat. I began to hold it up to view its shape from different angles. If I would lie it flat in my hand, it looked perfectly round. But if I held it upright and looked down at it, I could see an oval shape with scablike structures protruding from both ends. If I were to measure its size, I would say it was about two inches in diameter with a circumference of four inches. Holding it in my hand again, I noticed how firm it was to the touch yet how easy it would be to squash it with a pressured grip.

After class I took the kiwi home for a dissection. I placed it on a board on the kitchen table and sat down with my notepad. I took a knife and proceeded to cut it slowly into two perfectly even halves. The skin was tougher than I had expected and required more force than I had imagined necessary. As it opened, two individual pieces showed the faces of their inner beauty. Each center contained a wreath of ten or more black specks the size of poppy seeds on green flesh, the color of green-color crayons. Pastel green threads were visible through the darkened green shades; they appeared to be almost woven into the fruit. From its fine layer of outer skin to the direct center of the kiwi half, there was a spiral configuration. It looked to me as though someone had taken the fruit's insides, mashed it flat, then rolled it into a ball, and then sliced it down the center. Its pattern was very intriguing to me. The black specks seemed now more like blotches of black ink. As I moved my face closer to see it, its fragrance suddenly burst into my awareness; it was phenomenal: a fruity scent like a fresh piece of tropical-flavored bubble gum. I peeled off its skin, which was like taking off its winter coat. I put one half of the naked green fruit into my mouth. The taste was, as I had imagined, sour-sweet like a lime-flavored LifeSaver candy. The texture was soft and moist. I could crush out its juice by pressing my tongue against my palate. What a pleasant tasting experience! Then I quickly ate the second piece. And then I wished I had more.

Used with permission of Yvette Padilla.

EVALUATING YOUR WORK BY USING THE SCORING BOXES

The scoring box offers a simple consistent method for reviewing the assignment's objectives, for peer feedback, and draft revision. Finally, it might serve as a checklist for the instructor who assigns your grade.

A scoring box, like the one appearing below, follows all the Writing Application assignments in this book. The scoring box might also help you clarify what thinking skills the assignment is intended to foster. For instance, you will notice that you are given 20 points for writing two full typed pages of description of the fruit or vegetable. In other words, there is a reward for doing enough persistent observing to produce that much description. If your typed draft comes to less than two pages, then perhaps you will need to return to your subject in order to observe more.

The scoring boxes can serve first as a checklist to help you determine the strengths and weaknesses of your first draft. Second, they can be used in class to guide you and your classmates in assessing one another's works. Such an assessment might lead you to decide to revise your work once more before submitting it. Finally, and only if your instructor so chooses, the boxes might serve for the final grading of your paper. In summary, the scoring boxes have the following purposes:

1. To emphasize each assignment's skill-building components.
2. To clarify priorities and criteria.
3. To offer standards for a peer critical analysis in class.
4. To enable you to turn in your best work for a grade.

Scoring for Description of Fruit or Vegetable

1. Two full pages. 20 points
2. All senses used. 24 points
   (3 points each)
   Touch/texture
   Taste
   Smell
   Temperature
   Sound
   Color
   Shape
   Changes that occur during description

3. Physical description at least 2/3 of paper. 10 points
4. Language accuracy. 10 points
5. Crucial aspects not omitted. (Skin, seeds, interior aspects and design) 10 points
6. Inner process described. 10 points
7. No distracting errors of spelling, punctuation, or sentence structure. 16 points

---

ALTERNATE CORE DISCOVERY WRITING APPLICATION

Observing the Unfamiliar: A Tool

Bring to class some household tool whose function may be unfamiliar or difficult for most people to identify. This could be a cooking implement, a highly specialized tool for some craft, a cosmetic tool, or any interesting item from your kitchen drawer or tool chest. Do not select anything that has sharp points or blades. Carry this object to class in a paper sack so that no one else can see it. Do not discuss what you have brought with anyone else.

Step 1 The instructor will ask you to exchange your bag with someone else. Sitting at your desk with your eyes closed, put the bag on your lap under your desk and take the object out of the bag quietly. Spend at least fifteen minutes exploring your subject with your hands, getting to know its shape and texture by touch. Set aside your concerns about how to label it. Your perceiving mind will want to categorize it immediately according to some mental stereotype. "Oh," it will say, "that is just a can opener. All can openers are the same. I know what this looks like already." When this happens, just notice what your mind is doing and go on exploring the object as though you were a child, enjoying its touch, its smell, temperature, and taste (if you dare!). Remember, this is not a guessing game whose purpose is to label an object, but an exercise in gaining information about an object through your senses. Get all the data you can without looking. Try to guess its color. Take notes as you go along.

Step 2 When the instructor gives the signal, put the tool on top of your desk and open your eyes. Notice and write down your first reaction. Now spend at least fifteen minutes observing the visual details of your object and taking more notes. Gather all the information you can now from seeing.

Step 3 After class, put all your information together to write at least a one-page typed description that enables readers to imagine the object. (You can also provide a drawing.) Organize your information so that the reader can follow your process of exploration. In a final paragraph, or as you go along, describe what it felt like for you as you worked. Were there different stages in your process? Did you feel frustrated and anxious if you couldn't label your object?

Scoring for the Tool Exercise

1. One full page minimum. 15 points

2. Exploration includes (6 points each totaling 42 points)
   temperature
   texture
   weight
   smell
   general shape and parts
   colors
   sounds
   visual design elements such as scratches, trademarks, thumbprints

3. Inferences or guesses regarding its function. 18 points

4. Physical description is complete. 13 points

5. No distracting errors of spelling, punctuation, sentence structure. 10 points

6. Personal process described. 10 points

Student Writing Example

UNDERCOVER TOOL

Kenneth Wong

My partner handed me the brown paper bag that contained some unidentified tool. I placed the bag under my desk and reached inside, took it out, and dropped the bag to the floor. I immediately knew that what I was holding was a plastic disposable spoon. I was extremely disappointed that my partner did not take the time and effort to look for something more challenging. In my mind I imagined that she forgot to bring her tool and ran down to the cafeteria to see what she could scrounge up.

Although I was displeased with my object, I decided to make the best of the situation. I began my investigation through touch. My first observation was that the tool felt smooth and concave. I thought it resembled the shape of a half lemon without all the pulp. Judging from the smoothness of the object, I imagined it to be as clean and glossy as glass. As I felt my way up the object, I noticed it had a stem extending from its head. The extension was also relatively smooth except for what appeared to be a border about 2 mm thick along its edges. I could also feel a rough surface on the hind side of the stem. I assumed it was an imprint of the manufacturer's name. I identified a "D" in the writing and continued to survey the rest of this new terrain. In a valiant attempt to entertain myself, I attempted to decipher the rest of the writing. However, I failed miserably. After exploring the head and stem, my mind went blank. I assumed that was all there was to know about this typical plastic spoon.

After sitting still for about a minute, I decided to continue my investigation. I began examining the object with greater precision and concentration. I tried flicking the object and noticed it made a peculiar "click." Then I tried flicking it harder and harder. The noise would get louder but the tone and pitch of the click remained constant. My action of flicking the spoon then made me notice its flexibility, which led me to conclude that it was definitely not made of metal. I also began feeling for warmth. The object wasn't cold, however, it wasn't exactly warm either. I knew then for sure that the object was made of flexible plastic.

My mind went numb again until I had another great idea. I began playing catch with the tool, still keeping it under the table, of course. I realized it was very light in weight, almost weightless. It had a very airy sensation. The tool landed in my palms gently and with great ease. Then I tried bending the object and realized it was not as flexible as I first had imagined. After a certain point the object felt suddenly stiffer as though it were about to snap: so I let go. I realized that this spoon was not as flexible as ones I had used before. It was much stronger and more solid. However, the longer I played with it, the more flexible it became. It also seemed to get warmer. I placed my thumb in the concave head of the spoon and left it there while I continued to examine the object with my other hand. When I released my thumb, I could feel that the tool was much warmer in that area. Then I remembered to smell the tool. I couldn't detect any scent I could describe, either of plastic or of food.

The fifteen-minute examination time was finally over, thank God. I was about to go out of my mind with boredom. I brought my spoon up to my eyes and immediately a rush of images flooded my head. Though I wasn't exactly surprised by the identity of my object, little things like the reflection that came off the shine of the spoon captured my attention. I was stunned by the piercing glow of its white plastic: its shimmering whiteness resembled strong sunlight reflecting off fresh snow. I now also saw small dents and scratches that my fingertips had not detected. The curves of the spoon were also more detailed than I had pictured. Next I flipped the spoon on its backside to see what had been written there. I read "DIXIE."

I took the object home for a closer examination, but I didn't notice any other features I had overlooked. However, I did use the plastic spoon to shoot roasted peanuts at my brother. The spoon later snapped when I tried shooting a peanut across my living room.

I realized afterwards that even though I didn't need my vision to discover the identity of my object, there was a lot in that tool that I would have overlooked if I had used my vision first. After spending so much time first depending on touch, the final use of my vision brought me into a heightened relationship to the tool. Truly then I was seeing the tool with my own eyes.

Reprinted with permission of Kenneth Wong.

THE OBSERVATION PROCESS: SENSING, PERCEIVING, THINKING

When you can slow down sufficiently to experience your own sensing, perceiving, and thinking in operation, then you can begin to use each one with more skill.

When you worked with your fruit, vegetable, or tool, you went through a process of collecting data, seeing patterns, and drawing conclusions. As you learned in the opening Discovery exercise, this process is called inductive reasoning. If you observed your own mental processes as you proceeded in this simple task, you might have noticed that you went through different stages, using different skills.

So what are the parts of this process? When we take in data without preconceptions we are *sensing;* when we focus on particular sensations and categorize them according to our memory system, we are *perceiving;* and when we draw conclusions about their patterns and meaning, we are *thinking.*

Sensing occurs through sense organs such as the eyes and skin. When our sense organs become activated by stimuli—such as by a bright, warm light—they send this information through the nervous system to the brain. When we sense something, we *feel* it; we feel certain about the presence of something. As we sense, we may not yet have the words to identify or explain what is happening, because in order to find words, we have to think. *Yet, when we begin to think, we risk cutting ourselves off from our sensations.* We cannot fully sense and think at the same time. If we open the front door in the morning to sense how warm

---

THINKING

Thinking comes from the root Indo-European word *thong,* a word related to *thing.*

When we think, we *thing-a-fy;* we make "things" of nature and events from our perceptions of them.

Perceive comes from the Latin words *percipere,* meaning to receive—*per,* meaning thoroughly, and *capere,* meaning to catch, seize, or hold. When we perceive something, we catch and hold it in consciousness until we recognize patterns and find meaning.

Sensing comes from the Latin *sentire,* to feel.

the day is, we have to stop thinking in order to sense the temperature of air on face and skin. If we want to truly hear music, we can't be absorbed in our thoughts.

In everyday speech, the word *perceiving* is often used loosely as a synonym for sensing, although there are distinct differences. Perception is both passive and active; it holds sensations in consciousness long enough to interpret them. This holding allows the time needed to find patterns, to organize, and interpret the sensations. A study of the diagram below

PERCEIVING PERCEPTION

If you want to experience how your perception works stare at this form for a few minutes. What happens to the shape as you look? When do you begin to see some patterns you can identify? When do you make comparisons or give names to what you see?

> *Thinking is an active process whereby people organize their perceptions of the world. (Jean Piaget)*

will show you how your own perception operates to interpret space, dimension, and shape.

Perception helps us move through the physical world. When we are walking, we use perception to tell us the level of the surface below our feet; without perception, we would fall over curbs. Perception also helps us detect dimensions: to tell the difference between a lamp and its shadow. It enables us to identify sounds and estimate their location.

Now all of us sense, perceive, and think continually. But what *is* thinking? Philosopher Alan Watts uses the etymology of the word to show us how the earlier peoples (who gave us our language) explained thinking. The root word *thong* tells us that thinking is used to make "things" of nature and of events. We give a name to what we perceive, thus making it into a thing we can move around in our heads. A psychologist, Jean Piaget, defined thinking as "an active process whereby people organize their perceptions of the world." In both these definitions thinking is explained in terms of what people do with their perceptions.

Our intention in studying these definitions has been to help us become more aware of the observing process. When we can match precise words to inner experience, we can better observe and think about it. We can monitor and direct what was previously unidentified and invisible. Its stages can be consciously directed as

- we take in data from sensing,
- perceive as we interpret this data,
- think as we draw conclusions and communicate.

BARRIERS TO OBSERVATION

The barriers lie inside us.

We can well empathize with Scudder's experience in learning how to observe. His first mistake was his hurry. ("In ten minutes I had seen all that could be seen in that fish.") All of us know how difficult it can be to slow down, especially when we value striving for speed and efficiency. Yet our senses require a much slower speed than our thinking in order to process information. Therefore the need to shift down can feel highly uncomfortable at first. It might even make us feel impatient, anxious, or irritable. Yet if we stay on task and simply observe our feelings, we may soon become absorbed in deep concentration. *This phenomenon occurs when we move from left brain over into right brain dominance.* Here concern about time is lost; words are lost; there is just silence and presence. And at this point, we begin to make discoveries. Yet typically this exciting interval will continue for only about six minutes. Then we reach a plateau where nothing new emerges. Again we will feel restless. However, should we just hang in there or take a short break, a new cycle of interest will begin again, leading to new discoveries—until there arises still another plateau. Yet, just as Scudder discovered, each time he returned to observing, a new cycle would begin, leading to additional understandings.

Like Scudder, our experiencing—even suffering through—such a process can teach us that we have a far greater capacity to discover than we knew; it can show us that we *can* rely more on ourselves.

Short Break Study Questions

1. Did you ever feel uncomfortable while working on your tool or fruit? How did you handle it?

2. Discuss other historical examples where people feared and opposed new discoveries.

HOW DISCOMFORT LEADS US TO THINK

In our daily lives, when we are presented with a problem, our first reaction may be one of denial and inertia. We may try first to explain this situation in a way that will not require any change or effort from us. Let's take the case of a young man who tries one job after another, only to always find himself bored or fired.

"I haven't been able to get a decent job since I left high school; maybe I just need more luck."

As time goes by, if he continues to fail, he may begin to review his situation all over again. In short, he may really begin to think about it. Perhaps he might consider more that training or college would get him a better job. Should returning to school work for him, he will find himself feeling better. His thinking will have taken him out of a problem that was causing him more and more discomfort.

Let's look again at Jean Piaget's definition of thinking as "an active process whereby people organize their perceptions of the world." At one point, Piaget described this process as involving both **assimilation** (or easily inserting new data into an existing mental folder) and **accommodation** (or having to create a new folder). When we cannot grasp a new idea or make it fit with what we already know, we feel discomfort or what Piaget called "disequilibrium." We may not even realize that this discomfort stems from our inability to assimilate that new idea. Indeed, we may blame something or someone else for our discomfort. But if we can create

A Choice for Thinking

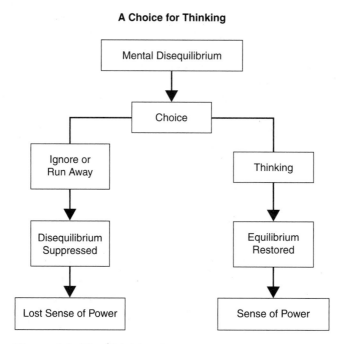

Figure 1.2 The Thinking Process

a new file drawer to rightly accommodate this new idea, we will then feel immediately better. Our equilibrium has been restored.

Should we run away from the problem, our discomfort will still remain there on a suppressed level. Basically, we human beings feel good when we can make sense of things, but uncomfortable when we don't. And that discomfort can push us to think.

Short Break Study Questions

1. Think of a problem that was hard for you to solve. How did it feel when you couldn't? How did it feel when you succeeded?

THE REWARDS OF SKILLED OBSERVATION

Sensitive accurate observing is an essential skill of scientists as well as artists. The following reading is taken from a book on art design. This book consists of exercises for developing design perception and control. Dorr Bothwell, a woman painter who was born in 1904, wrote this essay, "The Innocent Eye." At age 97 she was still exhibiting her works and winning national awards. Her essay serves as a reminder of what you

BUILDING ARGUMENTS

OBSERVATION SKILLS

This is the first of a series called "Building Arguments" which runs through each chapter. Each is designed to show you how that chapter's concept applies to the construction of an argument. This chapter will help prepare you for Chapter 9 when you will need to integrate all you have learned from each chapter into the analysis and writing of arguments.

Here are some Key Terms related to arguments that you will need to understand:

> **Parts of an argument**—An argument consists of two parts: a *principal claim* (also called a conclusion) which is justified by *reasons* which form the second part.

> **Principal claim** is the thesis of an argument. It is the conclusion that the argument wants you to accept.

> **Reasons** support or justify the principal claim through evidence or other claims. Observation skills furnish us with one form of evidence. (Other forms include records, testimony, or statistics.)

> **Hypotheses**—When we observe, we collect data and form tentative ideas or *hypotheses* about the data's meaning. Notice how Christopher Columbus makes a hypothesis from his observations.

Reading

They came swimming to the ships' boats, where we were, and brought us parrots and cotton thread in balls, and spears and many other things. They all go naked as their mothers bore them . . . they were very well built, with very handsome bodies and very good faces. Their hair is coarse almost like the hairs of a horse's tail and short; they wear their hair down over their eyebrows, except for a few strands behind, which they wear long and never cut. Some of them are painted black, and they are the colour of the people of the Canaries, neither black nor white, and some of them are painted white and some red and some in any colour they can find. . . . They do not bear arms or know them, for I showed to them swords and they took them by the blade and cut themselves through ignorance. (So far all these sentences are claims presented as evidence gained from observation.) *They should be good servants and of quick intelligence, since I see that they very soon say all that is said to them, and I believe that they would easily be made Christians, for it appeared to me that they had no creed.* (Hypothesis, conclusion, or principal claim drawn from evidence.)

Study Questions

1. Give your reaction to Columbus' conclusion. What were the historical consequences?
2. What other possible hypotheses would have taken history in a totally different direction?

From the Journal of Christopher Columbus, October 12, 1492.

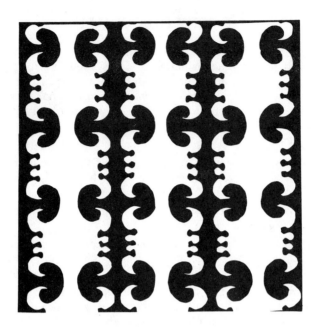

Figure 1.3 Can you see in this design the interaction between positive and negative space described in "The Innocent Eye"? Is either less important than the other?

may have already discovered: that although observing may require self-control and patience, it nevertheless can lead to the rapture, power, and wonder we feel when immersed in the creative process.

READING

THE INNOCENT EYE
Dorr Bothwell

Creative observation of our surroundings revives in us a sense of the wonder of life. 1
Much of this discovery involves the recovery of something that we all once had in childhood. When we were very young we were all artists. We all came into this world with the doors of perception wide open. Everything was a delightful surprise. Everything, at first, required the slow, loving touch of our tongues and our hands. Long before we could speak we knew the comfort of our mother's warm body, the delightful feel of a furry toy. Smooth and rough surfaces, things cold and hot surprised and en-

chanted us. Touch by touch we built up our store of tactile impressions, keenly sensed in minute detail.

Later on, this tactile sensing was transferred to our eyes, and we were able to "feel" through the sense of vision things beyond the grasp of our hands. This kind of seeing was not the rapid sophisticated eye sweep of the well informed. This kind of seeing was a slow, uncritical examination in depth. The more we looked the more lovely and surprising things appeared, until we were pervaded by that wordless thrill which is the sense of wonder. **2**

None of us has lost our store of tactile memories. Nor have we lost our sense of wonder. All that has happened is that we have substituted identifying and labeling, which can be done very rapidly, for the tactile sort of feel-seeing which requires much more time and concentration. For example, if you were asked to look at the edge of your desk and estimate its length, it would only take you a few seconds to flick your eyes back and forth and say it is so many inches long. But suppose you were asked to run the tip of your finger along the edge of the desk and count every tiny nick? You would press your finger along the edge and move it very, very slowly, and your eye would move no faster than your finger. This slow, concentrated way of feeling and seeing is the first step towards regaining our sense of wonder. **3**

There was a time when man moved no faster than his feet or the feet of some animal that could carry him. During that period the artistic or creative spirit seemed to have free expression. Today, in order to be creative and yet move smoothly and efficiently through our fast-paced world, we must be able to function on two different speed levels. The mistake we have made, often with tragic results, is to try to do *all* our living at the speed our machines have imposed upon us. **4**

In order to live at this speed we must scan the surface of things, pick out salient aspects, disregard secondary features; and there is certainly nothing wrong in this if we are driving on a busy freeway. But when we allow this pressure to invade every aspect of our life, we begin to "lose touch," to have a feeling that we are missing something, and we are hungry for we don't know what. When that happens, we have begun to suffer from aesthetic malnutrition. Fortunately, the cure for this condition is very pleasant, and although it takes a little self-discipline at the beginning, the results are worth the effort. **5**

When we see as design artists, we become especially aware of the interaction between positive and negative space. In architecture we are suddenly aware of the spaces between the windows, at the ballet we notice how the spaces between the dancers open and close, and in music we realize that rhythm is made by the shapes of silence between the notes. **6**

Everywhere we look we see this principle in action. Trees are not silhouetted against blank air, but hold blue spangles between their leaves while branches frame living shapes of sky. Space seems to be pulled between the leaves of a fern. We delight in the openings between the petals of a flower or the spokes of a wheel. This endless exchange between form and space excites us. Once more we feel in touch with our world; our aesthetic sense is being fed and we are comforted. **7**

We may have been taught that butterflies are lovely and toads are ugly, so we admire the butterfly and shrink away from the toad without really examining it to find **8** out if what we had been taught is true. Or we are taught that flowers are good and weeds are bad, so we pull up the latter without a glance. To the artist's eye there is no good or bad. There is just the inappropriate. In the garden, weeds are not appropriate, but in the vacant lot they offer a world of enchantment. And after we have learned to see the beauty in weeds, even though we have to pull them out of the garden, we can first admire their design.

When no preconceived ideas keep us from looking and we take all the time we $\quad$ **9** need to really "feel" what we see—when we are able to do that—the universe opens up and we catch our breath in awe at the incredible complexity of design in the humblest things. It is only when this happens that we regain our sense of wonder.

From Dorr Bothwell and Marlys Mayfield, *Notan: The Dark Light Principle of Design.* New York: Dover, 1991. Used with permission of Dorr Bothwell.

Study Questions

1. Explain the statement, "When we were very young we were all artists."
2. Explain what the author means by the expression "aesthetic malnutrition" that comes from high-speed living.
3. Describe what is meant by the "interaction of positive and negative space."
4. Explain what is meant by the statement, "To the artist's eye, there is no good or bad. There is just the inappropriate." When you were writing your descriptions of objects, was there a feeling of dislike for the object that kept you from making contact with it fully? Did your attitude change as you continued to work?

CHAPTER SUMMARY

1. If we want to develop more conscious thinking habits, we have to first observe our own thinking processes so we can recognize our strengths and weaknesses.

2. Careful observation can help us see details that contain the key to unlocking problems or arriving at insights. It can also help us discover new knowledge.

3. Observation is a process of sensing, perceiving, and thinking. Sensing is collecting data through the sense organs. Perceiving is holding sense data in consciousness until we can categorize and interpret it. Thinking organizes our perceptions.

4. Careful observation requires us to stay awake, take our time, give full attention, suspend thinking in an attitude of listening.

5. The rewards of cultivating observation skills are self-understanding, creativity, rapture, power, and wonder.

CHAPTER QUIZ

Rate each of the following statements as *true* or *false.* Justify your answer with an example or explanation to prove and illustrate your understanding. *Do not omit this part of the test. True/false* answers can be guessed. But when you defend your answer by example or explanation, you demonstrate not only your memory and understanding but also that you can apply what you have learned to life. The first question is answered for you.

FALSE 1. Observation skills are learned mainly through book learning.

Support for Answer. On the contrary, observation is learned from participation, which is more active and spontaneous than reading. Samuel Scudder learned observing through the active coaching of his teacher Agassiz, as well as from his own efforts, curiosity, and persistence in studying his fish.

_____ 2. The standard academic study of all the physical sciences requires observation skills, whether in the field or laboratory.

_____ 3. In thinking, the correctness of our conclusions usually depends on the clarity of our perceptions.

_____ 4. Observation skills can be extended to observing how you observe.

_____ 5. An insight is an experience of understanding that can occur spontaneously after we observe something intently for a while. One illustration of this experience is the story of Archimedes, who, while in his bath, discovered the means of measuring the volume of an irregular solid by the displacement of water.

_____ 6. Agassiz was simply too busy to give his student all the assistance he needed.

_____ 7. *Perception* and *sensation* are synonyms.

_____ 8. It is difficult to feel sensation and to think at the same time. If we want to feel whether a pair of new shoes fits properly, we have to pay attention.

_____ 9. *Assimilation,* according to Piaget, is an experience of easily understanding something that readily fits into our preexisting schemes or world view.

_____ 10. The word *thinking,* according to the dictionary, has only one meaning.

COMPOSITION WRITING APPLICATION

Survival As a Result of Observing: A Descriptive Narrative Essay

Describe an experience in which your safety, welfare, or survival depended upon your ability to observe a situation or problem clearly. This could involve a danger in city life, in camping, or in sports, or perhaps a life decision where observation skills were crucial. Write from three to five pages, telling your story as a narrative. (See F. Bruce Lamb's story as a model.) Remember that the theme that should tie your story together is the theme of observation. Be sure to emphasize in your story where you observed and where you did not and what the consequences were.

Review of Assignment Guidelines

1. *Form:* A story or narrative
2. *Theme:* How observation skills helped you survive
3. *Length:* Three to five typed pages or until you feel the story is complete.

Scoring for Narrative Essay

1. Minimum of three typed pages. 20 points
2. Story offers enough specifics to enable the reader to go through the experience. 20 points
3. Story flows; the reader can follow it without difficulty. 10 points
4. The language is accurate, appropriate, and appears carefully chosen. 10 points
5. The use of observation skills is clearly a theme in the story. 25 points
6. Free of errors in spelling, sentence structure, and punctuation. 15 points

READING

WIZARD OF THE UPPER AMAZON: THE STORY OF MANUEL CORDOVA-RIOS

F. Bruce Lamb

First published in 1971, this book was written by an American forest engineer who, while working in South America, met the narrator of this story, Manuel Cordova-Rios, then a famous Peruvian healer. Manuel's story begins in 1907, when at the age of

15, he was captured by a tribe of Amazon Indians and taken into a remote jungle area. During the course of the seven years he lived with them, he gradually began to recognize that he was undergoing a long apprenticeship. In this reading excerpt, he begins to learn what he needs to know in order to survive as a hunter. Note as you read what he has to learn.

1. First we chose a location between four small trees where a palm-leaf roof could be built on a vine-and-pole framework. Material for this we gathered from the forest around us. By the time the scouts had returned at dusk, the shelter was ready with space for six small hammocks and a fire burning in the middle under a meat-smoking platform of interwoven green sticks.

2. Each of the scouts had brought back game: two partridges, a small forest deer and a pair of monkeys. These were cleaned and the choicest tidbits put low over the fire for fast roasting for our first camp meal. The rest were prepared for slow-roasting and smoking on the platform.

3. That night, lying in our hammocks, we heard the minutest details of the hunt in addition to a review of hunting conditions that had been observed in the area. . . .

4. After this recital of the hunting stories was finished, the men listened to the sounds of the night jungle and explained them to me. Their hearing was much more acute than mine. Much of what they described I could not hear. This was true also of my sense of smell. Gradually we drifted off to sleep, all except the one assigned to tend the smoking fire and the turning of the meat on the smoke rack. Sleep was never continuous in a hunting camp—men were up and down and the fire watch changed several times.

5. The man on guard, I learned, was also expected continually to be aware of the sights, sounds, smells of the surrounding jungle as the guard changed during the night hours. Animal activity at night is often more intense than during daylight hours in the tropical forest.

6. As I was settling down to sleep I went over in my mind everything that had happened on the hunting expedition so far. I realized that I had learned more about the forest in these few days out with the Indians than during all my previous experience. I was also well aware that by comparison my knowledge was extremely limited and the acuity of my senses far below that of my companions. This I was determined to change.

7. The next day Nixi and I went off with Txaxo Anika to look for his band of wild pigs. One man was left in camp and the other two were to go to the tree with ripening fruit. There they would build covered hunting platforms up in the tree crown. These would make it easy to take the large birds and monkeys that came to eat the fruit.

8. Single file we went through the forest undergrowth, with me in the middle. Immediately my bodily coordination and sense perceptions were taxed to the utmost to keep up with the pace set and remain alert to the jungle signs I was learning to recognize. We came to the place where Txaxo had observed the trail of the wild pigs and we stopped briefly for consultation to decide what to do next. Before we moved off opposite to the direction the band of pigs had taken I was given additional hunting information.

They explained that in hunting a large band of pigs the timing of approach and an understanding of the animal signals were the major factors in the success of bagging these animals. The two principal signals of this species were imitated and explained to me. At a certain type of grunt from the leader, the band would break into a wild run and scatter in all directions. At a loud clicking of the teeth and a high-pitched squeal, the whole band would immediately bristle and attack any moving object that was not part of the band. To protect oneself in the hunt and obtain meat it was necessary to anticipate and recognize these signals. **9**

We went off again at a killing pace that required all my attention. It seemed we went at this fast speed for a long time and exhaustion was beginning to show on me, when we came to fresh tracks and stopped to look, sniff the air and discuss the signs. The odor I now associated with wild pig was strong here. Tracks and disturbance of the earth gave my companion considerable information—the approximate size of the band, what they were eating, how fast they were traveling and in what direction. **10**

This time we set off at an angle to what appeared to me to be the traveling direction of the pigs. After going up over a hill and down into a small valley with no sign of game, my companions came abreast and strung their bows with arrows. I did the same without sensing any reason why. Suddenly with a loud grunt there were wild pigs all around us, running and squealing in utter confusion. I managed to shoot one arrow and get strung up for another shot when I realized that as suddenly as the pigs had appeared they had gone without a sound. I looked around and my hunting companions were gone also. **11**

My quarry was nearby, gasping his last breath and kicking feebly with my arrow in his side. Soon Txaxo and Nixi came back, each with two pigs and each with a daub of blood on both cheeks. This was another good-luck charm for future hunts, and they insisted that I daub blood on my own cheeks from the animal I had killed and that I also rub some on my new bow. **12**

My first kill with a bow and arrow gave me a feeling of satisfaction. Nixi and Txaxo both showed their pleasure at my accomplishment. We immediately made vine slings and started back to camp with loads on our backs. On the way the animals were gutted, but only one at a stop in order to leave the least evidence at any one location in case a possible enemy might wander by. . . . **13**

From these discussions and from my own daily experience in the village I became aware of how closely these Indians were molded to their environment. Their muscular coordination and visual sense of their surroundings in the forest made it possible for them to move quickly and with ease through the most tangled undergrowth. They could anticipate the hazards and difficulties and avoid most of them. They reacted to the faintest signals of sound and smell, intuitively relating them to all other conditions of the environment and then interpreting them to achieve the greatest possible capture of game. Development of the other senses compensated for the limited visibility found in the forest. Often on the ground in the forest, visibility is no more than fifteen feet or so. Looking upward into the canopy, one may see one hundred **14** feet but seldom any farther. Most of the jungle animals have protective coloring or camouflage that make them difficult to see even close at hand.

The Indians had great patience when it was required and they used it, together **15** with knowledge and intuition, to capture game with the least possible expenditure of energy. Many of the best hunters seemed to know by some special extra sense just where to find the game they sought, or they had developed some special method of drawing game to them. Knowing how to imitate and to use the signals the animals made to communicate between their kind in various situations helped in locating game and drawing it within sighting range of an astute hunter. It took skill, keen development of all the senses, patience and experience to enable a hunter to provide, constantly, sufficient game to feed a family.

Study Questions

1. How did the Indians train their ability to observe in order to survive?
2. Given the limited visibility of the jungle, how did the hunters learn to compensate in order to succeed?
3. What skills enabled them to kill the pigs?
4. What habits, attitudes, and traits of character did the Indians develop in order to survive?
5. How does this reading help you better understand why today large numbers of Amazon Indians are committing suicide as they lose their lands and hunting grounds to encroaching miners and ranchers?

CHAPTER 2

Word Precision

How Do I Describe It?

"I liked it because you can read it with both the TV and the radio on." Used with permission of Richard Guindon.

When we want to share our experiences with others through writing, we need to give thought to our choice of words. This chapter takes a close look at that process of translation. It will describe how:

- words interconnect with thinking and perceiving;
- a good dictionary helps thinking;
- words are defined;
- words suggest feelings;

- concepts abstract thought;
- critical reading works.

This chapter cannot cover everything a college student needs to know about words. But when you have finished this chapter, you should know more about how well you actually work with words, how word confusion and word clarity affect your thinking, and how word precision can satisfy the spirit.

Discovery Exercise

Words Matching Senses

This exercise may be done independently at home or in class with four other people. If you are working with others, take turns reading this selection aloud. Then answer the study questions in writing or in discussion with your group.

READING

THE HOT SPRING

Barry Lopez

This reading is the second chapter of Desert Notes, *a short book of lyric prose that is the first of a trilogy followed by* River Notes *and* Field Notes. *Barry Lopez is best known for his book* Arctic Dreams (1986) *for which he received the National Book Award.*

I.

The man would set off late in the spring, after the dogwood had bloomed, in the blue   1
'58 Chevy pickup with the broken taillight and the cracked Expando mirrors. He would take a thin green sleeping bag and a blue tarpaulin, a few dishes and a one-burner stove. He would take his spoon and only cereal to eat and tea to drink. He would take no books, no piece of paper to write on.

He would stop only for gas and would pick up no hitchhikers. He would drive   2
straight through on the two-lane, blacktop roads, cracked and broken with the freeze of last winter, without turning the radio on. He would lift his damp buttocks from the hot naugahyde seat and let the wind, coming in through the window that was stuck halfway down, cool him.

It would take seven hours to drive the 278 miles. First, over the mountains, past   3
the great lava flows at the ridge, past the slopes of black obsidian glass, down into the sweet swamp of thick air in the ponderosa forest.

He would drive out then into the great basin over arroyos and across sage flats **4** dotted with juniper and rabbit brush, past the fenced squares marked Experimental Station where the government was trying to grow crested wheat grass, trying to turn the high desert into grassy fields for bony Herefords with vacant eyes. He would see few cows. He would see, on a long stretch of road, a golden eagle sitting on a fence post.

There would be more space between the towns and more until there were no **5** towns at all, only empty shacks, their roof ridges bowed, their doors and windows gone.

He would come around the base of another range of mountains, slip down on **6** the southeastern side and drive on a one-lane dirt road along the edge of the alkaline desert for twenty miles until he came to the hot spring. There he would stop. He would stop the truck, but he would leave the motor running to keep the engine cool. He would always arrive by one in the afternoon.

II.

He inhaled the tart, sulphurous fumes rising up from the green reeds, the only bit of **7** green for miles. He watched the spiders spinning webs in the wire grass and the water bugs riding the clots of yellow bubbles. He stared at the bullet-riddled walls of tin that surrounded the sandy basin where the water collected.

When he had seen these things, that they had weathered the winter, the man put **8** the truck in gear and rolled down over the sagebrush and onto the desert floor. He drove out over the dry, bleached soil for a mile before he put the truck in neutral and let it coast to a stop. He was careful with the silence. He could hear his fingers slide over the plastic steering wheel. He could feel the curve of his lips tightening in the dryness.

He took off his clothes, all of them, and put them in a zippered airlines bag on **9** the floor of the truck. Then he put his sneakers back on and went naked across the desert back to the hot spring with a pair of linen socks in his hand. The cool breeze from the mountains raised his flesh into a lattice of pin-pricked hills.

He removed his shoes. He lay on his back in the hot water, his toes grazing the **10** shallow, sandy bottom of the pool. He could hear the water lapping at the entrance to his ears, the weight of water pulling on his hair; he could feel the particles of dust falling off his flesh, floating down, settling on the bottom of the pool; he could feel the water prying at the layers of dried sweat. He concentrated and tried to hear the dirt and sweat breaking away from his body. The tips of his fingers wrinkled, and he stared at the water pooling in the cavity of his chest and falling away as he breathed.

He wanted to stay until the sun set but he couldn't: he could feel himself sink- **11** ing. He climbed out of the pool and walked out of the roofless tin shelter onto the floor of the desert. The wind began to evaporate the water and his pores closed like frightened mussels and trapped the warmth beneath his skin.

When his feet were dry he put on only the linen socks and left. He could feel **12** the wind eddying up around him like a cloak and his feet barely touched the ground. His eyes felt smoother in their sockets and he could tell, without looking, how his fingers were curled; he could see the muscles of his legs tied beneath his kneecaps, feel the patella gliding over the knot. He felt the muscles anchored on the broad, flat plate of his hipbones and the wind soft deep in the roots of his hair. He felt the pressure of his parting the air as he walked.

When he got back to the truck he poured a cup of water and placed a handful **13** of cereal into an earthen bowl. He ate and looked out across the desert and imagined that he had come to life again.

From Barry Lopez, *Desert Notes: Reflections in the Eye of a Raven.* New York: Avon Books, 1976. Copyright 1976 by Barry Holstun Lopez. Reprinted with permission of Andrews and McMeel and Barry Lopez.

Study Questions

1. What is simple about this writing? What is complex about it?
2. How does this reading affect your body and feelings? Do you identify with the protagonist? If so, how did the author manage to get you to feel you were inside the man?
3. Read paragraphs 7, 8, and 9 and notice how the verbs, nouns, and adjectives convey sensory information. Make a list of these sense-conveying words under columns headed *verbs, nouns,* and *adjectives.*
4. Notice the use of the verb *would* in the first paragraphs conveying a habitual action. Why do you think this man would regularly take such a long drive to a desert location?
5. Explain his last statement: "He ate and looked out across the desert and imagined that he had come to life again."
6. Do you think the author chose a boring subject? What makes a subject boring?
7. Working on your own or with a partner, choose any *two paragraphs* of "The Hot Spring" to analyze. Make column headings for word categories that convey different kinds of sensory information. Use the format given in the example that follows, which covers the first two sentences. Put parentheses around sensations that are associative or implied. Then create other word categories to match sensations as you find them.

Images	Texture	Kinesthetic	Color	Time	Size	Sound
dogwood	(soft)	bloomed	blue	late	thin	cracked
Chevy pickup	(slick)	broken	green	spring		
taillight	(shiny)					
mirrors	(reflecting)					
sleeping bag	(soft)					
tarpaulin	(rough)					
dishes	(smooth)					

ON FINDING THE RIGHT WORD

It is a highly complex mental operation to keep an experience in mind as a constant, while searching through memory and dictionary for the right words to describe it. Writing is a mental discipline that requires us to capture words. Yet, interestingly enough, the more words we master, the more of the world we see.

You have just learned something about the word artistry of a skilled professional author, who, like you, wrote from observations. Looking back at your descriptive writing in the last chapter, you may have noticed that there were also different stages involved in your word search. The first was probably one of silent absorption. If words came to you at that time, they could have interfered with your sensing process. Nevertheless—once you were ready to write down your experiences—you may have been surprised to find yourself at a loss for words. You knew what you had seen or touched or felt, but you also realized that any word choices would only result in *translations* into another medium that would never fully duplicate your silent experience. It took a lot of effort to keep your translation as true as possible to your experience.

If you were describing an orange, you might have found that although you had held hundreds of oranges, you still could not describe its color, texture, smell, and taste. For instance, if you wrote down, "It tastes like an orange," you knew already that the word *orange* was inadequate. To erase this and write down "citrus flavor" would have been still more abstract, including the taste of lemons, grapefruit, and tangerines. You could have picked up the orange to taste it again, giving more studied awareness to your senses. This round of savoring could have summoned up such words as *sticky-sweet, tangy-flesh, spicy-warm.* If you still were not satisfied, you could have gone to *Random House Word Menu* or *Roget's International Thesaurus* and looked under the lists of words for *sweetness* and *sourness,* finding choices like *pungent, acidic,* and *fermented.* Here you would have also discovered more words to describe the colors in the orange's rind: *reddish-yellow, ocher, pumpkin, gold, apricot, carrot, yellow-orange, gilt, canary, beige, saffron, topaz-yellow, green, emerald, olive, chartreuse,* or *nut-brown, fawn, rusty, bronze,* and *chestnut.*

Keeping an experience in mind as a constant, while searching both through word memory and thesaurus to find appropriate word correspondences, is a complex mental operation. Writing challenges you to stretch your abilities to use the words you know and to find new ones. Through this process you will move in time toward greater word mastery. In addition, learning more words enables you to actually *see* more. To learn the words for things, you have to pay more attention to them. And once you recognize by name a Washington navel orange and a Valencia orange, you also perceive more of their details: the navels' shapes, the rinds' different textures, the subtleties of their shades of color. When someone offers you an orange, you enjoy appreciating its characteristics and talking about them, for your perception, together with your vocabulary, has enabled you to make finer differentiations. *The advantage of having a precise vocabulary to describe your experience also enables you to learn and experience even more.*

Discovery Exercise

Sorting Out Confusion about Dictionaries

Rate each of the following statements as *true* or *false*. Be prepared to defend your answers in writing or in a class discussion.

1. Dictionaries are like phone books; basically, they all offer the same information.

2. If a dictionary is named Webster's, that means it is one of the best.

3. Experts who decide how we should speak English write dictionaries.

4. Small pocket dictionaries are the best kind to use for an in-depth study of words, because they eliminate unnecessary, confusing information and make understanding easier.

5. Since a dictionary can confuse us with so many definitions for any single word, it is better to try to figure out a word's meaning from its context or ask someone else.

6. Dictionaries are like cookbooks; a family needs to buy only one for the family's lifetime.

7. Dictionaries give us information about spelling and definitions, but that is about all they offer.

8. Dictionaries list word definitions in the order of most frequent use. Therefore, it is usually best to choose the first definition given.

Here is a discussion of the correct answers. Read this only *after* you've completed the quiz.

1. False. A comparative study of several dictionaries—for instance, *The American Heritage Dictionary, Webster's Collegiate Dictionary,* and *Webster's New World Dictionary*—will make this apparent.

2. False. Noah Webster was a nineteenth-century American lexicographer. The Merriam Company purchased the rights to his book, which has continued, under the name Merriam-Webster, to publish and revise the large *Webster's New International Dictionary.* However, since the name Webster's is not protected by a copyright, many other

companies have used it to put out both excellent and inferior products. The most prestigious and scientifically researched dictionary is the *Oxford English Dictionary*, bound in versions that range from two to twenty volumes.

3. False. Dictionaries serve as authoritative reference sources; however, they are not authoritative in the sense of being infallible but in the sense of offering reliable historical information about words and their use. In the case of *The American Heritage Dictionary*, this information is based on the opinions of a panel of lexicographers, linguists, writers, and scientists. Dictionaries are not written to dictate dogma but only to reflect agreements and standards about how people use their language, both in popular speech and formal writing.

4. False. Pocket dictionaries may be more convenient to carry and use for understanding simpler words or spellings, but they are too condensed for use in the more serious study of word ideas, concepts, and usage. Moreover, their definitions can sometimes be oversimplified to the point of being misleading. Finally, and more obviously, a pocket dictionary containing 30,000 words cannot offer you as much as an unabridged dictionary with 600,000 words or a college desk-sized one with 60,000 words.

5. False. Although most study skill texts suggest this, and most English composition-reading texts select the vocabulary for you, a guess based on your view of the context may be mistaken, and your friend may be even more confused than you. The result may be to "unlearn" a misunderstood word later. If you are skilled in dictionary use, it is not a chore to confirm a guess or a friend's definition by consulting the dictionary. Furthermore, certainty about a word's meaning can enable you to cement it more confidently into your memory.

6. False. If your dictionary is more than fifteen years old, it is time to buy a new one. The English language acquires or invents thousands of new words each year, and our customs about word usage change also.

7. False. It's worth spending a little time just browsing through your dictionary to find out all it has to offer. You'll find a concise history of the English language, for one thing.

8. False. This is true of *The American Heritage Dictionary* but not of *Webster's Collegiate Dictionary, Webster's New World Dictionary*, or the *Oxford English Dictionary*. These dictionaries begin with the oldest meaning of the word, which, in some cases, has already become obsolete. Thus, if you choose the first definition regardless of the type of dictionary you are using, you might not be able to make yourself understood. It is important, therefore, to make sure you know which system is being used in your dictionary.

HOW WELL DO YOU USE YOUR DICTIONARY?

Bring to class a college desk-sized dictionary. If you need to buy one, the following are recommended. These are comprehensive, hard-cover, up-to-date dictionaries that will help you through all your college courses.

> *The American Heritage College Dictionary,* third edition (Houghton Mifflin, 1997).

> *Webster's New World College Dictionary,* fourth edition (Macmillan, 1999).

Working with a partner, take turns finding three random entries to discuss. Explain to your partner every piece of information that you find there, including every symbol and every abbreviation. If you do not understand something, take the time to look it up. (If, for instance, you do not understand what is meant by the abbreviation *OF,* find out where your dictionary explains its abbreviations.) Work together to understand *all* the information given, and do not let one another off the hook until you sense everything interpreted is fully understood.

Finally, one of you should write down your answers to the following questions:

1. State the name of the dictionary you own and its date of publication. How many pages does it have? How many entries are there? Is it a desk-sized dictionary?

2. Do you feel you have had sufficient instruction in school to know how to make use of an unabridged or a desk-sized dictionary?

3. Test your knowledge of the history of the English language by explaining what your dictionary means when it refers to a word as *Anglo-Saxon* or *Middle English, Late Latin,* and *Indo-European.*

4. Look up *Pago Pago.* Write down how it is pronounced. Pronounce it for your partner. Was this easy or difficult for you?

5. Have you ever discovered that you had misunderstood a familiar word and were misusing it? Give an example and explain how you found out.

6. How does the word *plan* differ from the words *design, project,* and *scheme?* The *Webster's New World Dictionary* will explain how they differ in connotation. What are word connotations, and why are they important to consider when you make your selection?

7. Describe the mental signals that show you, in dictionary study, that you have fully understood a new word. Do you usually persist in word study until you have these signals?

8. If you can't find a word or clear definition of a word in one dictionary, do you usually think to consult another dictionary? Explain why or why not.

9. When do you use a thesaurus? How is it helpful when you do not know the word for something?

CLEAR THINKING DEPENDS ON CLEAR WORD DEFINITIONS

Persistent confusion about words actually makes us less conscious and aware. We can be as confused about unfamiliar words as familiar ones.

Clear thinking and expression depend on clear word understanding. Yet, as obvious as this idea may seem, word clarity is not necessarily common. It takes dedication to make the effort to truly understand all the words that pass through your day. Yet the effort need not be so great if based on a commitment to certain habits. The first simply involves noticing how you feel when you do not fully understand a word; the second is just taking out the time to clear things up. In conversation, word confusion stands out more. If a friend were to suddenly say you were *contumacious,* you would have to ask what that word meant before you could respond. But in reading it can be easier to ride over word confusion, just as it is in listening to radio or television. Moreover, a person can be just as confused about familiar words as unfamiliar ones. Unfamiliar words are easier to recognize, such as when we first hear the word *libertarian;* however, we may not recognize our actual perplexity about a word heard as often as *liberal.*

Words that describe the thinking process fall in this latter category of being familiar but not commonly well understood. Such words are given special attention in this text, as you will have noticed in reading the previous chapter's discussion of such words as observing, perceiving, sensing, and thinking.

Dictionaries are our resource for fully understanding words. Yet few are in the habit of using them as automatically as a napkin at a meal. Of course it can feel annoying to stop whatever we are doing to look up a word. Yet word confusion actually creates mental disequilibrium. If you hear or see a word that you do not understand, you might tell yourself that if you keep going, you would eventually understand it from the context. Indeed, reading study guides often advise that. However, if understanding does not occur, you will actually find yourself *losing consciousness,* or becoming drowsy. The knack here is to recognize the early inner signs of word confusion before drowsiness takes over and to exert sufficient willpower to clear up misunderstanding through dictionary study. Although this special effort is needed, once the meaning is clarified, the perceptible sense of relief makes the effort worthwhile. It may even take referring to more than one dictionary, diagramming the word, or using it in sentences. But when you have finished you will find yourself more alert, with a renewed energy for continuing your work.

The definitions of key concepts in every chapter of this text are designed to emphasize the importance of gaining better word-understanding habits. However, you will also come across many unfamiliar words as you read this textbook. *It will remain your responsibility to use the dictionary to understand any unfamiliar words that you may find while reading this textbook and thus to reinforce this important critical thinking habit.*

WHAT MAKES A DEFINITION?

Definitions clarify words through boundaries.

The etymology, or history, of the word **definition** shows us something interesting; it comes from the Latin roots *de,* meaning off or away from, and *finis,* meaning end or boundary; the Latin word *definire* means to set bounds to. So when we *define* something, we discover or establish its boundaries. When we learn a new word, the definition shows us what boundaries separate it from every other word. For example, let's take the word *cheesecake.* If we only go for its meaning as a dessert, we see (Figure 2.1) how it can be defined through six boundaries that classify the word:

> *baked desserts*
>
> *a cake that looks like a pie*
>
> *egg-based, not flour-based, with a thin crumb crust*
>
> *sweetened cottage or cream cheese as chief ingredient*

In a definition, the word to be defined is called a **term.** Every term can be included in a **class,** or the largest family to which it is related within this particular boundary. Thus the term *cake* belongs in the class of baked desserts whose boundaries also include baked custard or baked Alaska. In addition, cheesecake has three other distinguishing characteristics, each of which create smaller boundaries that gradually separate it from every other kind of baked dessert. Thus, when we define a thing, we methodically set it apart from everything else.

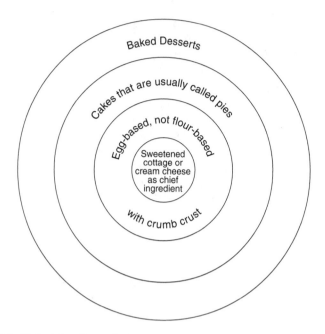

Figure 2.1 Definition Boundaries

Exercise

Word Boundaries

Set up a piece of paper with three columns headed *Term, Class,* and *Characteristics*. For each of the words below, list the class and characteristics, and diagram the boundaries as we did for *cheesecakes*.

Example

Term	Class	Characteristics
1. Scissors	Is a cutting tool	with two blades, each with a loop handle joined by a swivel pin

2. mailbag

3. moppet

4. November

5. pneumonia

6. cat

KINDS OF DEFINITIONS

Not all definitions are dictionary definitions.

When you looked up the word *cat,* you probably found it described as a mammal of the family felidae, or of the genus and species *Felis catus.* This taxonomic description indicates the boundaries that differentiate cats from all other animals. The cat family includes lions and tigers as well as house cats, while a particular breed name distinguishes a Siamese from a Persian cat. The rules that govern this system of classification are based on a science called **taxonomy.** This science, established by an international commission, enables us to know what *agreements* have been made to identify all plants and animals so that no two can be confused. Just as taxonomy helps us distinguish one living thing from another, **dictionary definitions** describe terms according to the boundaries established by shared and separate characteristics. Both taxonomy and dictionary definitions owe their value to agreements that everyone can refer to.

This is especially important for **scientific definitions,** which remain more fixed than other kinds of definitions because they are specific and technical. Nurses or medical students who study the heart have to learn definitions of words such as *aorta, atrium, diastole, endocardium.* And, indeed, a large part of scientific training is word training in a vocabulary handed down from one decade or century to the next.

At the other extreme are **stipulative definitions** based on individual or group agreements. The term *middle-class* no longer has any commonly agreed-upon meaning in the United States. Most Americans call themselves middle class whether they live in a mansion or a trailer. When considering a tax cut in 1995, the Democrats made a *stipulative* definition of the middle class as making up to $75,000 a year, while the Republicans set that amount at $200,000. Other commentators suggested that middle class could be better defined in terms of financial stability, rather than income, and the debate continues. Other areas in which stipulative definitions are based on agreements have to do with *functional illiteracy, disability,* and *sexual harassment.* In all these cases, definitions need to be reached for reasons such as law, research, or policy implementation. In these instances, dictionary definitions are not of much use.

Definitions can also be **inventive,** expressing previously unrecognized categories or concepts. This might be said for the word *'tweens* for young people of middle school age, or the term *living wage* which conveys the idea of a minimum wage more commensurate with the actual living costs.

"I don't know what you mean by 'glory,'" Alice said.

Humpty Dumpty smiled contemptuously. "Of course you don't—till I tell you. I meant 'there's a nice knock-down argument for you!'"

"But 'glory' doesn't mean 'a nice knock-down argument,'" Alice objected.

"When *I* use a word," Humpty Dumpty said in rather a scornful tone, "it means just what I choose it to mean—neither more nor less."

"The question is," said Alice, "whether you *can* make words mean so many different things."

"The question is," said Humpty Dumpty, "which is to be master—that's all."

People can also take familiar concepts and give them **personal definitions.** In an essay called "A Few Fine Words for Envy," the author describes his boyhood experiences of envy, and then has this to say:

> Envy is apparently more easily felt than defined. . . . Envy and jealousy, envy and emulation, envy and invidiousness, envy and ambition, envy and desire, the distinctions, the connections, the shades of meaning. . . . The standard dictionaries, I fear, are not very helpful on this troublesome word either. I have, therefore, decided to supply my own definition: envy, I say is desiring what someone else has—a desire usually heightened by the knowledge that one is unlikely to attain it. (Joseph Epstein, *A Line Out for a Walk*)

Definitions may also be **poetic** and **whimsical,** like "Happiness is a commute before the rush hour," or **philosophical,** like "Death is the invisible companion of life." Below this level are **eccentric** definitions that disregard the kind of agreements that make communication possible. A classic dialogue illustrating the eccentric definition takes place between Alice and Humpty Dumpty (from Lewis Carroll's *Through the Looking Glass*).

Another final category of definitions might be called **persuasive definitions.** These are definitions which advocate an opinion. Examples of these would be such statements as the following:

"A state lottery is a form of voluntary taxation."

"A state lottery is stealing from the poor."

"To be anti-abortion is to be pro-life."

"To be for abortions is to be pro-choice."

All these equations are opinions offered as though they were given truths in order to win others over to the same opinion. Obviously, they are far removed from dictionary definitions.

THE CONNOTATIONS OF WORDS

Word connotations are about feelings.

An important aspect of definitions is the **connotations** of words or the *associations* that they suggest to us. These associations can evoke reactions, images, emotions, or thoughts. For instance, let's take the word *snake.* The *denotation* of this word, or its literal meaning, is a reptile without legs. There it is: simply a "thing," nothing to get excited about. But for many people the word *snake* carries many negative *connotations,* such as being slimy, treacherous, poisonous, or evil. These common reactions can nevertheless be overcome through conscious familiarity with snakes.

Do dictionaries explain connotations? Not so in the case of the snake, where such connotations are universally understood. A few, but not all, dictionaries help us understand the connotations a defined word carries by discussing subtle differences among its synonyms. For instance, if you look up the word *lying* in the *Webster's New World Dictionary of the American Language,* you would find explanations of the connotative differences among *lie, prevaricate, equivocate,* and *fib.* If you were to arrange these synonyms on a scale of their potential for emotional impact, *lying* would be at the top and at the bottom.

Class Discussion

1. Explain the meaning and connotative differences among *disinformation, misspeaking,* and *falsifying.*
2. Make a list of the synonyms for *cheating,* and rank their connotations as negative, positive, neutral, or phony neutral (a euphemism that hides a true negative meaning).
3. Repeat the procedure for the word *stealing.*

In later chapters of this book we will look at how connotations show our judgments of things and how they can be used to manipulate others to accept the same evaluations. But for now simply consider connotations in your word choices and reading by asking questions or by dictionary study.

THE LADDER OF ABSTRACTION

Do not perambulate the corridors in the hours of repose in the boots of ascension. (Sign in Austrian ski resort)

The above statement was written by an Austrian who used an English dictionary to translate what he wanted to say word for word. His dictionary did not tell him that *perambulate* and *repose* are not used currently, but words carried over from the past that only now appear in prose to suggest formality and quaintness.

The English language allows us to choose between synonyms that are socially more formal or informal, between these more **abstract** or **concrete.** Many words that we use to convey formality are of Latin or Greek origin. This convention allows us to choose words like ascension for climb, tepid for warm, and inconvenience for bother. In the list given below, which of the words would you select as formal and abstract, and which would you consider more concrete and informal?

felicitations	nodding and handshaking
vehicle	car
frozen	petrified
sexy	libidinous

Many social conventions surround our choices for words of greater or lesser formality. We say "Motor Vehicle Bureau" rather than "Car, Truck and Motorcycle Office" because it engenders more respect. In the United States we consider the word "toilet" too gross a word to use in public, and so we say "men's room/ women's room." In the past we used a word derived from Latin: "lavatory." Thus we also use abstract words as euphemisms, or more formal codes of meaning.

In addition, we use Latin and Greek words to express more abstract or technical ideas. Such words enable us to say "economic assets" instead of repeating "my car, my house, my furniture, my bank account, etc." Having concept words allow us to use less language to communicate more general and complex ideas. Indeed, those who cannot express abstract

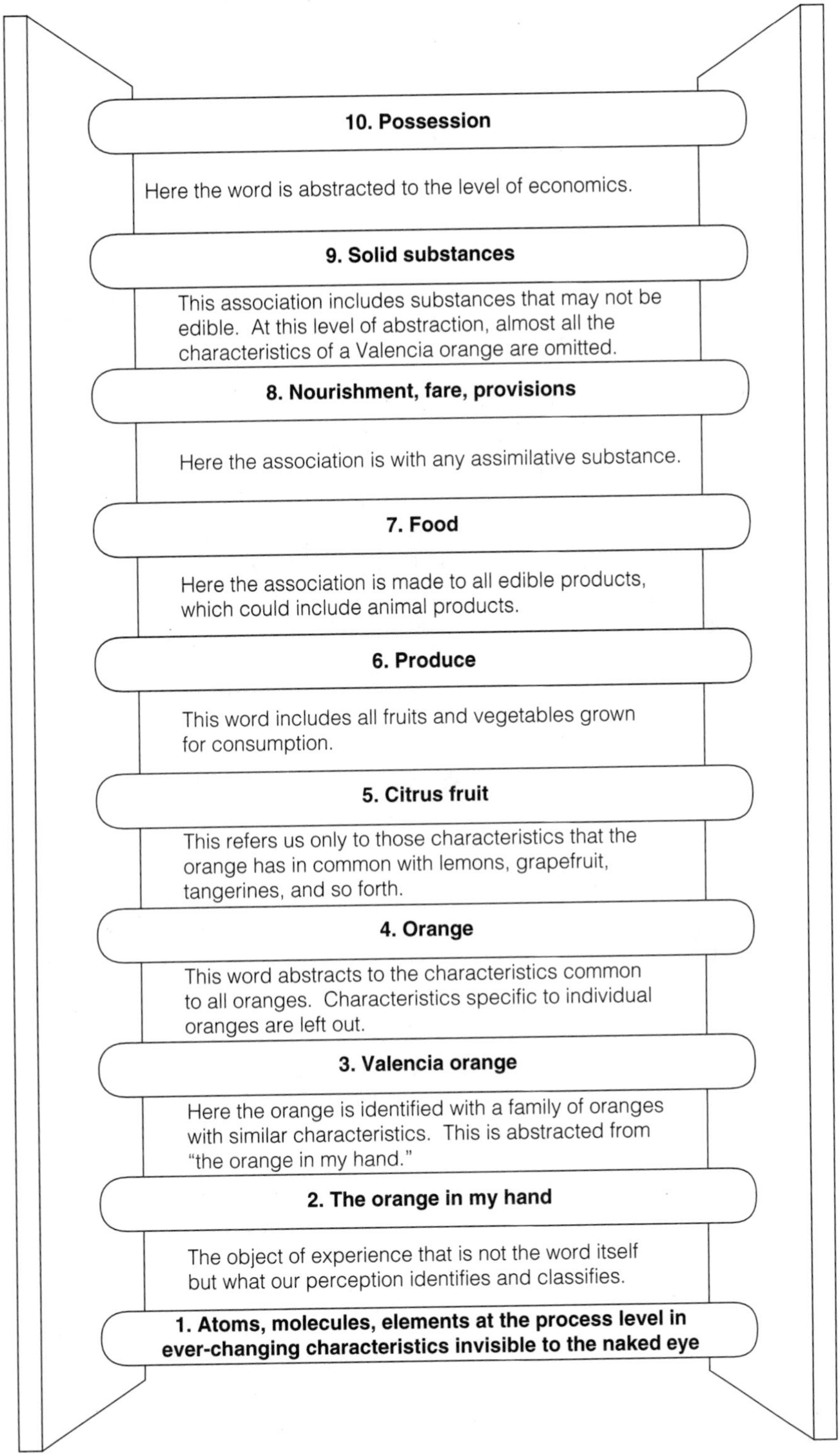

10. Possession

Here the word is abstracted to the level of economics.

9. Solid substances

This association includes substances that may not be edible. At this level of abstraction, almost all the characteristics of a Valencia orange are omitted.

8. Nourishment, fare, provisions

Here the association is with any assimilative substance.

7. Food

Here the association is made to all edible products, which could include animal products.

6. Produce

This word includes all fruits and vegetables grown for consumption.

5. Citrus fruit

This refers us only to those characteristics that the orange has in common with lemons, grapefruit, tangerines, and so forth.

4. Orange

This word abstracts to the characteristics common to all oranges. Characteristics specific to individual oranges are left out.

3. Valencia orange

Here the orange is identified with a family of oranges with similar characteristics. This is abstracted from "the orange in my hand."

2. The orange in my hand

The object of experience that is not the word itself but what our perception identifies and classifies.

1. Atoms, molecules, elements at the process level in ever-changing characteristics invisible to the naked eye

Figure 2.2 The Word *Orange* in a Ladder of Abstraction

ideas are handicapped. A child who says, "My tummy hurts" will require a lot of questions from parent or doctor to determine whether the problem is gastric or intestinal. Precise diagnoses require precise language.

On the other hand, abstract words may also be misused to deceive oneself or others:

> You always write it's bombing, bombing, bombing. It's *not* bombing! It's air support! (Col. David Opfer, U.S. air attaché in Cambodia, in talking to reporters)

Here the colonel seems to think that if he can persuade the reporters to use the more remote abstraction of "air support," he can make the bombings' effects abstract as well. The expression "air support" suggests military defense tactics rather than the horrors of mangled bodies. Perhaps the colonel believes that by using abstract language he can also magically remake such events into abstractions.

The relationship of words to perception and thought can best be explained through the "Ladder of Abstraction" first developed by the semanticist Alfred Korzybski. In this diagram, the word *orange* is used to illustrate the range of abstraction possible for any word that describes an object or living thing (Figure 2.2).

We can see how wide the boundaries may become for anything that exists; although abstractions are valuable for categorizing and conceptualizing, they can take us very far away from the concrete and specific that we can touch, observe, and verify. We need to develop word sensitivity so that we can make word choices align to our purposes, our perception, and our thinking. But to do this we have to begin with a clear awareness of our thoughts and perceptions.

THE IMPORTANCE OF DEFINING KEY IDEAS

Both study and debate need to begin with clear definitions.

The French philosopher Voltaire once said, "If you would argue with me, first define your terms." What he was talking about was not arguing in the sense of quarreling but in the sense of persuasive reasoning. He did not say *how* terms should be defined but that one should be very clear about what one has decided that key ideas mean. For example, if you wanted to argue in defense of the unregulated use of drugs, you should first define what you mean by *drugs*. Do you mean aspirin, or heroin, or both? How you define the term affects not only what you include within your boundaries to consider but also what remains outside to ignore. Undefined words have to be confronted sooner or later, and that is better done by you than by your opponent, because an argument based on un-defined words collapses when challenged.

Clear definitions are an essential part of all fields of learning. For ex-ample, in law, definitions help juries decide the difference between crimes and misdemeanors, between sanity and insanity. In public affairs, debates over definitions can generate controversy, as was the case with the mean-ing of "family values." In addition, definitions comprise a large part of any subject of learning. If you study political science, you have to begin by asking what the familiar word *political* really means. From that point, you can move into learning more unfamiliar words like *plebiscite*.

In order to study our terms, we must study more than one dictionary and use each well, beginning always with a good college desk-sized dic-tionary. Unfortunately, many students have formed the habit of only using pocket dictionaries which are helpful for spelling, but not helpful for a real study of words. Indeed, their terse definitions can be so over-simplified as to create misunderstandings. However, not all full-sized dic-tionaries are equally well written. Sometimes all we need to do is switch from one dictionary to another in order to understand a word fully. There-fore it is desirable to have some knowledge about what kinds of dictio-naries there are as well as to have the skills to explore them.

WORD CONCEPTS

Concepts abstract experience.

The study of critical thinking begins with a review of many concepts. Each chapter of this book is titled by a concept. The word *concept* comes from the Latin *conceptus*, a thing conceived, suggesting a mental cre-ation. Concepts convey abstractions of experience from the past like *plu-ralism, aristocracy, hegemony*, or they convey new ideas like *cultural di-versity, postmodern, ecology*, and *ergonomics*. Learning the key concepts from any field of learning comprises an important part of higher educa-tion. If we want to study economics, we begin by learning the difference between microeconomics and macroeconomics. Concepts help us make distinctions, as between a *heuristic* and an *algorithm* in problem solving. Concept learning not only conveys complex ideas, but also enables us to talk about them.

If we want to truly understand new concepts, it can be helpful to be-gin with the word's etymology or history, with its earliest root idea. This idea can give us a concrete sense of the word's original conception. Tra-ditional aids for concept study are encyclopedias, textbooks, and books

DEFINING REALITY

Reality comes from the Latin word *res*, which means thing, property, possession. Related to *res* is *reri*, which means to reason and from which we derive the words *reason, ratio, realize*. The past participle of *reri* is *ratus*, which means fixed by calculation, established, for certain. The ideas etymologically involved in the word *reality* therefore involve thought balancing and certainty. Here is what other noted thinkers have said about reality:

> *Everything flows.* Heraclitus, Greek philosopher

> *The world was created by the word of God so that what is seen was made out of things which do not appear.* St. Paul

> *Reality is what we bump against.* William James, American psychologist

> *Reality is something as it actually is, independent of our thoughts about how it is.* Mortimer J. Adler, American philosopher

> *Reality is an unknown and undefinable totality of flux that is the ground of all things and of the process of thought itself, as well as the movement of intelligent perception.* David Bohm, philosopher and physicist

DEFINING TRUTH

The word *true* comes from the Old English form of *troewe*, which means loyal, trustworthy, which in turn comes from the Indo-European base *deru*, meaning firm, solid, steadfast. Related to the base word *deru* is *dru*, meaning firm as a tree, hard as wood. This etymology suggests that *truth* is something as hard and firm and as steadfast as a tree or its wood. Here are some definitions and descriptions of truth:

> *Truth suggests conformity with the facts or with reality, either as an idealized abstraction ("What is truth?" said jesting Pilate) or in actual application to statements, ideas, acts, etc. ("There is no truth in that rumor").* The American Heritage Dictionary

> *Truth is a correspondence or agreement between our minds and reality.* Mortimer J. Adler

> *The ordinary mode of language is very unsuitable for discussing questions of truth and falsity, because it tends to treat each truth as a separate fragment that is essentially fixed and static in its nature. . . . However, truth and falsity have to be seen from moment to moment, in an act of perception of a very high order.* David Bohm

> **Concept:** A word that organizes and abstracts a body of related experience. A general idea.
>
> From the Latin *conceptus*, meaning a thing conceived.

written by leading thinkers in their special fields of knowledge. Yet, even scholars cannot always agree on the definition of a term. *Critical thinking*, as mentioned earlier, has as many definitions as people who write on the subject or teach it. Yet each definition contributes a dialogue, which may one day reach consensus as to which boundaries this new field of study should include or exclude.

Defining terms is a dynamic process in any field of learning. And there are some words that challenge each new generation. Two of these words, *truth* and *reality*, appear in the insert boxes on these pages. They are both ordinary but profound words; they both remain elusive, yet they are the standards for measuring our ways of knowing and proceeding in the world and for thinking critically about the world.

WHAT IS CRITICAL READING?

Accurate comprehension has to precede a critical analysis of a reading.

When we read a detective story, we enjoy getting lost in another world; when we read a training manual, we follow and memorize. In both cases, we rarely question what we read. It is more like boarding a train: we get on and then we get off. However, if we were to apply this attitude to newspaper reading, we might believe either everything or nothing. A critical reader does not soak up information but interacts and asks questions.

The process of critical reading, however, does not begin with questions but with making sure the reading is accurate. An attitude of receptivity is first needed to ensure *accurate comprehension*. Challenging or questioning has to be delayed until the reader has made an accurate mental reconstruction of the information. And sometimes this process of accurate comprehension takes more than one reading.

This first reading takes a special restraint if the topic is controversial. If we disagree, it can be too easy to misread what is being said. It can be really difficult to hold the reins on a mind that wants to jump immediately to judgments. *Receptive reading* faithfully and accurately records the message, regardless of whether it agrees with the reader's personal values, experiences, or expectations or not.

In reading this book, you will not always feel receptive to the controversies it presents. When an argument goes against our values, it can be painful to hear it out. Many psychological studies have shown that in reading we tend to accept the views we already hold and minimize those that we do not. *Thus both effort and discipline are needed to maintain neutrality, even with what we favor.* Yet we also have to realize that neutrality or objectivity can never be perfectly achieved. At best, we can only hold off our habitual personal reactions. Objectivity need not mean that you have changed what you feel, but it does mean that your reactions have been consciously taken into account and weighed for bias.

The critical reading phase begins with its analyzing and evaluating once the material is accurately understood. This second stage also can not be hurried; it is a slow and careful process led by questions. Again we return to the definition of *critical* whose original idea was to *sift* and *separate*. When one reads critically, one studies and reflects in order to sift out words and ideas. Thus critical reading must begin with an accurate reproduction of the message. When we are critical too soon, we lose the focus needed to make an accurate reading of the material. And a criticism of information or argument based on an inaccurate reading is a waste of time.

As you study this book, you will be learning in each chapter the questions that a critical thinker uses in order to assess information. In this chapter, you have been considering *four questions:*

Is this the most accurate word choice?

What is the connotation of this word?

What is the level of abstraction of this word?

Is this word clearly defined?

The reading selections offered in this text are intended to stimulate critical thinking. You are encouraged to read each selection at least twice—once for comprehension and once for critical interaction before you begin to answer the study questions that follow each one. If it is helpful, think of your first reading as a sponge reading and your second as a sifting. Consult your dictionary regularly as you read, and write down questions you need to ask to clarify or challenge what is said. Make your reading an active thinking endeavor.

BUILDING ARGUMENTS

WORD CHOICES

When we make a **claim,** each word appearing in the claim needs careful thought and definition. (*"If you would argue with me, first define your terms."* Voltaire) Word choices vary according to the values and purposes of the speaker. Notice how this author uses his definition of *Indians* to sway others to accept his beliefs.

Mr. Baily:

With the narrative enclosed, I subjoin some observations with regard to the animals, vulgarly called Indians. *(definition of key term)*

In the United States Magazine in the year 1777, I published a dissertation denying them to have a right in the soil. **(principal claim, conclusion, or thesis)**

The whole of this earth was given to man, and all descendants of Adam have a right to share it equally. There is no right of primogeniture in the laws of nature and of nations. (moral reasoning made through further claims to back principal claim)

What use do these ringed, streaked, spotted and speckled cattle make of the soil? Do they till it? Revelation said to man, "Thou shalt till the ground" . . . *I would as soon admit a right in the buffalo to grant lands, as in Killbuck, the Big Cat, the Big Dog, or any of the ragged wretches that are called chiefs.* . . . *What would you think of going to a big lick or place where the beasts collect to lick saline nitrous earth and water, and addressing yourself to a great buffalo to grant you land?* (analogy used to support principal claim)

(H. H. Brackenridge, 1782)

Exercise

1. The *issue* here is whether Indians should have the right to their land. What is the author's claim on this issue?
2. How does the author use his definition of Indians to help his argument?
3. What reasoning does he offer to prove Indians are not human?
4. What is *primogeniture?*
5. What is unfair about this argument?
6. Write a one-paragraph argument in which you make a claim about anything. Make either a neutral or controversial definition of your key term or subject. Then offer two reasons to support your definition.

CHAPTER SUMMARY

1. An accurate use of words improves our thinking. They give forms to our thoughts so that we can make use of them. Words enable us to communicate with others and ourselves. Knowing the words for things and experiences helps us see and perceive more.

2. Writing helps us learn more about words and how to use them. When we struggle to select words that will describe our experiences, we realize that words are only *translations* of experience and not the experience itself.

3. Clear thinking depends on a clear understanding of the words we use. Word confusion leads to less consciousness, or disequilibrium, which can only be restored through word clarification.

4. We need to understand what dictionaries can and cannot offer us; we need to use them skillfully and frequently.

5. The thesaurus helps us when we are writing and translating nonverbal experiences and ideas into words; the dictionary helps us when we are reading and interpreting the words of others.

6. Definitions set boundaries for word ideas and show us their specific and general characteristics and how they are related to or distinguished from one another.

7. Dictionary definitions show us the agreements that society has made about a word's meaning. But we may also compose our own personal or stipulative definitions of experiences or compose persuasive definitions to sway the opinions of others. In critical thinking it is important not to confuse these different kinds of definitions, or to believe that personal, persuasive, or stipulative definitions carry the same agreements as those to be found in a dictionary.

8. The test of our understanding of a word is our ability to define it. This ability is particularly important for words representing key ideas that we wish to explain or defend. Taking the time to define the words we use is an essential preliminary to genuine communication.

9. A study of a word's etymology can help us trace a word back to its earliest root idea and can give us an image that conveys a more concrete sense of the word's logic. Learning a word's etymology can also help us recognize its relationship to other words with the same root meanings.

10. The connotations of a word are its associative meanings, which can be positive, negative, or neutral. These associations can take the form of feelings, ideas, images, or thoughts. Thus, although politicians

might rarely admit to *lying* or being *confused,* it is quite acceptable for them to admit they *misspoke.*

11. The first stage of critical reading is objective receptivity to the material; this means having the technical ability as well as the willingness to accurately reproduce its content without alterations or distortions. If we question and interact with material that we have not accurately interpreted, our criticisms will not be fair or worthwhile.

12. To communicate well we need to understand the difference between concrete and abstract words and to choose appropriately from either category. The ladder of abstraction shows us how one word for a thing can range from a specific perceived directly to a concept that is part of a much larger collective.

CHAPTER QUIZ

Rate each of the following statements as *true* or *false.* To answer some of these questions, you will need to consult your dictionary.

_____ 1. Abstract words convey meaning better than concrete words.

_____ 2. Words can be used to do a better or worse job of describing experiences but can never be more than translations of the experiences themselves.

_____ 3. A dictionary can help us think better when we use it to clear up word confusion.

_____ 4. Definitions of a word show the word's boundaries.

_____ 5. Knowing the words for things helps us see them better.

_____ 6. We do not fully understand a word unless we can define it.

_____ 7. When people debate a topic, understanding is greatly helped by their taking the time to define the key terms.

_____ 8. Etymology gives us word histories.

_____ 9. Pocket dictionaries are sufficient guides for a critical study of word meanings.

_____ 10. The word *ohm* comes from the Sanskrit language and means the sound of creation.

_____ 11. According to most dictionaries, there is more than one acceptable spelling of the word *cooperate.*

_____ 12. The term *French leave* means to say good-bye with a big kiss.

_____ 13. The prefix *in* in the words *insignificant* and *inflammable* means *not* in Latin.

_____ 14. The following words all contain the sound called a schwa: *mass, polite, placement, bogus, visible.*

_____ 15. The word *nausea* can be pronounced at least three different ways.

_____ 16. The word *round* can function as six different parts of speech: adjective, noun, transitive and intransitive verb, adverb, and preposition.

_____ 17. *Egregious* comes from a Latin word meaning standing out from the herd.

_____ 18. The word *nadir* in the phrase "the nadir of politics" means the highest point.

_____ 19. A *cogent* argument is a convincing one.

_____ 20. The word *decimate* means to dice something up into pieces.

COMPOSITION WRITING APPLICATION

A Short Essay of Definition

Write an essay based on an extended definition or full discussion of a word or phrase, with the support of examples. It should also be an **essay of exposition,** *which is a form of writing that explains something. In this case you will want to* explain your definition *as fully as you can through stories, examples, or specific information. The thinking tasks of making definitions followed by explanations play a frequent part in our daily conversations. If you are having a conversation with a friend and say, "She just isn't* mature," *your friend may reply, "What do you mean by* mature?" *Thus, you are challenged to respond with a definition together with an explanation of how you use that term.*

The directions for this assignment, and for all the other writing assignments in this book, are designed to make you conscious of the thinking elements involved in solving it as a given problem, much like a problem in mathematics. However, you must follow the instructions exactly as they define its parameters.

Summary of Instructions for This Assignment

1. *Objective:* To give your own definition of a word, and to explain that word's meaning through your own experience.
2. *Form and length:* Write at least one typed page.
3. *Structure:* Begin with a topic sentence and end with a conclusion.

Step 1 Suppose you choose the first topic—defining *adult*. Think of what the word has come to mean to you in your own life. Think about how you have heard others use this word. Look up its definition in several dictionaries. Now turn back to the diagram of the word *cheesecake*. Draw and define the boundaries for the word *adult* using dictionary definitions or whatever you can add in terms of your own experience.

Step 2 Now try *clustering* with the word *adult*. Clustering (or mapping) is a warm-up exercise that invites both hemispheres of the brain to work with an idea. It can be a magical way to quickly release all the ideas, memories, and associations you have on a particular subject.

Step 3 Next, take the information you discovered from your cluster, and begin to write a good paragraph about the various meanings and boundaries of the word *adult*. Contrast what you feel to be the true meaning of the word with some false meanings. Bring together your findings into one sentence that announces all you want to say about the definitions and boundaries of *adult*. This is a *topic sentence,* which generalizes your findings into a kind of conclusion. The rest of the sentences in the paragraph should support, or provide examples that support, the topic sentence. In this paragraph you can see how well you think about words while also working on the college level in expository writing.

Peer Review

In class read your essays of definition to one another in small groups. For each paper, write a critique that answers these questions:

1. Was each of the parameters observed?
2. Did you understand all that was said? Did anything need to be explained more?
3. Did you honestly find the writing interesting?

Scoring For Essay of Definition

1. Essay shows dictionary study of word. 10 points
2. Body of essay defines and explains word from own experience. 30 points
3. The exposition seems complete and easy to follow. 10 points
4. Topic sentence opens essay. 10 points
5. Conclusion is clearly stated. 10 points
6. One full typed page. 20 points
7. Work reasonably free of spelling and sentence errors. 10 points

---

CLUSTERING

To begin **clustering,** place an oval in the center of a page and write your key word inside that oval. Focus on that word. As thoughts, symbols, memories, or new word associations come as you focus, draw lines to new ovals that contain these new words. As words stimulate still further associations, draw lines to these. In time you will have a number of new clusters, all radiating from the key word. Notice how this is done with the word *family*.

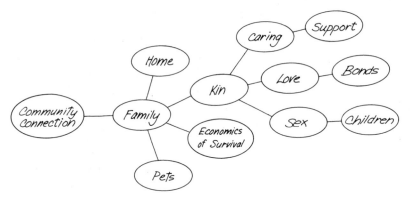

Clustering allows us to use both of our brain hemispheres at once. This method can feel more natural than restricting ourselves to the left brain by making an outline first. When we list or outline thoughts, we use our left brain to force our thinking into a sequence before we know all we could think about that subject. In clustering, we invite input from the right brain as well as the left at the beginning of our work and thus achieve a visual sense of the whole picture. Clustering is a free-association method that is best done without censorship, allowing discoveries and surprises at the results.

Student Writing Example

MUSIC

Gary Aguirre

The word music comes from the Greek word mousike, meaning "art of the muses." Its simplest dictionary definition is "a rhythmic sequence of pleasing sounds." However, neither the original word idea nor these simplest definitions suggest the meaning of music in my life. To me music is the axle around which all human spiritual experience revolves. It is the common thread linking all religions and cultural expressions. From Spanish *cante hondo*, or deep song, to Balinese *gamelan*, to American jazz, musicians use song to define their heritage and their interpretation of the human experience. Music is a tangible representation of what I consider to be the unexplainable central creative force in the world that some call God.

The word music's deeper meaning becomes clearer when you find that some synonyms given in Roget's Thesaurus are order and universe. Music is an improvised creative expression, or melody, skillfully woven over a tapestry of mathematically juxtaposed rhythms and harmonies. It mimics the relationship of an individual's life experience against the solid background of history and culture. For instance, when American jazz great John Coltrane plays the standard "My Favorite Things," he begins with the familiar melody that accompanies the words "raindrops on roses and whiskers on kittens." The audience is drawn in because they have experienced this "place" before; in other words, they recognize the tune. From this starting point Coltrane soars into a whirl of spontaneous improvisation, while the drums, piano, and bass continue to pound out the original background collage of sound and rhythm. When he sees fit, Coltrane returns to the original melody, completing a cycle not unlike that of birth and death. The musician, in his expertise, provides a higher order to a world of sound that can, at times, seem completely chaotic.

Songs begin, travel through time and space, and then end. They live and die, like everything in the universe, serving no practical purpose. But like Coltrane's "My Favorite Things," the universe began, and may eventually end, also serving no practical purpose but to host those of us who were lucky enough to be here.

To me music is not just "the art of combining tones to form expressive compositions" but a universe within itself that we humans can use to define our place in the infinite. Growing up in a non-religious family, music was my sole (or soul) connection with spirituality. The painstaking hours of teaching myself to play have afforded me the opportunity to worship in the only way I know how. As a song composer, I can offer my little bit to that which was here long before me and will continue long after I'm gone. Making music to me is prayer. Life and music are not separate entities; neither reflects the other, nor could either continue without the other. They are two parts of the greater whole, the everything.

Used with permission of Gary Aguirre.

READINGS

FIGHTING FOR OUR LIVES
Deborah Tannen

In this reading Deborah Tannen defines an invented term, "argument culture." This excerpt serves as an introduction to the book The Argument Culture: Moving from Debate to Dialogue, *which was published in 1998. Throughout this book, Deborah Tannen develops this same concept, explaining how a negative approach to argument harms American life, in its press, its politics, education, and attitudes toward gender.*

Deborah Tannen is an internationally recognized scholar and university professor of linguistics at Georgetown University in Washington, D.C. Her book on gender problems of communication called You Just Don't Understand Me *was on the* New York Times *bestseller list for nearly four years.*

This is not another book about civility. "Civility" suggests a superficial, pinky-in-the-air   1
veneer of politeness spread thin over human relations like a layer of marmalade over toast. This book is about a pervasive warlike atmosphere that makes us approach public dialogue, and just about anything we need to accomplish, as if it were a fight. It is a tendency in Western culture in general, and in the United States in particular, that has a long history and a deep, thick, and far-ranging root system. It has served us well in many ways but in recent years has become so exaggerated that it is getting in the way of solving our problems. Our spirits are corroded by living in an atmosphere of unrelenting contention—an argument culture.

The argument culture urges us to approach the world—and the people in it—   2
in an adversarial frame of mind. It rests on the assumption that opposition is the best way to get anything done: The best way to discuss an idea is to set up a debate; the best way to cover news is to find spokespeople who express the most extreme, polarized views and present them as "both sides"; the best way to settle disputes is litigation that pits one party against the other; the best way to begin an essay is to attack someone; and the best way to show you're really thinking is to criticize.

Our public interactions have become more and more like having an argument   3
with a spouse. Conflict can't be avoided in our public lives any more than we can avoid conflict with people we love. One of the great strengths of our society is that we can express these conflicts openly. But just as spouses have to learn ways of settling their differences without inflicting real damage on each other, so we, as a society, have to find constructive ways of resolving disputes and differences. Public discourse requires *making* an argument for a point of view, not *having* an argument—as in having a fight.

The war on drugs, the war on cancer, the battle of the sexes, politicians' turf   4
battles—in the argument culture, war metaphors pervade our talk and shape our thinking. Nearly everything is framed as a battle or game in which winning or losing is the

main concern. These all have their uses and their place, but they are not the only way—and often not the best way—to understand and approach our world. Conflict and opposition are as necessary as cooperation and agreement, but the scale is off balance, with conflict and opposition overweighted. In this book, I show how deeply entrenched the argument culture is, the forms it takes, and how it affects us every day—sometimes in useful ways, but often creating more problems than it solves, causing rather than avoiding damage. As a sociolinguist, a social scientist, I am trained to observe and explain language and its role in human relations, and that is my biggest job here. But I will also point toward other ways for us to talk to each other and get things done in our public lives.

From *The Argument Culture* by Deborah Tannen. Copyright © 1998 by Deborah Tannen. Reprinted by permission of Random House, Inc.

Discussion Break Questions

1. How does she introduce her subject in the first paragraph?
2. How is her second paragraph constructed around the refutation of an assumption?
3. What point does she make about conflict in the third paragraph?
4. What does she mean about war metaphors?
5. How does she state the thesis of her book in the final paragraph?
6. Explain whether or not you found this concept to be a useful one.

SAVED

Malcolm X

Interest in the life and work of Malcolm X continues to grow. The recognition he achieved during his lifetime as a provocative thinker and public speaker was short; he died, at age 40, the victim of a political assassination. In this selection, now a classic, Malcolm X describes how he managed through self-education to pull himself out of a life of street hustling and prison into literacy and power.

It was because of my letters that I happened to stumble upon starting to acquire some   1
kind of a homemade education.

I became increasingly frustrated at not being able to express what I wanted to   2
convey in letters that I wrote, especially those to Mr. Elijah Muhammad. In the street, I had been the most articulate hustler out there—I had commanded attention when I said something. But now, trying to write simple English, I not only wasn't articulate, I wasn't even functional. How would I sound writing in slang, the way I would *say* it, something such as, "Look, daddy, let me pull your coat about a cat, Elijah Muhammad."

Many who today hear me somewhere in person, or on television, or those who   **3**
read something I've said, will think I went to school far beyond the eighth grade. This
impression is due entirely to my prison studies.

It had really begun back in the Charlestown Prison, when Bimbi first made me   **4**
feel envy of his stock of knowledge. Bimbi had always taken charge of any conversation he was in, and I had tried to emulate him. But every book I picked up had few
sentences which didn't contain anywhere from one to nearly all of the words that
might as well have been in Chinese. When I just skipped those words, of course, I really ended up with little idea of what the book said. So I had come to the Norfolk
Prison Colony still going through only book-reading motions. Pretty soon, I would have
quit even these motions, unless I had received the motivation that I did.

I saw that the best thing I could do was get hold of a dictionary—to study, to learn   **5**
some words. I was lucky enough to reason also that I should try to improve my pen-
manship. It was sad. I couldn't even write in a straight line. It was both ideas together
that moved me to request a dictionary along with some tablets and pencils from the
Norfolk Prison Colony school.

I spent two days just riffling [sic] uncertainly through the dictionary's pages. I'd   **6**
never realized so many words existed! I didn't know *which* words I needed to learn.
Finally, just to start some kind of action, I began copying.

In my slow, painstaking, ragged handwriting, I copied into my tablet everything   **7**
printed on that first page, down to the punctuation marks.

I believe it took me a day. Then, aloud, I read back, to myself, everything I'd writ-   **8**
ten on the tablet. Over and over, aloud, to myself, I read my own handwriting.

I woke up the next morning, thinking about those words—immensely proud to   **9**
realize that not only had I written so much at one time, but I'd written words that I
never knew were in the world. Moreover, with a little effort, I also could remember
what many of these words meant. I reviewed the words whose meanings I didn't remember. Funny thing, from the dictionary first page right now, that "aardvark" springs
to my mind. The dictionary had a picture of it, a long-tailed, long-eared, burrowing
African mammal, which lives off termites caught by sticking out its tongue as an
anteater does for ants.

I was so fascinated that I went on—I copied the dictionary's next page. And the   **10**
same experience came when I studied that. With every succeeding page, I also learned
of people and places and events from history. Actually the dictionary is like a minia-
ture encyclopedia. Finally the dictionary's A section had filled a whole tablet—and I
went on into the B's. That was the way I started copying what eventually became the
entire dictionary. It went a lot faster after so much practice helped me to pick up handwriting speed. Between what I wrote in my tablet, and writing letters, during the rest
of my time in prison I would guess I wrote a million words.

I suppose it was inevitable that as my word-base broadened, I could for the first   **11**
time pick up a book and read and now begin to understand what the book was
saying. Anyone who has read a great deal can imagine the new world that opened.
Let me tell you something: from then until I left that prison, in every free moment I
had, if I was not reading in the library, I was reading on my bunk. You couldn't have

gotten me out of books with a wedge. Between Mr. Muhammad's teachings, my correspondence, my visitors—usually Ella and Reginald—and my reading of books, months passed without my even thinking about being imprisoned. In fact, up to then, I never had been so truly free in my life.

The Norfolk Prison Colony's library was in the school building. A variety of classes **12** was taught there by instructors who came from such places as Harvard and Boston universities. The weekly debates between inmate teams were also held in the school building. You would be astonished to know how worked up convict debaters and audiences would get over subjects like "Should Babies Be Fed Milk?"

Available on the prison library's shelves were books on just about every general **13** subject. Much of the big private collection that Parkhurst had willed to the prison was still in crates and boxes in the back of the library—thousands of old books. Some of them looked ancient: covers faded, old-time parchment-looking binding. Parkhurst, I've mentioned, seemed to have been principally interested in history and religion. He had the money and the special interest to have a lot of books that you wouldn't have in general circulation. Any college library would have been lucky to get that collection.

As you can imagine, especially in a prison where there was heavy emphasis on **14** rehabilitation, an inmate was smiled upon if he demonstrated an unusually intense interest in books. There was a sizable number of well-read inmates, especially the popular debaters. Some were said by many to be practically walking encyclopedias. They were almost celebrities. No university would ask any student to devour literature as I did when this new world opened to me, of being able to read and *understand*.

I read more in my room than in the library itself. An inmate who was known to **15** read a lot could check out more than the permitted maximum number of books. I preferred reading in the total isolation of my own room.

When I had progressed to really serious reading, every night at about ten P.M. I **16** would be outraged with the "lights out." It always seemed to catch me right in the middle of something engrossing.

Fortunately, right outside my door was a corridor light that cast a glow into my **17** room. The glow was enough to read by, once my eyes adjusted to it. So when "lights out" came, I would sit on the floor where I could continue reading in that glow.

At one-hour intervals the night guards paced past every room. Each time I heard **18** the approaching footsteps, I jumped into bed and feigned sleep. And as soon as the guard passed, I got back out of bed onto the floor area of that light-glow, where I would read for another fifty-eight minutes—until the guard approached again. That went on until three or four every morning. Three or four hours of sleep a night was enough for me. Often in the years in the streets I had slept less than that.

Small-Group Discussion Questions

1. Why, do you think, Malcolm X could be so confident and articulate as a hustler, yet have so much difficulty writing "simple English"?

2. What do you think of his practice of copying out every word in a dictionary?
3. Why did Malcolm X find it so empowering to learn new words?
4. What motivated him to read in his cell in semi-darkness late through the night?
5. Why do you think Malcolm X wanted others to hear this story?

ADVANCED OPTIONAL WRITING ASSIGNMENT

Write an essay of about three typed pages in which you describe a significant learning experience in your life—or someone else's—that involved your use of language. What was easy for you? What was difficult? Highlight one or two significant experiences where your sense of self and personal power changed through a greater or lesser mastery of language.

CHAPTER 3

Facts

What's Real?

© Jared Lee 1985. Reprinted with permission of Jared Lee.

Why is it funny to find fresh milk confirmed as fact through observation? Is it because we find cows' udders embarrassing? Or does it remind us that the fresh milk claims we usually accept may not be factual?

This is an easy problem compared to some of the difficulties we run into when trying to establish facts. Because facts are judged on the basis of "truth" and "reality," establishing them can be a tricky business. But we *can* learn to recognize pitfalls and to apply standards in gathering them. These are the skills that this chapter aims to teach.

Discovery Exercises

The following three Discovery Exercises can be done on an individual or collaborative basis; they can be done outside class in preparation for discussion or in class itself.

Beginning with the Word *Fact*

After consulting at least two dictionaries, write down your own definitions of the following words:

1. Know
2. Certain
3. Verified
4. Existence
5. Real
6. Fact

Then read your definitions of *fact* aloud in class. Which definitions seem to cover all kinds of facts? Does your definition of **fact** contain the following elements?

1. **Fact** comes from the Latin *factum,* meaning a deed, something done.
2. A fact is something known with certainty through experience, observation, or measurement.
3. A fact is something that can be objectively demonstrated and verified.
4. A fact becomes a fact when we can get another source or person to *agree* that it corresponds to a reality.

Learning to Recognize Facts

Answer the following questions in writing, in preparation for a class discussion.

1. Make a list of five facts about yourself, beginning with your birth date.
2. Make a list of five facts about your neighborhood.
3. List five facts about the room you are in right now. Do not just name objects or events (such as lights, door), but make statements describing what you see in its context. For instance, do not say "Four windows" but "There are four open windows on the south wall of this room."
4. Which of the following are statements of fact?

    (a) Water freezes at 0 degrees Celsius and 32 degrees Fahrenheit at sea level or under standard pressure.

(b) The major religion in Mexico is Roman Catholicism.

(c) The food is awful in the cafeteria.

(d) No volcanoes are located in North America.

(e) Everybody should have Internet access.

(f) She must have forgotten her lunch; it is still on the table.

(g) Advertisement: "Johnson's Music offers you the best buys in records and tapes."

5. Explain why items 4c through 4g are not facts.

Verifying Facts

One characteristic of facts is that they can be objectively verified—proven to be true—through the testimony of witnesses, through observations, or through records or documentation. Read the facts listed below. Select three to study. How would you go about verifying that each is indeed a fact?

1. Captain James Cook arrived in Hawaii in 1778.

2. One hundred percent of Japanese graduating high-school seniors have taken at least six years of English-language classes.

3. The mean height and weight for children between one and three years old in the United States are 35 inches and 29 pounds.

4. Tallahassee is the capital of Florida.

5. It takes 90 minutes to hard-boil an ostrich egg.

6. Gravity is a force that tends to draw all bodies in the earth's sphere toward the center of the earth.

7. Water is wet.

8. The word *bible* comes from the Greek word *biblia*, meaning a collection of writings.

9. There is a job available as a receptionist in the college president's office.

10. State laws allow right turns at stoplights.

FACTS AND REALITY

What we call facts do not necessarily represent what is real and true.

If you were to stand on a street corner and ask each passerby to tell you what a fact is, most people would tell you that a fact is what is real and true. However, this common notion is mistaken. Facts are our **interpretations** of what is real and true, but the problem with interpretations is that they can be wrong. Human history provides us with many examples.

Every school child knows that the long-accepted "fact" that the earth was flat was an error based on limited perception. In every century mistaken notions taken for fact come and go, such as the idea that bathing is unhealthy, that blood-letting cures the sick, that women are inferior to men, that some races are inferior to others. Toward the end of the twentieth century, science and government assured us that pesticides would not harm human beings, nor lead paint, nor buried toxic wastes. Such horrendous misjudgments remind us that what we call facts are the creations of human minds, and, for this reason, subject to error. Most of us grew up believing that 98.6 degrees Fahrenheit represented normal body temperature. This medical "fact" was commonly accepted until 1992, when new investigations revealed that 98.6 wasn't normal at all; indeed, it was downright unusual. Indeed, it was found that healthy people thrive between 96.0 and 99.9, depending on the individual, time of day, sex, and race. Science moved forward in this case because facts long assumed to be true were re-examined. We need to continually re-evaluate what we call our "facts" in the light of the feedback received from their tests against reality.

Now, what then is reality?

Reality is another term that we all use every day, yet few of us can define. It remains a mystery illusive of a definition that can be agreed upon. In the previous chapter, you were offered a number of very different definitions, some by philosophers who have long debated the nature of reality. Philosophers have divided themselves into two camps: those who consider reality to be relative, and those who view reality as absolute. In other words, some say the observer determines what reality is, while others say that reality is what it is—regardless of what people may think about it. Yet, no matter what side we may lean toward ourselves, we must concede that our judgments do change about the truth of some facts.

In summary, facts are not the equivalent of truths or reality; they are, at best, only our decisions about what seems to be most real. Human beings need facts because they need certainties in order to proceed through the world. But we should not forget that human beings are fallible.

Discussion Break Questions

1. State two facts that you are certain are true.
2. State two facts that you are certain will never change.
3. State two facts that you are certain will change.

FACTS ARE NOT ABSOLUTES

**The most we can say about any fact is that it has a higher
or lower level of probability of certainty.**

Facts that are most useful to us are those that have been repeatedly verified by many sources over time. Our lives and welfare depend on these certainties. We know the facts of gravity limit what we can do and not do safely; we know we can plan our daily schedules around the rising and the setting of the sun. But none can say that the orbit of this planet or its condition of gravity will always remain the same. We can know that this is the case now. We live in a physical universe that is eternally changing—from the invisible-to-the-eye subatomic level to obvious levels of wrinkles in our skin, the courses of rivers, the growth of children, and the motion of the sun and stars. Furthermore, modern technology is accelerating all manner of unexpected environmental changes.

The sciences have their own way of coming to terms with our problem of absolute certainties. Many statements that most people would call facts are considered *probability* statements by the sciences. If a thermometer says the temperature is 65 degrees, a scientist would say that there is a 99 percent chance that the temperature is between 62.5 and 67.5 degrees. This would take into account any inaccuracies of the instrument. *Certainty* in science usually means probability that approaches certainty.

In the world outside of science, facts are based on social agreements that can and do change as human knowledge evolves. The invalidation of old "facts" and the acceptance of new ones ended the burning of witches and practice of human slavery. Some of today's most accepted ideas may be found mistaken as well. For such reasons a healthy society needs to preserve the freedom to debate, the right to investigate, the license to disagree with one another's claims about "realities." Indeed, this is the only kind of environment in which critical thinking can flourish. A government that seeks absolute power over its citizens suppresses every stimulus to critical thinking. It buys out the media, censors a dissident press, discourages public protests, closes down schools, and kills those who

© by Nita Winter Used with permission of Nita Winter.

© by Nita Winter. Used with permission of Nita Winter.

dissent. Critical thinking is a fragile product of civilizations that value the freedom to search for truth. For the advancement of human knowledge and welfare, we need to value the right to continually reexamine whatever equations are made between reality and the "facts."

Discussion Break Questions

1. List some facts you correctly took for granted that enabled you to be reading this book at this minute.
2. Give an example of some methods used intentionally to suppress critical thinking.

DISCERNING FACTS FROM FICTION

Surprisingly enough, we can sometimes be led to believe the difference between fact and fiction doesn't really matter.

In the Introduction to this book you met the Thomas family. The majority of those who take this quiz never realize that they are making not one but two assumptions when they accept the statement "This is graduation day for the Thomas family." In their preoccupation with whether the photo really depicts a graduation day for one or all family members, they overlook assumptions made about the actuality of family name and family status. Yet, if they go along with the assumption that this is a family with the name "Thomas," they fall into believing that most of the following statements are true as well. The photo is actually an advertisement designed to sell Amway products. The "family" consists of paid models taken to the Stanford University campus to have their picture taken. (Actually, three of the older adults were related; the little girl was borrowed from a family next door.) This was a *contrived* situation, not a real one, yet had the photo appeared contrived, it would not have succeeded in its purpose of convincing magazine readers that selling Amway products would make them feel as successful and happy as this family.

Commercial advertising uses a lot of sophisticated knowledge about how to get consumers to accept fakery. Actors in television commercials have to convince us that they are not actors: they should look "real"—like one of us. They have to persuade us that it is natural for two homemakers doing aerobics together to share advice on laundry detergents or that a celebrity is sincere in making a product testimonial.

The blurring of fact and fiction extends beyond commercials, sometimes with little concern for the distinctions. We watch documentaries that alternate between actual news footage and reenactments. We watch adventure stories that use news footage with pseudo-newsreels. Consider the following instances of fact mixed with fiction.

1. Ronald Reagan was known for his "presidency by photo ops." When he went to the demilitarized zone in Korea, his video managers wanted to get footage of Reagan at the most exposed American bunker, Guardpost Collier, which overlooked North Korea. However, the Secret Service vetoed the idea for fear of sharpshooters or infiltrators. After several days of negotiation, the problem of protection was solved by erecting posts strong enough to hold 30,000 yards of camouflage netting in front of the bunker. Then, to get the most dramatic shots, the army built camera platforms on the hill beyond the guardpost so Reagan could be snapped standing there at the front. In the final shot, he was to be seen surrounded by sandbags, peering with his binoculars toward North Korea, evoking the memory of General Douglas MacArthur (from "The Storybook Presidency," *Power Game: How Washington Works*, by Hedrick Smith, 1988).

2. In a newspaper cartoon a father is changing a flat tire in the rain while his two children complain from the car window. The father says, "Don't you understand? This is *life;* this is what is happening. We *can't* switch to another channel."

3. Some TV stations regularly reenact true local crime events for the news, using actors to play the parts on the exact locations. They claim this is done as a public service.

4. A film star who regularly played the surgeon Colonel Potter on the TV series "M*A*S*H" appeared, wearing a doctor's white coat, in an aspirin commercial to endorse the product.

5. In the summer of 1985 the House Democratic Task Force on Agriculture brought in three Academy Award–winning actresses to testify about the problems facing American agriculture. They were—Jessica Lange, star of the movie *Country*, Sissy Spacek, who portrayed a farm wife in *The River*, and Jane Fonda, who played the part of a rural woman in the movie *The Dollmaker*.

6. In 1990 both the Mexican government and some U.S. Drug Enforcement Administration agents protested gross factual inaccuracies in the NBC miniseries *Drug Wars: The Camarena Story*. In defense, a DEA spokesperson said, "We're not going to go through it all with a fine-tooth comb. In our view, it captures the spirit of events."

FEELINGS CAN BE FACTS

Feelings can deceive as well as illuminate us.

We often hear that we should be objective and not subjective in order to determine facts. This warning is needed to remind us that anger, fear, envy, and prejudices can distort our perceptions and keep us from seeing things fairly as they really are. However, many interpret this familiar

Photo by Aaron Hale. Used with permission of the photographer.

advice to mean that all feelings are "subjective"—and therefore irrational and unreliable—or that they invariably keep us from knowing what is true. This is a false assumption. There are times when feelings lead us to make a more careful investigation of a situation, such as when we feel mistrust. Therefore, it would seem wiser not to deny or suppress our feelings, but instead to examine our *attitude* toward an issue. Is it objective or subjective? We can hate the taste of a bitter medication, yet decide to take it because our health depends on it. This would be assuming an objective attitude in spite of our feelings. A subjective attitude, on the other hand, would only choose what feels most comfortable despite the long-term consequences. Thus attitude can be objective in the sense of being under conscious control, or subjective in terms of remaining under unconscious influence. An ambulance attendant, police officer, or firefighter may flinch when they see a maimed or burned person, but nevertheless carry on with their work. Personal reactions of aversion cannot be allowed to interfere with such professional duty. Yet this does not mean that professionals need to deny what they are feeling in order to function well.

There are many circumstances in which a careful consideration of our feelings offers vital information. We need this sensitivity in human relationships, and we need sensitivity to interpret art. Look for instance at the photo on page 83.

Suppose you notice that you react to the photo by feeling both uneasy and curious. Such feelings might draw you to look more closely in order to learn more. You might even wonder if the photographer intended to lure your interest in this way.

When we are studying art, we give attention to our feeling reactions, since they can lead us to better understand a work's meaning. Artists, like the photographers whose pictures appear in this book, intentionally try to provoke reactions. Indeed, you cannot come into objective contact with a work unless you first assess how it affects you. When we listen to a salsa, our mood is affected and we feel enticed to dance. The release of joy we feel inside, when recognized, becomes a fact. Such experiences, when shared with others, can be especially powerful. We have all attended public performances where we laughed and cried together in an audience that was sharing the same feeling response. Here the feelings became a shared reality, a fact.

Let's then go back to the terms objective and subjective. Some believe that in order to be objective, a person must deny or suppress any feelings, since feelings keep one from being coolly rational and observant. Certainly this belief expresses an ideal. But, without faking, can it be achieved? Let us then consider how we might proceed with more honest realism about our feelings. We can learn how to observe, rather than react, to our feelings—to observe while feeling them at the same time. This means simply allowing feelings to be present without ignoring, denying, or suppressing them. When we are subjective about feelings, we are driven by them, we are unaware of how they are influencing our thoughts and decisions; and we react blindly to their directives. Unrecognized feelings can distort our reasoning and lead us to deceive others and ourselves. When subjectivity rules us, we cannot clearly discern what is real and true. However, when we take our feelings into account, staying present both with them and what lies before us, we come closer to that ideal of objectivity.

FACTS AND SOCIAL PRESSURE

Our need to have our perceptions verified by others also makes us susceptible to manipulation.

Some facts can only be determined by our senses and perceptions. To test their accuracy, we need confirmation from other sources. Then we try to achieve certainty through confirmation.

1. JOHN: "Tell me, am I asleep or awake?"
   MARY: "You are awake."
2. BILL: "Did that woman make a pass at me or did I imagine it?"
   JANE: "She made a pass, alright."
3. EMILY: "I think this suit is too large for me. What do you think?"
   MAY: "Much too large."
4. VERNA: "My checking account balances."
   NORMA: "My figures show you are correct."

In each of these examples, a personal examination alone could not determine what was real. To test the perception accuracy, confirmation was needed from others. Confirmation takes us out of disequilibrium and restores us to equilibrium. The reverse side of this principle is that a contradiction of our perceptions can make us feel uncomfortable, angry, self-doubting, even crazy.

5. JOSE: "I didn't have too much to drink last night."
   WANDA: "Yes, you did! You were drunk!"
6. CHILD: "I don't want to eat my carrots. They taste icky."
   PARENT: "Yes, you do want to eat them. You are just imagining things. They taste good."

Figure 3.1 Standard and Comparison Lines in the Asch Experiment

As these examples illustrate, disagreements about perceptions cause conflicts. Sometimes they can be settled by various arbiters: an umpire in a game, a speedometer in a car, or a thermometer on the wall. But without an arbiter, we can be left feeling unsure of ourselves.

This human need for confirmation leaves us vulnerable to manipulation. The truth of this principle was demonstrated by American psychologist Solomon Asch, who conducted some simple experiments to test how a group could affect the perceptions of an individual. He found that in a small group, people are willing to deny the evidence of their own senses if the other members of the group interpret reality differently. In one experiment, Asch assembled groups of seven to nine college students in what was described as a test of visual judgment. In each group, only one of the students was actually a subject in the experiment; the others were the researcher's secret accomplices. The researcher informed the students that they would be comparing the lengths of lines. He showed them two white cards. On the first was a single vertical black line—the standard—whose length was to be matched. On the second white card were vertical lines of various lengths. The subjects were to choose the one line of the same length as the standard line (see Figure 3.1).

A series of eighteen trials was conducted. When the first pair of cards was presented, the group gave a unanimous judgment. The same thing happened on the second trial. In twelve of the remaining sixteen trials, however, all of Asch's accomplices agreed on what was clearly an incorrect answer. The real subject of the experiment was left to react.

In about a third of the cases, the subject yielded to the majority and conformed to its decision. In separate experiments with a control group consisting of only genuine subjects, Asch found that people made mistakes less than 1 percent of the time. Subsequent interviews with those who yielded to the majority revealed that only a few of them had actually believed that the majority choice was correct. They admitted that they thought they had judged the length of the lines correctly but did not want to "rock the boat" or "spoil the results" by giving the right answer. And then there were those who had doubted their own perceptions and had concluded that they had better hide this from the others. The test made a significant demonstration of the power of consensus to bring about conformity and to make a person invalidate his or her own perception.*

Class Discussion

1. Why did a third of the subjects in Asch's experiments conform to the incorrect majority even when their perceptions told them they were correct?
2. Did these subjects have any other means of judging the correctness of their perceptions than from the others in the group?
3. If group pressure can affect us this much in such a simple problem as determining the relative length of a line, what do you think are the implications in more complex problems such as public opinion on controversial issues?
4. If you are familiar with the story "The Emperor's New Clothes," what parallels do you see between its theme and Asch's experiment?

*Figure and text adapted from Solomon Asch, "Effects of Group Pressure upon Modification and Distortion of Judgments," in H. Proshansky and B. Seidenberg (eds.), *Basic Studies in Social Psychology* (New York: Holt, Rinehart & Winston, 1965), pp. 393–401. Used with permission of CBS College Publishing.

FACTS AND OUR LIMITED SENSES

Both science and wisdom are needed to help us compensate for the limitations of our senses.

We have seen how consensus and conformity influence perception and thus limit our ability to know the facts. But even aside from the influence of social pressure, we are limited in our ability to know the facts because of the limits of our senses. We now know that dogs can hear levels of pitch that we cannot and that butterflies can see colors invisible to us. If we look at a chart of the electromagnetic spectrum, the portion visible to us is only a tiny slit in the whole band. We have to use instruments—X-rays, radar, the seismograph, smoke detectors—to compensate for our sense limitations.

But aside from all this, our senses are affected by many other variables such as mental preoccupations, distractions, or our varying degrees of alertness in different circumstances. How much do you actually see on your commute route? How much attention do you pay to background sounds when you live in the city? Has a friend ever complained you didn't notice when he shaved off his beard?

Another human failing is that we interpret what we perceive on the basis of our experience. Moreover, this experience may be too narrow and limited to embrace what lies before us. The Buddha once succinctly illustrated this point and more in the following wise parable.

READING

THE BLIND MEN AND THE ELEPHANT

Once upon a time a king gathered some blind men about an elephant and asked them to tell him what an elephant was like. The first man felt a tusk and said an elephant was like a giant carrot; another happened to touch an ear and said it was like a big fan; another touched its trunk and said it was like a pestle; still another, who happened to feel its leg, said it was like a mortar; and another, who grasped its tail, said it was like a rope. Not one of them was able to tell the king the elephant's real form.

Study Questions

1. What do you think the elephant represents?
2. Why did each of the blind men think in terms of comparisons?
3. What was wrong with their comparisons?
4. Can you think of examples in your life where you could not experience something new because you were comparing it to something familiar?

STATEMENTS OF FACT

How we state a fact makes all the difference.

As the preceding sections have demonstrated, it is not always easy to determine some facts. Moreover, facts depend on the language used to express them. There is a considerable difference between these two sentences: "There is a male football player in this photograph" and "I see the rear of an individual dressed in a football uniform in this photograph." The first statement makes assumptions about sex and sport activity that are probable but not necessarily factual. The second statement uses language that reflects the limitations of certainty.

When we make statements of fact, our language needs to be quite specific and guarded against assumptions. This does not mean we must use tentative language all the time. But if we are stating facts, our language has to reflect the limits of our data as well as the measure of our certainty.

Study the photograph on page 89. Then read the following statements, and notice how those in italics differ from those in regular type.

1. *This is a lone football player.*

   Prominent in the center of this black-and-white photograph is a rear view of an individual wearing smooth white knee-length pants and a

Photo by John Pearson. Used with permission of the photographer.

dark jersey. The texture of bare skin can be seen below the elbows and calves. A white mop-like covering hides the back of the head; its spaghetti strands hang down over the person's shoulders and back. A light-colored padding, suggestive of leather because of its smoothness and solidity, lies beneath these strands. The padding extends over the scapula and into flaps over the shoulders. A single white vertical line on a horizontal base that suggests the letters *T* or *I* appears on his back. This is the dress usually worn as a football uniform. From this view it is not possible to guess whether this person is male or female, but I will assume male.

2. *He is acting like a clown on roller skates.*

He is wearing high white socks and high-top shoes with small wheel shapes visible beneath each. The left leg extends back, raised at an angle. The right leg is bent forward at the knee, and the foot is parallel to the surface. In the whole body, no bulge of fat or muscle is visible. The left arm is swinging outward, and a dark triangular shape extended from the hand resembles a swimming flipper. The right elbow appears to be close to the torso; extending from the fist is a dark rod connected to an oval gray canopy that resembles an umbrella.

3. *He is trying to catch up with the school bus.*

On the far right of the photo, parallel with the man's head and torso, is a large white-domed square. Below it are dark perpendicular curves suggesting tires. Across the white shape's upper part extends a dark rectangle interrupted by two white vertical lines. The black material has the reflective translucent quality of windows. The whole has the shape of the back of a school bus.

4. *He is in a parade in New York City.*

The central figure is perpendicular to a plane of gray diagonals with one thin white diagonal between them. This surface also contains a random arrangement of larger white squares and tiny white rectangles that resemble pieces of paper and confetti. To his left and in front of the figure, extending through the top of the picture, horizontal and vertical lines suggest office building floors and windows. To the left of the skater at the lower perimeter of one dark rectangular building are white blobs and vertical lines, suggesting the heads, chests, arms, and legs of four standing individuals. Three of these blobs appear beneath a prominent white number, 7000.

As you probably have guessed, the statements in regular type are statements of fact, while the italicized sentences are interpretations of these facts, or inferences. Given the information available, they may or may not be reliable. From looking at this photograph alone we cannot tell if the figure is male, a clown, or a football player, whether he is acting like a clown, trying to catch up with the bus, or in New York City.

The factual statements in regular type, on the other hand, have the following characteristics:

1. Factual statements show an awareness of the limitations of the information available. If a photo is being described, the writer does not forget this is not a life situation where one can see all angles or ask questions.

    "From this view it is not possible to guess whether this person is male or female, but I will assume male."

2. Factual statements use appropriate qualifiers to indicate uncertainties, such as the words and phrases *probably, generally, may, might, possibly, suggest, likely, it seems to be, there's a chance that, it could be.*

    ". . . white blobs and vertical lines, suggesting the heads, chests, arms, and legs of three standing individuals."

3. Factual statements state the obvious.

    "black-and-white photograph"

4. Factual statements show a disciplined effort to describe what is present and restrain the impulse to jump to conclusions.

    "a dark triangular shape . . . resembles a swimming flipper."

5. Factual statements are not inappropriately cautious, such as to say,

    "This individual *appears* to have arms and legs."

6. Factual statements are not guesses assumed to be certainties.

    "He is in a parade in New York City."

7. Factual statements provide specific details that others can verify.

    "The central figure is perpendicular to a plane of gray diagonals."

Class Discussion

1. How do the detailed statements resemble police reports? Why are police taught to write like this?
2. If you were on a jury, how could it be useful to know the difference between factual statements and claims that are interpretations of data?
3. Why would it be important to know the difference if you were an attorney or judge, a witness, or a defendant?
4. Why would a reporter be concerned with the difference between facts and interpretations?
5. Why would the difference matter to (a) a doctor, (b) a car mechanic, (c) a biologist, (d) a pharmacist?

CORE DISCOVERY WRITING APPLICATION

Using a List of Facts to Describe a Photograph

This is an exercise that challenges your mental and verbal awareness. Its task seems simple: to describe a photograph by making a list of at least ten factual statements about it. This exercise is best done first by the whole class working together on one photograph. Then small groups can work with other photographs.

1. Choose one photograph from this book for your group to study that has not already been described by the author. Each person should

work quietly alone, then discuss his or her effort when everyone is finished. Spend some time absorbing the photograph, then take notes. Imagine that you are writing for someone who cannot see the photograph. Be as specific and detailed as you can, even about the picture's most obvious aspects. Be on guard against jumping to conclusions. Stay with your evidence. Arrange your list in some kind of logical order. (Don't jump around from the background to a person's clothes to another's hair.)

2. Write out your list of ten or more factual statements. Then compare your list with others in your group who worked on the same picture. How do you agree or differ about the facts you found? Star the facts you can agree upon.

Scoring for Using a List of Facts to Describe a Photograph

1. Obvious details not ignored. 20 points

2. Things are described, not just labeled. (To say "bus" is not to describe the evidence of the clues you actually see; besides, this label could be a mistaken inference.) 20 points

3. Facts are stated in at least 10 sentences. 10 points

4. Inferences are not stated. 30 points

5. Systematic presentation of data. 10 points

6. No distracting errors of spelling, punctuation, or sentence structure. 10 points

---

STANDARDS WE USE TO DETERMINE FACTS

Verifiability, Reliability, Plausibility, Probability

When we need to think critically in any situation, we first have to determine what the facts are. We solve practical problems through facts, such as proving the payment of a bill; we seek facts in every form of investigation, whether in a court of law or a geographical survey. This primary need for facts has led to the development of standards for determining both their existence and their reliability. When we think critically, we fully understand and use these standards, many of which have already been suggested in this chapter. Let's now look directly at four of them: verifiability, reliability, plausibility, and probability.

Verifiability means the data can be confirmed by another source. This source can be a reference source (like a dictionary), a record (like a marriage license), or a standard (like Greenwich mean time). Another source could be the testimony of a witness or of an expert. Data can be verified by the senses, by agreements, by measurements, or by documentation.

A second standard for determining facts is **reliability.** When we obtain agreements or disagreements about facts, we have to consider their degree of dependability. To do this we have to ask some critical questions. Is the witness biased? Do we need a larger survey? Were the senses used carefully and consciously? Were they adequate to the task? Were the measurements accurate? Were the documents genuine?

Another standard used to determine reliability is the test of time and repetition (probability). If the weather pattern in one region alters radically over a period of several years, this phenomenon of change becomes a fact. If things always drop when they fall on this planet, gravity remains a fact. Still another standard test for reliability is to consider whether a given fact confirms or contradicts other known facts (plausibility). If a person claims to be over twenty-one, whereas his ID and birth certificate show he is now eighteen, this contradiction calls into question his statement. The same can be said of a senator who claims to support a particular issue but whose voting record demonstrates no support at all.

The standards of **plausibility** and **probability** are familiar ones that we all use but may not always recognize as standards. It does not seem plausible or probable that a person is actually twenty-one if he offers up an ID that says he is eighteen. For facts to be accepted, they have to make sense to us or seem to be the most likely possibility.

CHAPTER SUMMARY

1. By definition, a fact is something known with certainty through experience, observation, or measurement. A fact can be objectively demonstrated and verified. A fact depends on other sources to agree that it corresponds to reality.

2. It is not easy for us to determine whether facts correspond to reality. This can only be determined over time with repeated feedback and testing.

3. We need to be alert to discern facts from fiction.

4. Feelings can be facts. Feelings about art can offer us clues to the artist's intentions.

5. Facts are not absolutes but statements of probability.

6. Because we are dependent on confirmation from others in our search for facts, social pressures can we lead us to distrust or distort our own perceptions.

7. Our senses are limited both in range and capacity and are affected by many factors, such as selective focus and mental preoccupations.

8. Facts must be expressed in carefully formulated statements that have the following characteristics:
   (a) They define their own limitations.
   (b) They are objectively stated.
   (c) They use appropriate qualifiers.
   (d) They state the obvious.
   (e) They are not inappropriately cautious.
   (f) They do not include guesses or inferences.
   (g) They are specific and offer their evidence for others to verify.

9. The standards traditionally used to determine facts are verifiability, reliability, plausibility, and probability. Facts have to undergo the test of time and repetition and not contradict other known facts.

CHAPTER QUIZ

Rate each of the following statements as *true* or *false*. In class discussion or in writing, give an example to substantiate your answer in each case.

_____ 1. Some facts can be determined by measurements.

_____ 2. Some facts can be confirmed by the senses, others by records.

_____ 3. The most reliable facts are those that have been repeatedly confirmed by tests over time.

_____ 4. Facts often consist of obvious details that are seen but not consciously recognized.

_____ 5. Sometimes what we claim to be facts are untrue because the human perceptions used to determine them are limited and fallible.

_____ 6. A person educated in critical thinking qualifies statements to reflect probabilities and uncertainties using provisional phrases such as "it appears that . . . ."

_____ 7. Often it is hard to make a decision because we do not have enough facts.

_____ 8. The study of many subjects consists of memorizing facts, because they are the nearest things we have to certainties.

_____ 9. All newspapers can be depended upon as reliable sources of facts about world events.

_____ 10. An atmosphere that permits disagreements about widely accepted perceptions and beliefs helps critical thinking to flourish.

COMPOSITION WRITING APPLICATION

Writing a Short Fact-Finding Report

Think of a problem that you might solve by getting whatever facts you need to make a decision or take effective action. This could involve buying a used car, selecting a college, agreeing to a date, getting insurance, finding affordable housing, or making a complaint before the city council. Write a simple report on the subject. Here is a summary of the parameters:

1. *Objective:* Write a report concerning a problem that could be solved through knowing or verifying more facts. Also describe how determining and verifying these facts would help you make better decisions or take more effective action.
2. *Structure:* Begin with a topic sentence and end with a summary statement. Your content should include three parts:
   (a) Describe the problem.
   (b) Describe what facts you need, where you found them, and how you interpreted them.
   (c) Describe the final outcome. Explain how getting these facts affected your perspective of the problem and helped you make a decision or take action toward solving the problem.
3. *Length:* The length of your report should be at least one typed page.

Scoring for the Fact-Finding Report

1. The problem is clearly explained. 10 points
2. There is a systematic assessment of the missing or needed facts. 20 points
3. There is a description of how the facts were found, what information was discovered, and how these facts were verified and interpreted. 20 points
4. A conclusion shows how these facts aided understanding, made a decision or action possible, or solved the problem. 20 points
5. The report is at least one typed page in length. 20 points
6. There are no distracting errors of spelling, punctuation, or sentence structure. 10 points

Student Writing Example

A PROBLEM SOLVED BY FACTS

Anthony Choy

I am an auto mechanic; a large part of my job requires skills in observing, investigating, and determining facts. Often people bring in cars with problems they can't identify, much less repair. In such cases, they hire me to get the facts. And the final test of whether or not I got the facts right is a car that runs right. Let me illustrate this with a story.

One day a customer brought in a 1977 Ford Pinto. His complaint was about the awful noise in his V-6 engine, which was louder when it revved high and quieter when it revved low. I began my inspection by locating the noise at the front of the engine area. I checked the alternator, water pump, valve adjustment, cam gears. Nothing was out of the ordinary. I was stumped.

I then removed the timing chain cover. I noticed there was a gear-to-gear system that is known to make a racket, but nothing comparable to the sound this engine was producing. Again the gears checked out okay. I was stumped again.

Then I started looking at the obvious. I retraced my diagnosing steps to study the engine some more. I noticed an excessive amount of silicone on the oil pan gasket where the bottom of the timing chain cover meets the oil pan. I noticed some broken gears inside the oil pan. I wondered: "Why didn't the last mechanic take care of this?"

I examined the gears again and noticed how hard it was to remove the crank gear. The only way to remove that gear would be to remove the oil pan by lifting the engine off its mounts first. I realized then that the last mechanic who replaced the cam and crank gears did not do the job correctly: if the mechanic had removed the gears, there would not have been an excessive amount of silicone on the oil pan gasket. The gasket had not been replaced, otherwise the broken pieces in the oil pan would have been cleaned out. Why did the mechanic omit doing this? I realized it was probably because he or she could not figure out how to remove the oil pan.

Well, I replaced the parts and proceeded to repair the vehicle the way I was taught. I started up the engine, checked for leaks, and there were none. Then I revved the engine high for a moment and left it at idle, and the noise was completely gone. It purred like a kitten. I felt good to have corrected the problem. When my customer returned, he shook my hand and gave me a bonus.

Used with permission of Anthony Choy.

READINGS

THE ACCIDENT AND AFTERMATH
Hayden Herrera

"I made two terrible mistakes in my life: the one was a bus accident and the other was Diego Rivera." Thus did Frida Kahlo, a Mexican artist of great charismatic beauty, sum up her life. Her writing and paintings had a lot to say about these two events: the first was a disaster suffered at age eighteen that left her crippled, and the second was her stormy marriage to Diego Rivera, the most famous Mexican muralist of this century. This reading selection describes her first "mistake"—the bus accident. Although the trauma would seem to have been so terrible as to be unbearable, through its telling and retelling, Kahlo achieved a measure of transcendence over its impact. In the years that followed, she managed to lead a highly creative life. Her own healing seemed to have begun with simply confronting the reality of the facts.

It was one of those accidents that make a person, even one separated by years from the actual fact, wince with horror. It involved a trolley car that plowed into a flimsy wooden bus, and it transformed Frida Kahlo's life. 1

Far from being a unique piece of bad luck, such accidents were common enough in those days in Mexico City to be depicted in numerous *retablos.* (Small votive paintings offering thanks to a holy being, usually the Virgin, for misfortunes escaped.) Buses were relatively new to the city, and because of their novelty they were jammed with people while trolley cars went empty. Then, as now, they were driven with toreador bravado, as if the image of the Virgin of Guadalupe dangling near the front window made the driver invincible. The bus in which Frida was riding was new, and its fresh coat of paint made it look especially jaunty. 2

The accident occurred late in the afternoon on September 17, 1925, the day after Mexico had celebrated the anniversary of its independence from Spain. A light rain had just stopped; the grand gray government buildings that border the Zócalo looked even grayer and more severe than usual. The bus to Coyoacán was nearly full, but Alejandro [Frida's boyfriend] and Frida found seats together in the back. When they reached the corner of Cuahutemotzin and 5 de Mayo and were about to turn onto Calzada de Tlalpan, a trolley from Xochimilco approached. It was moving slowly but kept coming as if it had no brakes, as if it were purposely aiming at a crash. Frida remembered: 3

> A little while after we got on the bus the collision began. Before that we had taken another bus, but since I had lost a little parasol, we got off to look for it and that was how we happened to get on the bus that destroyed me. The accident took place on a corner in front of the San Juan market, exactly in front. The streetcar went slowly, but our bus driver was a very nervous young man. When the trolley car went around the corner the bus was pushed against the wall.
>
> I was an intelligent young girl, but impractical, in spite of all the freedom I had won. Perhaps for this reason, I did not assess the situation nor did I guess the kind of

wounds I had. The first thing I thought of was a *balero* (Mexican toy) with pretty colors that I had bought that day and that I was carrying with me. I tried to look for it, thinking that what had happened would not have major consequences.

It is a lie that one is aware of the crash, a lie that one cries. In me there were no tears. The crash bounced us forward and a handrail pierced me the way a sword pierces a bull. A man saw me having a tremendous hemorrhage. He carried me and put me on a billiard table until the Red Cross came for me.

When Alejandro Gómez Arias describes the accident, his voice constricts to an almost inaudible monotone, as if he could avoid reliving the memory by speaking of it quietly: **4**

"The electric train with two cars approached the bus slowly. It hit the bus in the middle. Slowly the train pushed the bus. The bus had a strange elasticity. It bent more and more, but for a time it did not break. It was a bus with long benches on either side. I remember that at one moment my knees touched the knees of the person sitting opposite me, I was sitting next to Frida. When the bus reached its maximal flexibility it burst into a thousand pieces, and the train kept moving. It ran over many people.   **5**

"I remained under the train. Not Frida. But among the iron rods of the train, the handrail broke and went through Frida from one side to the other at the level of the pelvis. When I was able to stand up I got out from under the train. I had no lesions, only contusions. Naturally the first thing that I did was to look for Frida.   **6**

"Something strange had happened. Frida was totally nude. The collision had unfastened her clothes. Someone in the bus, probably a house painter, had been carrying a packet of powdered gold. This package broke, and the gold fell all over the bleeding body of Frida. When people saw her they cried, '*La bailarina, la bailarina!*' With the gold on her red, bloody body, they thought she was a dancer.   **7**

"I picked her up—in those days I was a strong boy—and then I noticed with horror that Frida had a piece of iron in her body. A man said, "We have to take it out!" He put his knee on Frida's body, and said, "Let's take it out." When he pulled it out, Frida screamed so loud that when the ambulance from the Red Cross arrived, her screaming was louder than the siren. Before the ambulance came, I picked up Frida and put her in the display window of a billiard room. I took off my coat and put it over her. I thought she was going to die. Two or three people did die at the scene of the accident, others died later.   **8**

"The ambulance came and took her to the Red Cross Hospital, which in those days was on San Jeronimo Street, a few blocks from where the accident took place. Frida's condition was so grave that the doctors did not think they could save her. They thought she would die on the operating table.   **9**

"Frida was operated on for the first time. During the first month it was not certain that she would live."   **10**

The girl whose wild dash through school corridors resembled a bird's flight, who jumped on and off streetcars and buses, preferably when they were moving, was now immobilized and enclosed in a series of plaster casts and other contraptions. "It was a strange collision," Frida said. "It was not violent but rather silent, slow, and it harmed everybody. And me most of all."   **11**

Her spinal column was broken in three places in the lumbar region. Her collarbone was broken, and her third and fourth ribs. Her right leg had eleven fractures and her right foot was dislocated and crushed. Her left shoulder was out of joint, her pelvis   **12** broken in three places. The steel handrail had literally skewered her body at the level of the abdomen; entering on the left side, it had come out through the vagina. "I lost my virginity," she said.

Study Question

1. This excerpt gives two observers' accounts of the bus accident—its impact and aftermath. Compare and contrast the details given from the two viewpoints. How do you account for their different assessment of the most important facts?

ADVANCED OPTIONAL WRITING ASSIGNMENT

Write an essay of about four typed pages in which you describe an event in your own life or family life that involved facing and dealing with "hard facts." Were the facts subject to different interpretations? Did you go through different stages before you could come to acceptance? What changes resulted in your life because of these facts?

LIES MY TEACHER TOLD ME

James W. Loewen

This reading is taken from the Introduction to Lies My Teacher Told Me: Everything Your American History Textbook Got Wrong. *In the mid-nineties, this book was a best-seller, reflecting a new interest in re-examining accounts of American history for the racist and ethnocentric biases. As you read this excerpt, consider what it has to say about facts, shared realities, fiction, and propaganda.*

HIGH SCHOOL STUDENTS HATE HISTORY. When they list their favorite subjects, history invariably comes in last. Students consider history "the most irrelevant" of twenty-one subjects commonly taught in high school. *Bor-r-ing* is the adjective they apply to it. When students can, they avoid it, even though most students get higher grades in history than in math, science, or English. Even when they are forced to take classes in history, they repress what they learn, so every year or two another study decries what our seventeen-year-olds don't know.   1

African American, Native American, and Latino students view history with a special dislike. They also learn history especially poorly. Students of color do only slightly worse than white students in mathematics. If you'll pardon my grammar, nonwhite students do more worse in English and most worse in history. Something intriguing is going on here: surely history is not more difficult for minorities than trigonometry or Faulkner. Students don't even know they are alienated, only that they "don't *like*   2 social studies" or "arently any good at history." In college, most students of color give history departments a wide berth.

Many history teachers perceive the low morale in their classrooms. If they have **3** a lot of time, light domestic responsibilities, sufficient resources, and a flexible principal, some teachers respond by abandoning the overstuffed textbooks and reinventing their American history courses. All too many teachers grow disheartened and settle for less. At least dimly aware that their students are not requiting their own love of history, these teachers withdraw some of their energy from their courses. Gradually they end up going through the motions, staying ahead of their students in the textbooks, covering only material that will appear on the next test.

College teachers in most disciplines are happy when their students have had sig- **4** nificant exposure to the subject before college. Not teachers in history. History professors in college routinely put down high school history courses. A colleague of mine calls his survey of American history "Iconoclasm I and II," because he sees his job as disabusing his charges of what they learned in high school. In no other field does this happen. Mathematics professors, for instance, know that non-Euclidean geometry is rarely taught in high school, but they don't assume that Euclidean geometry was *mistaught*. Professors of English literature don't presume that *Romeo and Juliet* was misunderstood in high school. Indeed, history is the only field in which the more courses students take, the stupider they become.

Perhaps I do not need to convince you that American history is important. More **5** than any other topic, it is about *us*. Whether one deems our present society wondrous or awful or both, history reveals how we arrived at this point. Understanding our past is central to our ability to understand ourselves and the world around us. We need to know our history, and according to C. Wright Mills, we know we do.

Outside of school, Americans show great interest in history. Historical novels, **6** whether by Gore Vidal (*Lincoln, Burr,* et al.) or Dana Fuller Ross (*Idaho!, Utah!, Nebraska!, Oregon!, Missouri!,* and on! and on!) often become bestsellers. The National Museum of American History is one of the three big draws of the Smithsonian Institution. The series "The Civil War" attracted new audiences to public television. Movies based on historical incidents or themes are a continuing source of fascination, from *Birth of a Nation* through *Gone with the Wind* to *Dances with Wolves* and *JFK*.

Our situation is this: American history is full of fantastic and important stories. **7** These stories have the power to spellbind audiences, even audiences of difficult seventh-graders. These same stories show what America has been about and are directly relevant to our present society. American audiences, even young ones, need and want to know about their national past. Yet they sleep through the classes that present it.

What has gone wrong? **8**

We begin to get a handle on this question by noting that the teaching of history, **9** more than any other discipline, is dominated by textbooks. And students are right: the books are boring. The stories that history textbooks tell are predictable; every problem has already been solved or is about to be solved. Textbooks exclude conflict or real suspense. They leave out anything that might reflect badly upon our national character. When they try for drama, they achieve only melodrama, because readers know that everything will turn out fine in the end. "Despite setbacks, the United States overcame these challenges," in the words of one textbook. Most authors of history textbooks don't even try for melodrama. Instead, they write in a tone that if heard aloud might be described as "mumbling lecturer." No wonder students lose interest.

Textbooks almost never use the present to illuminate the past. They might ask **10** students to consider gender roles in contemporary society as a means of prompting students to think about what women did and did not achieve in the suffrage movement or in the more recent women's movement. They might ask students to prepare household budgets for the families of a janitor and a stockbroker as a means of prompting thinking about labor unions and social classes in the past and present. They might, but they don't. The present is not a source of information for writers of history textbooks.

Conversely, textbooks seldom use the past to illuminate the present. They por- **11** tray the past as a simple-minded morality play. "Be a good citizen" is the message that textbooks extract from the past. "You have a proud heritage. Be all that you can be. After all, look at what the United States has accomplished." While there is nothing wrong with optimism, it can become something of a burden for students of color, children of working-class parents, girls who notice the dearth of female historical figures, or members of any group that has not achieved socioeconomic success. The optimistic approach prevents any understanding of failure other than blaming the victim. No wonder children of color are alienated. Even for male children from affluent white families, bland optimism gets pretty boring after eight hundred pages.

Textbooks in American history stand in sharp contrast to other teaching materials. **12** Why are history textbooks so bad? Nationalism is one of the culprits. Textbooks are often muddled by the conflicting desires to promote inquiry and to indoctrinate blind patriotism. "Take a look in your history book, and you'll see why we should be proud," goes an anthem often sung by high school glee clubs. But we need not even look inside. The titles themselves tell the story: *The Great Republic, The American Way, Land of Promise, Rise of the American Nation.* Such titles differ from the titles of all other textbooks students read in high school or college. Chemistry books, for example, are called *Chemistry* or *Principles of Chemistry,* not *Rise of the Molecule.* And you can tell history textbooks just from their covers, graced as they are with American flags, bald eagles, the Statue of Liberty.

Between the glossy covers, American history textbooks are full of information—— **13** overly full. These books are huge. The specimens in my collection of a dozen of the most popular textbooks average four and a half pounds in weight and 888 pages in length. No publisher wants to lose an adoption because a book has left out a detail of concern to a particular geographical area or a particular group. Textbook authors seem compelled to include a paragraph about every U.S. president, even Chester A. Arthur and Millard Fillmore. Then there are the review pages at the end of each chapter. *Land of Promise,* to take one example, enumerates 444 chapter-closing "Main Ideas." In addition, the book lists literally thousands of "Skill Activities," "Key Terms," "Matching" items, "Fill in the Blanks," "Thinking Critically" questions, and "Review

Identifications," as well as still more "Main Ideas" at the ends of the various sections within each chapter. At year's end, no student can remember 444 main ideas, not to mention 624 key terms and countless other "factoids." So students and teachers fall back on one main idea: to memorize the terms for the test following each chapter, then forget them to clear the synapses for the next chapter. No wonder so many high school graduates cannot remember in which century the Civil War was fought!

None of the facts is remembered, because they are presented simply as one **14** damn thing after another. While textbook authors tend to include most of the trees and all too many twigs, they neglect to give readers even a glimpse of what they might find memorable: the forests. Textbooks stifle meaning by suppressing causation. Students exit history textbooks without having developed the ability to think coherently about social life.

Even though the books bulge with detail, even though the courses are so busy **15** they rarely reach 1960, our teachers and our textbooks still leave out most of what we need to know about the American past. Some of the factoids they present are flatly wrong or unverifiable. In sum, startling errors of omission and distortion mar American histories.

From James W. Loewen, *Lies My Teacher Told Me*. New York: A Touchstone Book Published by Simon & Schuster, 1996. Copyright ©1995 *Lies My Teacher Told Me* by James W. Loewen. Reprinted with permission of The New Press.

Study Questions

1. What support does he offer for his claim that high school students hate history?
2. State three criticisms he makes of high school American history textbooks.
3. Explain what he means when he says that nationalism is one of the reasons history textbooks are so bad. How does nationalism result in biased and distorted thinking?
4. Explain whether your own experience studying history in high school coincides with what he describes. What facts did you learn that you can still remember?
5. Explain what you understand this quotation to mean: "Textbooks stifle meaning by suppressing causation. Students exit history textbooks without having developed the ability to think coherently about social life."

BUILDING ARGUMENTS

FACTS

One powerful form of argument is to simply state the facts, allowing the facts to support for an inevitable but implied conclusion. (This is generally known as "letting the facts speak for themselves.") Notice how this is accomplished in the reading given below. It offers the words of a Blackfoot woman from the year 1835, who offers only (her version of) the facts to explain why she left her husband to live with a white trapper.

I was the wife of a Blackfoot warrior, and I served him faithfully. (principal claim) *I brought wood in the morning, and placed water always at hand. I watched for his coming; and he found his food cooked and waiting. If he rose to go forth there was nothing to delay him. I searched the thought that was in his heart, to save him the trouble of speaking. When I went abroad on errands for him, the chiefs and warriors smiled upon me, the braves spoke soft things, in secret; but my feet were in the straight path, and my eyes could see nothing but him.*

When he went out to hunt, or to war, who aided to equip him but I? When he returned I met him at the door; I took his gun; and he entered without further thought. When he sat and smoked, I unloaded his horses; tied them to stakes, brought in their loads, and was quickly at his feet. If his moccasins were wet I took them off and put on others which were warm and dry. I dressed all the skins that were taken in the chase. . . . I served him faithfully; and what was my reward? A cloud was always on his brow, and sharp lightning on his tongue. I was his dog; and not his wife. Who was it scarred and bruised me? It was he.

Exercise

1. Put into words the conclusion the Blackfoot woman leads you to draw for yourself from her story. (This is called an **implicit conclusion.**) What claims does she present as fact in order to support this conclusion?
2. Compose an argument in which you state two paragraphs of facts that give compelling support to a conclusion.

CHAPTER 4

Inferences

What Follows?

"If I am right in my guess that this is the Atlantic then we're the biggest fish in the world." Used with permission of Richard Guindon.

O f course the fish are only the biggest fish in their own world, but they don't know that, only we do. We can be excellent observers, we can have some facts plainly before us, but still err in our inferences. We have to remember that inferences stand on even shakier ground than facts. When we learn to give them conscious attention, our thinking becomes more skillful. This chapter is dedicated to helping you do just that.

Cartoon by John Heine. Used with permission of John Heine. Taken from *A Good Planet is Hard to Find*. Birmingham: Menasha Ridge Press, 1991.

Cartoon by John Heine. Used with permission of John Heine. Taken from *A Good Planet is Hard to Find*. Birmingham: Menasha Ridge Press, 1991.

Discovery Exercises

Recognizing Inferential Thinking

Study the cartoons on these pages. What kind of thinking is going on in the cartoons? How does the humor relate to this kind of thinking?

Defining Infer

After consulting a dictionary, write down your own definitions of the following words:

1. Reasoning
2. Conclusion
3. Guess
4. Explanation
5. Imagine
6. Infer
7. Inference
8. Interpret

UNDERSTANDING THE WORDS
INFER AND *INFERENCE*

When we infer, we imagine, reason, guess, surmise, speculate, estimate, predict, and conclude.

Infer The word infer comes from the Latin root *inferre,* meaning to bring in or to carry.

When we infer, we bring in our imaginations to fill in for missing facts. We make guesses to form a bridge between what we know and don't know.

We use inferences every hour of the day in all its forms of imagining, guessing, estimating, predicting, and concluding. Inferences govern our simplest actions. Let's look at a simple example, such as giving a graduation gift. You want to find a gift that will both surprise and please your girlfriend. Therefore you have to imagine (infer) what she would like. Suppose you decide (infer) that since most high school girls like the Backstreet Boys, she might want their latest CD. The test would come when she opens the package. If she smiles, jumps up and down, and throws her arms around you, you can infer you made a good choice. However, you might guess (infer) that she could be acting in order to please you. If you ask her if she *really* likes it, and if she jumps up and down some more, you could conclude (infer) you really made a good choice for her. You had predicted (inferred) successfully. Thus an inference enables us to imagine, decide, guess, conclude, and predict about things unknown. But we still need feedback to confirm our inferences.

Discovery Exercises

Drawing Inferences from Evidence

Read the following scenarios and think of three inferences you could make to explain each situation:

1. Your neighbors have regular habits and spend a lot of time at home. One day you notice that no lights have been on in their house in the evenings for at least a week.

2. In an airport waiting room, you sit down next to a nun wearing a dark blue dress, starched white collar, and starched white headdress. You notice she is reading *Playboy* magazine.

3. Your child, age four, usually has a good appetite. However, she says no this morning when you offer her a dish of applesauce.

4. You are on a Greyhound bus. A man gets on and sits beside you. He is carrying an expensive briefcase although he is shabbily dressed, unshaven, and perspiring heavily. When you suggest he place his briefcase on the rack overhead, he refuses, saying he doesn't mind holding it in his lap.

5. You are looking in your wife's closet for your missing shoe, and you notice a new and expensive man's sports jacket hanging there.

6. After a class you go to see your professor about an error in addition on your test score. You explain to him respectfully that 100 minus 18 is 82, not 79. He tells you to get the hell out of his office.

7. You are driving through a valley on a spring morning in a heavy rainstorm. You are on a two-lane highway, and you notice that only about half the cars that pass you head-on have their lights on.

8. You want to buy a used car but your first priority is that it be smoke-free. The owner of the car assures you that she is a nonsmoker. You notice small holes the size of cigarette ends in the upholstery of the front seats and the car has a strong smell of lemon deodorant.

Drawing Inferences from Facts

When we interpret the meaning of facts, we draw inferences about them. How many inferences can you draw from the following facts? Note if you can experience your mind making inferences as they take place.

Largest Countries with Increasing Populations

In millions	1999	2050
1. China	1,266.8	1,477.7
2. India	998.1	1,528.8
3. United States	276.2	349.3
4. Indonesia	209.2	311.9
5. Brazil	168.0	244.2

Source: *UN 1998 Revision of World Population Estimates and Projections* as reprinted in *San Francisco Chronicle,* 10/11/99.

Countries Most in Debt to the World Bank (1998)

(In trillions)

1. Mexico	165,743
2. Brazil	159,139
3. Russia	120,461
4. China	118,090
5. Indonesia	107,831

Source: *World Bank* as quoted in *Top 10 of Everything 2000.* N.Y: D.K. Publishing Co, 1999.

Top Employers in the United States (1998)

1. US Postal Service	898,354
2. Wal-Mart Stores	825,000
3. General Motors	608,000
4. United Parcel Service	331,000

Source: *Fortune 500* as quoted in *Top 10 of Everything 2000.* New York: DK Publishing, 1999.

© by Jennifer Leigh Sauer. Used with permission of Jennifer Leigh Sauer.

DISTINGUISHING INFERENCES
FROM FACTS

**Good writing distinguishes inferences from facts,
description from interpretation.**

Inferences are very often confused with facts, as you may well have discovered from taking the quiz on the mythical Thomas family in the Introduction.

_____ 1. This is graduation day for the Thomas family.

_____ 2. The father is proud of his son.

_____ 3. The sister looks up to her brother.

_____ 4. This is a prosperous family.

_____ 5. The son has just graduated from law school.

If you said *true* to any of these assertions, you were confusing inferences with facts. And if you had recognized this, you would have realized that you had no facts but were basing your answers on a guess about missing details. The only right response in each case is *can't answer* because all five statements are inferences.

As you learned when you described a photograph in the last chapter, the work of identifying the facts by stating details instead of substituting inferences made *about* these details is the primary challenge of descriptive writing. Usually, specific details are the most conspicuous and obvious information we can see; indeed, they can be so obvious that we do not even realize that we are seeing them. One of the most difficult things about learning how to write descriptive reports is to remember to give the details and let them speak for themselves as much as possible instead of substituting our inferences or *interpretations* of what they mean.

To review the difference between statements of fact and those of inferences, suppose three people were asked to describe what they saw when they looked at a photograph of a man who was wearing overalls and lying with eyes closed under a tree. Suppose each person just gave you one statement:

- This is a picture of a man who is dead drunk.
- This is a farmer resting during his lunch hour.
- This is a picture of a man who just had a car crash.

Although each person might think they were correctly sizing up the situation, none was carefully examining or describing the evidence. Instead, only final *interpretations* were offered. Each statement might seem to be a plausible explanation of why the man is lying under the tree, but none

© by Jennifer Leigh Sauer. Used with permission of Jennifer Leigh Sauer.

of these conclusions can be verified. Therefore, we have to present our evidence carefully, which is what we do in description. Our facts are our evidence. And facts can often lie in the *obvious*—or ordinary details that we take for granted. When we describe, we need to set forth our perceptions without assuming that others see or interpret things as we do.

The practice of stating the obvious also helps the writer draw better inferences. When we review our evidence, we may discover that we had rushed to hasty conclusions such as those offered above. A man dressed in overalls lying under a tree is just a man dressed in overalls lying under a tree; he is not a drunk, not a lunch time loafer, and not a car wreck victim. Such labels are not facts, only interpretations. However, this does not mean we should never make interpretations. It is just that we need to draw only those which our facts can support. Yet such a practice goes contrary to human inclinations, or the preference to rush to interpretations. Thus, descriptive writing can become a discipline for the mind; it stretches our capacities to state our facts and think about them with care. And it requires slowing down and taking our time. Nevertheless, the results are worth it, for descriptive writing that presents its facts with responsible clarity is also *interesting* writing. When we clearly describe what we observe and think, our work naturally becomes concrete and specific, and therefore more alive and interesting to ourselves and to others.

Short Break Study Questions

1. Which of the following statements are descriptive statements and which are interpretations?
   (a) She is a strange person.
   (b) You are brilliant.
   (c) When you don't pass the ketchup when I ask, I wonder why.
   (d) Whenever I see him, I feel angry inside.
2. How would you translate the statements you decided were interpretative into descriptive statements?

HOW INFERENCES CAN GO RIGHT AND WRONG

We make inferences to help us fill in for missing facts and in order to make sense of the facts we have. As we make inferences, we have to keep checking them against our facts, otherwise we can build one faulty inference on top of another.

We solve problems by asking questions, gathering facts, making inferences from them, and then letting these inferences suggest strategies for finding new facts, which in turn lead to new inferences. Each inference directs us toward our objective. When we use inferences consciously and imaginatively, they give us the certainties we need to move forward.

Inferences are *essential* mental operations in the search for knowledge. But we have to learn how to make them soundly. The greatest difficulties occur when inferences are confused with facts or acted upon

© by Ken Graves/Jeroboam. Used with permission of Ken Graves.

as though they were facts. Inferences used with conscious skill lead us to knowledge. When used without conscious awareness, they lead us to confusion and illusion.

Let us now consider contrasting examples of how inferences can either create knowledge or confusion. Let's begin with a reading selection showing the thinking of that master of skillful inference, Sherlock Holmes.

READING

A STUDY IN SCARLET

Sir Arthur Conan Doyle

"I wonder what that fellow is looking for?" I asked, pointing to a stalwart, plainly dressed 1
individual who was walking slowly down the other side of the street, looking anxiously
at the numbers. He had a large blue envelope in his hand, and was evidently the
bearer of a message.

"You mean the retired sergeant of Marines," said Sherlock Holmes.   **2**

"Brag and bounce!" thought I to myself. "He knows that I cannot verify his guess."   **3**

The thought had hardly passed through my mind when the man whom we were   **4**
watching caught sight of the number of our door, and ran rapidly across the roadway.
We heard a loud knock, a deep voice below, and heavy steps ascending the stair.

"For Mr. Sherlock Holmes," he said, stepping into the room and handing my friend   **5**
the letter.

Here was an opportunity of taking the conceit out of him. He little thought of this   **6**
when he made that random shot. "May I ask, my lad," I said in the blandest voice,
"what your trade may be?"

"Commissionaire, sir," he said, gruffly. "Uniform away for repairs."   **7**

"And you were?" I asked, with a slightly malicious glance at my companion.   **8**

"A sergeant, sir, Royal Marine Light Infantry, sir. No answer? Right, sir."   **9**

He clicked his heels together, raised his hand in salute, and was gone. . . .   **10**

"How in the world did you deduce that?" I asked.   **11**

"Deduce what?" said he, petulantly.   **12**

"Why, that he was a retired sergeant of Marines."   **13**

"It was easier to know it than to explain why I know it. If you were asked to prove   **14**
that two and two made four, you might find some difficulty, and yet you are quite sure
of the fact. Even across the street I could see a great blue anchor tattooed on the back
of the fellow's hand. That smacked of the sea. He had a military carriage, however,
and regulation side whiskers. There we have the marine. He was a man with some
amount of self-importance and a certain air of command. You must have observed
the way in which he held his head and swung his cane. A steady, respectable, middle-aged man, too, on the face of him—all facts which led me to believe he had been
a sergeant."

"Wonderful!"   **15**

From Sir Arthur Conan Doyle, *A Study in Scarlet.* New York: Penguin Books, 1982. (Originally published
in 1887.)

Study Questions

1. Where in the story does Sherlock Holmes make an inference about the profession of the man seen walking down the street?
2. On what observations does he base this inference?
3. Describe a situation in which one of the following individuals would need to
   make skillful inferences:
   (a) A physician
   (b) A salesperson
   (c) A car mechanic
   (d) A cook

The fascination that Holmes holds for us lies in his uncanny ability
to draw correct inferences. He is a fictional hero, not of physical, but

mental prowess. His appeal endures because we all know wrong inferences can hurt us, whereas correct inferences give us power, vision, and speed. The danger is that even one faulty inference can get us into trouble. Moreover we can build a wobbly leaning tower of inferences on the foundation of one mistaken one. Let's look now first at a simple example of how two different people confronted this challenge.

Neighbor 1

Facts observed:

1. I see John sitting on the front steps of his house.

2. It is Monday morning. He usually is at school by this time.

Chain of inferences:

1. He could be sick.

2. He could be playing hooky.

3. Maybe he has some good reason to be home.

4. In any case, I don't think he'd mind talking to me.

Conclusion

I'll go over and ask him what's up.

Neighbor 2

Facts observed:

1. I see John sitting on the front steps of his house.

2. It is Monday morning. He usually is at school at this time.

Chain of inferences

1. He's pretending to be sick.

2. He was probably out late partying last night.

3. I'll bet he is hung over from drugs and alcohol.

4. I'll bet his parents don't know.

New chain of inferences

1. If this keeps up, he'll get kicked out of school.

2. Maybe he's been suspended already.

Conclusion

I had better call up his parents at work and tell them he's in real trouble.

Class Discussion

1. Why do the inferences drawn by Neighbor 1 and Neighbor 2 go in such different directions?

2. What is the difference between the way Neighbor 1 and Neighbor 2 work with their facts and inferences?

Now, moving from a life situation where inferences can be verified, let us consider how inferences can go wrong in a writing sample. Read the following story, which describes the photo on page 109. What happens here in terms of inferences, and at what points does this description go off course?

This photo shows a special and scary moment in the life of a woman who is about to jump out of a plane. Her eyes are closed and her head is uplifted as she prepares for her fall to earth. Her friends are about to give her the extra push she needs to get out of the door, but she shows no fear that her parachute will not open.

Discussion Break Question

1. Write or relate verbally to your partner a short description of this photo that avoids any stories or interpretations of its situation. Why do you suppose this is difficult to do?

DRAWING INFERENCES FROM CAREFUL OBSERVATION

Though we may not have all the facts about a photograph, we can learn a lot by recording the details we can observe and by drawing careful inferences from them. Since it is easier to show than describe how this is done, we'll examine how one person used observation and inference to describe the photo on page 117. As you read this description of the reading woman, notice these features:

1. The facts appear first, followed by the inferences that can reasonably be drawn from them.
2. More than one inference can be drawn from each set of facts.
3. The factual information groups together the details of one segment or feature of the photograph at a time. (For instance, it does not first describe the person's hair, then jump to the background, then jump back to her posture.)
4. The conclusion draws together the facts and the possible inferences into a plausible explanation of the message, purpose, and meaning of the photograph.

Facts

My attention is drawn first to the human figure seated flat on a plane with her legs straight out in front, forming a right angle on the central right side of this black-and-white photograph. Most prominent is the body covering that forms a dress pattern of bold gray-and-white stripes. Emerging from the dress are the pale flesh shades of her neck and face, one bent arm, and both legs; the latter are in a darker shade capped by black ovals. Most striking are the values of white; the lightest comes from

Photo by John Pearson. Used with permission of the photographer.

a stack of straight-edged shapes on her lap. There are also a white spot at her wrist, some specks of white over her ear, and finally from a flash of white streaks from the top of her ear to her eye speck where it meets a perpendicular curved line. Another curved line appears in front of the other eye. Her shoulders are rounded, and her head is bent forward toward her lap where the stack of white shapes rests.

Inferences

1. This is a woman with gray hair and glasses who is wearing a dress, low-heeled shoes, and stockings while seated on a floor reading. She wears a wristwatch and glasses and is bent over a stack of three hardback books that she holds on her lap.

2. Although she is seated on the floor, she does not seem to mind since she is absorbed in her reading.

Facts

Her dress forms a pattern of horizontal stripes that intersect at the wide lapels and ripple across her lap. This wide-banded, striped pattern with short sleeves was a conservative summer dress style in the 1950s. Her hairstyle forms shapes close to her head that curve like curly waves, ending at the nape of her neck.

Inferences

1. She is middle aged. Her sensible dress, hairstyle, shoes, and stockings suggest middle-class values of neatness, conservatism, practicality, and modesty.
2. She could be stereotyped as a schoolteacher, nun, or homemaker.
3. Although her appearance is conservative, her behavior is nonconformist. She is an eccentric scholar.

Facts

Only one angle of gray, an eye, appears at the edge of her glasses. Her lips are one tight line. Her visible left arm rests on her upper thigh, and her hand rests, fingers hidden, at the bottom of a curved dark line that appears to be a half-open page.

Inferences

1. She finds her reading so interesting that she does not care how awkward this bent position must feel to her body; she does not even notice that the floor may be dirty and cold. She reads rapidly and can hardly wait to turn the next page.
2. She is resting from standing and reading in the store.
3. She cannot sit in a cross-legged position because she is wearing a skirt.

Facts

Above her on her right is a tall shelf with seven full rows of paperback-sized books. The covers of a few of the books face forward, revealing the name of one mystery author, Agatha Christie. Above her feet, a display stand offers popular magazines such as *People* and *Harper's*.

Inferences

1. This is a public place but not a library. It is a magazine and newspaper store that also carries books or a bookstore that also sells magazines.
2. The store offers no chairs so that its patrons keep moving.
3. She is a mystery fan.
4. She is reading the books so that she will not have to pay for them.
5. She wants to buy one of these books but has to do some reading in order to make her selection.
6. She doesn't care what people think.

Facts

The floor upon which the woman is seated shows the lines of tile squares decorated with a speckled paint pattern and spattered with some larger dark spots and streaks. About three feet away from the woman's feet lies a dark shell-shaped crumpled object of two contrasting textures and shades of color. No other people are visible in this scene.

Inferences

1. It is a linoleum floor and dirty. Perhaps it is just before cleaning time; or perhaps the store has such constant traffic that it does not attempt to keep the floor spotless.
2. The crumpled object is her coat; she was so excited to get on with her reading that she forgot that she had dropped it there.
3. On the other hand, she appears to be too tidy a person to have scattered her belongings in public; perhaps it belongs to a second reader out of the camera's view.
4. If other people are in the store, this woman is not inhibited by what they may think. Nor does she seem concerned as to whether she is taking up too much space or blocking other customers from the shelves. She is lost in her books.

Conclusion

This photograph plays with some incongruities of public and private, formality and informality. Here a conventionally dressed woman is behaving unconventionally in a public bookstore. Although one would expect her to seek to remain clean and inconspicuous, here she is sitting legs stretched out on a dirty floor, blocking access to at least part of the store. Moreover, although one might expect her to browse standing up, later taking her books home to read, she seems to be absorbed by a stack of books that she may not even pay for. The photographer pokes fun at the social expectations that make this situation seem strange.

CORE DISCOVERY WRITING APPLICATION

Using Facts and Inferences to Describe a Photograph

1. This is a mental exercise that uses writing. Choose a photograph in this book not described by the author. (Do not use the photos already described by the author.) For your notes, make yourself a page with columns like this:

Facts of the Photograph	Inferences I Make About This Fact
My description of a detail: a form, texture, shade, relationship, or configuration that I see.	What I imagine this detail represents or what I interpret it to mean.

2. Survey the photograph in a systematic way, beginning with what is central, then moving to relationships of the parts and the background.

3. Write out your list using the columns in step 1 to match each statement of fact with an inference. (Actually, in your thinking, the inference will probably come to mind first. If so, write it down, then restudy the photo to discover and describe the evidence upon which this inference was based.)

4. Write a conclusion that draws your list of facts and inferences together into an explanation of the photograph. (See the example on page 119.) This summary should not introduce new information or provide a story that your evidence cannot support.

5. Now write your description in the paragraph form illustrated for you in the preceding exercise on pages 117–120. Remember to end with a summary.

6. The length should be about two typed pages.

Scoring Using Facts and Inferences to Describe a Photograph

1. Obvious details not ignored. 10 points

2. Statements of fact described rather than just named or interpreted. 10 points

3. Facts not confused with inferences. 20 points

4. Systematic organization of data: systematic sectioning of photo-small groupings of related facts, shown with inferences clearly drawn from each grouping. 20 points

5. Some imaginative use of inferences beyond the obvious. 10 points

6. Conclusion brings given facts and inferences together in a logical interpretation (not introducing new facts or a fantasy). 10 points

7. No distracting errors of spelling, punctuation, sentence structure. 10 points

8. Minimum length of two typed pages. 10 points

GENERALIZATIONS ARE INFERENCES

A good scientist, like a good writer, knows how much evidence is needed to support a generalization.

Samuel Scudder, whose encounter with a fish was described in Chapter 1, stated that "Agassiz's training in the method of observing facts and their orderly arrangement was ever accompanied by the urgent exhortation not to be content with them. 'Facts are stupid things,' he would say, 'until brought into connection with some general law.'" We can apply this statement to our concerns about thinking and writing: it is not enough to collect and state facts and inferences alone; we need to look for patterns in them and see how we can make generalizations to describe their organizing principles or "laws."

"Do you perhaps mean," I asked, "that the fish has symmetrical sides with paired organs?"

His thoroughly pleased "Of course! Of course!" repaid the wakeful hours of the previous night.

In science, laws are **generalizations** that are based on observations and that deal with recurrence, order, and relationships. Generalizations, in turn, relate individual members of a class or category to a whole. To arrive at laws or generalizations, we must look for information, then look for patterns or configurations, analyze them, and finally draw conclusions about the relationships, recurrences, and order of the gathered data.

These were the complex mental actions you followed when drawing conclusions in the last exercise.

It takes experience to know when you have gathered enough information to make accurate generalizations. Beginners, like Scudder, may decide they have seen everything after 10 minutes or, at the other extreme, refrain from drawing conclusions for too long. A good scientist, like a good writer, recognizes how much evidence is needed to support reliable generalizations.

When you first listed only facts about a photograph, you may have experienced the sense of the "stupidity" of facts that Agassiz referred to. Perhaps you had a sense of not knowing where to stop or how to separate the relevant details from the irrelevant. However, this first stage of simple-minded observing and collecting is important.

In the second stage of writing and of thinking, we begin to separate, compare, categorize, and organize our information. In the photograph description our intuition may first put everything together. Eventually, we are able to formulate all this into a generalization that is a summary statement. In paragraph writing, this statement becomes our **topic sentence.** This (usually first) sentence states in a general way the main idea to be proven or explained. What then follows is the evidence—the facts and inferences that support the main idea. Therefore what we do is present our topic sentence, which is actually our conclusion, *first* in our writing, although we arrived at it *last* in our thinking. This is exactly what you did in the exercise where you first wrote down your facts and inferences in columns and then drew a conclusion at the end that summarized all your information.

The topic sentence serves both a statement of commitment as well as a guide, aiding us in sorting out what support is needed and relevant. A topic sentence functions like a magnet in this respect. It also *tests* our facts and our inferences about them. We may even discover that the evidence we have selected does not support our topic sentence very well at all. In such cases, we stop and begin again.

The willingness to loop back and forth between the evidence and the generalization takes persistence fueled by a resolve to arrive at truth as best we can. Such a process must be familiar to you from your own writing experience, although you may never have looked at what you were doing in this conscious way before. The final exercise is designed to have you write with this conscious awareness in mind.

COMPOSITION WRITING APPLICATION

Writing a Paragraph from Facts, Inferences, and Generalizations

Choose a photograph from this chapter that you have not described before or study the Doonesbury cartoon on page 123. Working alone, observe your photograph or

Doonesbury

G. B. TRUDEAU

Questions

1. What is the professor trying to teach his students?
2. What inferences does he expect them to make?
3. What inferences do they make?
4. What clues led you to your own conclusions about this cartoon?
5. How would you describe the professor's teaching style?

the cartoon for a while, noticing what is plainly visible. Make notes by listing your facts and seeing what inferences you can draw from them.

Putting this information together, draw a conclusion about the whole. What message, what statement about life do you think is being conveyed here? Write this conclusion at the top of your page. Use this sentence as a topic sentence for a paragraph to follow that makes a general statement or conclusion about your evidence. Now write the rest of the paragraph in sentences. Describe the photograph or cartoon using all the facts you can to support your topic sentence. Link these facts to your inferences appropriately throughout. At the end, bring everything together into a second conclusion or a summary of what you have demonstrated.

Read your paragraph aloud to one to three other students who selected the same photo or cartoon. Do you find that you supported your topic sentence adequately?

CORE DISCOVERY WRITING APPLICATION

Analyzing the Use of Facts and Inferences in a Newspaper Article

1. Work with the article on pages 125–126 called "Tougher Grading Better for Students" or with another article assigned to you by the instructor. Read the article carefully. Then make yourself a chart with four headings in columns. After you read each sentence, choose the column that seems appropriate for entering quotes or comments. The example at the end should explain the analysis format and help you get started. Proceed as in this example, working sentence by sentence, analyzing each one.

2. To save time, you can make a photocopy of the article and cut and paste some sentences into the appropriate columns. When working with quotations, note that although the public statement may be a fact, its content could be an inference. In such cases, put the quote in the first column, and in the second column, note that it expresses an inference.

3. Line for line, as you proceed through the article, notice if you find any information missing. Consider what you or an ordinary reader would need to have in order to understand and believe its claims. Is enough information given about the source of the facts so that they could be verified? Are there enough facts, enough inferences, sufficient explanations? As you read, notice the times you feel puzzled, curious, confused, or suspicious. Then consider if these reactions could be due to pertinent missing information.

4. In the last column, record your thinking about each recorded fact and/or inference. Write down your conclusions, questions, comments, and reactions.

5. When you have finished going through the whole article systematically, prepare your chart in final form by typing and/or by cutting and pasting.

6. On a final sheet of paper, sum up what you learned through your analysis in one paragraph. Did you conclude that the article offers reliable information? Did your final impressions differ from your first?

Data Claimed to be Factual in this sentence	Inferences expressed in this sentence	Pertinent Missing Information	My own inference about this sentence
	"Tougher Grading Better for Students"		Wow! I didn't know that. This must be true since it is based on research.
	"America's high school students may not be getting smarter, but their teachers are getting more generous—at least when it comes to grading."	Who arrived at this conclusion? Was that the unanimous opinion of the teachers surveyed? Or is it the opinion of one or more researchers?	This statement is a rather broad unqualified generalization. Surely there must be a significant number of exceptions.
A national survey released this month showed that a record 28 percent of incoming college freshmen had A averages, up from only 12.5 percent in 1969.		Both private and public college freshmen? And do students take the same high school courses now with the same content and standards offered in 1969?	Maybe teachers don't grade as hard as they used to because students complain more about their grades. Maybe students receive better instruction and training in how to improve their study habits now than in 1969.

READING

TOUGHER GRADING BETTER FOR STUDENTS

America's high school students may not be getting much smarter, but their teachers 1
are getting more generous—at least when it comes to grading.

A national survey released this month showed that a record 28 percent of in- **2** coming college freshmen had A averages, up from only 12.5 percent in 1969. During much of that period, ironically, student scores on standardized tests actually declined.

Higher grades and lower test scores may be related, according to new research **3** by economists Julian Betts and Stefan Boedeker at the University of California, San Diego. They find a strong relationship between school grading standards and student achievement: The tougher a school grades, the harder its students work and the more they learn.

Their finding is enormously significant. "For thirty years, social scientists have been **4** trying to decide why some schools are good and some are bad," said Betts. "They looked at class size, teacher education and per pupil spending, none of which seem to matter much. So I decided to look at standards set in the schools."

If Betts and Boedeker are right, spending more money on schools may help a lot **5** less than simply changing the incentives facing students. If they are allowed to slack off and still earn good grades, most will take it easy. But holding them to higher standards costs nothing and can motivate them to achieve more.

Betts and Boedeker studied the math and science performance of roughly 6,000 **6** middle- and high-school students nationwide over five years, starting in 1987. Students were tested each year to measure how much they were learning. The researchers also had information on grading standards, amount of homework assigned and other factors.

The two scholars found large differences in grading standards between schools **7** and a strong relationship between those standards and how much students learned each year. Over five years, otherwise similar students at tough schools scored about 6 points more than students at easy schools on standardized tests with 100 as the top score. A 6-point difference is huge, Betts said.

Stronger students seem to benefit the most from tougher standards, suggesting **8** that other policies must also be sought to "help the weaker students match the gains in achievement of their (better) prepared counterparts."

One solution to uneven grading standards would be to hold standardized state **9** or national graduation exams to test high school achievement and thus give students more incentive to take their studies seriously. Such exams are routine in Europe and Japan, where graduating students are much further advanced than their American counterparts.

Bishop tested this theory by comparing the math performance of 13-year-olds **10** (measured by an international test administered in 1991) in Canadian provinces that have standardized graduation exams and in those that don't.

His findings were striking. In Canadian provinces with testing, students learned **11** about two-thirds of a grade level more than those in provinces without.

"One of the most cost-effective methods of improving achievement in American **12** schools would be to create curriculum-based exams for each state," Bishop said.

BUILDING ARGUMENTS

INFERENCES

No reasonable man can for one moment believe that such a Beautiful country (America) was intended by its Author (God) to be forever in the possession and occupancy of serpents, wild fowls, wild beasts and savages who derive little benefit from it. (Caleb Atwater, 1850)

Exercise

1. Above is a claim based on an inference. Put the claim into your own words. Explain how its reasoning is an inference.
2. What conclusion is implied?
3. What evidence offered in support of the claim?
4. Explain how the claim justifies the author's values.
5. Make a claim that is based on an inference.

Scoring for Analyzing Facts and Inferences in a Newspaper Article

1. Correct identification of all facts and inferences appearing in the article. 30 points

2. Does not confuse own inferences with those made in article. 10 points

3. Shows an understanding that although a quotation may be presented as fact, its content may express an inference. 10 points

4. Shows understanding that estimates, predictions, and opinions are inferences. 10 points

5. Missing information column shows thoughtful reflection on *pertinent* missing data. 10 points

6. Own inferences are drawn systematically, item for item, and show careful reflection on the data. 10 points

7. Format is systematic, methodical, and easy to read. 10 points

8. Final conclusion assesses how the information is presented in the article. 10 points

CHAPTER SUMMARY

1. The word *infer* means (a) to derive by reasoning; (b) to conclude; (c) to guess. When we infer, we use imagination or reasoning to provide explanations for situations where all the facts are either not available or not yet determined.

2. Responsible report writing or descriptive writing lets the facts speak for themselves as much as possible. This often means taking the time to find the right words to describe the obvious and abandoning inferences drawn too hastily that cannot be supported.

3. Writing that offers specific detailed support for its conclusions makes interesting writing. When we perceive and think clearly, we interest both ourselves and others.

4. Reasonable inferences can be used in descriptive writing to tie facts together. Care must be taken to distinguish facts from inferences, nevertheless.

5. In solving problems, inferences can be used as a strategy in planning and choosing alternatives. When we think well, we assess all facts, derive as many inferences as we can, and devise strategies for confirming or obtaining more information.

6. Detectives and consultants of all kinds are valued for their ability to examine facts and make the best inferences from them.

7. Inferences tend to build on inferences in chains of association. Unless each inference is tested for its support of evidence, a series of inferences can mislead us into flights of imagination, away from reliable knowledge.

8. Facts and inferences are linked together through generalizations. Facts have little significance in themselves until generalizations or laws can be derived from them. Generalizing too soon, before we have gathered a sufficient number of facts, is hazardous; this does not mean that we should not generalize at all. It simply means that we should learn how to draw generalizations that can be supported.

9. The topic sentence of a paragraph is a generalization that summarizes the main idea to be demonstrated in that paragraph. When we think, we usually arrive at this generalization last, after we have examined all our facts and inferences; nevertheless, we state it first, at the beginning of the paragraph. The topic sentence is a kind of conclusion, which is repeated again in another form at the end of the paragraph.

10. By the time you have finished this chapter, you should understand more about the thinking operations involved in constructing a paragraph or

doing descriptive writing. You will understand how observation helps determine facts, imagination, and reasoning to link the facts with explanations, and how a generalization ties all this information together into a meaningful whole.

CHAPTER QUIZ

Write two inferences to explain each of the following events:

1. You see a little girl pushing an elderly woman being pushed down Main Street in a large baby carriage.

2. Your best friend leaves you a note saying she has joined the Marines.

3. You have received no mail for the past two weeks.

4. A recent study found that men between fifty and seventy-nine years old married to women one to twenty-four years younger tended to live longer or had a mortality rate 13 percent below the norm.

5. The same study found that men married to older women died sooner or had a death rate that was 20 percent higher than the norm.

Rate each of the following statements as *true* or *false*. Explain your choice in each case or give an example to defend your choice.

_____ 6. To state that "annual beef consumption in the US is 96.8 pounds per capita in 1998, as compared to 11 pounds in China" is to make a generalization without facts.

_____ 7. To state the obvious is to state the sensory details of what is actually seen, as opposed to what is *thought* or interpreted about what is seen.

_____ 8. Good thinking does not continue to build inferences on top of inferences but stops whenever possible to check these inferences against the original facts or to find new ones.

_____ 9. One should always avoid making inferences in every kind of writing.

_____ 10. To state that the United States has the highest per capita use of motor vehicles in the world is to make a generalization without offering the supporting facts.

READINGS

THE THREE PERCEPTIVES
Idries Shah

This is an old teaching story of the Sufis, a mystic Muslim sect that claims to be far older than Islam. Their stories are parables told to help people understand the nature of the mind and how to use it to gain wisdom. The term perceptives *might also be translated as wise men. This reading was translated by Idries Shah, one of the leading interpreters of Sufi philosophy in the West. As you read it, take note of how accurately the three men connect their inferences to their observation skills and their past experiences.*

There were once three Sufis, so observant and experienced in life that they were **1** known as The Three Perceptives.

One day during their travels they encountered a camelman, who said, "Have you **2** seen my camel? I have lost it."

"Was it blind in one eye?" asked the first Perceptive. **3**

"Yes," said the cameldriver. **4**

"Has it one tooth missing in front?" asked the second Perceptive. **5**

"Yes, yes," said the cameldriver. **6**

"Is it lame in one foot?" asked the third Perceptive. **7**

"Yes, yes, yes," said the cameldriver. **8**

The three Perceptives then told the man to go back along the way they had come, **9** and that he might hope to find it. Thinking that they had seen it, the man hurried on his way.

But the man did not find his camel, and he hastened to catch up with the Per- **10** ceptives, hoping that they would tell him what to do.

He found them that evening, at a resting-place. **11**

"Has your camel honey on one side and a load of corn on the other?" asked the **12** first Perceptive.

"Yes," said the man. **13**

"Is there a pregnant woman mounted upon it?" asked the second Perceptive. **14**

"Yes, yes," said the man. **15**

"We do not know where it is," said the third Perceptive. **16**

The cameldriver was now convinced that the Perceptives had stolen his camel, **17** passenger and all, and he took them to the judge, accusing them of the theft.

The judge thought that he had made out a case, and detained the three men in **18** custody on suspicion of theft.

A little later, the man found his camel wandering in some fields, and returning to **19** the court, arranged for the Perceptives to be released.

The judge, who had not given them a chance to explain themselves before, asked **20** how it was that they knew so much about the camel, since they had apparently not even seen it.

"We saw the footprints of a camel on the road," said the first Perceptive. **21**

"One of the tracks was faint; it must have been lame," said the second Perceptive. **22**

"It had stripped the bushes at only one side of the road, so it must have been blind in one eye," said the third Perceptive. **23**

"The leaves were shredded, which indicated the loss of a tooth," continued the first Perceptive. **24**

"Bees and ants, on different sides of the road, were swarming over something deposited; we saw that this was honey and corn," said the second Perceptive. **25**

"We found long human hair where someone had stopped and dismounted, it was a woman's," said the third Perceptive. **26**

"Where the person had sat down there were palm-prints, we thought from the use of the hands that the woman was probably very pregnant and had to stand up in that way," said the first Perceptive. **27**

"Why did you not apply for your side of the case to be heard so that you could explain yourselves?" asked the judge. **28**

"Because we reckoned that the cameldriver would continue looking for his camel and might find it soon," said the first Perceptive. **29**

"He would feel generous in releasing us through his discovery," said the second Perceptive. **30**

"The curiosity of the judge would prompt an enquiry," said the third Perceptive. **31**

"Discovering the truth by his own enquiries would be better for all than for us to claim that we had been impatiently handled," said the first Perceptive. **32**

"It is our experience that it is generally better for people to arrive at truth through what they take to be their own volition," said the second Perceptive. **33**

"It is time for us to move on, for there is work to be done," said the third Perceptive. **34**

And the Sufi thinkers went on their way. They are still to be found at work on the highways of the earth. **35**

Study Questions

1. Make a list with two columns. On one side, state the inferences made by the three men. On the other side show the facts to which they related these inferences.
2. Why were the men so restrained in defending themselves?
3. What do you think of their statement: "It is our experience that it is generally better for people to arrive at truth through what they take to be their own volition." Can you apply this to learning and teaching?
4. What would you say is the most important value of the three men?

READING

"FRIENDS"

Tim O'Brien

This short story is taken from The Things They Carried. *Tim O'Brien was born in Minnesota and was a foot soldier in Vietnam in 1969. The book is dedicated to the men of the Alpha Company with whom he served. Reading this story aloud is the best way to appreciate its beauty. What you may find surprising is how such a bare style can still convey such powerful feelings. In your second reading, consider how the author uses the interplay of facts and inferences tell his story.*

Dave Jensen and Lee Strunk did not become instant buddies, but they did learn to 1
trust each other. Over the next month they often teamed up on ambushes. They covered each other on patrol, shared a foxhole, took turns pulling guard at night. In late August they made a pact that if one of them should ever get totally fucked up—a wheelchair wound—the other guy would automatically find a way to end it. As far as I could tell they were serious. They drew it up on paper, signing their names and asking a couple of guys to act as witnesses. And then in October Lee Strunk stepped on a rigged mortar round. It took off his right leg at the knee. He managed a funny little half step, like a hop, then he tilted sideways and dropped. "Oh, damn," he said. For a while he kept on saying it, "Damn oh damn," as if he'd stubbed a toe. Then he panicked. He tried to get up and run, but there was nothing left to run on. He fell hard. The stump of his right leg was twitching. There were slivers of bone, and the blood came in quick spurts like water from a pump. He seemed bewildered. He reached down as if to massage his missing leg, then he passed out, and Rat Kiley put on a tourniquet and administered morphine and ran plasma into him.

There was nothing much anybody could do except wait for the dustoff. After we'd 2
secured an LZ, Dave Jensen went over and kneeled at Strunk's side. The stump had stopped twitching now. For a time there was some question as to whether Strunk was still alive, but then he opened his eyes and looked up at Dave Jensen. "Oh, Jesus," he said, and moaned, and tried to slide away and said, "Jesus, man, don't kill me."

"Relax," Jensen said. 3

Lee Strunk seemed groggy and confused. He lay still for a second and then mo- 4
tioned toward his leg. "Really, it's not so bad. Not terrible. Hey, *really*—they can sew it back on—*really*."

"Right, I'll bet they can." 5
"You think?" 6
"Sure I do." 7
Strunk frowned at the sky. He passed out again, then woke up and said, "Don't 8
kill me."
"I won't," Jensen said. 9
"I'm *serious*." 10

"Sure." 11

"But you got to promise. Swear it to me—swear you won't kill me." 12

Jensen nodded and said, "I swear," and then a little later we carried Strunk to the 13
dustoff chopper. Jensen reached out and touched the good leg. "Go on now," he said.
Later we heard that Strunk died somewhere over Chu Lai, which seemed to relieve
Dave Jensen of an enormous weight.

Discussion Break Questions

1. What inferences do Strunk and Jensen make about how they would react if they were seriously wounded? What inferences do they make about how they should best take care of one another?
2. What stages of reaction does Strunk go through after stepping on the rigged mortar round?
3. How does Jensen react as his friend?
4. How did their experience with the facts and realism of injury transform them both?
5. What inferences do you make as to why Jensen seemed relieved at the end?

OBJECTIVES REVIEW OF PART I

When you have finished Part I, you will understand:

1. The following concepts on an experiential basis: observing, labeling, describing, interpreting, facts, inferences, sensing, perceiving, thinking.
2. That it is possible to maintain awareness of one's own thinking-feeling-perceiving process.
3. How clear thinking depends on "staying awake" to what is.

And you will have practice in developing these skills:

4. Suspending thinking in order to freshly sense and gather data.
5. Describing the obvious evidence without substituting labels and interpretations.
6. Recognizing when you and others are formulating facts and when you are formulating inferences.
7. Recognizing how facts and inferences can become confused.

PART II

Problems of
Critical Thinking

CHAPTER 5

Assumptions

What's Taken for Granted?

"She was eager to meet her e-mail 'partner,' knowing that the man who possessed such rare sensitivity online would be just as appealing in person."
Used with permission of Andrew Toos.

No matter how funny it may be, there's always a shock in discovering we have made a wrong assumption. In this chapter, we will take a fresh look at that familiar term, assumption, and see how it operates in our thinking. We will study types of assumptions and build on what we have learned about aware observing and inferences. We will also consider their useful role in scientific reasoning and creativity. In short, we will continue to build the skills of critical thinking.

Used with permission of Richard Guindon.

Discovery Exercises

The following three exercises can be done with a partner or alone, depending on your instructor's directions.

What Is an Assumption?

Using at least two dictionaries, write your own definition of *assumption*.

Finding Assumptions in Cartoons

Study these cartoons and state what assumptions brought humor to these situations.

Finding Assumptions in Stories

As you read the stories recounted in each of the paragraphs below, think how each depends on an assumption. Write your answers to the questions that follow each paragraph, in preparation for a class discussion.

1. You are a guard at Alcatraz. One day a prisoner was found to be missing. When you inspected his cell, you found a hole dug through the

Used with permission of Universal Press Syndicate.

concrete under his bed. All that was next to the hole was a bent metal spoon. What assumptions of the guards did the prisoner exploit in order to escape?

2. You are a guard at a station on the border of the country of Mesamania. Your duty is to inspect for smuggled goods. Every day some notorious smugglers pass through carrying heavy loads of goods on donkeys. You always examine their loads carefully for contraband but never find anything. What are the smugglers smuggling?

3. You have a dinner guest from a foreign country who belches loudly all through the meal. You find him disgusting and want to get rid of him. But he insists that he be allowed to return your hospitality. So you go to his house for dinner. There everyone but you belches loudly

"...so we began asking ourselves, does it really make sense to pay you fifty million when there are C.E.O.'s in Korea and Mexico who would do the same job for twenty-five."

Used with permission of David Sipress.

all through the meal. Before you leave, your host says, "I am sorry you did not like my dinner, but you didn't have to be so rude about it." What was the assumption of the foreign guest?

4. George Bernard Shaw was once approached by a woman who proposed marriage. "Imagine a child," she said, "with my body and your brains." "Yes," he said, "but what if the child has my body and your brains?" What was his assumption?

5. In his struggles to receive backing for the voyage of his ships to the Far East by sailing west, Christopher Columbus once spent some hours trying to persuade a nobleman to lend his support. The nobleman maintained that he was trying to do the impossible, like making an egg stand on end. Then the nobleman called for an egg and handed it to Columbus, who was sitting across from him at a table. Taking up the challenge, Columbus tried wobbling the egg on one end and then the other, while the nobleman laughed in derision. Then, picking

© 1997 Andrew B. Singer. Used with permission of Andrew B. Singer.

up the egg, Columbus gently smashed its end on the table, allowing it to stand firmly in position, while its contents oozed out. What assumption about the problem did the nobleman make that Columbus did not?

6.   In California, a bank holdup was staged by a man wearing a Levi's jacket and pants, a beard, and hair in dreadlocks. He waved a hand grenade and pointed to some sticks of "dynamite" strapped to his waist, which were actually road flares. After leaving the bank he ran into a warehouse next door where he shed his wig, beard, the flares, and clothing and changed into a blue, pin-striped suit. Stopped by a police officer outside, he insisted, "I'm not the one!" And because he didn't look the same as the robber, the police officer let him go. What assumptions did the robber count on in his strategy?

> The word **assume** comes from the Latin *assumere*—to take, adopt, accept. To assume is to take and accept something. In time, this word came to mean accepting something without sufficient inspection. When we assume, we make a faulty inference.

UNDERSTANDING ASSUMPTIONS

Assumptions are hasty or forgotten inferences.

Our study of inferences in Chapter 4 prepares us for understanding assumptions better. Assumptions might be defined as hasty or forgotten inferences. For example, most tourists visiting San Francisco in foggy July are easily recognizable: they are the people you see on the streets shivering in their light summer clothing. When they packed their shorts and T-shirts for their visit, they had inferred that since most places are warm in July, and since California has a reputation for sunny weather, light clothing would be suitable. They may not remember this inference until met with the facts of the cold damp fog typical of the northern coast's summer season. And every year more tourists arrive who have made the same assumption, enabling shops that sell them warm clothing to flourish.

We can choose—or not choose—to learn from discovering our assumptions. Some of these tourists may do a little research to double-check the weather before packing for their next destination. Others will not deem such inconvenience that important. Thus our priorities will determine how careful we might be next time. If we survive being hit by a car after assuming we could cross an intersection against a red light, we would not dare make the same assumption again. Nevertheless, none of us can avoid the effects of wrong relationships entirely because of the factors of probability and randomness. A person may be hit by a red-light runner while crossing an intersection with a green light. Yet we can prevent many assumptions by making it a habit to stop to review any that we do make. Indeed, our survival can depend on our ability to learn from mistaken assumptions.

Discussion Break Questions

1. Write down or turn to your neighbor and give an example of an assumption you made that resulted in a lot of trouble.
2. Did you learn something from this experience that would help you not make such an assumption again?

TYPES OF ASSUMPTIONS

Critical thinking helps us make creative use of conscious assumptions and avoid more of those that are unconscious and unwarranted.

Not all assumptions cause us problems. There are forms of assumptions that guide the scientific method and allow discoveries, inventions, and creative problem solving. There are **conscious and unconscious assumptions** as well as **warranted and unwarranted ones.**

Unconscious assumptions are what have been discussed thus far: mistaken inferences.

If you take something for granted, you are making an *unconscious assumption.* If you go to a party expecting to see your usual friends and find a room full of strangers, you might wish you had first asked your host who was coming.

A *conscious assumption,* on the other hand, is an intentional strategy, which is also called a working assumption. It is used in order to gain more information or to achieve a clear goal. To go back to the example of the party, suppose you decide not to leave the company of strangers but make new friends there instead. You conceive a working assumption: you will go into the kitchen and put together a tray of snacks to distribute among the crowd. This strategy will enable you to survey the crowd and decide whom you want to spend time with. You also know this plan may not succeed, but even if you don't meet people this way, you won't be disappointed, since your strategy was a conscious assumption, not an unconscious one.

Here is another example of a conscious assumption. Suppose your parents want to make an investment decision. They decide to invest in real estate, *assuming* that property values will continue to rise in the years to come. Since their assumption is conscious, they recognize there is a risk that they may be wrong. Should property values fall, they may be disappointed, but they will not be left with the shock or surprise of having taken a profit for granted. The same factors operate in any area of life where people take action based on calculated risks.

In mathematics, conscious assumptions are essential. For example, $2 + 2 = 4$ is not a fact but a conclusion or theorem based on axioms that are *assumed* to be fundamental. An *axiom* is defined as a statement assumed as a basis for the development of a subject. Usually, axioms are very acceptable assumptions—not outlandish ones—that can be applied to the real world. Sometimes, as in this case, they are said to be self-evident, but basically they are labeled "assumptions." We will return in the chapter on Inductive Reasoning to the topic of creating working assumptions—or where they are called **hypotheses.**

Warranted and unwarranted assumptions have some similar parallels to those that are conscious and unconscious; warranted assumptions depend on a knowledge of standards, codes, and customs. In the United States, if you buy a carton of milk—dated for use within a week—at your neighborhood grocery, you can make a *warranted assumption* that it will not be sour when you open it. If you find the milk to be sour, you can return it to the store for a refund. The same can be said of assumptions that the city buses will arrive and leave on schedule, that the post office will be open on weekdays but not holidays, and that gas and electricity will be available at the flick of a switch. When such events do not occur, citizens can and do complain to those responsible for their maintenance. Thus, warranted assumptions offer us a lot of public convenience for dealing with routine matters.

Unwarranted assumptions show a disregard or ignorance about standards, codes, or agreements. If you expect milk to remain fresh in your refrigerator for a month, that would be an unwarranted assumption. If you expect city buses to arrive every half-hour after midnight, that would be unwarranted; and if you go to the post office to mail a package on Christmas day, that assumption would be unwarranted. Critical thinking helps us avoid unconscious or unwarranted assumptions because they lead to faulty reasoning and poor decisions.

Discussion Break Question

1. Write down, or explain to your neighbor, the difference between a conscious and unconscious assumption, and a warranted and unwarranted assumption. Give your own examples of each.

IDENTIFYING HIDDEN ASSUMPTIONS IN REASONING

Good reasoning confronts its own assumptions.

- If your friend is Japanese, she must be moody.
- He is a good candidate for mayor since he looks sincere.
- If you love her, you'll give her diamonds.

All of the statements given above contain hidden assumptions—or silent unexpressed opinions—that influence and shape what is put into words. In each case, these assumptions not only remain silent, they may remain unrecognized as well. The first statement hangs on a stereotype, assumed to be true, about the moodiness of all Japanese. The second depends on two beliefs: (a) that the appearance of sincerity is actual sincerity; (b) that sincerity is a qualification for holding office. Finally, the third example contains an assumption intended as an advertising manipulation. All these assumptions are based on false stereotypes and **hasty generalizations.** If we accept these statements, we are also swallowing their hidden assumptions, although we may not even realize what we have done. Assumptions can remain hidden to one—or both—the speaker and the listener, or writer and reader.

When we think critically, we try not to base our reasoning on unexamined assumptions. We remember to ask ourselves: "Now when I say this, what am I taking for granted?" Moreover, in our reading and listening, we learn to sense hidden assumptions, the way a fisherman senses fish lurking under water. The bait that brings the fish to the surface is the question: "What would someone have to believe in order to reason in this way?" As we formulate this belief, we put the hidden assumption into words. Once the assumption is exposed through words, its reasoning can be examined together with its implications.

Learning how to identify hidden assumptions is an important critical thinking skill, but like any skill, it is one that takes practice. Such practice will be offered in the exercises that follow, but first let us review the types of assumptions.

Stereotypes are one form of hidden assumption already considered. Stereotypes might be described as data classified automatically, without close inspection, into familiar mental categories. Stereotypes are hasty generalizations made about people or situations that serve to cause prejudice. Should a child firmly decide that all dogs are vicious, this belief will prevent her from ever learning how to learn more by relating to them. Most familiar are the stereotypes that assume the superiority of a particular race, nationality, religion, or gender.

"Indians do not eat cows because they are superstitious."

"Americans eat hamburger and steak because they are ignorant."

This first statement judges Indians according to Western beliefs, lacking familiarity with Hindu beliefs and traditions: the second is the reverse of the other. Both viewpoints are ethnocentric and religiocentric, terms used to describe ideas that assume that truth lies only within one's own culture and religion. We will examine such *isms* in more detail in the chapter called "Viewpoints." For now, it's important to recognize when such beliefs take the form of hidden assumptions in reasoning.

To return to the two remaining opening examples—the sincere mayor and the gift of diamonds—each also represents ideas based on stereotypical assumptions.

"He is a good candidate for mayor since he looks sincere."

This claim assumes that people who appear sincere are honest people. Yet a person could also be sincerely deluded or sincerely malevolent. Moreover, many other more crucial qualifications are needed to hold public office.

"If you love her, you'll give her diamonds."

This statement assumes that love can only be proven through a gift of expensive stones. For over a century, the diamond industry has succeeded in persuading millions to believe (1) that the little stones called diamonds are rare and deserve a high price and (2) that they offer public proof of a pledge of love. The advertising message, moreover, prods the consumer to feel guilty if not conforming to expectations cultivated by such propaganda.

Discussion Break Questions

Identify and express the hidden assumptions underlying each of the following statements. The first one is provided as an example:

1.   What's a nice girl like you doing in a place like this?

Hidden underlying assumptions: 1. I am a nice girl. 2. This is a bad place. 3. You can offer me protection. 4. I should trust you. 5. I would fall for a pick-up line as old as this one.

2.   I couldn't visit a Buddhist temple because they worship idols there.
3.   How can that marriage counselor help people if he himself is divorced?
4.   You go into a pharmacy and see a young woman standing behind the counter. You ask her if you can speak to the pharmacist. She tells you she is the pharmacist.
5.   You shouldn't be critical of corporations. Aren't you in favor of free enterprise?
6.   I can't understand why I haven't met my soul mate this year. My astrologer said I would.
7.   Villagers in the Fiji Islands live in poverty and hardship. They do not have running water, baths, and toilets in their homes. It will take them a hundred years to catch up with the rest of the world.
8.   In a television program about earthquake preparedness, an expert demonstrated his gas-driven generator. "In the event of a major disaster," he said, "this generator would run our children's television set so that they would have something to do."

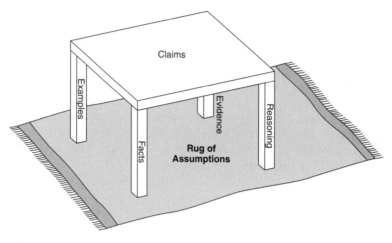

Figure 5.1

HIDDEN ASSUMPTIONS IN ARGUMENTS

Good arguments are not based on assumptions.

Arguments, as defined in critical thinking, are claims supported by reasoning, facts, examples, and evidence which are are offered with the intent to be persuasive. A successful argument is based on a careful structure of its reasoning. An argument lacks careful construciton when it rests on unexamined assumptions. A clever debater can pull the rug out from under any argument by pointing out its dependence on unexamined assumptions. Thus, as said previously, if you want to write an effective argument, you need to learn how to locate your own assumptions. Learning how to spot assumptions is a fundamental critical thinking skill.

> The purpose of an **argument** is to be persuasive. An argument consists of **claims** supported by reasoning, by facts, examples, and evidence. **Facts** take the form of statistics, testimony, records, and verified information. A **good argument** sets forth its claims and reasoning clearly and openly. It does not contain hidden assumptions.

Discovery Exercise

Articulating Hidden Assumptions Underlying Arguments

Write down the hidden assumptions you find in the following quotations, to share in a later class discussion. The first is done for you by way of explanation.

1. A Senator, concerned about the high mortality rate of children in the United States from gunshot wounds, introduced legislation that would require manufacturers to install childproof locks on all handguns.

Hidden Assumptions

   (a) It is all right for adults to shoot guns but not for children to shoot guns.
   (b) Accidental deaths caused by children shooting children is the major preventable cause of death of children.
   (c) Children fire the guns that kill children.
   (d) Adults know how to use guns with discretion.
   (e) Parents will procure their guns from law-abiding manufacturers and dealers.
   (f) Children only get shot by handguns.

2. I am worthless; I do not have a college degree.

3. "I'm nothing," he said. "You understand that, nothing. I earn $250,000 a year, but it's nothing, and I'm nobody. My expenses range from maintaining an apartment on Park Avenue for $20,400 a year to $30,000 a year for private schools for my children. My total expenses come to over $300,000 a year, leaving nothing left over for dinner parties, paintings, furniture, a mistress, psychiatrists, or even a week in Europe." (from Lewis Lapham, "The Gilded Cage," *Money and Class in America*. New York: Random House, 1988)

4. In Chicago, a high school basketball player was dropped from his team after being arrested for two alcohol-related offenses, including drunk driving. Later he filed a lawsuit for reinstatement under the Americans With Disabilities Act, pleading that he was a recovering alcoholic who also had an alcoholic father and therefore he was suffering from discrimination because of his disability.

5. In China, there is a popular religious sect called Falun Gong that practices meditation and meditative physical exercises, which its members say bring them health and spiritual well-being. When the government tried to discourage its continuation, massive silent non-violent protests were held. The Chinese government banned the sect by passing a law against "superstitious sects and secret societies that violate laws or administrative regulations."

6. A federal judge ruled that schools violate the Constitution by requiring fundamentalist Christian children to use textbooks that offend their religious beliefs. He ordered the Hawkins County Tennessee public schools to excuse fundamentalist children from reading class to avoid books that their parents say promote feminism, pacifism, and other themes that they regard as anti-Christian.

VALUE OR BELIEF ASSUMPTIONS

Value assumptions are basic beliefs that lie even deeper in our consciousness than ordinary assumptions. Sometimes these beliefs or values are so fundamental that they defy recognition.

Value assumptions are beliefs we never question. We assume they represent common sense or universal truths. They can be so fundamental to our thinking that we take them as for granted as gravity. However, a visit to another culture can sometimes bring them to the surface. An example from the life of the author Jean Liedloff will serve as an illustration.

Liedloff spent two-and-a-half years living with a Stone Age tribe, the Yequana Indians of the rain forests of Brazil. One thing that puzzled her was that the tribe did not have a word for *work*, nor did members distinguish work from other ways of spending time. She observed the women thoroughly enjoying the task of going down to a stream for water several times a day, even though they had to descend a steep bank with gourds on their heads and babies on their backs. Gradually the author came to realize that the idea that work is unpleasant and leisure is pleasant is only a Western value assumption. She had to consider that this idea was not necessarily a truth about life, but a cultural attitude. This insight led her to reexamine other Western beliefs, such as the idea that progress is good and that a child belongs to its parents.

Another account of a woman's discovery of her Western value assumptions appears in *Mutant Message Down Under* by Marlo Morgan. In the first chapter of this novel, the storyteller finds herself in a jeep being driven across a hot Australian desert to meet a tribe of Aborigines gathered for a ceremony in her honor. Since she is expecting a ceremony and banquet, she is wearing stockings, a suit with a pink silk blouse, and carrying a tape recorder, 35mm camera, and a purse with credit cards. Much to her surprise, the jeep comes to a stop beside a small, corrugated tin shed where the tribe waits for her. They greet her warmly, then give her one wrap-around rag to wear and send her inside the shed to cleanse herself of all her garments and possessions. When she emerges, much to her amazement, the tribe members throw all of her possessions into the fire—camera, credit cards, and all. Finally, they offer her their greatest token of trust: an invitation to join them on a barefoot walkabout across Australia. With courage, she accepts their gift and begins a new adventure. She learns how to live with a people who trust nature to provide them with all their necessities for life.

Discussion Break Questions

1. What one value assumption shaped the way Marlo Morgan approached the Aborigines?
2. What value assumption did they demonstrate to her?
3. Why do you think we consider work to be so different from leisure?

All of us live from the guidance of our value assumptions—sometimes well, sometimes poorly. The cartoon called "The 6 Virtues of Consumer Culture" depicts some values that are commonly accepted in our time. Their effect can be startling when we recognize that these values are what our great grandparents called the seven deadly sins. (This cartoon omits lust.) It awakens us to the possibility that, without awareness, we have transformed what once were sins into virtues. Moreover, the implication is that past traditional virtues (such as thrift, sobriety, generosity, and modesty) are now sins in a consumer culture. Thus, value assumptions differ not only from culture to culture but can even reverse themselves over time within a society. Bringing these value assumptions to conscious awareness allows us to choose if we want to continue to live by them.

Discussion Break Questions

1. Why do you think Westerners separate work so radically from leisure?
2. What possessions do you consider to be necessities? What values do they represent? What values do you consider to be luxuries? What values do they represent?

ASSUMPTION LAYERS IN ARGUMENTS

A value assumption can form the foundation for a pyramid that supports many layers of hidden assumptions, all of which provide support for one thought expressed at the top.

THE 6 VIRTUES OF CONSUMER CULTURE

Used with permission of Kirk Anderson.

Once we understand the meaning of both hidden assumptions and value assumptions, we can engage in the kind of archeological search needed to find them in multiple layers beneath a stated claim. Consider this example of a statement once made by Ronald Reagan. When he heard that twelve million Americans were unemployed, this is how he responded:

"If you women would stay at home, maybe we could solve America's unemployment problem."

Now why, you may wonder, would he make such a statement? First we have to list some of the assumptions he was making.

1. All women could have men to support them.
2. Women are taking jobs away from men.
3. Women do not really need jobs since they can stay at home.
4. Men want and will take women's jobs (and pay).
5. Work for all women is a kind of indulgence allowed by their men.

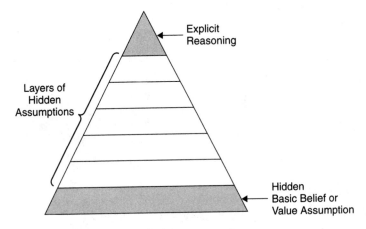

Figure 5.2 Pyramid of Value Assumptions

Finally, the question remains: what basic belief or value assumption would lead him to make all these assumptions? One conviction he might have held, common to his generation, was this idea:

A woman's place is in the home.

Discussion Break Questions

Consider the following statements and list the hidden assumptions you can find they include. After you have listed these hidden assumptions. See if you can articulate at least one underlying basic belief or value assumption.

1. Schools should teach children to believe in the Bible.

2. Hospitals shun the poor and suffering. John Andrews, who was severely beaten, was brought to a private hospital by a friend. He was suffering from a collapsed lung, concussion, and broken rib. Because he couldn't prove he had insurance, he was turned away and dumped on a county hospital.

3. "The cruelest thing you could say to a woman who is pregnant, poor, alone, and afraid is that she has the right to terminate her child." (Vatican representative at UN Women's Conference in Beijing, 1995)

Photo by Arthur Rothstein. Courtesy Library of Congress.

4. "The first thing you do is sit down with your wife and say something like this: 'Honey, I've made a terrible mistake. I've given you my role. I gave up leading this family.' I'm not suggesting that you ask for your role back, I'm urging you to take it back. . . . Be sensitive. Listen. Treat the lady gently and lovingly. But lead!" (Tony Evans, *Seven Promises of a Promise Keeper*)

5. "The government has painted all their helicopters black. These helicopters are monitoring patriotic Americans and are prepared to take their arms away, round them up, and put them in internment camps." (Statement by a member of a militia group)

6. "The anti-environmental forces in Congress are escalating their all-out war on America's environment. If they succeed, they will rob us

of our national heritage, pollute our air and water, cut down our forests, close some of our beloved national parks, and threaten the health and quality of life of thousands of Americans." (Sierra Club newsletter, 1995)

ASSUMPTIONS, INCONGRUITIES, AND THINKING

First we have to be alert enough to recognize incongruities, then we need to think in order to reconcile them.

When we see two little girls dressed up in their Sunday best to have their picture taken, we expect to see happy smiling faces as well. But what we see instead challenges our assumption. It may even make us feel uncomfortable. Yet, if instead of turning away from the picture, we become curious about the incongruity, we might then discover something new. When we can allow ourselves to just go through the discomfort of having assumptions challenged, we learn and grow.

This topic brings us back to Chapter 1 and the ideas of the psychologist, Jean Piaget, about learning. Piaget says that when we have experiences that we cannot easily assimilate, we then are provoked to think. We think when we re-order old mental categories. This process is what Piaget calls accommodation. It is provoked by an inner sense of disequilibrium. We experience disequilibrium when our assumptions are challenged by momentous experiences like witnessing a birth or a death, or in mundane matters, like discovering we have a flat tire. It can happen when we see a woman in a hard-hat pounding nails at a construction site. Suddenly we have a new understanding about what women can do. When our assumptions are challenged, we feel actual physical discomfort; but when we can reorganize our mental categories to accommodate a new experience, our equilibrium is restored. Thus a feeling of equilibrium is a reward for successful thinking.

While describing many of the photographs in this book so far, you may have felt especially uncomfortable. This is because all of them, whether you realized it or not, are *based on incongruities*. In studying the photographs, you have had the choice of either avoiding the disequilibrium they aroused, or of staying with the task long enough to reach a satisfactory explanation for their incongruities—and thus finding a way to restore your equilibrium.

To return to the picture of the little girls, you might seek an explanation for their frowns by inferring (1) they were given dolls they didn't like; (2) they did not want to pose for the picture; (3) the picture was taken when they were off guard; (4) the photographer only wanted to make a statement of ironic contrasts. If this last explanation seems the most promising, you might wonder if perhaps the photographer was purposely playing with some incongruities. Perhaps the whole composition was intentional: to contrast Hollywood play dolls against two girls dressed up as dolls; to contrast a false concept of little girls, with real little girls; to contrast false faces with real faces reflecting the stresses of life.

Sometimes we have to hang in there through a period of doubt and confusion before we can reach an explanation that reconciles all our facts, until we can bring our information into a satisfying pattern of order. And although we may never be able to confirm the final truth of our explanation, we at least have the satisfaction of having reconciled all the available information. Piaget says that persistence in this process of moving from disequilibrium to equilibrium develops our thinking skills.

Thinking comes about in life through provocation: when we meet situations that do not fit a familiar pattern, that do not fall into familiar stereotypes, that do not meet expectations. In such cases, we have the personal choice to deny or ignore—or to think, to learn, and to grow. When we were toddlers, if we touched a hot stove, the experience of being burned was an unpleasant encounter with reality. And yet, even then, if we had not stopped to analyze even in a simple way what caused the pain, we would have had to suffer the same pain over and over again. Even if we decided to always depend on someone else to think for us and protect us, we would eventually have found such a solution to be impractical. We survive best when we can think for ourselves. And the more we think, the more willing, open, and able we are to accept life's challenges of our assumptions.

Discussion Break Questions

1. Give an example of an incongruity that you have experienced that has challenged one of your assumptions.
2. Can you describe the disequilibrium you felt when you saw this incongruity?
3. How did you restore your equilibrium?
4. Have you experienced disequilibrium at times while studying this textbook? How was your equilibrium restored?

BUILDING ARGUMENTS

ASSUMPTIONS: BUILDING AN ARGUMENT

Some of our chiefs make the claim that the land belongs to us. It is not what the Great Spirit told me. He told me that the lands belong to Him, that no people owns the land; that I was not to forget to tell this to the white people when I met them in council. (Kannekuk, Kickapoo prophet, 1827)

Exercise

1. What claim is being refuted here?
2. What assumption lies in the claim?
3. What counterclaim is being made?
4. State a claim that you feel contains an assumption. State why you believe it is an assumption. Formulate your own counterclaim.

CHAPTER SUMMARY

1. An assumption is something we take for granted, something we buy before checking it out carefully. Often, we do not recognize that we have made an assumption until it causes a problem for us.

2. Assumptions can be conscious or unconscious, warranted or unwarranted. Unconscious and unwarranted assumptions can lead to faulty reasoning, whereas conscious and warranted assumptions can be useful tools for problem solving. We need to recognize the difference.

3. Hidden assumptions are unconscious assumptions that form the basis for reasoning that leads to a particular conclusion. Common forms of hidden assumptions are stereotypes, where we file new experiences in old categories; belief in the superiority of a particular race, nationality, religion, or gender; and assumptions based on value judgments, known as value assumptions.

4. Arguments are the use of reasoning to defend an idea or to persuade someone else to believe in the idea. Arguments that contain assumptions are easily demolished, so it is important to make an argument as conscious a mental construction as possible.

5. Incongruities are things we observe that do not meet our expectations or assumptions. When our assumptions are challenged by incongruities, we can choose to reexamine our assumptions in order to regain our equilibrium. This is the process of growth and learning.

6. Someone who brings a fresh perspective to a problem that has stumped others is often able to find a solution because he or she does not buy the assumptions that restrain others. As a conscious tool, we can look for assumptions when we are confronted with a problem to solve.

CHAPTER QUIZ

Rate each of the following statements as *true* or *false*. Justify your answer with an example or explanation.

_____ 1. When we articulate hidden assumptions, we simply read what we find in print before us.

_____ 2. A good argument invariably contains a few hidden assumptions.

_____ 3. To make a value assumption is to offer a line of reasoning based on a value or belief assumed to be shared by everyone.

_____ 4. "Can you believe it? She is twenty-three years old and not even thinking of getting married." This statement, made by a Puerto Rican mother, contains no value assumption.

_____ 5. Assumptions are often recognized only in retrospect because of the problems they cause.

_____ 6. In mathematics, conscious assumptions are called *axioms*.

_____ 7. A *conscious* assumption can be used as a strategy to lead us to new information. If a child does not come home from school at the usual time, we might first decide to call the homes of the child's friends; if that turns up no information, we might call the police.

_____ 8. Stereotypes contain no assumptions.

_____ 9. To be uncomfortable is to be in disequilibrium. Thinking through a problem restores the comfort of our mental equilibrium.

_____ 10. Incongruities can provoke us into thinking in order to resolve their conflict with our assumptions and expectations.

COMPOSITION WRITING APPLICATION

Expository Essay: Solving a Problem by Uncovering Assumptions

Think of a major problem from your own life (or someone else's) that was solved by the discovery of one or more hidden assumptions. If you prefer to use historical examples from the lives of explorers, artists, or scientists, do some research on the kinds of problems they succeeded in solving. (Besides using ordinary encyclopedias, you might also look for some special science encyclopedias in the library.) Write in sketch form your basic findings, searching for the following elements to develop and emphasize:

1. What particular problem concerned your subject?
2. What assumptions were embedded in the problem?
3. How were these assumptions discovered?
4. What restraints did these assumptions impose?
5. What, if any, wrong assumptions were made?

Prepare a working outline for an essay of about three typewritten pages. Then begin your essay with a thesis statement that explains what you concluded from your research and analysis.

The **thesis statement,** also called the *thesis,* has some similarity to the topic sentence in that it states a generalization. However, as it is introduced, it may be stated through several sentences instead of one, as it proposes an idea that will be developed, explained, and illustrated over many paragraphs and pages. By definition, the thesis is the idea that the essay intends to prove. Again, in the process of thinking, the thesis, like the topic sentence, may only be mentally formulated after some time has been spent studying the subject. However, when the essay is written in an academic style, the thesis is stated in the first paragraph. A thesis is also called the *controlling idea* because everything written in the essay is based on the dictates of its objective. We can visualize the thesis as a frame, like a picture frame: everything that will appear in that picture—the essay— is contained in and limited by the thesis. (See Figure 5.3.)

The act of stating the thesis also helps us organize our thoughts around one main purpose; it can also serve for us like a magnet to help us decide what information is relevant for support. Every statement and every fact appearing in the essay should either support or develop the thesis.

Let's look at an example of a thesis. Suppose you decided to write an expository essay to explain a problem you solved at work through the discovery of a hidden assumption. Your thesis might be introduced in this manner:

(1) All of us have heard fables about villages that suffered long and hard from a particular problem, like a famine or a wayward dragon. (2) Then one day a stranger appeared and solved the problem simply, quickly, and miraculously. (3) In such stories, what seemed to be a miracle to the villagers was only a matter of a newcomer's bringing a fresh perspective, unbiased by any past assumptions. (4) My own life had a parallel situation several years ago when I went to work for the municipal utilities district. (5) And although I did not arrive on a horse or in a suit of armor, I did bring a fresh perspective that solved an "insoluble problem."

These five sentences comprise the thesis statement. The first two introduce the topic and invite reader interest. The third states a principle

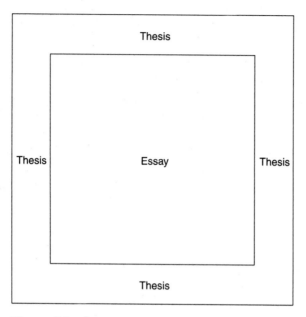

Figure 5.3 Thesis as a Frame.

and a limitation of focus. The fourth makes the transition to a personal incident that will illustrate this principle. And the fifth sentence states the actual thesis that the narrative will develop, support, and illustrate.

Here is a summary of the parameters for this assignment:

1. *Topic:* How one creative individual challenged the restraints of some mistaken assumptions in solving a problem.

2. *Objective:* To describe and explain through a narrative a personal or historical achievement from the perspective of how inherent assumptions were worked through.

3. *Form:* Essay using personal or researched information for illustration and exposition to support the thesis statement.

4. *Length:* At least three typed pages.

Submit your working outline with your paper if your instructor requests that you do so. To follow up in class, read your essays to one another in pairs or small groups. Check over one another's work to see whether the parameters were followed. Critique each essay with the following questions.

Scoring for Expository Essay on Assumptions

1. Does the writer state the thesis clearly and develop it through narrative and exposition? 40 points

2. Does the essay really stay with the topic of illustrating how an individual solved one major problem through working with some mistaken assumptions? 25 points

3. Is the length at least three typed pages? 10 points

4. Is the thesis supported with personal or researched information? 15 points

5. Is the work free of distracting errors in punctuation, spelling, and sentence structure? 10 points

Student Writing Example

A MISPLACED ASSUMPTION

Terry Ruscoe

All of us have heard fables about villages that suffered long and hard from a particular problem, like a famine or a wayward dragon. Then one day a stranger appeared and solved the problem simply, quickly, and miraculously. In such stories, what seemed to be a miracle to the villagers was only a matter of a newcomer's bringing a fresh perspective, un-biased by any past assumptions. My own life had a parallel situation several years ago when I went to work for the municipal utilities district. And although I did not arrive on a horse or in a suit of armor, I did bring a fresh perspective that solved an "insoluble problem."

My work as a storekeeper was to receive and distribute merchandise, such as plumbing supplies, to our work crews. Here was the problem: after our trucks rolled out of the yard to make deliveries, we would often get calls asking for a modification in the order. But, we had no way of getting in touch with the trucks once they left. This could mean even more frustration for the frantic caller who needed just one more of those special pipeline fittings to complete the job and get traffic moving again.

"Radios, that's what we need," said the foreman as he burst into the office. He had just been chewed out by the supervisor of maintenance for a work delay of two hours because of some missing material. "The only problem is the budget. How can we afford $800 right away to put a radio in each of the trucks?" Carl, the receiving clerk, who was instructing me on the proper manner of keeping stock records, looked up and quipped, "Yeah, not only is that too much money, but say the driver is out of his truck unloading . . . he may not even hear the thing."

Later that day at lunch, several of us were in the break room. We began tossing the problem around. One of the guys came up with a good idea, suggesting that we augment the radios with an attachment to automatically sound the horn of the truck when it was called. But this would be even more expensive and still be useless if the driver was out of range or was out in a pool vehicle.

Another problem that arose was the lack of firsthand communication; every message would have to be channeled through the base station operator unless we bought our own base station transmitter, which would cost even more money. And then there was the question of privacy: what if we wanted the driver to stop on the way back to pick up some doughnuts? We didn't need the whole district to know about it. "It's the same old problem," moaned one driver. "Face it, we're just going to have to pop for the whole deal, base station and all, and be done with it. Consider it a long-term investment into our sanity."

I had been listening, just listening, for about twenty minutes when I realized that what we had here were two misplaced assumptions: the first was that we had to reach the truck; and the second was that we had only one way of communicating. It's the driver we need to reach, I reasoned. And what else was there besides radios? Telephones? He couldn't carry a phone around with him but . . . what about a beeper? That way, when he got our message, he could go to any nearby phone and call us. (Remember that this was back in the times when only doctors carried beepers.) "Okay," I said, "why not supply each driver with a remote-controlled beeper, so that when he gets our message he can go directly to a phone and call us. As they say, 'phoning is the next best thing to being there.'" And guess what? It worked. If we wanted to contact a driver we simply beeped him. It was far less expensive, and we were able to rent the beepers immediately. Above all, the troops could now get what they wanted without any of those old-fashioned glazed-or-chocolate mix-ups.

Used with permission of Terry Ruscoe.

READINGS

LATERAL AND VERTICAL THINKING
Edward de Bono

Edward de Bono has been a professor at Cambridge, Oxford, and Harvard and has written many innovative books about thinking, maintaining it is a learnable and teachable skill. He was the first to develop the term lateral thinking, *which is particularly useful for creative problem solving. Lateral thinking allows a person to overcome binding assumptions and see a problem in an entirely different way, thus allowing novel solutions. In the illustrative story presented here, Edward de Bono explains the differences between lateral and vertical thinking.*

Many years ago when a person who owed money could be thrown into jail, a merchant in London had the misfortune to owe a huge sum to a money-lender. The money-lender, who was old and ugly, fancied the merchant's beautiful teenage daughter. He proposed a bargain. He said he would cancel the merchant's debt if he could have the girl instead. **1**

Both the merchant and his daughter were horrified at the proposal. So the cunning money-lender proposed that they let Providence decide the matter. He told them that he would put a black pebble and a white pebble into an empty money-bag and then the girl would have to pick out one of the pebbles. If she chose the black pebble she would become his wife and her father's debt would be canceled. If she chose the white pebble she would stay with her father and the debt would be canceled. But if she refused to pick out a pebble her father would be thrown into jail and she would starve. **2**

Reluctantly the merchant agreed. They were standing on a pebble-strewn path in the merchant's garden as they talked and the money-lender stooped down to pick up the two pebbles. As he picked up the pebbles the girl, sharp-eyed with fright, noticed that he picked up two black pebbles and put them into the money-bag. He then asked the girl to pick out the pebble that was to decide her fate and that of her father. **3**

Imagine that you are standing on that path in the merchant's garden. What would you have done if you had been the unfortunate girl? If you had to advise her what would you have advised her to do? **4**

What type of thinking would you use to solve the problem? You may believe that careful logical analysis must solve the problem if there is a solution. This type of thinking is straight-forward vertical thinking. The other type of thinking is lateral thinking. **5**

Vertical thinkers are not usually of much help to a girl in this situation. The way they analyze it, there are three possibilities: **6**

1. The girl should refuse to take a pebble.
2. The girl should show that there are two black pebbles in the bag and expose the money-lender as a cheat.

3. The girl should take a black pebble and sacrifice herself in order to save her father from prison.

None of these suggestions is very helpful, for if the girl does not take a pebble **7** her father goes to prison, and if she does take a pebble, then she has to marry the money-lender.

The story shows the difference between vertical thinking and lateral thinking. Ver- **8** tical thinkers are concerned with the fact that the girl has to take a pebble. Lateral thinkers become concerned with the pebble that is left behind. Vertical thinkers take the most reasonable view of a situation and then proceed logically and carefully to work it out. Lateral thinkers tend to explore all the different ways of looking at something, rather than accepting the most promising and proceeding from that.

The girl in the pebble story put her hand into the money-bag and drew out a **9** pebble. Without looking at it she fumbled and let it fall to the path where it was immediately lost among all the others.

"Oh, how clumsy of me," she said, "but never mind—if you look into the bag you **10** will be able to tell which pebble I took by the colour of the one that is left."

Since the remaining pebble is of course black, it must be assumed that she has **11** taken the white pebble, since the money-lender dare not admit his dishonesty. In this way, by using lateral thinking, the girl changes what seems an impossible situation into an extremely advantageous one. The girl is actually better off than if the money-lender had been honest and had put one black and one white pebble into the bag, for then she would have had only an even chance of being saved. As it is, she is sure of remaining with her father and at the same time having his debt canceled.

Vertical thinking has always been the only respectable type of thinking. In its ulti- **12** mate form as logic it is the recommended ideal towards which all minds are urged to strive, no matter how far short they fall. Computers are perhaps the best example. The problem is defined by the programmer, who also indicates the path along which the problem is to be explored. The computer then proceeds with its incomparable logic and efficiency to work out the problem. The smooth progression of vertical thinking from one solid step to another solid step is quite different from lateral thinking.

If you were to take a set of toy blocks and build them upwards, each block rest- **13** ing firmly and squarely on the block below it, you would have an illustration of vertical thinking. With lateral thinking the blocks are scattered around. They may be connected to each other loosely or not at all. But the pattern that may eventually emerge can be as useful as the vertical structure.

From Edward de Bono, *New Think.* New York: Basic Books, 1971. Copyright 1967 by Edward de Bono; reprinted with permission of Basic Books, a member of Perseus Books, L.L.C.

Study Questions

1. What role do assumptions play in vertical thinking?
2. How does lateral thinking work with assumptions?

3. "Vertical thinkers take the most reasonable view of a situation and then proceed logically and carefully to work it out. Lateral thinkers tend to explore all
   the different ways of looking at something, rather than accepting the most
   promising and proceeding from that." Look again at the story of Columbus and
   the egg cited in the Discovery Exercises at the beginning of this chapter. Was
   Columbus a vertical or lateral thinker?
4. Is the author saying that vertical thinking is wrong?
5. Can lateral and vertical thinking be used creatively together to solve a problem? Give an example.
6. In the state-operated health care program offered in China, village physicians
   are paid not for their services to the sick but for the number of their assigned
   patients who stay well. How does this represent a lateral thinking solution?
   What do you think are its advantages and disadvantages? What is just interesting about this idea?
7. A persistent U.S. problem is illegal drug use. One unsuccessful solution has
   been the "war on drugs." Do you think this was a vertical or lateral solution?
   If you feel it is vertical, suggest some lateral solutions. If you claim it is lateral,
   then describe some vertical solutions.

WINTERBLOSSOM GARDEN

David Low

*The following is an excerpt from an autobiographical short story. Born in 1952 in
Queens, New York, David Low now lives in the East Village of New York City. This
story may be viewed from many dimensions, including as a study of the frustrations
of a mother and son separated by their different value assumptions. The short story
"Winterblossom Garden" appeared in an anthology,* Under Western Eyes *(New York:
Doubleday, 1995), edited by Garrett Hongo.*

My mother pours two cups of tea from the porcelain teapot that has always been in 1
its wicker basket on the kitchen table. On the sides of the teapot, a maiden dressed
in a jade-green gown visits a bearded emperor at his palace near the sky. The maiden
waves a vermilion fan.

"I bet you still don't know how to cook," my mother says. She places a plate of 2
steamed roast pork buns before me.

"Mom, I'm not hungry." 3

"If you don't eat more, you will get sick." 4

I take a bun from the plate, but it is too hot. My mother hands me a napkin so 5
I can put the bun down. Then she peels a banana in front of me.

"I'm not obsessed with food like you," I say. 6

"What's wrong with eating?" 7

She looks at me as she takes a big bite of the banana. **8**

"I'm going to have a photography show at the end of the summer." **9**

"Are you still taking pictures of old buildings falling down? How ugly! Why don't **10** you take happier pictures?"

"I thought you would want to come," I answer. "It's not easy to get a gallery." **11**

"If you were married," she says, her voice becoming unusually soft, "you would **12** take better pictures. You would be happy."

"I don't know what you mean. Why do you think getting married will make me **13** happy?"

My mother looks at me as if I have spoken in Serbo-Croatian. She always gives **14** me this look when I say something she does not want to hear. She finishes the banana; then she puts the plate of food away. Soon she stands at the sink, turns on the hot water and washes dishes. My mother learned long ago that silence has a power of its own.

She takes out a blue cookie tin from the dining-room cabinet. Inside this tin, my **15** mother keeps her favorite photographs. Whenever I am ready to leave, my mother brings it to the living room and opens it on the coffee table. She knows I cannot resist looking at these pictures again; I will sit down next to her on the sofa for at least another hour. Besides the portraits of the family, my mother has images of people I have never met: her father, who owned a poultry store on Pell Street and didn't get a chance to return to China before he died; my father's younger sister, who still runs a pharmacy in Rio de Janeiro (she sends the family an annual supply of cough drops); my mother's cousin Kay, who died at thirty, a year after she came to New York from Hong Kong. Although my mother has a story to tell for each photograph, she refuses to speak about Kay, as if the mere mention of her name will bring back her ghost to haunt us all.

My mother always manages to find a picture I have not seen before; suddenly I **16** discover I have a relative who is a mortician in Vancouver. I pick up a portrait of Uncle Lao-Hu, a silver-haired man with a goatee who owned a curio shop on Mott Street until he retired last year and moved to Hawaii. In a color print, he stands in the doorway of his store, holding a bamboo Moon Man in front of him, as if it were a bowling trophy. The statue, which is actually two feet tall, has a staff in its left hand, while its right palm balances a peach, a sign of long life. The top of the Moon Man's head protrudes in the shape of an eggplant; my mother believes that such a head contains an endless wealth of wisdom.

"Your Uncle Lao-Hu is a wise man, too," my mother says, "except when he's in **17** love. When he still owned the store, he fell in love with his women customers all the time. He was always losing money because he gave away his merchandise to any woman who smiled at him."

I see my uncle's generous arms full of gifts: a silver Buddha, an ivory dragon, a **18** pair of emerald chopsticks.

"These women confused him," she adds. "That's what happens when a Chinese **19** man doesn't get married."

My mother shakes her head and sighs.　　　　　　　　　　　　　　　　**20**

"In his last letter, Lao-Hu invited me to visit him in Honolulu. Your father refuses **21**
to leave the store."

"Why don't you go anyway?"　　　　　　　　　　　　　　　　　　**22**

"I can't leave your father alone." She stares at the pictures scattered on the cof- **23**
fee table.

"Mom, why don't you do something for yourself? I thought you were going to **24**
start taking English lessons."

"Your father thinks it would be a waste of time."　　　　　　　　　　**25**

While my mother puts the cookie tin away, I stand up to stretch my legs. I gaze **26**
at a photograph that hangs on the wall above the sofa: my parents' wedding picture.
My mother was matched to my father; she claims that if her own father had been
able to repay the money that Dad spent to bring her to America, she might never have
married him at all. In the wedding picture she wears a stunned expression. She is
dressed in a luminous gown of ruffles and lace; the train spirals at her feet. As she
clutches a bouquet tightly against her stomach, she might be asking, "What am I doing? Who is this man?" My father's face is thinner than it is now. His tuxedo is too
small for him; the flower in his lapel droops. He hides his hand with the crooked pinky
behind his back.

I have never been sure if my parents really love each other. I have only seen **27**
them kiss at their children's weddings. They never touch each other in public. When I
was little, I often thought they went to sleep in the clothes they wore to work.

Study Questions

1. Working individually or in small groups, take a piece of paper and draw a vertical line down the center in order to make two columns. Write the words
   Mother at the top of one column and *Son* at the top of the other. Then reread
   the story carefully, this time taking particular note of the value assumptions
   that underlie their thinking. As you read, compose statements that express
   these assumptions (they will usually take the form of "shoulds," like "People
   should like to eat"). In the first list, write out the assumptions the mother holds
   about what her young Chinese-American son should do, how he should live,
   and what he should understand. In the second column, write down the assumptions held by the son about what she should do, how she should live,
   and what she should understand.

2. When you have finished, compare and discuss your lists.

3. Do you find that one is more aware than the other of these assumptions?
   How does this awareness level affect their relationship?

ADVANCED OPTIONAL COMPARISON AND CONTRAST WRITING ASSIGNMENT

Write an autobiographical essay of about four typed pages in which you show how you discovered some of your value assumptions through conflicts with another person, your own culture, a visited culture, or a newly adopted culture. Explain what the conflicts were and explain how they resulted from different value assumptions that you may or may not have been aware of at the time. Show how you were able to resolve or not resolve these differences.

Begin the essay with a thesis that involves some statement about value assumptions. Work from an outline that will appear on the first page of this assignment. Construct a draft outline or cluster to help you set up the symmetries for your comparison (how alike) and contrast (how different). You might decide to use a story to describe the conflict, contrasting your value assumptions in conclusion. Or you might want to state the value assumptions first, and then compare and contrast each person on the basis of each value assumption, followed by a summary conclusion at the end.

CHAPTER 6

Opinions

What's Believed?

"ARE THERE ANY OTHER WRONG OPINIONS SOMEONE ELSE WOULD CARE TO EXPRESS?"

Used with permission of Ted Goff.

Oddly enough, we can hold contradictory attitudes about opinions. We might fondly repeat the cliché "Everyone is entitled to an opinion," but that does not mean we agree to listen. Thus, when a cartoon character does not disguise intolerance, such honesty can be funny.

This chapter explores that familiar word *opinion* and examines how it affects our ability to think critically. By definition, opinions might be considered to be our inferences—or decisions—about life. We collect them from our experiences—or from those of others—and store them in our memory files. They may be based on a careful study of evidence, or they may not. They may even be confused with facts. Yet we all tend to cherish our own collection of nuggets and pull them out from time to time to show to others. In this chapter, we will take a lighter look at opinions, their characteristics and problems.

Discovery Exercises

The three discovery exercises that follow can be done either alone or with a partner in preparation for class discussion of this chapter.

Comparing a Sample of Opinions

Study the following statements of opinion:

1. "It's a proven fact that capital punishment is a known detergent [sic] to crime." (Archie Bunker, in the TV series *All in the Family*)

2. "Those who indulge in sex for sheer excitement and physical pleasure get exactly what they bargained for and nothing more. After the fleeting moments of pleasure, they are spent and empty." (*Ann Landers Talks to Teenagers About Sex*, Crest Books, 1963)

3. "'I need to meet a new woman. I need to have an affair. I may not look the part, but I'm a man who needs romance. I need softness. I need flirtation. I'm not getting any younger, so before it's too late I want to make love in Venice . . . and exchange coy glances over red wine and candlelight. You see what I am saying?'"

   "Dr. Mandel shifted in his chair and said, 'An affair will solve nothing. You're so unrealistic. Your problems run much deeper.'" (Woody Allen, "The Kugelmass Episode," *Woody Allen Side Effects*, Random House, 1980)

4. "Chinese Communists have this view that only after the liberation of the whole world can one liberate oneself. But I believe that if each person would liberate himself first, then the world could liberate itself." (Shen Tong, Chinese student leader at Tiananmen Square)

5. Any person on welfare is a bum.

6. "All this . . . persuades us that the word 'person' as used in the Fourteenth Amendment does not include the unborn. . . . We need not resolve the difficult question of when life begins. When those trained in the respective disciplines of medicine, philosophy, and theology are unable to arrive at any consensus, the judiciary, at this point in the development of man's knowledge, is not in a position to speculate as to the answer." (U.S. Supreme Court, *Roe* v. *Wade*, 1973)

In writing or class discussion, answer these questions about the statements:

1. What do these opinions have in common?

2. How are they different?

3. Do they all have equal weight and value?

Why Do We Get Confused by the Word *Opinion?*

Find at least three different meanings in a dictionary for the word *opinion*. (Be sure to look at the word's etymology.) Write down each definition, and compose a sentence that clearly expresses each meaning. Do you find that some of these meanings of *opinion* seem to contradict one another? Explain exactly how.

After you have finished, compare your different meanings to those given here:

1. A judgment that, though open to dispute, seems probable to the speaker.

   No one can say if our weather has changed permanently for the worse or not, but it's my *opinion* that it has.

2. A belief held with confidence but not substantiated by proof.

   There'll always be an England.

3. A *claim* or statement about what is considered to be true, supported by reasoning.

   This editor is of the *opinion* that the community colleges' enrollment of students would not be seriously affected by charging tuition if this estimate is not based on initial enrollments but final enrollments. A payment of tuition implies a commitment that may make even more students stay with their courses who might drop out casually otherwise.

4. A judgment formed by an expert.

   As your doctor of long standing, it is my *opinion* that you should not have surgery at this time.

5. Prevailing sentiment.

   Public opinion supports more environmental protection.

6. A formal statement of a judgment drawn after a legal hearing.

   It is the *opinion* of the court that the defendant is guilty.

An Exercise in Evaluating Opinions

Rate the following opinions as:

A. An opinion I would accept and act on.

B. Worthy of consideration.

C. I'd want another opinion.

D. Forget it!

_____ 1. Your doctor says you need surgery immediately to remove your _____.

"I'd say it's your gallbladder, but if you insist on a second opinion, I'll say kidneys."
Used with permission of Universal Press Syndicate.

_____ 2. A psychiatrist testifies in court that the defendant is not guilty by reason of insanity.

_____ 3. The weather forecaster says it will rain tomorrow.

_____ 4. Your attorney says you should sue your neighbor for damages.

_____ 5. You want to rent an apartment but the neighbor next door says the landlord is a weirdo.

_____ 6. Your best friend tells you your fiancée is tacky.

_____ 7. Your English instructor says you don't know how to think and should see a psychiatrist.

_____ 8. Your astrologer tells you not to go on any long trips in May.

_____ 9. The judge says you are guilty of driving under the influence of alcohol.

_____ 10. An engineer says you can prevent your basement from flooding by blasting holes for drainage in your foundation.

_____ 11. Your utility energy advisor says you can conserve energy by having your floors insulated.

_____ 12. A Pentagon general advised we should bomb Mexico.

TYPES OF OPINIONS

Opinions can take the form of judgments, advice, generalizations, or sentiments. Each type has to be evaluated differently.

Let's review what you may have discovered so far by categorizing opinions into types. First, there are what could be called the *judgments:* this is *good,* this is *bad;* this is *right,* this is *wrong;* this *should be,* this *should not be.* Look at the two following examples and provide a third example of your own.

1. Men and women should not share college dorms.

2. That car you bought was a lemon.

3.

Judgments are based on personal or collective codes of values. They are conclusions, arrived at through a long chain of reasoning. Judgments can also be simple *evaluations* of good and bad, desirable and undesirable. These are all discussed fully in the next chapter, on evaluations. At root, all forms of judgments are based on values or belief systems not necessarily shared by everyone. However, a person can state a judgment as a personal opinion without needing to offer support for it.

A second type of opinion could be seen in the *advice* category: *you should do this; you should not do this*. Examples of such opinions are as follows:

1. I wouldn't advertise for a roommate if I were you.

2. You need a new car.

3.

As you must have concluded from the earlier rating exercise, whether one chooses to accept advice is an individual matter.

A third category of opinions includes simple *generalizations,* typically preceded by the word *all, no,* or *some*. In this manner, the opinion is housed in a generalization to suggest that it represents a general truth.

1. Children in the United States are pressured to grow up too fast.

2. Nothing comes without a price.

3.

Here again, support for the opinion may be offered or not. Those who take more responsibility for their opinions do volunteer reasons in order to prove that they have examined all the evidence. A person trained in critical thinking makes an effort to gather evidence before generalizing about it, and, in turn, examines all generalizations for their basis in evidence.

A final category of opinions is *personal taste* or *sentiments: I like this; I don't like that. Such opinions do not need to be defended with evidence or reasons.* They are matters of preference that do not need to be justified. Examples of such opinions would be:

1. Movies aren't much fun without popcorn.
2. Backpacking is the best kind of vacation.
3.

DISTINGUISHING BETWEEN RESPONSIBLE AND IRRESPONSIBLE OPINIONS

Not all opinions deserve careful consideration.

You are probably wondering at this point how we can manage to communicate about opinions when we use the same word to convey so many different meanings:

1. An expert's judgment
2. An unsubstantiated belief
3. An argument that is well supported
4. A final legal judgment
5. Prevailing sentiment (feeling) on a topic

When we study critical thinking, we take these differences into account and recognize that we have to evaluate each type differently. A popular truism, which would seem to contradict this idea, is the one that states "Everyone is entitled to an opinion." Some might believe that this expression means that all opinions are relative truths and should therefore not be judged. Others believe that "Everyone is entitled to an opinion" only means that every person has a right to free speech. Critical thinkers might be willing to give most—but not all—opinions a full hearing, but never promise blanket tolerance. Moreover, a critical thinker would expect any opinion offered with the intent to persuade to meet the standards for an argument.

Let's give an ordinary example that illustrates a need to evaluate opinions. Suppose you want to decide how to vote on a safe drinking water bond issue. After reading a number of pro and con arguments in the Voter Information Pamphlet, you wonder whose opinion you should respect the most. Would it be that of the League of Women Voters? Of your assembly representative? Of the Save-Us-from-More-Taxes Association? Of your Uncle George? Actually, from all these four choices, your Uncle George might turn out to be the most knowledgeable source you could find. To determine the value of his contribution, you would need to know how well and recently he had studied the subject, how much inside knowledge he had, and what sources he had consulted. You would also want to know whether his viewpoint was independent of vested interests and how sound his reasoning appeared. These questions represent the same standards that we use for a serious evaluation of any opinion offered to influence us.

On the other hand, opinions that are only expressions of personal taste or belief do not require justification or evaluation. If you prefer yogurt to ice cream, jazz to pop music, you do not really need to explain why. The same may be said of personal beliefs. You do not have to defend a statement that you believe in God. However, if you wanted to persuade someone to agree with you, then you would want to use the standards of an argument, that is to say, you would offer the support of reasons. In evaluating opinions, therefore, the first step is to distinguish between opinions that require responsible support and those that do not.

To sum up, critical thinkers have standards for judging which opinions are worthy of their time and consideration and which are not. Thus when we read a newspaper editorial, we expect it to meet the standards of an argument. When we go to a physician, attorney, or financial advisor, we assume they have the training and experience to offer sound opinions. We can assume they know what facts are available and which are missing, what the variables are, and how much risk is involved in judging and predicting the odds. However, as critical thinkers, we do not assume that all the authorities we consult are always right; in the last analysis, we make our own decisions on the basis of our own judgments about others' opinions.

LOOKING AT PUBLIC OPINION POLLS

Public opinion polls can be used unfairly to determine public opinion as well as to manipulate it.

Some congressional representatives and senators regularly poll their constituents by sending questionnaires with questions like the following:

Of every dollar now spent by state government, how much do you feel is wasted?

1. None
2. 0–10 cents
3. 10–20 cents
4. 20–40 cents
5. 40–50 cents
6. Over 50 cents

On the whole, do you consider the following institutions and people to be trustworthy and credible?

1. Major industry and corporations	Yes	No
2. Small businesses	Yes	No
3. Labor unions	Yes	No
4. Government bureaus and agencies	Yes	No
5. Elected officials	Yes	No
6. JudgesYes	No	
7. Print journalists	Yes	No
8. TV journalists	Yes	No

Here, the constituent is asked to give opinions without the assistance of any facts. Moreover, judgments are requested on the basis of general impressions or feelings. The government representative who formulated this poll appears to have relinquished the expectation that an electorate should give informed consent. And thus the polled constituents might also draw the same conclusion. In tabulating the poll's results, legitimacy and weight will be given equally to conclusions based on vague impressions and to those based on study and knowledge.

Unfortunately, such polling practices are becoming more common in the United States. Indeed, with citizens voting less and less, polls provide at least some kind of feedback for representatives. Nevertheless, polls carry none of the legal safeguards of a public vote or election. Poll results can also be influenced by many factors that do not affect voting, such as how the question was phrased, how the sampling was taken, and how the poll was interpreted. Finally, although election results must be released, the release of poll results depends upon the discretion of individuals. Poll results can be published for the calculated purpose of *creating* public opinion. (Remember what Solomon Asch taught us?) Thus, their purpose need not necessarily simply reflect public sentiment. In sum, polls are not equivalent to public elections in terms of legal safeguards, the extent of their representation, or even the measure of responsibility assumed for them by either pollsters or the public.

Discussion Break Questions

1. If the president announced that a recent poll has shown that three out of every five Americans favor invading Canada, do you think this should give the president a mandate to go ahead?
2. Do you think it is becoming too complex for most Americans to be well informed on public issues and that this is why many tend to fall back on sentiments and feelings?

OPINIONS AS CLAIMS IN ARGUMENTS

Opinions function as primary claims in arguments which are supported by facts, other claims, and reasoning. In an essay, the thesis is a statement of opinion.

Arguments begin with opinions. Having an opinion that we want to express and defend motivates us to build an argument. Yet, a mere statement of opinion alone is not an argument.

Americans are overworked.

To serve as an argument, this statement needs support. An opinion only becomes an argument when it provides supporting reasons which might persuade others to agree with this opinion.

> Unemployment in Americans is growing while the employed are overworked. (opinion that is a conclusion or principal claim) Employers are hiring fewer workers because they can use their existing workforce for more hours. (supporting claim or reason) In the Detroit area the average workweek is 47.5 hours; Saturn workers have a regular 50-hour week, and in some plants, workers are doing 60 hours a week. The United Auto Workers (UAW) estimates that 59,000 automobile jobs would be created if the plants were on a 40 hour week. (supporting claims offering verifiable statistics) (Juliet Schor, *A Sustainable Economy for the Twenty-first Century,* 1995)

Thus, an argument consists of an opinion supported by reasons. To explain an argument we return again to the metaphor of a table; the tabletop holds the opinion or principal claim, whereas its legs are supporting claims, also known as reasons (Figure 6.1). More simply, an argument is a conclusion supported by reasons.

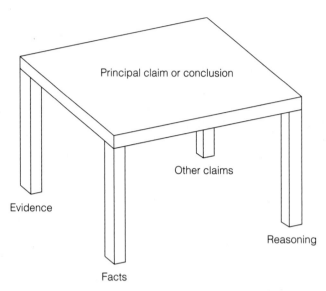

Figure 6.1 Argument Structure

The principal claim in an essay is called a **thesis:**

Unemployment in America is growing while the employed are over-worked.

In the language of argument, this thesis is also called a **conclusion.** It is not a conclusion in the sense that it is a final summary but in the sense that it is the conclusion of a line of reasoning:

Employers are hiring fewer workers because they can use their existing workforce for more hours.

The argument's credibility is greatly increased by the support of additional claims offering verifiable statistics about the working hours of autoworkers. This is what is known as **evidence:** data that can be verified as factual. Evidence includes statistics, testimony, personal experience, witnesses, and records: information whose accuracy can be examined independently.

In the Composition Writing Application that follows, you are asked to write an essay in which you make a short argument in support of an opinion, express an opinion, or analyze three opinions. Such an exercise can remind you how opinions function as primary claims in an argument and how the support of evidence, other claims, and reasoning gives these opinions credibility and persuasiveness.

COMPOSITION WRITING APPLICATION

First Option: A Short Argument Supporting an Opinion

Write a one- to two-page essay stating and defending an opinion you believe in. Follow these steps:

1. *What:* State the opinion or principal claim in one sentence.
2. *Support:*
   (a) Give three or more reasons why you believe this opinion to be true or false.
   (b) Also provide evidence in the form of facts or statistics or specific examples to support your claim.
3. *Persuasion:* Explain why you feel others should accept or reject this opinion.
4. *Conclusion:* Bring your ideas together in a summary or a generalization.

Second Option: A Short Expository Essay About an Opinion

Write a short essay describing an opinion of your own. Follow these steps:

1. *What:* State an opinion.
2. *Source:* Was this opinion based on your own experience or something you heard or read? Be specific about the circumstances within which you formulated it.
3. *Reasons:* Why is it a good opinion or a poor one? What tests of life and time has it survived? Have any experiences suggested that you need to alter this opinion?

The length of your essay should be two to three typed pages. It should take the form of an essay with a thesis. The first paragraph should cover step 1. The second or next two paragraphs should cover step 2. The main part of your essay (two to three paragraphs) should offer the support of reasons described in step 3. The final paragraph should sum up the whole.

Third Option: A Short Essay Analyzing Three Opinions

Study your local newspaper's editorial pages to find some editorials and letters to the editor that interest you. Select three to analyze, and photocopy them. For each, paste your photocopy at the top of a page and then analyze the piece of writing by answering these questions:

1. Is the opinion a judgment, advice, an expression of taste or sentiment, a belief, or a generalization? Support your answer in each case, providing an example and explaining it fully in these terms.
2. Is this opinion just a personal expression of taste or sentiment, or is it offered in an attempt to influence others? Explain fully.

3. Does the person giving this opinion show any special expertise regarding the subject or have any special qualifications? Explain what information you have and what is lacking.
4. Is the opinion backed up by evidence and sound reasoning? Show why or why not.
5. Does this opinion appear to be based on an objective study of the facts, or does it seem to be motivated by vested interests or a profit motive? Explain your judgment.
6. Would you call this a responsible opinion? Why or why not?

Peer Review

To follow up in class, form groups of two or more and read your papers aloud. Check one another's work to determine whether all the parameters given were observed. Evaluate the assignment according to the scoring sheet given below.

Scoring Sheet for Any One of the Three Opinion Essay Options

1. The opinion or opinions are clearly stated. 10 points
2. The support offered is adequate and relevant (or, in the case of option three clearly stated and analyzed). 30 points
3. Each parameter is followed and/or each question considered. 30 points
4. The essay is clearly organized around a purpose to describe, state and defend, or analyze, depending on the option chosen. 20 points
5. There are no distracting errors of punctuation, spelling, or sentence structure. 10 points

---

CHAPTER SUMMARY

1. Although the word *opinion* is a common one, it is just as commonly misunderstood, since the same word covers so many varieties of thoughts, ranging from expert judgments to expressions of sentiment or personal taste.

2. Opinions can be well substantiated or not. They can be based either on reasons or solely on whim, feelings, emotions, or prejudice.

3. Critical thinking requires that we recognize the difference between responsible and irresponsible opinion and that we distinguish statements based on evidence from statements based solely on feelings.

4. People enjoy expressing and reading opinions.

5. Expert opinion is based on an understanding of evidence and risks in a situation and is important and highly valued.

6. Public opinion polls can be used to *determine* public sentiment on social and political issues as well as to *manipulate* public sentiment. This occurs when we forget that sentiment is not the same as informed opinion and that opinion polls are not subject to the same safeguards as public elections.

7. Opinions should not be confused with facts.

8. Arguments consist of supported opinions; the intent of an argument is to persuade.

9. In an essay, a statement of opinion can be the thesis or its principle claim.

BUILDING ARGUMENTS

OPINIONS

Indians ought not to buy whiskey. It is hot in his heart for a little while, then it is gone; the Indian is cold, his head is sore, and he does not remember what he did when the poison was in him. Whiskey is hot poison for the Winnebagoes. My head is like the snow with age, I have seen the ruin that it has brought upon our nation, and I advise them to buy no more whiskey. (Decori, Winnebago chief, 1828)

Exercise

1. What is the principal claim made here?
2. What reasons are given to support it?

CHAPTER QUIZ

Rate each of the following statements as true or false. Justify each answer.

_____ 1. Expert opinion calculates the risk involved in spacing the gap between the known and the unknown for a particular situation.

_____ 2. Giving advice is a not a way of offering an opinion.

_____ 3. The results of public opinion polls are equivalent to votes in elections.

_____ 4. Opinions in the form of judgments state what is right and wrong, bad and good.

_____ 5. Some opinions are based on generalizations, such as stereotypes, as in the statement "All Chinese look alike."

_____ 6. Responsible opinions are based on a careful examination of the evidence.

_____ 7. Opinions are the same as facts.

_____ 8. Gossip is opinion sharing without any requirement for substantiation.

_____ 9. Everyone is entitled to his or her own opinion because all opinions carry equal value.

_____ 10. Opinions do not express feelings.

READINGS

THE OVERSPENT AMERICAN

Juliet B. Schor

Juliet Schor is an author, lecturer, and director of womens' studies at Harvard University. She made the bestseller list with her book The Overworked American. *This reading is taken from the introduction to her most recent book,* The Overspent American. *Consider this essay as a scholar's presentation of an opinion drawn from her own sociological research.*

In 1996 a best-selling book entitled *The Millionaire Next Door* caused a minor sensation. In contrast to the popular perception of millionaire lifestyles, this book reveals that most millionaires live frugal lives—buying used cars, purchasing their suits at JC Penney, and shopping for bargains. These very wealthy people feel no need to let the world know they can afford to live much better than their neighbors. 1

Millions of other Americans, on the other hand, have a different relationship with spending. What they acquire and own is tightly bound to their personal identity. Driving a certain type of car, wearing particular designer labels, living in a certain kind of home, and ordering the right bottle of wine create and support a particular image of themselves to present to the world. 2

This so not to say that most Americans make consumer purchases solely to fool others about who they really are. It is not to say that we are a nation of crass statusseekers. Or that people who purchase more than they need are simply demonstrating 3 a base materialism, in the sense of valuing material possessions above all else. But it is to say that, unlike the millionaires next door, who are not driven to use their wealth to create an attractive image of themselves, many of us are continually comparing our own lifestyle and possessions to those of a select group of people we respect and want to be like, people whose sense of what's important in life seems close to our own.

This aspect of our spending is not new—competitive acquisition has long been an American institution. At the turn of the century, the rich consumed conspicuously. In the early post-World War II decades, Americans spent to keep up with the Joneses, using their possessions to make the statement that they were not failing in their careers. But in recent decades, the culture of spending has changed and intensified. In the old days, our neighbors set the standard for what we had to have. They may have earned a little more, or a little less, but their incomes and ours were in the same ballpark. Their house down the block, worth roughly the same as ours, confirmed this. Today the neighbors are no longer the focus of comparison. How could they be? We may not even know them, much less which restaurants they patronize, where they vacation, and how much they spent for their living room couch. **4**

For reasons that will become clear, the comparisons we make are no longer restricted to those in our own general earnings category, or even to those one rung above us on the ladder. Today a person is more likely to be making comparisons with, or choose as a "reference group," people whose incomes are three, four, or five times his or her own. The result is that millions of us have become participants in a national culture or upscale spending. I call it the new consumerism. **5**

Part of what's new is that lifestyle aspirations are now formed by different points of reference. For many of us, the neighborhood has been replaced by a community of coworkers, people we work alongside and colleagues in our own and related professions. And while our real-life friends still matter, they have been joined by our media "friends." (This is true both figuratively and literally—the television show *Friends* is a good example of an influential media referent.) We watch the way television families live, we read about the lifestyles of celebrities and other public figures we admire, and we consciously and unconsciously assimilate this information. It affects us. **6**

So far so good. We are in a wider world, so we like to know that we are stacking up well against a wider population group than the people on the block. No harm in that. But as new reference groups form, they are less likely to comprise people who all earn approximately the same amount of money, and therein lies the problem. When a person who earns $75,000 a year compares herself to someone earning $90,000, the comparison is sustainable. It creates some tension, even a striving to do a bit better, to be more successful in a career. But when a reference group includes people who pull down six or even seven-figure incomes all aspire to be part of one urban literary referent group, which exerts pressure to drink the same brand of bottled water and wine, wear similar urban literary clothes, and appoint apartments with urban literary furniture, those at the lower economic end of the reference group find themselves in an untenable situation. Even if we choose not to emulate those who spend ostentatiously, consumer aspirations can be a serious reach. **7**

Advertising and the media have played an important part in stretching out refer- **8** ence groups vertically. When twenty-somethings can't afford much more than a utilitarian studio but think they should have a New York apartment to match the ones they see on *Friends,* they are setting unattainable consumption goals for themselves, with dissatisfaction as a predictable result. When the children of affluent suburban and impoverished inner-city households both want the same Tommy Hilfiger logo emblazoned on their chests and the top-of-the-line Swoosh on their feet, it's a potential disaster. One solution to these problems emerged on the talk-show circuit recently, championed by a pair of young urban "entry-level" earners: live the *faux* life, consuming *as if* you had a big bank balance. Their strategies? Use your expense account for private entertainment, date bankers, and sneak into snazzy parties without an invitation. Haven't got the wardrobe for it? No matter. Charge expensive clothes, wear them with the tags on, and return them the morning after. Apparently the upscale life is now so worth living that deception, cheating, and theft are a small price to pay for it.

These are the more dramatic examples. Millions of us face less stark but prob- **9** lematic comparisons every day. People in one-earner families find themselves trying to live the lifestyle of their two-paycheck friends. Parents of modest means struggle to pay for the private schooling that others in their reference group have established as the right thing to do for their children.

Additional problems are created by the accelerating pace of product innovation. **10** To gain broader distribution for the plethora of new products, manufacturers have gone to lifestyle marketing, targeting their pitches of upscale items at rich and nonrich alike. Gourmet cereal, a luxurious latte, or bathroom fixtures that make a statement, the right statement, are offered to people almost everywhere on the economic spectrum. In fact, through the magic of plastic, anyone can buy designer anything, at the trendiest retail shop. Or at outlet prices. That's the new consumerism. And its siren call is hard to resist.

The new consumerism is also built on a relentless ratcheting up of standards. If **11** you move into a house with a fifties kitchen, the presumption is that you will eventually have it redone, because that's a standard that has now been established. If you didn't have air conditioning in your old car, the presumption is that when you replace it, the new one will have it. If you haven't been to Europe, the presumption is that you will get there, because you deserve to get there. And so on. In addition to the proliferation of new products (computers, cell phones, faxes, and other microelectronics), there is a continual upgrading of old ones—autos and appliances—and a shift to customized, more expensive versions, all leading to a general expansion of the list of things we have to have. The 1929 home I just moved into has a closet too shallow to fit a hanger. So the clothes face forward. The real estate agents suggested I solve the "problem" by turning the study off the bedroom into a walk-in. (Why read when you could be buying clothes?) What we want grows into what we *need,* at a sometimes dizzying rate. While politicians continue to tout the middle class as the heart and soul of American society, for far too many of us being solidly middle-class is no longer good enough.

Oddly, it doesn't seem as if we're spending wastefully, or even lavishly. Rather, **12** many of us feel we're just making it, barely able to stay even. But what's remarkable is that this feeling is not restricted to families of limited income. It's a generalized feeling, one that exists at all levels. Twenty-seven percent of all households making more than $100,000 a year say they cannot afford to buy everything they really need. Nearly 20 percent say they "spend nearly all their income on the basic necessities of life." In the $50,000–100,00 range, 39 percent and one-third feel this way, respectively. Overall, half the population of the richest country in the world say they cannot afford everything they really need. And it's not just the poorer half.

This book is about why: About why so many middle-class Americans feel mate- **13** rially dissatisfied. Why they walk around with ever-present mental "wish lists" of things to buy or get. How even a six-figure income can seem inadequate, and why this country saves less than virtually any other nation in the world. It is about the ways in which, for America's middle classes, "spending becomes you," about how it flatters, enhances, and defines people in often wonderful ways, but also about how it takes over their lives. My analysis is based on new research showing that the need to spend whatever it takes to keep current within a chosen reference group—which may include members of widely disparate resources—drives much purchasing behavior. It analyzes how standards of belonging socially have changed in recent decades, and how this change has introduced Americans to highly intensified spending pressures.

And finally, it is about a growing backlash to the consumption culture, a move- **14** ment of people who are downshifting—by working less, earning less, and living their consumer lives much more deliberately.

Excerpt from *The Overspent American* by Juliet Schor. Copyright © 1998 by Juliet B. Schor. Reprinted by permission of Basic Books, a member of Perseus Books, L.L.C.

Study Questions

1. Write out an outline of this essay. See if you can divide the whole into four major parts.
2. Notice how she introduces her subject by making a comparison in the first three paragraphs.
3. What sentence best expresses her thesis in the third paragraph?
4. Notice how she builds her essay on the definitions of three invented terms: competitive acquisition, new consumerism, and reference group. Explain what each of these terms mean.
5. What does she say are the problems caused by the new consumerism?
6. What does she mean by "the relentless ratcheting up of standards" in the eleventh paragraph?
7. Explain whether you agree or disagree with her opinion. Are Americans overspent?

A NATION OF VICTIMS

Charles J. Sykes

Charles J. Sykes has written several books critical of U.S. higher education. In this excerpt from the first chapter of A Society of Victims, *he expresses his opinions about "the decay of American character." (Notes to the original reading have not been included here.)*

Something extraordinary is happening in American society. Criss-crossed by invisible trip wires of emotional, racial, sexual, and psychological grievance, American life is increasingly characterized by the plaintive insistence, *I am a victim.* 1

The victimization of America is remarkably egalitarian. From the addicts of the South Bronx to the self-styled emotional road-kills of Manhattan's Upper East Side, the mantra of the victims is the same: *I am not responsible; it's not my fault.* 2

Paradoxically, this don't-blame-me permissiveness is applied only to the self, not to others; it is compatible with an ideological puritanism that is notable for its shrill demands of psychological, political, and linguistic correctness. The ethos of victimization has an endless capacity not only for exculpating one's self from blame, washing away responsibility in a torrent of explanation—racism, sexism, rotten parents, addiction, and illness—but also for projecting guilt onto others. 3

If previous movements of liberation may have been characterized as Revolutions of Rising Expectations, this society is in the grips of a Revolution of Rising Sensitivities, in which grievance begets grievance. In the society of victims, individuals compete not only for rights or economic advantage but also for points on the "sensitivity" index, where "feelings" rather than reason are what count. This ethos is fueled by a hypersensitivity so delicately calibrated that it can detect racism in the inflection of a voice, discover sexism in a classroom's seating pattern, and uncover patriarchal oppression in a mascara stick or a Shakespeare sonnet. 4

The new culture reflects a readiness not merely to feel sorry for oneself but to wield one's resentments as weapons of social advantage and to regard deficiencies as entitlements to society's deference. Even the privileged have found that being oppressed has its advantages. On the campuses of elite universities, students quickly learn the grammar and protocols of power—that the route to moral superiority and premier griping rights can be gained most efficiently through being a victim—which perhaps explains academia's search for what one critic calls the "unified field theory of oppression." 5

Americans, of course, have a long tradition of sympathy for the downtrodden; compassion for the less fortunate has always been a mark of the nation's underlying decency and morality. But our concern for the genuine victims of misfortune or injustice is sorely tested as the list of certifiable victims continues to grow; victim status is now claimed not only by members of minority groups but increasingly by the middle class, millionaire artists, students at Ivy League colleges, "adult children," the obese, 6 codependents, victims of "lookism" (bias against the unattractive), "ageism," "toxic parents," and the otherwise psychically scarred—all of whom are now engaged in an elaborate game of victim one-upmanship. Celebrities vie with one another in confessing graphic stories of abuse they suffered as children, while television talk shows feature a parade of victims ranging from overweight incest victims to handicapped sex addicts. "A Martian would be forgiven for thinking," columnist Barbara Amiel wrote in *McLean's*, "that the primary problem of North Americans is a population of females totally absorbed with their personal misery—addictions, abuse experiences and pain. . . . We are suffocating in our own pain."

Describing the new "politics of dependency" of the poor in the 1990s, Lawrence **7** Mead notes that its practitioners "claim a right to support based on the injuries of the past, not on anything that they contribute now. Wounds are an asset today, much as a paycheck was in progressive-era politics. One claims to be a victim, not a worker."

Everybody wants in on this. **8**

But the competition is stiff: If you add up all the groups—women, blacks, youths, **9** Native Americans, the unemployed, the poor, etc.—that consider themselves to be oppressed minorities, Aaron Wildavsky calculates, their number adds up to 374 percent of the population. The media continue to create new categories of victimization. A recent CBS report, for example, breathlessly revealed the existence of "the hidden homeless"—people living with their relatives. As a reporter for *The Washington Post* pointed out, "Once we called these situations *'families.'*"

Study Questions

1. Underline the thesis of the essay.
2. In an outline show how each paragraph contains generalizations that develop that thesis.
3. Outline in detail paragraph 6, showing how the author supports the claim made in his topic sentences. Name the types of support he chooses from the possibilities of illustration, description, listing, specific examples, facts and statistics, testimony, and authoritative corroborating opinions.
4. What underlying assumptions do you find in his argument? What value are assumptions?
5. Did he persuade you to agree with his opinion or not?

ADVANCED OPTIONAL WRITING ASSIGNMENT

Opinion on Sykes' Essay

Write an essay of opinion in which you analyze this essay, then agree or disagree with its thesis. Provide your own examples and explain your criteria for deciding between instances where victims deserve attention and legal recourse and where victimization has become a racket.

CHAPTER 7

Evaluations

What's Judged?

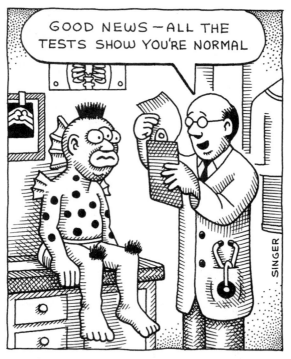

"Good News—All the tests show you're normal."
© 1998 Andrew B. Singer. Used with permission of Andrew B. Singer.

Now what does the physician mean by "normal"? We are left to wonder. This is a chapter about that variety of opinion called **evaluations,** which can appear in single words like "normal." Evaluations can be based on explicit or vague criteria, clear or vague feelings. When we mistake them for facts, we get into trouble. This chapter teaches both how to recognize and detach from *evaluations*.

Discovery Exercises

Both Discovery Exercises can be studied alone or with a partner in preparation for class discussion of this chapter.

Defining *Evaluate*

First, study the etymology of the word *evaluate*. What do its prefix and root mean? Then, write out definitions of the following words:

1. Judge
2. Appraise
3. Estimate
4. Value
5. Evaluate

Based on your work, answer these questions either in writing or in class:

1. What does *evaluate* mean?
2. Is an evaluation an inference?
3. Is an evaluation an opinion?
4. Can an evaluation be based on an assumption?

Recognizing Evaluative Words

Circle the words in the following passages that express evaluations, or the judgment that something is bad or good, desirable or undesirable. Note whether any evidence or reasons are given to support the evaluations.

A reminder before you begin: remember that these Discovery Exercises are not tests in which you are expected to know all the answers; they are meant only to help you acknowledge what you already know and to inspire you to learn more.

1. "I think contraception is disgusting—people using each other for pleasure." (Director, Pro-Life Action League)
2. Gun control is an aggressive cancer based on Nazi weapons laws. (Jews for the Preservation of Firearms Ownership.)
3. "*Random Hearts* is Hollywood hit-making at its efficient, formulaic worst . . . [It is] pablum, a piece of boilerplate cinema with no ambition but to sedate and pacify us." (Edward Guthmann, *San Francisco Chronicle*, 10/8/99)
4. "THE NEW 2000 MAXIMA. Once you slip behind the wheel of the new Maxima, once you begin to pilot the formidable 222 horsepower V6, amazing things happen." (Ad 1999 Nisan North America. 11/99)

Used with permission of Universal Press Syndicate.

ON EVALUATIONS

**Our values shape our ideals, decisions, judgments,
and they direct our lives.**

> **Evaluate** comes from the Latin *ex* = from, and *valere* = to be strong, to
> be of value. To evaluate, then, is (1) to determine or fix the value or
> worth of something or (2) to examine and judge, appraise, estimate.

To evaluate, appraise, and estimate value according to a standard is a
complex thinking task. It involves making comparisons and measuring
them against ideals that may be either conscious or unconscious, or both.
We like or dislike people, and judge them on the basis of standards that

we may or may not recognize. In turn, others judge us, sometimes fairly, sometimes unfairly. Yet it is essential that we learn to make evaluations, for without them we would not be able to improve our performance on tasks, decide what car to buy, what food to eat. When we do "comparison shopping," we evaluate products. We also survey and compare in order to decide what job to accept, what physician to trust. We develop personal criteria from our needs, values, and priorities. We draw comparisons from our experiences and memories in order to decide what candidate we want to vote for, what beliefs to hold, what friends we want to spend our time with, what movies we like, what books we read. Our evaluations determine the direction of our lives. In addition our lives are affected by the evaluations of others: the teacher who assigns grades, the boss who hires or fires us, the friends who give or withhold their loyalties. For all these reasons, it is worthwhile for us to give close attention to evaluations and make the evaluating process more skilled and conscious.

PREMATURE EVALUATIONS

Since our minds like to size up situations quickly, such a tendency can lead us into premature evaluations.

Premature evaluations are evaluations made before we have taken enough time to make a fair study of a situation. They bypass the observing and thinking process, substituting prejudice or vague impressions instead:

> Alex: "I knew before I spoke to him that he was too young for the job."
> Corey: "How do you know he is too young for the job?"
> Alex: "Well, he has acne, for one thing . . . Okay, okay, I'll give him an interview."

Sometimes an evaluator may not be that obliging. A lot of moral conviction can be attached to evaluations:

> Alice: "He looks like a turkey to me."
> Ruth: "What do you mean by a *turkey?*"
> Alice: "You know—a TURKEY!"

Instead of offering reasoning or evidence, Alice keeps repeating her evaluation as though it were a self-evident fact that needed no justification. In critical thinking terms, what she is doing is committing the *fallacy of circular reasoning*, which means repeating the conclusion as though that same conclusion provided its own support. (We will learn more about this fallacy in Chapter 10.) We hear such evaluations, expressed as though they were facts, everyday:

"He's a genius."

"She's a psychopath."

"They're just jerks."

Discussion Break Questions

Premature evaluations bypass close observing and thinking. What observing and thinking could alter the following evaluations?

1. She drives an old VW van. We'd better not take her in as a housemate.
2. He has bleached blonde hair. Don't go out with him.
3. A couple is driving down a road early one morning when they pass a Cadillac parked on the curb. A man is standing, bent forward, in front of the car with one hand on the hood. He is swaying slightly and violently ill. The woman in the car remarks, "Look at that drunk."
4. You buy a new answering machine and it cuts off your messages. Your brother says, "That machine is no good. You should ask for your money back."

EVALUATIONS ARE NOT FACTS

Critical thinkers separate evidence from evaluations.

Connie: "This sausage pizza I just made is good. That's a fact!"

John: "What do you mean, 'That's a fact'? It is not a fact as far as I am concerned."

Connie: "Well, you're vegetarian! Well, let me see how I can better explain what I mean. I like sausage and I like food that tastes fresh. That's a fact. When I took the sausage and cheese out of the refrigerator, they both smelled fresh to me. These are facts."

John: "I agree. These are all facts."

Connie: "And I added oregano and marjoram—spices that I love. That's a fact. So 'This sausage pizza is good' is my *evaluation*, based on the facts of my tastes and standards."

John: "Hey! You're right."

In this example, Connie is showing how our minds tend to operate: the evaluation comes easily and instantly, but inspection takes time and effort. This tendency to evaluate quickly may well be a survival mechanism. If we see a huge rock about to fall on top of us, an immediate evaluation of danger is all that is needed. Yet there are also many situations

"The Country's Toughest Beauty College" Used with permission of Universal Press Syndicate.

where we are better off reserving judgment until we can make a careful investigation of a situation. This is one reason we have developed courts of law to hold objective inquiries before arriving at judgments.

We need to learn how to evaluate as well as re-evaluate in order to learn from personal and collective experience. The reading offered at the end of Chapter 3, *Lies My Teacher Told Me*, re-evaluates many historical assumptions. Yet both the making and the remaking of evaluations are difficult because evaluations can contain intense feelings. To think critically, we have to acknowledge the feelings involved, but not let them dominate. Most of all, we need to remember that evaluations are not facts but require the support of evidence and clear reasoning.

EXPECTATIONS INFLUENCE EVALUATIONS

False expectations can lead us to make mistaken evaluations.

Psychologist John Enright tells the following story that illustrates the influence of expectations on evaluations.

> This morning I had a longing for some orange juice. I knew there must be some in the freezer, since my roommate went shopping yesterday. I took an orange-labeled can out of the freezer, and made myself a glass; as I did so, I noticed that it was a little darker than usual, but I concluded that it must just be another variety of orange or a different mix of rind and juice. Then when I tasted it, it was just *awful*. I spit it out in the sink and really made a mess of things, but I was sure it was spoiled, and I didn't want to make myself sick. Then I decided that I might as well take it back to the grocer's and get our money back. I fished the can out of the garbage and looked at the label. To my surprise it said "Tangerine Juice." I couldn't believe it. I tasted some of the juice left in the glass and . . . it was *good tangerine juice*!

Discussion Break Questions

1. Why did the evaluation change?
2. Neither the liquid nor the taste buds of the person changed. How can you explain what happened?
3. What information was missing in the first evaluation?
4. What can you conclude from this story about the effect of expectations on our perceptions and evaluations?
5. Describe an instance where new information made you backtrack toreconsider an earlier evaluation.

RECOGNIZING EVALUATIONS IN WORD CONNOTATIONS

Word connotations can manipulate us to accept evaluations we may not arrive at through our own thinking.

Evaluations are opinions that can be openly or covertly expressed. Compare these two statements:

- I believe electric cars are impractical because they can't be driven on the freeway at high speeds, and they can only be driven a limited number of miles before needing a recharge.
- Electric cars are just weird kiddy-cars for environmental Puritans.

The first example is an up-front evaluation that clearly expresses a personal opinion. It allows us to agree or disagree. The second example is a covert opinion since it evaluates through a choice of words with negative connotations such as "weird," "kiddy-cars, and "environmental Puritans." It does not invite us to agree or disagree because it implies that these words represent facts.

Word connotations were introduced in Chapter 2, "Word Precision." At that time we were studying how to select words with connotations appropriate for what we wanted to communicate. In this chapter our focus is on the way in which word connotations carry evaluations that influence feelings and opinions. Sometimes these connotations are so subtle as to influence us without our awareness. Let's look now at some simple word choices that carry positive or negative word connotations.

Discussion Break Questions

Show how the connotations of each of the following words differ by writing a plus or minus beside each word that carries either a positive or a negative connotation. Then answer the questions that follow either in writing or with your neighbor in class.

1. girl	doll	lady
2. undependable	flake	carefree spirit
3. cheat	rip-off	defraud
4. drinker	wino	alcoholic
5. soldier	terrorist	military advisor

- Are there significant differences in the meaning of the words within each set of three?
- Does the difference between a flake and a carefree spirit lie in the person thus described or in the person choosing these words?
- If you call me a flake, does that mean that I am, in fact, "a flake" or does it simply mean you see me in a negative light?

Discovery Exercise

Recognizing Evaluative Words' Persuasive Powers

Underline the words in the following passages with connotations that could be chosen to sway feelings and thus opinion as well.

1. "I listen to the feminists and all these radical gals—most of them are failures. They've blown it. Some of them have been married, but they married some Caspar Milquetoast who asked permission to go to the

bathroom. These women just need a man in the house. That's all they need. Most of these feminists need a man to tell them what time of day it is and to lead them home. And they blew it and they're mad at men. Feminists hate men. They're sexist. They hate men—that's their problem." (Rev. Jerry Falwell)

2. "We saved these helpless pets from being butchered for 'gourmet' food in South Korea. You can help us save thousands more from the cruel 'Cages of Despair.'" (International Fund for Animal Welfare)

3. (Photograph of a happy white middle-class family walking into the arms of a grandfatherly figure) *"All these years we've been protecting you.* When you walk into our insurance office, you'll learn how we can protect the lives of a husband and wife. Your children. Or even the lives of your business associates."

4. "Some environmentalists are retrograde. . . . Trapped in their own brand of fundamentalism, they refuse to play a constructive role in shaping the future of American forestry." ("Forest Puritans Want It All" by William Wade Keye, *San Francisco Chronicle*, 10/15/99)

5. "This city does not need our vote for a ballpark shopping mall complex that would only be a megashrine to cookie-cutter consumerism."

6. "A Real Life Bigot. A former leftist earns a place on the wild-eyed right." (Jack E. White, *Time*, 8/30/99)

SKILLED USE OF EVALUATIONS

An expert is a person who has a reputation for making dependable evaluations.

So far in this chapter we have looked mainly at examples of premature or manipulative evaluations; however, that does not mean that evaluations should be avoided. On the contrary, skilled evaluations are highly important creations. Experts in any profession, such as law or medicine, are highly paid because they are highly skilled evaluators. We read editorials in newspapers because we expect editors to offer evaluations of public issues that are worth consideration. We read film, book, art, and music reviews because we respect the reviewers' expertise. Good editorials and reviews can lead us to form our own opinions and make our own choices. Such examples follow in the two readings given on the following page, which were written by two skilled evaluators. The first is by a professional film reviewer; the second is by a famous paleoanthropologist.

READINGS

THE MALTESE FALCON

Humphrey Bogart at his most cynical, director John Huston at his nastiest, and the detective genre at its most hard-boiled and case-hardened (faithfully adapted from Dashiell Hammett's novel). Bogart's Sam Spade is the original Looking Out for Number One carrying on an affair with his partner's wife, shedding not a tear when his partner is murdered, and selling his private eye skills to the highest bidder in the search for the jewel-studded Maltese Falcon. Everything Bogart does in this film is galvanizing—from the casual way he wraps the priceless bird in newspaper and deposits it with an old man in a checkroom, to the magnificent rage he throws for Sydney Greenstreet (archvillain) and Peter Lorre, a rage which evaporates the instant he slams the door on them and steps into the corridor with a self-satisfied grin on his face, the satisfaction of a job well-done, a rage well-acted. With Mary Astor as the love interest Bogart sends to Death Row (1941).—M.C.

From *Express*, September 7, 1984, p. 2. Used with permission of the publisher.

DISCARDING THE CONCEPT OF MAN AS "KILLER APE"

Richard Leakey

Richard Leakey is a world-renowned paleoanthropologist. He has made major contributions to the study of human evolution.

"Evidence for Aggression Does Not Exist"

I am concerned about the widespread belief that humans are innately aggressive. 1
Many people think that there is good anthropological evidence for this. But when you actually look at the past, the evidence for aggression and violence does not exist.

The only evidence of what people did in that primitive period is what they left 2
behind, and no weapons of death and destruction—no clubs—have been found. The archeological record tells us what people used to eat and to gather things, but there is no evidence of their behavior. Behavior doesn't fossilize. So where does the view of violent and aggressive man come from? It's obviously created to explain present-day problems.

The popularity of the concept of man as "killer ape" and macho male was needed 3
to explain the terrible atrocities that occurred in World War II. Even before that, there was a feeling in Western culture that Neanderthal man was primitive and brutish. Many people grew up with images drawn from comics of the cave man as the hairy brute

with a club who used to beat fellow brutes on the head in the course of stealing women and dragging away victims.

These developments have created psychological acceptance of violence and ag- **4** gression rooted in a primitive past. It's a dangerous perspective that leads to the conclusion that such behavior is inevitable. But I would argue very strongly that violence and its acceptance are purely cultural.

Today, given what we know about the working of the mind and about techniques **5** of education, we could take an infant from any family anywhere in the world and by involvement in a particular cultural environment make the child *this* or *that*. The child's attitudes are not innate; they are learned. We could just as easily insist that everybody be taught from childhood that everyone is beautiful and that everybody should love everyone else as that people should hate each other.

I'm not necessarily taking a moral position on these matters. I'm simply saying **6** that what happens to this world is within our power to determine.

From *U.S. News & World Report*, February 15, 1982. Copyright © 1982 U.S. News & World Report, Inc. Used with permission of the publisher.

Study Questions

1. In his article Leakey is correcting a mistaken evaluation. How does he say it came about? How has it affected us?
2. For what different purpose are evaluations used in the review of *The Maltese Falcon*?

HOW HIDDEN EVALUATIONS APPEAR IN PROPAGANDA

The best defense against propaganda is to stay awake.

The word **propaganda** has a negative connotation; it means to manipulate public opinion for the benefit of the propagator. Propaganda uses many techniques, one of which is to hide evaluations inside powerful images and words. Advertisers know that words and images, especially those connected with sex and death, can be embedded into the unconscious mind within seconds.

The influence of propaganda is not as distant as an airplane dropping pamphlets on the enemy, but as close as your television set or the checkout stand in your neighborhood supermarket. Propaganda is most effective when you are most off guard, while half dozing during a TV program or while thumbing through those magazines as you wait your turn in line.

When we are tired or bored, evaluations have appeal: they serve to spice things up. Consider these magazine headlines:

Thugs Mourn the Death of Their Dictator

Senator X Grovels for Votes

John John's Secret Sex Life

Unfortunately, since our lives seem to be in more and more of a hurry, news magazines and TV news programs that promise to both entertain us and save our time are appealing even though they may distort with oversimplifications and slant with opinions. It can feel easier to allow them to do our thinking for us.

Advertisers also prefer to evaluate for us about their products. One useful technique is to just keep repeating the desired evaluative words. This technique has the additional advantage of not requiring evidence. It is only necessary to get the message imprinted in our brains during the seconds it takes to turn a page or glance at a TV commercial.

"Tiggerrific!" "What a gem! A fun, heartwarming story for the whole family. A gem of a movie! The Tigger Movie. What a gem!"

Discerning propaganda demands more painstaking attention many readers may feel willing to give. For those whose only reading time is while commuting or when the children are in bed, careful attention is not always easy to muster. The same may be said for our television viewing, which occurs when we need "to relax" in front of TV. Yet both fatigue and lethargy play right into the hands of the propagandist. When viewers are tired, they are less aware, and at that time words and images can be more easily imprinted directly on the unconscious memory. But the next day, they will find themselves reaching automatically for the advertised products on the shelves—never fully aware that they have been programmed to do so. Simple messages filed under the mental category of "good" make purchasing decisions easy.

What has happened is the advertiser's evaluations were transmitted to their subjects while they were in a trance state. Trance reception, also called hypnotism, is a routine event, if *hypnotism* is defined as altering a person's state of consciousness and making the person prone to suggestion. Hypnotism is not, as commonly believed, something performed only by a magician on stage or by a psychiatrist, but a routine event in which a person ceases to ward off someone else's suggestions.

Television, according to the book *The Plug-In Drug* (by Marie Winn, Bantam, 1978), induces an immediate trance state in viewers, regardless of the subject matter. Induction into an altered state is achieved by the television projection itself, by the manner in which it affects our eyes and consciousness. Perhaps you have become aware of this phenomenon

---

BUILDING ARGUMENTS

EVALUATIONS

Yet, while there were whites who preferred to live like Indians, there are few, if any, Indians who regarded a completely civilized form of living as superior to their own way of life. This is true even of Indian children who were educated in the schools of the white colonists and who were later permitted to return to their own people. With the opportunity of choosing between the two ways of life, they rarely cast their lot with civilization.

The reason for this decision was because the Indian was convinced that the white man's style of life, with its lack of freedom; innumerable laws and taxes; extremes of wealth and poverty; snobbish class divisions; hypocritical customs; private ownership of land; pent-up communities; uncomfortable clothing; many diseases; slavery to money and other false standards, could not possibly bring as much real happiness as their own ways of doing the great mass of white people and the great mass of Indians realized that their two ways of life were directly opposed. Each race looked upon the other as inferior; neither felt inclined to adopt the ways of the other; and that is why the Indians and the whites could not get along together. (Alexander Henry, American trader, 1764)

Exercise

1. What is the principal claim made in the first paragraph?
2. What behavior is cited to support this claim?
3. What characteristics of the white man did the Indians find objectionable? What do these evaluations tell us about the values of the Indians?

---

yourself when you found you had to make an extreme effort to get up out of your chair and turn the television off. And if that were not enough, commercials themselves use all the techniques associated with hypnotic induction: an object waved in front of the eyes and a pleasant, comforting, slow-speaking voice repeating evaluations over and over again. "Reach for aspirin for relief, aspirin for relief, for relief. Reach for aspirin for relief whenever you have those awful headaches, those awful headaches again. Aspirin."

Thinking critically requires that we simply *wake up*. Advertisers use extremely sophisticated psychology to make you associate desirable qualities with their products. If you want to retain the power of making your own choices you have to remain alert to propaganda strategies. In short, you have to continuously reclaim the right to think for yourself.

CHAPTER SUMMARY

1. Making evaluations is a complex thinking task that requires making judgments about worth according to standards that are both conscious and unconscious.

2. Premature evaluations bypass observing and thinking.

3. Evaluations appear sometimes as instinctive reactions that can help us survive. The problem is to distinguish sound instinct from hasty conclusion. The feelings invoked in evaluations have to be sorted out carefully.

4. Evaluations are not facts. Factual reports keep the distinction between facts and evaluations clear.

5. Expectations affect our perceptions and evaluations. We need to guard against making premature evaluations based on unconscious expectations.

6. All of us need to learn how to make skilled evaluations since they affect all our decisions. Experts are those who are well paid because they can provide skillful evaluations.

7. Connotative words convey evaluations that can be used to sway us toward a bias. When we think critically, we recognize their hidden emotional appeals.

8. Evaluations are used in advertising and journalism to persuade us, sometimes hypnotically, to make positive associations with products.

9. Critical thinking requires that we stay alert to manipulative advertising techniques, which are most effective when we are not alert—or when we are in a trance state.

10. Propaganda is an art with many sophisticated techniques for manipulation. One of these is the use of hidden evaluations. A critical thinker knows how to recognize and detach from the influence of propaganda.

CHAPTER QUIZ

Rate the following statements as *true* or *false*. Give an example to substantiate your answer in each case.

_____ 1. Evaluations are not facts but judgments based on conscious as well as unconscious standards.

_____ 2. Premature evaluations bypass observing and thinking.

_____ 3. The use of highly connotative words to influence opinion can be a form of hidden evaluation.

_____ 4. Evaluations should never be used in writing reviews, such as of films and books.

_____ 5. Repeating evaluations, as is done in advertising, is a way of hypnotizing and swaying opinion.

_____ 6. A critical thinking skill is the ability to detect evaluations substituted for evidence.

_____ 7. Prior expectations influence perceptions and our evaluation of these perceptions.

_____ 8. Our first reactions, before we have had time to examine the evidence, are always the most reliable.

_____ 9. To evaluate wisely, we first have to observe and then compare, and then be clear about our standards.

_____ 10. Advertisements encourage us to soak up their own evaluations of their products.

COMPOSITION WRITING APPLICATION

First Option: Observing and Analyzing Evaluations in Advertisements

Select two printed advertisements of the same product or type of product and circle all the evaluative words used. Photocopy them to hand in with your paper, or save the originals to hand in. Write at least a one-page analysis of each advertisement; then compare the ads to one another in a final page. Write a summation at the end that states your thesis. Try to decide which ad uses evaluations less responsibly, with distortions or confusing language that might mislead or trick the reader. Which ad is the more honest? Which is the more effective as an advertisement?

In your one-page analysis of each, go over every major evaluative word you have circled and thoroughly discuss both its literal and connotative (associative) meanings. Notice what appeals they carry to make you want to buy the product. Do the words make a pattern of evaluation that conveys a subliminal message? Is one key or primary evaluation repeated a lot, reinforced by secondary or lesser evaluations?

In review, the parameters are:

1. *Topic*: Comparison of the use of evaluative language in two advertisements of the same or related products. The originals, or photocopies of the same, should be attached.
2. *Method*: Descriptive analysis using exposition, comparison, and evaluation.

3. *Length*: Three typed pages.
4. Summation at the end can state your thesis.

Second Option: Writing a Critical Review

Write a review that evaluates a film, music album, or concert. Be conscious of your standards for evaluation. Try working with just three criteria, such as exciting, *enter-taining, and* instructive. *Be sure to define each. Describe strengths as well as weak-nesses. Make this into a one-page paragraph, like the review of* The Maltese Falcon *that you read in this chapter. Let your topic sentence be your recommendation for (or against) consumption.*

In review, the parameters are:

1. *Topic*: A review of a film, music album, or concert.
2. *Method*: A summary and evaluation of an event or product on the basis of three criteria. The topic sentence states your recommendation as a reviewer.
3. *Length*: One-page paragraph.

Scoring for Evaluative Words in Advertising or a Critical Review

1. Directions followed for choice of comparison of two adver-tisements or the writing of a review. 25 points

2. Method directions followed for descriptive analysis—or a summary and evaluation in the review on the basis of three explicit criteria. 40 points

3. Length of three typed pages. 20 points

4. Summary states thesis. 15 points

READING

LIFE-ALIENATING COMMUNICATION
Marshall Rosenberg, PhD

Marshall Rosenberg, PhD, is a clinical psychologist, internationally known peace-maker, and founder of the Center for Nonviolent Communication. Every year he trav-els through twenty-two countries in order to train people in the communication skills, which will help them solve their differences peacefully. His work, which centers on teaching what he calls the language of compassion, has proven successful not only in war-torn countries, but also in families, schools, churches, businesses, and governments.

In studying the question of what alienates us from our natural state of compassion, I have identified specific forms of language and communication which I believe contribute to our behaving violently toward ourselves and one another. I use the term "life-alienating communication" to refer to these forms of communication. **1**

MORALISTIC JUDGMENTS

One kind of life-alienating communication is the use of moralistic judgments that imply wrongness or badness on the part of people who don't act in harmony with our values. Such judgments are reflected in language such as, "The problem with you is that you're too selfish." "She's lazy." "They're prejudiced," "It's inappropriate." Blame, insults, put-downs, labels, criticism, comparison, and diagnoses are all forms of judgment. **2**

An item from the *New York Times*, June 23, 1983; "At the annual Lower East Side Jewish Festival yesterday, a Chinese woman ate a pizza slice in front of Ty Thuan Duc's Vietnamese grocery store. Beside her a Spanish-speaking family patronized a cart with two signs; 'Italian Ices' and 'Kosher by Rabbi Alper.' And after the pastrami ran out, everybody ate knishes." **3**

On the day before Memorial Day, 1983, a poet called me to describe a city he had just visited. He said that one section included mosques, built by the Islamic people who dwelled there. Attending his reading, he said, were large numbers of Hispanic people, 40,000 of whom lived in the same city. He was not talking about a fabled city located in some mysterious region of the world. The city he'd visited was Detroit. **4**

A few months before, as I was visiting Texas, I heard the taped voice used to guide passengers to their connections at the Dallas Airport announcing items in both Spanish and English. This trend is likely to continue; after all, for some southwestern states like Texas, where the largest minority is now Mexican-American, Spanish was the first written language and the Spanish style lives on in the western way of life. **5**

Shortly after my Texas trip, I sat in a campus auditorium at the University of Wisconsin at Milwaukee as a Yale professor—whose original work on the influence of African cultures upon those of the Americas has led to his ostracism from some intellectual circles—walked up and down the aisle like an old-time Southern evangelist, dancing and drumming the top of the lectern, illustrating his points before some Afro-American intellectuals and artists who cheered and applauded his performance. The professor was "white." After his lecture, he conversed with a group of Milwaukeeans—all of whom spoke Yoruban, though only the professor had ever traveled to Africa. **6**

One of the artists there told me that his paintings, which included African and Afro-American mythological symbols and imagery, were hanging in the local McDonald's restaurant. The next day I went to McDonald's and snapped pictures of smiling youngsters eating hamburgers below painting that could grace the walls of any of the country's leading museums. The manager of the local McDonald's said, "I don't know what you boys are doing, but I like it." as he commissioned the local painters to exhibit in his restaurant. **7**

Such blurring of cultural styles occurs in everyday life in the United States to a **8**
greater extent than anyone can imagine. The result is what the above-mentioned Yale
professor, Robert Thompson, referred to as a cultural bouillabaisse. Yet members of
the nation's present educational and cultural elect still cling to the notion that the
United States belongs to some vaguely defined entity they refer to as "Western civilization," by which they mean, presumably, a civilization created by people of Europe,
as if Europe can even be viewed in monolithic terms. Is Beethoven's Ninth Symphony,
which includes Turkish marches, a part of Western civilization? Or the late-nineteenth-
and twentieth-century French paintings, whose creators were influenced by Japanese
art? And what of the cubists, through whom the influence of African art changed modern painting? Or the surrealists, who were so impress with the art of the Pacific Northwest Indians that, in their map of North America, Alaska dwarfs the lower forty-eight
states in size?

Are the Russians, who are often criticized for their adoption of "Western" ways by **9**
Tsarist dissidents in exile, members of Western civilization? And what of the millions
of Europeans who have black African and Asian ancestry, black Africans having occu-
pied several European countries for hundreds of years? Are these "Europeans" a part
of Western civilization? Or the Hungarians, who originated across the Urals in a place
called Greater Hungary? Or the Irish, who came from the Iberian Peninsula?

Even the notion that North America is part of Western civilization because our **10**
"system of government" is derived from Europe is being challenged by Native American historians who say that the founding fathers, Benjamin Franklin especially, were
actually influenced by the system of government that had been adopted by the Iroquois hundreds of years prior to the arrival of Europeans.

Western civilization, then, becomes another confusing category—like Third World, **11**
or Judeo-Christian culture—as humanity attempts to impose its small-screen view of
political and cultural reality upon a complex world. Our most publicized novelist recently said that Western civilization was the greatest achievement of mankind—an attitude that flourishes on the street level as scribbles in public restrooms; "White Power,"
"Niggers and Spics Suck," or "Hitler was a prophet." Where did such an attitude, which
has caused so much misery and depression in our national life, which has tainted even
our noblest achievements, begin? An attitude that caused the incarceration of Japanese-
American citizens during World War II, the persecution of Chicanos and Chinese Americans, the near-extermination of the Indians, and the murder and lynchings of thousands of Afro-Americans.

The Puritans of New England are idealized in our schoolbooks as the first Amer- **12**
icans," "hardy band" of no-nonsense patriarchs whose discipline razed the forest and
brought order to the New World (a term that annoys Native American historians). In-
dustrious, responsible, it was their "Yankee ingenuity" and practicality that created the
work ethic.

The Puritans, however, had a mean streak. They hated the theater and banned **13**
Christmas. They punished people in a cruel and inhuman manner. They killed children
who disobeyed their parents. They exterminated the Indians, who had taught them
how to survive in a world unknown to them. And their encounter with calypso culture,

in the form of a servant from Barbados working in a Salem minister's household, resulted in the witchcraft hysteria.

The Puritan legacy of hard work and meticulous accounting led to the establishment of a great industrial society, but there was the other side—the strange and paranoid attitudes of that society toward those different from the elect.   **14**

The cultural attitudes of that early elect continue to be voiced in everyday life in the United States; the president of a distinguished university, writing a letter to the *Times*, belittling the study of African civilizations; the television network that promoted its show on Vatican art with the boast that this art represented "the finest achievement of the human spirit."   **15**

When I heard a schoolteacher warn the other night about the invasion of the American educational system by foreign curricula, I wanted to yell at the television set, "Lady, they're already here." It has already begun because the world is here. The world has been arriving at these shores for at least 10,000 years from Europe, Africa, and Asia. In the late nineteenth and early twentieth centuries, large numbers of Europeans arrived, adding their cultures to those of the European, African, and Asian settlers who were already here, and recently millions have been entering the country from South America and the Caribbean, making Robert Thompson's bouillabaisse richer and thicker.   **16**

North America deserves a more exciting destiny than as a repository of "Western civilization." We can become a place where the cultures of the world crisscross. This is possible because the United States and Canada are unique in the world. The world is here.   **17**

In studying the question of what alienates us from our natural state of compassion, I have identified specific forms of language and communication which I believe contribute to our behaving violently toward ourselves and each other. I use the term "life-alienating communication" to refer to these forms of communication.   **18**

One kind of life-alienating communication is the use of moralistic judgments that imply wrongness or badness on the part of people who don't act in harmony with our values. Such judgments are reflected in language such as, "The problem with you is that you're too selfish." "She's lazy." "They're prejudiced." "It's inappropriate." Blame, insults, put-downs, labels, criticism, comparisons, and diagnoses are all forms of judgment.   **19**

The Sufi poet Rumi once wrote, "Out beyond ideas of wrongdoing and rightdoing, there is a field. I'll meet you there." Life-alienating communication, however, traps us in a world of ideas about rightness and wrongness—a world of judgments; it is a language rich with words that classify and dichotomize people and their actions. When we speak this language, we judge others and their behavior while preoccupying ourselves with who's good, bad, normal, abnormal, responsible, irresponsible, smart, ignorant, etc.   **20**

Long before I reached adulthood, I learned to communicate in an impersonal way that did not require me to reveal what was going on inside of myself. When I encountered people or behaviors I either didn't like or didn't understand, I would react in terms of their wrongness. If my teachers assigned a task I didn't want to do, they   **21** were "mean" or "unreasonable." If someone pulled out in front of me in traffic my reaction would be, "You idiot!" When we speak this language, we think and communicate in terms of what's wrong with others for behaving in certain ways, or occasionally, what's wrong with ourselves for not understanding or responding as we would like. Our attention is focused on classifying, analyzing, and determining levels of wrongness rather than on what we and others are needing and not getting. Thus if my partner wants more affection than I'm giving her, she is "needy and dependent." But if I want more affection than she is giving me, then she is "aloof and insensitive." If my colleague is more concerned about details than I am, he is "picky and compulsive." On the other hand, if I am more concerned about details than he is, he is "sloppy and disorganized."

It is my belief that all such analyses of other human beings are tragic expressions **22** of our own values and needs. They are tragic because, when we express our values and needs in this form, we increase defensiveness and resistance to them among the very people whose behaviors are of concern to us. Or, if they do agree to act in harmony with our values because they concur with our analysis of their wrongness, they will likely do so out of fear, guilt, or shame.

We all pay dearly when people respond to our values and needs, not out of a **23** desire to give from the heart, but out of fear, guilt, or shame. Sooner or later, we will experience the consequences of diminished goodwill on the part of those who comply with our values out of a sense of either external or internal coercion. They, too, pay emotionally, for they are likely to feel resentment and decreased self-esteem when they respond to us out of fear, guilt, or shame. Furthermore, each time others associate us in their minds with any of those feelings, we decrease the likelihood of their responding compassionately to our needs and values in the future.

It is important here not to confuse *value judgments* and *moralistic judgments*. **24** All of us make value judgments as to the qualities we value in life; for example, we might value honesty, freedom, or peace. Value judgments reflect our beliefs of how life can best be served. We make *moralistic judgments* of people and behaviors that fail to support our value judgments, e.g. "Violence is bad. People who kill others are evil." Had we been raised speaking a language that facilitated the expression of compassion, we would have learned to articulate our needs and values directly, rather than to insinuate wrongness when they have not been met. For example, instead of "Violence is bad," we might say instead, "I am fearful of the use of violence to resolve conflicts; I value the resolution of human conflicts through other means."

The relationship between language and violence is the subject of psychology pro- **25** fessor O.J. Harvey's research at the University of Colorado. He took random samples of pieces of literature from many countries over the world and tabulated the frequency of words that classify and judge people. His study shows a high correlation between the frequent use of such words and incidences of violence. It does not surprise me to hear that there is considerably less violence in cultures where people think in terms of human needs than in cultures where people label one another as "good" or "bad" and believe that the "bad" ones deserve to be punished. In 75 percent of the television programs shown during hours when American children are most likely to be watching, the hero either kills prople or beats them up. This violence typically constitutes the "climax" of the show. Viewers, having been taught that bad guys deserve to be punished, take pleasure in watching this violence.

In his book, *Out of Weakness*, Andrew Schmookler of the Conflict Resolution Department at Harvard University claims that at the base of all violence—whether verbal, psychological, or physical, whether among family members, tribes, or nations—is a kind of thinking that attributes the cause of conflict to wrongness in one's adversaries. Schmookler further implicates a corresponding inability to think of oneself or others in terms of vulnerability—what one might be feeling, fearing, yearning, missing, etc. We saw this dangerous way of thinking during the Cold War. Our leaders viewed Russians as an "evil empire" bent on destroying the American way of life. Russian leaders referred to the people of the United States as "imperialist oppressors" who were trying to subjugate them. Neither side acknowledged the fear lurking behind such labels. **26**

The Indian philosopher J. Krishnamurti once remarked that observing without evaluating is the highest form of human intelligence. When I first read this statement, the thought, "What nonsense!" shot through my mind before I realized that I had just made an evaluation. For most of us, it is difficult to make observations of people and their behavior that are free of judgment, criticism, or other forms of analysis. **27**

I became acutely aware of this difficulty while working with an elementary school where the staff and principal often reported communication difficulties. The district superintendent had requested that I help them resolve the conflict. First I was to confer with the staff, and then with the staff and principal together. **28**

I opened the meeting by asking the staff, "What is the principal doing that conflicts with your needs?" "He has a big mouth!" came the swift response. My question called for an observation, but while "big mouth" gives me information on how this teacher evaluates the principal, it fails to describe what the principal *said* or *did* that led to the teacher's interpretation that he "has a big mouth." **29**

When I pointed this out, a second teacher offered, "I know what he means; the principal talks too much!" Instead of a clear observation of the principal's behavior, this was also an evaluation—of how much the principal talked. A third teacher then declared, "He thinks only he has anything worth saying." I explained that inferring what another person is thinking is not the same as observing his behavior. Finally a fourth teacher ventured, "He wants to be the center of attention all the time." After I remarked that this too was an inference—of what another person is wanting—two teachers blurted in unison, "Well, your question is very hard to answer!" **30**

We subsequently worked together to create a list identifying *specific behaviors* on the part of the principal which bothered them, and made sure that the list was free of evaluation. For example, the principal told stories about his childhood and war experiences during faculty meetings, with the result that meetings sometimes ran 20 minutes overtime. When I asked whether they had ever communicated their annoyance to the principal, the staff replied they had tried, but only through evaluative comments. They had never made reference to specific behaviors—such as his storytelling—and agreed to bring these up when we were all to meet together. **31**

Almost as soon as the meeting began, I saw what the staff had been telling me. **32** No matter what was being discussed, the principal would interject, "This reminds me of the time..." and then launch into a story about his childhood or war experience. I waited for the staff to voice their discomfort around the principal's behavior. However, instead of Nonviolent Communication, they applied nonverbal condemnation. Some rolled their eyes; others yawned pointedly; one stared at his watch.

I endured this painful scenario until finally I asked, "Isn't anyone going to say **33** something?" An awkward silence ensued. The teacher who had spoken first at our meeting screwed up his courage, looked directly at the principal, and said, "Ed, you have a big mouth."

As this story illustrates, it's not always easy to shed our old habit and master the **34** ability to separate observation from evaluation. Eventually, the teachers succeeded in clarifying for the principal the specific actions which led to their concern. The principal listened earnestly and then pressed, "Why didn't one of you tell me before?" He admitted he was aware of his story-telling habit, and then began a story pertaining to this habit! I interrupted him, observing (good-naturedly) that he was doing it again. We ended our meeting developing ways for the staff to let their principal know, in a gentle way, when his stories weren't appreciated.

Excerpt from *Nonviolent Communication: A Language of Compassion.* Copyright © Marshall B. Rosenberg, 1999. Reprinted with permission of PuddleDancer Press. PO Box 1204, Del Mar, CA 92014.

Study Questions

1. Why does Rosenberg say that our analyses of other human beings are tragic expressions of our own values and needs?
2. What difference does he draw between value judgments and moral judgments?
3. Explain the point he makes about the relationship between language and violence?
4. In the story he tells at the end, why does he ask the teachers to describe exactly what behaviors of the principal they observed—and objected to—rather than to keep repeating their evaluations of the principal?

ADVANCED OPTIONAL WRITING ASSIGNMENT

Moralistic Judgments

Write a four-page typed essay in which you offer your own opinion on the advantages and disadvantages of moralistic judgments. Draw from your own experience, from what you have learned from others, and, if you wish, from your family and religion. Take a position stated in your thesis in which you agree, disagree, or partially agree with Marshall Rosenberg.

CHAPTER 8

Viewpoints

What's the Filter?

"It's too bad..."
Used with permission of John Heine.

When one's own viewpoint is identified with reality, there are no other viewpoints. In this cartoon, we see how such narrow awareness affects our lives on this planet. We might also wonder if the animals have the wiser perspective.

The ability to detach from one's own point of view and to assume another's is an important skill. Such an ability enables us to communicate better with others and gain new perspectives. However, if we forget that all information flows through the filters of human biases, we confuse information with reality. A person trained in critical thinking always looks for the source of any piece of information and evaluates that information within the context of its viewpoint and inherent bias. The purpose of this chapter is to demonstrate the value of such attitudes and skills.

Discovery Exercises

Understanding the Term *Viewpoint*

Using at least two dictionaries, formulate your own definitions of the following words:

viewpoint

point of view

attitude

bias

perspective

frame of reference

opinion

Discussion or Writing Questions

1. Explain how viewpoint can be both collective and individual.
2. Explain why the term viewpoint is far more than a synonym for the word "opinion."

What Types of Viewpoints Are There?

This is an exercise that will involve the whole class working in small groups. Each group will use brainstorming to construct one cluster or mindmap illustrating a viewpoint. The mindmaps may be drawn on sections of the blackboard or be drawn with crayons or felt-tip pens on large sheets of paper. Each group will begin by choosing to work with one of the categories of viewpoints listed below. Each mindmap will record all the different viewpoints the group could imagine would fit under the chosen category.

Type of Viewpont	Examples To Get You Started
Socioeconomic	Homeless, working class, middle class
Political	Republicans, Conservatives
National	Chinese, Korean
Ethnic	Native American
U.S. high school youth	Nerds, Goths
Gender roles	Mother, father

Type of Viewpont	Examples To Get You Started
Religious preference	Islam, Catholicism
Financial world	Corporate, banking, small business
Education	Students, administration, higher education
Occupation	Plumber, doctor, journalist
Citizenship	Immigrant, naturalized citizen, voter
Pasttimes	Bikers, museum-goers, shopping mall visitors
Consumer groups	Internet users, Ford owners, Harley-Davidson owners

Study Questions

1. What did you learn from this exercise?
2. Take any one sub-group within a viewpoint (i.e., nerds in high schools) and describe how its members identify themselves through clothing, symbols, possessions, language, or shared opinions.

VIEWPOINTS IN LITERATURE

When we study the elements of literature, one viewpoint that we look for is the point of view chosen to tell the story. In literature an author can choose a third person to tell the story—who may or may not be a character in the story—with a viewpoint that can range in awareness from omniscient to limited. Other choices of viewpoint range from using a first person narrative told by a character, or the multiple points of view of several characters. In each case, the author must decide how wise or how limited the person would be in awareness, and how this viewpoint will affect both the story and the reader. What follows now is an excerpt from a short story. As you read, consider what effects the author was able to achieve by allowing the story to be told solely through the viewpoint of its chief character.

READING

THIS IS MY LIVING ROOM

Tom McAfee

My Living Room

it ain't big but big enough for me and my family—my wife Rosie setting over there   1
reading recipes in the Birmingham *News* and my two girls Ellen Jean and Martha Kay

watching the TV. I am setting here holding *Life* magazine in my lap. I get *Life*, the *News*, and *Christian Living*. I read a lots, the newspaper everyday from cover to cover. I don't just look at the pictures in *Life*. I read what's under them and the stories. I consider myself a smart man and I ain't bragging. A man can learn a lots from just watching the TV, if he knows what to watch for and if he listens close. I do. There ain't many that can say that and be truthful. Maybe nobody else in this whole town, which is Pine Springs.

Yonder in the corner, to the other side of the Coca-Cola calendar, is my 12 gauge. **2** When I go in to bed, I take it with me, set it against the wall, loaded, ready to use, so I can use it if I need to. I've used it before and maybe will again. The only one to protect you is yourself and if you don't you're a fool. I got me a pistol and a .22 locked up in the back room. I could use them too.

Rosie can shoot, I taught her how, but she's afraid. The noise scares her. She said, **3** Don't make me shoot that thing one more time. We was in the forest. The girls was waiting for us in the car. Don't make me shoot that thing again, she said, and started to cry. I slapped her face and told her to shoot the rifle. She did. Then I took it and told her to go back to the car with the girls. She started to cry again, but I stayed a long time—till it was dark—and shot the rifle and pistol and shotgun.

You can't tell what people are going to do in a town like this. They want your **4** money and they're jealous of you. They talk about you in front of the courthouse and plan up schemes. You can't trust the police or sheriff. You got to watch out for yourself.

My Two Girls

are fourteen and sixteen year old. Both of them want to go on dates but I won't let **5** them. I know what the boys will do, what they want to get out of a girl.

Ellen Jean, the oldest, is a right good-looking girl but sassy and you can't hardly **6** do anything with her. She started to paint her face at school, so I took her out. I've got her working at my store.

I seen her passing notes to Elbert. I seen her get out of his car one night. She **7** said she was going to the picture show by herself. She's a born liar and sassy. Like as not he's had her. Like as not she's got a baby starting in her belly right now. She's a sassy bitch-girl and don't take after her ma or me. Sometimes I wonder if she's mine.

Martha Kay is like her ma. She cries all the time, minds good. I let her stay in **8** high school and will keep on letting her as long as she can act right. The first time I see lipstick, out she comes. She can work at the store too. I could use her to dust and sweep up. You can always use somebody to keep things clean.

I ask Martha Kay, Why're you late gettin' in from school? Where you been? Off in **9** the woods with some boy? She starts to cry. She's like her ma.

Martha Kay helps at the store on Saturdays but can't add up figures good. **10**

Ellen Jean is watching that man on TV make a fool of hisself and she's laughing. **11** She'll end up a Birmingham whore. Her sister is laughing too and they look like a bunch of fools.

People

in this town are like they are in any other town on earth. I was in the World War I and **12** seen a good many places. Since then I've stayed here most of the time. What's the good of moving? People are as mean one place as they are another and they're always out to get you. They won't get me because I won't let them.

Take Sam Coates who owed me twenty dollars for that fencing. Sam wouldn't **13** pay. I said to him pay up by first of the month or I'll make you pay. He says how will I make him. Sue him for twenty dollars? Won't no lawyer in town take it anyway, he says, because they're all looking out for election. You pay, I told him.

When first of the month come I got in my car and rode out in the country to his **14** front door. Where is your husband? I said to his wife. Milking, she said, and I went around to the barn with my .22, stuck it in his face, and told him to pay me or I'd blow the hell out of him. Sam turned as white as that bucket of milk. Him and his wife counted me out the money.

There ain't one on earth that wouldn't try to cheat you if they could. **15**

I use to think that women was worse than men but now I think just the oppo- **16** site. Women are easier to handle. About the worst they can do is talk and what does that matter?

Niggers are better than anybody because you can handle them. They don't hardly **17** ever give you any trouble. Except that one time with Ezmo. I didn't have no trouble handling him. . . .

Old Ezmo

was what you'd call a low class of nigger. He'd come into the store and say, Give me **18** a pound of sugar and I'll pay you Saturday evening. I wouldn't do it. I'd say, You give me the money. I give you the best prices in town. You give me the money.

One time Ellen Jean let him have a loaf of bread on credit. I smacked her for it **19** and told her she was a fool, which she is. On Saturday Ezmo come in and wanted some side meat for cooking greens. Pay me off, I told him, for that loaf of bread. What loaf? he wanted to know.

Ellen Jean, didn't you charge this nigger a loaf of bread? She said yes and he said **20** she didn't. You ain't calling my girl a liar, are you? Naw, he said, but he didn't get no loaf of bread. Somebody's a liar, I told him, and it ain't my girl.

He said he wouldn't pay me. You're a crooked, low-down nigger, I told him, and **21** they ain't nothing much worse than that. You ain't fit for making side meat out of. I told him if he had any younguns he better watch out. I didn't wants lots of black bastards like him growing up in my town. You get out of here right now.

That night I was setting in this chair where I am right now—this same chair. The **22** girls was watching TV. Rosie was shelling peas.

I heard somebody outdoors and I knew right off who it was. I got better ears **23** than most people. Any time somebody sets foot in this yard, I know it. Even if I'm asleep.

That's Ezmo, I said to myself. I got up, picked up my 12 gauge over in the cor- **24**
ner and said I was gonna clean it, went through the house without turning any lights
on, then eased out the back door.

There wasn't much moon but I spotted Ezmo right off, standing behind some **25**
hedge bushes over by my bedroom window. I got just this side of him without him
hearing. *Ezmo!* I hollered, and up he comes with a knife about eight inches long. I
was ready for him. I triggered my 12 gauge and got him square in the face.

Rosie and the girls come running to the back door. Get me a flashlight, I told **26**
them. I never seen such a blowed-up face. The girls started getting sick and Rosie
started crying. I want you to take a good look, I told Rosie, and see what this world is
coming to. You see that knife he had. I held Rosie's arm and made her stand there
till Ellen Jean could get Sheriff Claine.

Rosie

ain't exactly good-looking. She's got to be dried-up but once was on the fat side. She **27**
makes a good wife. I've been married to her for going on thirty years. Sometimes I
get fed up with her and go to my woman in South Town. I take her a couple of cans
of beans and some hose or a pair of bloomers. There ain't nothing much a woman
won't do for food or clothes.

Rosie knows about her, all about her. I talk about it sometimes when we're in **28**
bed. I wouldn't trade Rosie for her but Rosie don't know that.

Tomorrow's Saturday and I got to get some sleep. **29**

"Turn off the TV, girls. Get in yonder to bed. Tomorrow's Saturday." **30**

I stand in front of Rosie. "Go in yonder and get in bed." She starts to cry and that's **31**
all right. It wouldn't be a bit like her if she didn't.

From Tom McAfee, *Poems and Stories*. Used with permission of Jeanie K. McAfee and the Department
of English at the University of Missouri–Columbia on behalf of the Thomas McAfee Memorial Fund.

Study Questions

1. Why is this story entitled "This Is My Living Room"?
2. What kind of mental living room does the storyteller live in? How does he see his world and himself in it?
3. How does he justify his sexist and racist behavior?
4. How well does he understand his wife, daughters, and "Old Ezmo"? Does he observe or stereotype them?
5. What cliches do you find in his speech? What does this suggest about the way he views life?
6. Why isn't he capable of compassion or sympathy for others?

Used with permission of Mark Stivers.

ON UNCONSCIOUS VIEWPOINTS

**Viewpoints, like assumptions, opinions, and evaluations,
may or may not be consciously recognized.**

In earlier chapters of this text, distinctions were drawn between the conscious and unconscious uses of assumptions, opinions, and evaluations. To understand assumptions, we have to know that an assumption can be unconscious. To appreciate well-supported opinions, we need to distinguish them from superficial sentiment or fixed opinions immune to conscious reexamination. To make sound evaluations, we need to guard against premature judgments. In this chapter, as we work with viewpoints, the issue of conscious and unconscious use appears again.

The unconscious viewpoint is illustrated in the story just read where the central character lives in a viewpoint as narrow as one room, yet believes it is the whole world. One might say that he is not even aware that he has a viewpoint because he does not even grasp the concept. For this reason, he cannot imagine that viewpoints could exist beyond his own, much less enter into them. He cannot step outside of himself and say, "Well, I have a way of looking at things, but that does not mean that I am always right. Other people also have viewpoints, which I could assume and even learn from." Moreover, since he confuses the way he sees things with the way things are, he uses his "thinking" to rationalize feelings of fear and anger that others might evaluate as selfish, paranoid, racist, and sexist. He is what we call an *egocentric* person.

Egocentric individuals can rarely put themselves in someone else's shoes. Psychologist Jean Piaget, who studied learning stages in children, theorized that egocentrism is typical for most young children before the age of seven. The ability to grow beyond this cognitive limitation varies from one individual to another, depending on the measure of intelligence, emotional stability, or cultural and educational factors. As we grow out of egocentrism, we also develop the ability to be *exterior* to our own viewpoint—to see and recognize it from the outside, objectively. We learn how to see the world through the eyes of others. Such a capacity enables us to respect life more, and to separate who we are as human beings from how we sometimes think and behave. We learn the meaning of the word *compassion* and move from the unconsciousness of egocentrism to the consciousness of objectivity.

Other less conscious viewpoints that share this feature of self-identification, include ethnocentrism and religiocentrism. *Ethnocentrism*, in its milder forms, is an attitude that judges other people by one's own cultural practices, values, and standards, as though these were the only reasonable norm. The relativity of ethnocentrism becomes clearer to us when we go to live in another country and find that we can adapt to new cultural mores, such as eating with our hands, that we might have judged as backwards before. However, ethnocentrism also has tragic consequences, as has been seen within the country formerly called Yugloslavia, which coined the term "ethnic cleansing." The United States, in turn, shows its ethnocentricity when it justifies political actions such as bombing other countries as being "in America's best interests." Thus ethnocentricity is always easier to see in other nations, especially if they are considered enemies.

Religiocentrism is another form of ethnocentricity; in this case a total identification is made with a particular religious tradition or ideology. Again, the implicit assumption is that "we are right and everyone else is wrong; there is only one correct religious viewpoint and that is ours." Religiocentrism leads people to make statements that contain value assumptions:

> "All any couple needs to have a happy marriage is to be good Christians."

> "Women are morally crooked because they came from Adam's rib. It is best for a girl not to come into existence, but being born she had better be married or buried."

Finally, in recent times two newer concepts describing self-centered viewpoints have come into being: *androcentrism* and *anthropocentrism*. The women's movement drew attention to the prevalence of androcentric (male-dominated) thinking, whereas the animal rights proponents and environmentalists pointed out our pervasive anthropocentrism (human centeredness).

Discovery Exercise

Recognizing Political and Social Points of View

Read the following passages and notice how they express very different viewpoints based on different concerns, values, and priorities. See if you can assign each a political or social label, such as "radical left," "right conservative," or "feminist" on the basis of the language used and the ideas expressed.

1. "I never burned my bras in the sixties. But I wish I had." (*Ms.* magazine)

2. *"The Race to Save Our Earth* was written to excite students about alternative technologies and to encourage their participation in creative solutions to global problems." (*Solar Mind: Holistic Approaches to Technology & Environment*)

3. "It will be our own actions, our own ideas, our own well-designed laws, our own politicians that will end the feet dragging of AIDS funding, the raping of health options, the assurance of full civil rights and jobs for people, and an environment safe from violence . . . of bigotry." (*Frontiers*)

4. "There is a cultural war going on in America led by the elite of academia, the media, and the judiciary which has been infected with a philosophy of moral relativism that encourages and promotes abortion, homosexuality and other crimes and aberrations." (Rep. William Dannemeyer quoted in *San Francisco Examiner*)

5. "Black realists have little faith in the American justice system and believe armed, physical retaliation against racists who kill and abuse Blacks, then escape justice, is a just, viable option." (James Strong, *The Final Call*)

6. "Let's assassinate the CIA." (*Nation*)

Discuss these questions in writing or in class:

1. Which quotes were the most difficult for you to identify?

2. What were the clues that helped you decide how to label the viewpoint?

Figure 8.1 The Left-to-Right Political Spectrum

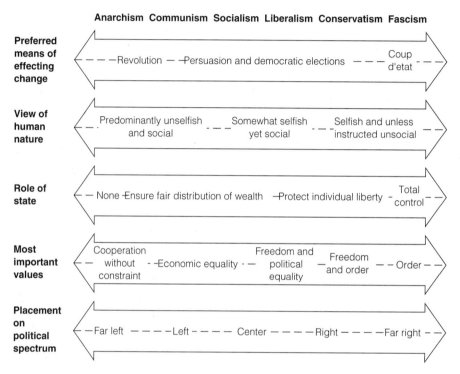

Figure 8.2 Traits of Political Systems on Left-to-Right Spectrum

Adapted from Kay Lawson, *The Human Polity: An Introduction to Political Science*. Boston: Houghton Mifflin, 1985, p. 118. Used with permission of the publisher.

RECOGNIZING VIEWPOINTS LEFT AND RIGHT

Even though their meanings keep shifting, the terms liberal and conservative, left and right, are still used as yardsticks to describe political viewpoint.

Today's students often find it both frustrating and confusing to understand, use, and apply the labels "left" and "right" to categorize shifting world patterns of political, social, economic, and religious values (see Figures 8.1 and 8.2). Perhaps this is because, as some political scientists

(Hamiltonian: favors nationalization, global interdependence, government-corporation cooperation)

BIG

Liberal

Democratic

Neoconservative

Conservative

Socialist

(favors equality and collective control)

LEFT

RIGHT

(favors liberty and private control)

Utopian communalist

Libertarian

Guild socialist

Anarcho-capitalist

Left-anarchist

SMALL

(Jeffersonian; populist, green perspective [peace and environmentalism]: favors liberty and equality, small cooperatives, community self-reliance)

Figure 8.3 The Two-Axis Model of Political Views

From Michael Marien, "The Two Post-Industrialisms and Higher Education," *World Future Society Bulletin*, May 1–June 1982, p. 20. Used with permission of World Future Society.

maintain, the use of the left-to-right spectrum as a paradigm (model of reality) to explain viable political positions is now obsolete. It was derived, they say, from the period of the French, American, and industrial revolutions, which conceived oppositions between monarchies and democracies, between more and less authoritarian control, and between open markets and free trade versus social protection from the market system's inequities.

Other models or viewpoints, besides the left-to-right spectrum, have been offered, such as the two-axis model depicted in Figure 8.3. This model has the advantage of including perspectives that do not fit on the single-axis left-to-right paradigm, such as anarchism, populism, libertarianism, and environmentalism.

In the United States, we have a two-party system; however, the Democratic and Republican parties include both right and left, conservative and liberal perspectives.

Unlike other developed democracies, the United States does not have a parliamentary political system in which voters cast their votes for parties. Parties in most countries have distinct commitments to differing national programs, differences easily discerned by voters. Citizens voting in those countries know that when they cast their ballots for a party's candidate they are voting for particular policies. In the United States, voters cast ballots for individual candidates who are not bound to any party program except rhetorically, and not always then. Some Republicans are more liberal than some Democrats, some libertarians are more radical than some socialists, and many local candidates run without any party identification. No American citizen can vote intelligently without knowledge of the ideas, political background, and commitments of each individual candidate. (Ben H. Bagdikian, *The Media Monopoly*, 1983, p. 176. Used with permission of the author.)

Americans also have difficulty defining many of the terms used to describe the range of views within any one party. The meanings of the words *liberal, conservative, radical left*, and *radical right* can shift from one decade to another. In addition, how one defines all these terms, whether *liberal, conservative, radical left*, or *radical right*, depends on one's own ideology and perspective within the whole political spectrum. The chart on U.S. Conservatives and Liberals attempts some generalizations.

The professed neutrality of the American mass media is perhaps another reason why it can be so difficult to categorize viewpoint today in America. Our largest city newspapers, national radio programs, and television networks generally claim to be objective and non-ideological, but all are now corporate-owned and reflect big-business commercial values and assumptions. This situation also no longer differs in European countries, where formerly political party and church-affiliated newspapers offered their own daily interpretations of news and issues. In the past, clear labels did not leave the reader wondering about a viewpoint's source, its stands on issues, or its sponsors. Moreover, by comparing their different interpretations of the same news events, the reader could draw his or her own conclusions.

In the United States, our large so-called "mainstream" city newspapers, network radio and television stations have not fully reflected this country's vast and diverse range of opinion. However, in the past decade, the Internet has filled this vacuum, offering an outlet for a dazzling range of viewpoints that grows daily. The Internet affords a medium for the free expression and distribution of every possible viewpoint; it allows access to a vast range of perspectives on all issues arising within a country as well as between people all over the world.

Libraries also offer access to viewpoints both online and in print that are underrepresented in the mainstream media. Most of these publications clearly identify their social, religious, or political affiliations. Browsing through such small newspapers and magazines can help you develop your own sense of what values, ideas, and rhetoric characterize right-wing

U.S. CONSERVATIVES	U.S. LIBERALS
1. Chief concern is preservation of wealth, assets, and resources both personal and national. Belief in personal initiative and responsibility.	1. Chief concern is protection of poor and less privileged from inequities of capitalist economic system.
2. Concern about safety, law and order: personal, national, and international. Believes in a strong police and military force with punishment for offenders.	2. Wants law and order but more concerned about justice and respect for human rights.
3. Concern about personal freedom: prefers least taxes, least government regulation and interference with private life.	3. Concern about social responsibility. Supports regulations and funding to assure community needs are fairly met.
4. Prefers Christian values and traditional social conformity.	4. Likes nonconformity; more tolerant of alternative lifestyles, ethnic diversity, and other religious orientations.
5. Patriotic. Supports a high defense budget and use of military solutions to problems.	5. Supports strong defense but wary of military-industrial complex and more critical of military interventions.
6. Supports legislation such as: less gun control, pro-business, school vouchers, tax refunds, no capital gains taxes, abortion controls, expansion of military spending.	6. Supports legislation such as: minimum wage increases, stricter gun control, less taxes for poor and middle class, more taxes on the rich, universal health care, federal subsidies to public schools and farmers, labor protection.
7. Dislikes high federal spending for welfare programs, universal health care programs, affirmative action, rights to abortions, student loans, public housing, public education, environmental protection.	7. Dislikes tax loopholes and subsidies for corporations; low fines for environmental pollution, federal deregulation of banks, huge corporate mergers, corporate control of media.
8. Prominent in Republican Party.	8. Prominent in Democratic Party.

opinion, left-wing opinion, green opinion, reform party opinion, etc. Making such a survey will help you discover the wide range of viewpoints available in the United States; you will also discover how they stimulate your thinking by presenting unfamiliar perspectives.

CORE DISCOVERY WRITING APPLICATION

A Survey of Two Alternative Viewpoints in Two Magazines or Newspapers

This is an assignment designed to broaden your familiarity with the wide spectrum of non-mainstream social and political opinion in the United States today. The following publications, listed below, cannot be bought at your neighborhood drugstore or grocery store, although a few may appear in some bookstores. This assignment can be done either online or in the magazine section of your library. Your choice of two publications will depend, of course, on which ones you can find available. First read through the list of magazines, and then read the directions that follow.

The Advocate (leading national gay and lesbian news magazine)

Arab American News

Arms Sales Monitor

Asian Week

The Beat Within (newsletter of writing and art by incarcerated youth)

Black Issues in Higher Education

Boycott Quarterly

Censorship News

Christian Science Monitor

Christianity Today

Consumer Reports

Dioxin Digest

Earth Island Journal

Emerge: Black America's News Magazine

Fifth Estate (anarchist)

High Times Magazine (Pot Party)

In These Times (Left Progressive)

Indian Country Today (*Lakota Times*)

Issues in Science and Technology

The Jewish Week

Korea Times

Latin American Perspectives

Media Culture Review

Ms. Magazine (feminist)

Mother Jones (left progressive journalism)

New American (John Birch Society)

News India

The New Republic (liberal)

The Nuclear Monitor

The People Magazine (Socialist Labor Party)

The Worker Magazine (Worker's Party USA Marxist-Leninist)

Sojourners (Christian Left)

Teen Voices Magazine

Tikkun (Jewish culture, philosophy, politics)

Tricycle: The Buddhist Review

Utne Reader (New Age liberal)

Welfare Mothers Voice

Zines (self-published magazines online)

Assignment Directions

Choose your two publications, and write down your notes about each in the following order:

1. *Magazine or newspaper name and date.*

2. *Cover page or front page*: Describe the cover or front page in sufficient detail so someone else might visualize its mood and impact on the reader. How does this cover page differ from such Time-Warner publications as *Time, Life, People Magazine, Money, Fortune,* and *Sports Illustrated?*

3. *Table of contents or headlines*: Study what subjects this magazine covers and write them down. What slant does this publication take on life? How would you describe its values and interests?

4. *Advertising*: If there are any advertisements, note them. Generalize about the types of advertisers, the products, and the way they are presented, and describe one that may be typical. Comment on what product ads are missing that would usually appear in mainstream magazines.

5. *Audience*: How would you describe the particular political, social, or ethnic group for which this publication seems to be written? What

might you infer, from the topics chosen and language used, about their level of education and income?

6. *Content*: What perspectives does this publication offer that is never or rarely found in mainstream publications or media? Write down one thing you learned from studying this magazine.

Write up your notes on these two magazines in a report of at least four typed pages. You can use an outline form, following through the six points for each one. Attach to your report either the magazines or newspapers themselves, or your print-outs, or a photocopy of each publication's cover and table of contents. Be prepared to give an oral summary of your work to the whole class or a small group.

Scoring for Observing Alternative Viewpoints in Magazines and Newspapers

1. Choice of two publications whose unfamiliarity poses some challenge. 10 points

2. Description of cover or front page conveys its calculated effort to attract readers through mood, choice of images, symbols, words, and topics. 20 points

3. Table of contents or headlines are not just listed; discussion shows thoughtful attention to the details that give evidence of the publication's interests, slant on life, values, and ideology. 20 points

4. Advertisements: specific examples are given to show the types of advertisers, the types of products and how they are presented. Speculations could be offered about what the ads, or lack of ads, suggest about the values of the magazine and its readers. 20 points

5. Audience: thoughtful conclusions are drawn about the social, ethnic, income, and educational level of the readers. 10 points

6. Content: Thoughtful conclusions offered about the uniqueness of this perspective. 10 points

7. No distracting errors of spelling, punctuation, sentence use, word use. 10 points

HIDDEN VIEWPOINTS:
THE USE OF NEWS FRAMING

News framing describes the way an editor uses layout design, placement, and headlines to sensationalize, downplay, exaggerate, or convey importance.

When we begin to understand that information is filtered through human viewpoints, we begin to ask more questions about "the daily news." We begin to wonder *who* decides *what* is news? Are they noble truth seekers dedicated to public service? A book such as *How to Watch TV News* (by Neil Postman and Steve Powers) says "no" in answer to this last question, casting doubt even on the assumption that the intention of any news media is to keep you informed. The media's purpose, these authors maintain, is to keep you entertained and sell you products:

> You may think that a TV news show is a public service and a public utility. But more than that, it is an enormously successful business enterprise. . . . The whole package is put together in the way that any theatrical producer would proceed, that is, by giving priority to show business values. (p. 161)

The authors then go on to say that acquiring media literacy means taking the time to inquire about the viewpoint, or the economic and political interests, of those who run TV stations:

> Keep in mind that other professionals—doctors, dentists, and lawyers, for example—commonly display their diplomas on their office walls to assure their clients that someone judged them to be competent. . . . But diplomas tell more than station "owners" and news directors and journalists tell. Wouldn't it be useful to know who these people are? Where they come from? What their angle is? And, especially, where they stand in relation to you? (p. 163)

Learning the identity of the owners of any given TV network (as well as magazines or newspapers) remains a challenge in this decade of constant and overlapping media mergers. It can require ongoing research to learn what combinations of business conglomerates (including banks, insurance companies, industries, publishers, and individuals) control which newspapers or television stations or which of these media groups are merging with still other media groups.

The Core Discovery Writing Application that follows is designed to introduce you to the technique of *news framing analysis*. A news frame is basically the layout, placement, and prominence given to any story in a publication. The editor, representing the policies and values of the publishers, owners, and advertisers, chooses the frame for any given story. The editor must decide what stories go on the front page, which will have pictures, which will be short, which long, which sensationalized, which minimized. Although journalists may write the stories, editors decide on the wording of the headlines, a comparison of two newspapers from the same day will show one how different stories are given different prominence and treatment.

When we conduct frame analysis we remove our attention from story content and bring our awareness to the influence of newspaper layout, story prominence, and headline language. Such analysis helps us to recognize which information one viewpoint will tend to emphasize, minimize, or omit. We then understand how all of these more subtle elements have a calculated effect on the reader. Frame analysis habits teach us to detach from the influence of the frame and gain a more objective perspective of the hidden viewpoint it expresses.

*The author is indebted to Ralph H. Johnson and William Dorman for their lectures on how to teach frame analysis.

Discovery Assignment

Observing How a Newspaper Frames Its Information

1. Each student should bring that day's newspaper to class for this exercise, which will involve small-group or a general class discussion. These newspapers could be *USA Today*, the *Wall Street Journal*, *The New York Times*, a local city newspaper, or an online newspaper.

2. Study the front pages of each. What subject was chosen for the main headline? How was the headline worded? What were the subjects of stories accompanied by pictures? What stories were given less prominence? What are the differences in depth of treatment?

3. Now study the inside pages. Which news stories are given less prominence in each? What stories do not appear in some papers? How do the editorials differ? How do the advertisements differ?

4. Choose one news item that appears in each newspaper to compare. Consider the following items:
   (a) How much prominence is given to this story?
   (b) Does the headline use words that suggest evaluations?
   (c) Does the story have balance, giving more than one point of view?
   (d) Are opinions and judgments mixed in with the facts?
   (e) Does the headline accurately reflect the article's data and conclusions?

5. What can you infer about the different values of each newspaper from the way in which each frames its information?

CHAPTER SUMMARY

1. Critical thinking means learning to recognize viewpoints and how they shape the content of any message.

2. Viewpoints—like assumptions, opinions, and evaluations—can either be consciously or unconsciously assumed.

BUILDING ARGUMENTS

VIEWPOINTS

Much has been said of what you term Civilization *among the Indians. Many proposals have been made to us to adopt your laws, your religion, your manners, and your customs. We do not see the propriety of such a reformation. We should be better pleased with beholding the good effects of these doctrines in your own practices than with hearing you talk about them, or of reading your newspapers on such subjects. You say, "Why do not the Indians till the ground and live as we do?" May we not ask with equal propriety, "Why do not the white people hunt and live as we do?"* (Old Tassel of the Cherokee tribe, 1777)

Exercise

1. What argument is Old Tassel refuting?
2. Given what you know about U.S. history from 1777 to the present, was Old Tassel's viewpoint heard or understood by the white men?
3. How can you explain that Old Tassel could describe and compare the two opposing viewpoints while the white men only saw their own?

---

3. We communicate best when we are aware of our own viewpoint and can understand and respect the viewpoints of others as well.

4. Writers shape their stories through their choice of a point of view; their choices include third person, first person, and multiple points of view. These viewpoints may be omniscient or humanly limited.

5. Unconscious viewpoints include the egocentric, ethnocentric, religiocentric, androcentric, and anthropocentric.

6. U.S. politics cannot be defined in terms of a simple left-to-right spectrum of viewpoints.

7. In alternative periodicals and on the Internet a far wider range of viewpoints is available than on U.S. network television and mainstream publications. Such viewpoints include third political parties, feminists, gays and lesbians, ethnic minorities, workers, environmentalists, religious groups, immigrants, and the political far right and left.

8. Periodicals can express viewpoints through images, words, and in the framing given to information. Framing decisions made by an editor can exercise a hidden influence over the reader.

CHAPTER QUIZ

Rate each of the following statements as *true* or *false*. Rewrite any false statements to make them true.

_____ 1. Viewpoints can be either consciously or unconsciously assumed.

_____ 2. To be exterior to one's own viewpoint is to see it objectively as just one viewpoint among many.

_____ 3. Egocentrism means being absorbed in one's personal viewpoint without being able to put oneself in other people's shoes.

_____ 4. Religiocentrism means believing one's country is morally superior to any other.

_____ 5. Nations tend to become more ethnocentric in wartime, righteously affirming their own national superiority while denouncing their enemies.

_____ 6. Authors only tell their stories from one viewpoint.

_____ 7. A *conservative* viewpoint is concerned with protecting personal freedom.

_____ 8. A *liberal* tries to avoid any drastic changes in the political, economic, or social institutions of a society.

_____ 9. In the United States some Republicans are more liberal than some Democrats and vice versa.

_____ 10. We communicate best when we ignore the viewpoints of others.

ADVANCED OPTIONAL WRITING ASSIGNMENT

Essay: Comparing and Contrasting the Reading Audience of Two Magazines

Magazines can target their readers not only by their interests and tastes, but also by their socio-economic groups. The publishers of such magazines may know more about you, the reader, than you do about them. On the basis of your zip code, they can predict how much disposable income you have, whether you rent or own your home, what kind of cars you like, and what brands of clothes you wear. They sell their advertising space to advertisers on the basis of their knowledge about their readers. This assignment is your opportunity to learn, from observing and inference, more about the viewpoint and intended audience of two magazines. A list of suggested magazines that you might study follows the directions given below.

In this essay you are to work with any two magazines of your own choice. Here are the parameters for your work:

1. *Form and length*: Essay of four typed pages.

2. *Topic*: Comparison of two viewpoints, their values and ideologies, as expressed in two magazines from the same month and year. Begin by taking notes on the issues they discuss, the ads they offer and for what products, and the general tone of the magazine: is it optimistic, paranoid, pessimistic, intellectual, bored, or superficial? Next, ask yourself, how much money would a person have to earn to consider buying the products advertised in this magazine. Or is this a magazine for those who would like to dream about having this much income? Is the appeal of the advertised products mainly that of impressing other people? What class values do they suggest? What might be the political views of its readers? What kind of travel or entertainment would be of interest?

3. *Thesis*: The thesis should represent the inferences you make about the type of readers who would buy this magazine. In your thesis statement generalize about their values, attitudes toward life, or anything else that you find to be distinctive.

4. *Evidence and support*: Give concrete examples from the materials you are using to illustrate your inferences and generalizations.

5. *Structure*: Comparison (how alike) and contrast (how different). One strategy is to describe the readers of one magazine or newspaper fully; a second would be to compare and contrast the main features in each. With the use of either strategy, both your thesis and conclusion should bring both periodicals together into one or several generalizations.

Suggested Magazines

If you choose not to use one of these magazines, do not substitute a trade magazine, glamor, travel, or sports, or teen magazine where the reading audience is obvious and easy to identify.

Atlantic Monthly, Harpers, U.S. News and World Report, Ebony, National Review, Newsweek, NY Times Magazine, New Yorker, Wired, The Smithsonian, Forbes, Better Homes and Gardens, Life, Vanity Fair, Talk, George.

READINGS

IF A TV NEWS ANCHOR TALKED STRAIGHT
Norman Solomon

The following excerpt is taken from a book entitled The Habits of Highly Deceptive Media. *Norman Solomon writes a nationally syndicated column, "Media Beat," distributed to daily newspapers. His viewpoint could be described as left liberal. He appears on radio and television and has written nine books on the media, including* Unreliable Sources: A Guide to Detecting Bias in News Media.

Warren Beatty's movie *Bulworth* has caused quite a stir. The plot features a successful politician who begins to speak with absolute candor—a notion so outlandish that it's apt to sound incredible.   **1**

But the scenario might seem even more far-fetched if the film's blunt protagonist were a TV news anchor instead of a U.S. senator. Imagine how astonished you'd be if you turned on a television and found a newscast like this one: **2**

"At the top of the news tonight—well, never mind. As usual, the script on my TelePrompTer is a scam. It's written to make money, not sense.   **3**

"Tonight, I'm supposed to say more about sorrow in the wake of the latest school tragedy. Yes, the sorrow is genuine. But the chances of your kid getting hit by a bullet at school are very small. During an average month in this country, four children die after being shot at school—while about 400 kids are killed by gunshots away from school grounds. Overall, poverty is a big risk factor.   **4**

"Meanwhile, television offers little to young people other than mediocre programs and a lot of commercials. As for TV news coverage: If it bleeds, it leads. But if it challenges social inequities, it rarely gets air time. We'd much rather run more footage of yellow police tape, grieving relatives and moralizing politicians.   **5**

"From the somber tone of some news stories, you might think that our network is appalled by violence. Don't make me laugh. This network adores violence. We broadcast plenty of it—in prime time—with guns often presented as the way to solve problems. And the conglomerate behind this network also owns a movie studio that puts out a continual stream of films glorifying murder and mayhem.   **6**

"During the last few years, White House conferences and newsmagazine covers have hailed scientific discoveries about the importance of the first years of a child's life. Duh. What did we think—that we could keep kicking kids around from year one and not have it affect them in crucial ways?   **7**

"While we've cheered the ascending stock market, children have seen us shortchanging their futures. I've been around long enough to know that lip service is meaningless compared to how we use our money.   **8**

"In many public schools, the students get little or no counseling—because, officials say, there's no money to hire more counselors. As for higher education, the Justice   **9**

Policy Institute points out that government decision-makers 'have been robbing our universities to pay for prisons we don't need.'

"Back in 1995—while media outlets were busy distracting us with endless reports **10** about O.J. Simpson—state governments made history by collectively spending more to build prisons than colleges. Prison construction went up by $926 million, to $2.6 billion, while university construction fell by $954 million, to $2.5 Billion. How's that for planning a future for our kids?

"The Census Bureau recently found that 11.3 million Americans under age 19 **11** had no health insurance (even though 92 percent of them had at least one working parent). Meanwhile, a study by the Center on Hunger, Poverty and Nutrition Policy at Tufts University calculated that more than 30 million Americans are going hungry—an increase of 50 percent since 1985.

"Today, among all the industrialized countries, the United States has the largest **12** gap between rich and poor. But we're not going to spend much time talking about such facts on our newscasts. Why should we?

"It's not rocket science: To watch out for my career, I've kept a lid on—playing it **13** safe—going along to get along with people more powerful than me. After all, I don't really work for journalists. I work for business executives. And the day I upset their apple cart is the day I'm looking at a pink slip with my name on it.

"Most of the news we put on television reminds me of the story about the em- **14** peror's new clothes—the royal guy parades around without a stitch on, but no one wants to take the risk of saying so out loud. Maybe you yell at your TV set. But believe me, the studio walls are just about soundproof. We can barely hear you. And we won't, unless you shout a whole lot louder."

"If a TV News Anchor Talked Straight" is by Norman Solomon, copyright © 1999, all rights reserved, used by permission of Common Courage Press.

Discussion Questions

1. How does the author contrast facts with network conventions, such as giving sensational prominence to school shootings?
2. Does he cite the sources for his facts? How could they be verified?
3. The whole excerpt consists of a series of contrasts between fact and the conventions of television news. Each example exposes the way in which network television exploits the sensational value of events and keeps its news coverage superficial. Which of the examples interested you most? Which did you agree or disagree with?
4. Why do you think that network news programs never explore the root causes of recurring problems, such as higher priorities placed on prisons rather than education, the widening gap between rich and poor in the United States, and the exploitation of violence for entertainment?
5. What value assumptions do you find in the author's argument spoken through the viewpoint of a fictional TV news anchor?

THE NATURAL WORLD
Rigoberta Menchú

The following excerpt is taken from the book I, Rigoberta Menchú: An Indian Woman of Guatemala. *The author, a young Mayan woman, received international attention when she received the Nobel Peace Prize at age 33 in 1992 for "her work for social justice and ethnocultural reconciliation based on respect for the rights of indigenous peoples." In this short chapter she offers the viewpoint of her own people with pride and simplicity.*

From very small children we receive an education which is very different from white 1
children, *ladinos*. We Indians have more contact with nature. We worship—or rather not worship but respect—a lot of things to do with the natural world, the most important things for us. For instance, to us, water is sacred. Our parents tell us when we're very small not to waste water, even when we have it. Water is pure, clean, and gives life to man. Without water we cannot survive, nor could our ancestors have survived. The idea that water is sacred is in us children, and we never stop thinking of it as something pure. The same goes for the earth. Our parents tell us: 'Children, the earth is the mother of man, because she gives him food.' This is especially true for us whose life is based on the crops we grow. Our people eat maize, beans and plants. We can't eat ham, or cheese, or things made with equipment, with machines. So we think of the earth as the mother of man, and our parents teach us to respect the earth. We must only harm the earth when we are in need. This is why, before we sow our maize, we have to ask the earth's permission.

Copal is a sacred ingredient for our people. We use it to express our feelings 2
for the earth, so that she will allow us to cultivate her. *Copal* is the resin of a tree. It has a smell like incense. We burn it and it gives off a very strong smell: a smoke with a very rich, delicious, aroma. We use the candle, water and lime a great deal in our ceremonies. We use candles to represent the earth, water and maize, which is the food of man. We believe (and this has been passed down to us by our ancestors) that our people are made of maize. We're made of white maize and yellow maize. We must remember this. We put a candle out for man, as the son of the natural world, the universe, and the members of the family join together in prayer. The prayers usually ask the earth for permission to plant our crops at sowing time, to give us a good harvest, and then to give thanks with all our might, with all our being, for a good harvest.

The prayers and ceremonies are for the whole community. We pray to our an- 3
cestors, reciting their prayers which have been known to us for a long time—a very, very long time. We evoke the representatives of the animal world; we say the names of dogs. We say the names of the earth, the God of the earth, and the God of water. Then we say the name of the heart of the sky—the Sun. Our grandfathers say we must ask the sun to shine on all its children: the trees, animals, water, man. We ask it to shine on our enemies. To us an enemy is someone who steals or goes into prostitution.

So, you see, it's a different world. This is how we make our pleas and our promises. It doesn't refer so much to the real world, but it includes part of our reality. A prayer is made up of all this. We make a definite plea to the earth. We say: 'Mother Earth, you who gives us food, whose children we are and on whom we depend, please make this produce you give us flourish and make our children and our animals grow . . .', and other things as well. Or we say: 'We make our vows for ten days so that you concede us permission, your permission, Mother Earth, who are sacred, to feed us and give our children what they need. We do not abuse you, we only beg your permission, you who are part of the natural world and part of the family of our parents and our grandparents.' This means we believe, for instance, that the sun is our grandfather, that he is a member of our family. 'We respect you and love you and ask that you love us as we love you'—those prayers are specially for the earth. For the sun, we say: 'Heart of the sky, you are our father, we ask you to give your warmth and light to our animals, our maize, our beans, our plants, so that they may grow and our children may eat.' We evoke the colour of the sun, and this has a special importance for us because this in how we want our children to live—like a light which shines, which shines with generosity. It means a warm heart and it means strength, life-giving strength. It's something you never lose and you find it everywhere. So when we evoke the colour of the sun, it's like evoking all the elements which go to make up our life. The sun, as the channel to the one God, receives the plea from his children that they should never violate the rights of all the other beings which surround them. This is how we renew our prayer which says that men, the children of the one God, must respect the life of the trees, the birds, the animals around us. We say the names of birds and animals—cows, horses, dogs, cats. All these. We mention them all. We must respect the life of every single one of them. We must respect the life, the purity, the sacredness, which is water. We must respect the one God, the heart of the sky, which is the sun. We must not do evil while the sun shines upon his children. This is a promise. Then we promise to respect the life of the one creature, which is man. This is very important. We say: 'We cannot harm the life of one of your children, we are your children. We cannot kill any of your creatures, neither trees nor animals.' Then we offer up a sheep or chickens, because we believe sheep to be sacred animals, quiet animals, saintly animals, animals which don't harm other animals. They are the most tranquil animals that exist, like birds. So the community chooses certain small animals for the feast after the ceremonies.

I, Rigoberta Menchú: An Indian Woman in Guatemala, edited and introduced by Elisabeth Burgos-Debray, translated by Ann Wright, Verso: London/New York 1984, pp. 56–58. Reprinted with permission of Verso Publications.

Discussion Questions

1. In the first paragraph she begins by contrasting the way in which white children and Indian children relate to nature. As you read, what insights occur to you concerning the environmental and social consequences of such different attitudes?

2. Why is it that she says they pray to ancestors, to animals, to the God of earth, the God of water, and the sun?

3. In one of the last sentences, she seems to be saying that Indians offer animal sacrifices of sheep or chickens while making the promise "We cannot kill any of your creatures. . . ." Why do you suppose, from her viewpoint, this action does not seem contradictory with a respect for life?

MY PARENT'S VILLAGE
Richard Rodriguez

This essay appears as the Introduction to the book Days of Obligation: An Argument with My Mexican Father *published in 1992. Many of Richard Rodriguez's writings deal with of the complexity of his viewpoint as an Anglicized Latino who holds an ambivalence for both cultures. Richard was born into a poor Mexican-American family in San Francisco, California. When he entered kindergarten, he was hardly able to speak in English. Yet he distinguished himself as a student, attended Stanford University, and eventually obtained a PhD. In the 1980s he became known for his opposition to bilingual education and affirmative action. Since the 1990's he has become a familiar face on the "Jim Lehrer NewsHour" where he continues to offer poetic visual essays on American life. This is another essay that can be best appreciated when read aloud.*

I am on my knees, my mouth over the mouth of the toilet, waiting to heave. It comes   1
up with a bark. All the badly pronounced Spanish words I have forced myself to sound during the day, bits and pieces of Mexico spew from my mouth, warm half-understood, nostalgic reds and greens dangle from long strands of saliva.

I am crying from my mouth in Mexico City.   2

Yesterday, the nausea began. Driving through Michoacan with a television crew, I   3
was looking for a village I had never seen. The production assistant fed a Bobby Brown tape into the car stereo.

We had been on the road since breakfast. I was looking for the kind of village my   4
parents would have known as children, the kind they left behind.

The producer was impatient—"What about that one?"—indicating with the disin-   5
terested jerk of his head yet another church spire, yet another configuration of tile roofs in the distance.

The British Broadcasting Corporation has hired me to serve as the "presenter" for   6
a television documentary on the United States and Mexico. A man who spent so many years with his back turned to Mexico. Now I am to introduce Mexico to a European audience.

For the last several years, I have told friends that I was writing a book about California and Mexico. That was not saying enough. I've been writing a book about comedy and tragedy. In my mind, in my life, Mexico plays the tragic part; California plays the role of America's wild child. **7**

The comedy of California was constructed on a Protestant faith in individualism. Whereas Mexico knew tragedy. **8**

My Mexican father, as his father before him, believed that old men know more than young men; that life will break your heart; that death finally is the vantage point from which a life must be seen. **9**

I think now that Mexico has been the happier place for being a country of tragedy. Tragic cultures serve up better food than optimistic cultures; tragic cultures have sweeter children, more opulent funerals. In tragic cultures, one does not bear the solitary burden of optimism. California is such a sad place, really—a state where children run away from parents, a state of pale beer, and young old women, and divorced husbands living alone in condos. But at a time when Californians are driven to despair by the relentless optimism of their state, I can only marvel at the comic achievement of the place, California's defiance of history, the defiance of ancestors. **10**

Something hopeful was created in California through the century of its Protestant settlement. People believed that in California they could begin new lives. New generations of immigrants continue to arrive in California, not a few of them from Mexico, hoping to cash in on comedy. **11**

It is still possible in California to change your name, change your sex, get a divorce, become a movie star. My Mexican parents live in a California house with four telephones, three televisions, and several empty bedrooms. **12**

How could California ever reconcile comedy and tragedy? How could there not have been a divorce between Mexico and California in the nineteenth century? **13**

The youth of my life was defined by Protestant optimism. Now that I am middle-aged, I incline more toward the Mexican point of view, though some part of me continues to resist the cynical conclusions of Mexico. **14**

Which leaves me with at least a literary problem to start with: How shall I present the argument between comedy and tragedy, this tension that describes my life? Shall I start with the boy's chapter, then move toward more "mature" tragic conclusions? But that would underplay the boy's wisdom. The middle-aged man would simply lord over the matter. **15**

No, I will present this life in reverse. After all, the journey my parents took from Mexico to America was a journey from an ancient culture to a youthful one—backward in time. In their path I similarly move, if only to honor their passage to California, and because I believe the best resolution to the debate between comedy and tragedy is irresolution, since both sides can claim wisdom. **16**

Yesterday, around noontime, I recognized it. We were driving along the two-lane Mexican highway and there it was—just off to the right, past a grove of eucalyptus—the village of childhood imagining. **17**

The production assistant radioed the other cars in our caravan to follow. We turned down a muddy road. **18**

The village was constructed around a central square. Passage toward the center **19** was narrow; just room enough for a van filled with our television equipment to pass. Most of the doors of the village were open. We saw few people about; those few more curious than friendly, more Indian than mestizo.

This is perfect, I kept saying from the back seat, perfect. **20**

I could imagine my father as a boy, dreaming of running away from just such a **21** village. I could see my mother's paradise—she of the sausage curls, the lampshade dress.

Ahead I spied a church on the south side of the square. There was a crumbling **22** fountain. Also a crowd of women in dark shawls. Market day? All the better.

The church bell was tolling. I don't wear a watch. It must be noon. **23**

And then I saw the reason for the crowd in the plaza—a tiny coffin was being **24** lifted from the bed of a truck. At the same moment, people at the edge of the crowd turned toward our noisy precession.

Bobby Brown panted Unh-oh-ahhhhhhhh from our rolled-down windows. **25**

A village idiot—a cripple—hobbled toward us, his face contorted into what was ei- **26** ther a grin or a grimace, his finger pressed against his lips.

Silencio. Silencio. **27**

"Turn off the music," the producer shouted. **28**

The production assistant radioed the rest of the convoy: Back up, back up. **29**

There was no room to turn. **30**

The van, the two cars shifted into reverse. Then my stomach began to churn. **31**

My vision of the Mexican village—yellow doors, wet gutters, children with preter- **32** naturally large eyes—floated backward. The crowd of mourners in the village square became smaller and smaller and smaller.

"Introduction: My Parents' Village," from *Days of Obligation* by Richard Rodriguez, copyright © 1992 by Richard Rodriguez. Used with permission of Viking Penguin, a division of Penguin Putnam Inc.

Discussion Questions

1. How would you contrast Rodriguez's style and world view with Rigoberta's style and world view?
2. What makes sense about beginning his essay with an act of vomiting?
3. How does he contrast the viewpoints of Mexican and American, Catholic and Protestant? How does he illustrate the consequences of these differences?
4. What makes sense about ending the essay with the film caravan's awkward intrusion into a Mexican funeral?

OBJECTIVES REVIEW OF PART II

When you have finished Part II, you will understand:

1. The concepts and complexities of assumptions, opinions, evaluations, and viewpoints.
2. How these concepts are mental experiences.
3. How they are problematical when confused with facts.
4. How a viewpoint frames information.
5. Some varieties of conscious and unconscious viewpoints.
6. And you will have practice in developing these skills:

   - Recognizing the mental formation of assumptions, opinions, evaluations, and viewpoints.
   - Checking for assumptions, reexamining opinions, evaluations, and viewpoints for their strengths and limitations.
   - Identifying underlying assumptions and value assumptions in discourse.
   - Separating opinions and evaluations from facts.
   - Recognizing opinions and evaluative words.
   - Using observing and inferring to identify characteristics of social and political viewpoint.
   - Analyzing the news frame.

PART III

Forms and Standards of Critical Thinking

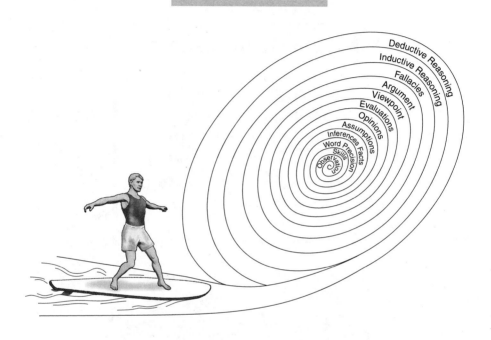

CHAPTER 9

Argument

What's a Good Argument?

Used with permission of Ben Dib.

Fighting may be easier than arguing, but even fighting can't proceed when viewpoints and ideologies become entangled. This chapter shows you how to disentangle before the fighting starts, or better, how to make fighting unnecessary. It will show you models of good and poor arguments in order to lead you toward writing arguments that are well constructed, well supported, and persuasive. In short, you will learn the skills of argument building, argument analysis, and argument evaluation.

You have been prepared for this chapter by studying the Building Arguments boxes, through many references to argument components, and some short argument writing assignments. When you finish studying this chapter, you will be able to prepare for the longer argument research assignments described in the Appendix of this book.

Discovery Exercise

Reading and Judging Arguments

Read the six points of view offered here on a controversial issue. Then answer the questions that follow in writing or class discussion.

Viewpoint 1

The NRA has always attacked us "politicians" for going after guns instead of criminals. Thankfully, the public has grown increasingly intolerant of this mantra. The challenge now for every law-abiding, peace-loving citizen is to use this momentum to enact a code of laws to better regulate and register all guns in this country. (Don Perata, California State Senator, supporter of legislation to ban assault weapons. Opinion Page, *San Francisco Chronicle*, 8/17/99.)

Viewpoint 2

Those who support law-abiding gun ownership feel that a war of misinformation is being waged against them. Citizens who support the Second Amendment know that it is they who are blamed for the criminal actions of a few. Every time some nut-case or felon wreaks mayhem, the media point their fingers at gun advocates, saying it is the proliferation of guns that leads to these events. But in times past, when almost every man owned a gun as a necessary tool for his survival, such wanton slaughter was rare. (Jarold Hayden, contractor and carpenter. Opinion Page, *San Francisco Chronicle*, 8/17/99.)

Viewpoint 3

Petition to Ban All Guns in the United States. We, the people, are tired of having our schools invaded by psychotic youngsters. We, the people, are tired of being robbed of our political leaders by some psychotic with a gun or rifle. We, the people, are tired of passing through metal detectors on our way to our courts, and our governmental buildings. We, the people, are tired of being victimized by gun carrying criminals. (Goodbye Guns Web site-www.Goodbyeguns.org.)

Viewpoint 4

I cannot imagine anyone suggesting that my wife and children are somehow "unworthy" of the most effective means of protection that a person can now have. Nor can I imagine that the safety of myself and my family should be potentially sacrificed in the name of "safer streets." . . . I love my family, and I will protect them as best I can, always. I think most Americans feel that way too. (Lee Miracle, *The Wolverine's [sic] The Newsletter of the Wayne County Michigan Militia.* 8/99)

Viewpoint 5

I find that just as criminals can be deterred by higher arrest or conviction rates, they can also be deterred by the fact that would-be victims might be able to defend themselves with a gun. Criminals are less likely to commit a crime if the probability is that a victim is going to be able to defend themselves increases. (John Lott, author of *More Guns, Less Crimes. Time* debate transcript, 7/1/98. Time.com)

Study Questions

1. How would you describe each of the viewpoints given here?
2. What is the basic pro or con position on gun control taken by each?
3. Take one viewpoint for analysis. What reasons are given to support its position?
4. Which do you find to be the most persuasive and why?

CRITICAL READING OF ARGUMENTS

Criticism of an argument should not begin until it has been given a fair and objective reading. Criticism can be guided by five questions.

As you will remember from the short discussion of critical reading in the second chapter, accurate comprehension must precede any criticism of the material. In reading arguments, maintaining openness is not always easy, especially when the arguments express values that differ from your own. It can require a lot of restraint to slow down those inner objections in order to make sure that you really understand what is being said. You may have found it a struggle to give a fair hearing to some of the viewpoints on gun control that opened this chapter. Yet critical analysis cannot be fair unless it is based on a careful and accurate reading of the material.

In this chapter you will be guided by some questions that will help you assess the arguments you read fairly. By using these questions, you will be able to make rapid evaluations of newspaper editorials, letters-to-editors, voter information pamphlets, and any other form of persuasive writing. The skills of critical analysis will also enable you to write more effective arguments yourself, whether in the form of simple letters of complaint, or in the longer argumentative essay assignments that appear in the Appendix of this book.

Here are the five guiding questions that will help you analyze any argument. After the analysis has been completed, you will know whether to accept the argument, to reject it or simply to suspend judgment for the time being.

1.   What viewpoint is the source of this argument?
2.   What is the issue of controversy that is being addressed?
3.   Is it an argument? Or is it a report?
4.   How is the argument structured in terms of reasons and conclusion?
5.   What are the strengths and weaknesses of this argument?

WHAT VIEWPOINT IS THE SOURCE OF THIS ARGUMENT?

Arguments represent the bias, interests, and objectives of a viewpoint.

This chapter's opening Discovery Exercise gave you an opportunity to apply what you learned in the previous chapter about the way in which viewpoint shapes content. You might have begun by first skimming through each argument, reading the names, titles, and affiliations of each speaker, then re-reading the argument in light of this information. From such clues, you might have been able to make inferences about the speaker's values, motives, and beliefs. You would have begun by asking the first question of critical reading: *What viewpoint is the source of this argument?*

WHAT IS THE ISSUE OF CONTROVERSY?

To assess an argument, we first must determine the issue that it addresses.

Arguments are based on *issues*. An issue is a controversial problem that evokes different arguments pro and con. Examples of topics that each contain many controversial issues are the death penalty, campaign

---

Issue: a problem of public concern that is subject to dispute, or debate.

Debate question: A question that states an issue, providing a focus for pro and con positions on that issue. Debate questions are expressed in neutral terms and often begin with the word "should."

---

finance reform, WTO policies, genetically modified foods, subsidies to tobacco farmers, physician-assisted suicide, universal health care. Daily newspapers continually offer information and opinions on new topics each of which can have many issues of controversy.

Every controversial topic generates many issues and many debate questions. The opening discovery exercise began with arguments pro and con on the issue of gun control. A close study of these arguments suggest they address one of two debate questions:

- Does the United States need stricter gun control laws?
- Should all private use of guns be banned?

You will note that the words used in these debate questions are free of biased connotations. The debate questions are prefaced by the words *does* and *should*. Such terms leave the question open. The phrase "stricter gun control laws" is also neutral, although one side might prefer to ask "Should the United States continue to put up with gun mayhem?" while the other might prefer "Should the United States government be allowed to take away our constitutional rights to defend ourselves?" The debate question, like a good polling question, needs to be carefully formulated in order to avoid slant or bias.

Both of these debate questions on gun control propose solutions to the problem of increasing gun violence: in one case the solution or stricter laws, and in the second, a ban. Sometimes a debate question is concerned with possible cause:

- What is the cause of gun violence in the United States?

Debate questions can also be less general than these three, dealing instead with specific aspects of the larger problem:

- Should there be stricter handgun (or assault gun) legislation?
- Should only U.S. police and military have access to guns?
- Does the United States only need better enforcement of its existing gun control laws?
- Should there be a ban on concealed weapons?
- Should gun manufacturers be sued?

Debate questions are clearly stated when we find pro and con arguments on newspaper editorial pages, or in magazines like the *Congressional Digest*. However, often the debate questions are not made explicit in arguments, requiring that we supply them from our own thinking. Consider this example:

> Americans receive almost 2 million tons of junk mail every year. About 44% of the junk mail is never even opened and read. Nonetheless, the average American still spends 8 full months of his or her life just opening junk mail. (*50 Simple Things You Can Do to Save the Earth*, Earthworks Press, 1989)

These two sentences comprise an argument around which debate questions could be posed, such as the following:

- Should junk mail be banned?
- Should consumers revolt against junk mail?

Class Discussion

Read each argument below and then, for each, (1) state its issue, (2) then formulate one debate question it would address:

1. Good cocoa cannot be made properly with water. Milk is essential.
2. Today millions of 40- and 50-year-old workers are being let go due to age discrimination. We need better enforcement of our discrimination laws.
3. Rail transportation carries at least ten times the number of people per hour as the average freeway. It should be obvious to city and state traffic planners that an investment in improved rail service is the best answer to traffic gridlock.
4. Republicans have been unfairly criticized for their vote against an international comprehensive test ban treaty. If we really want to eliminate the potential of a nuclear holocaust, the United States must continue to build up its military and thus persuade the rogue nations of the world to disarm.
5. Consumers who object to ATM fees can avoid payment by using the ATMs owned by their own banks.

IS IT AN ARGUMENT OR A REPORT?

Arguments and reports are each structured differently and have different objectives. We cannot analyze one according to the standards of the other.

ARGUMENTS AND REPORTS: DIFFERENT PURPOSES, STRUCTURES, AND STANDARDS

Report	Argument
Purpose: To inform	**Purpose:** To persuade
Structure:	**Structure:**
1. Data presented and/or explained.	1. Assertion of principal claim, thesis, or conclusion.
2. Support for data's accuracy and veracity offered in the forms of corroborating evidence independent studies examples expert testimony records surveys, polls, investigations statistics analogies	2. Support of reasons for conclusion. Includes all items on left as well as appeals to feelings and values such as justice, purpose, meaning, consistency, harmony, unity, responsibility
3. Different hypotheses that interpret data may be offered; one hypothesis might be supported with recommendations, but mood is one of openness.	3. Clearly committed position with effort to win agreement.
4. Summary of findings.	4. Summary repeats why this position is correct.
Standards:	**Standards:**
Objectivity Verifiability Reliability Rigorous scientific standards	Clarity about claims Adequate and convincing support Cogent reasoning Fairness of presentation

Although arguments and reports have very different objectives and forms, they can be mistaken for one another if their differences are not fully understood. Moreover, to add to the confusion, arguments can appear as reports in disguise, "reports" that only pretend to offer an unbiased perspective. (More will be explained about this hybrid later.)

The main purpose of **reports** is to offer information; this can be done offering facts and findings or relating and explaining events. Its objective is not to advocate an opinion, but to provide a balance of information about a situation. If the situation is controversial, the reporter should present arguments from all sides, but not favor one argument or another. In writing scientific reports, the author might make recommendations, but not advocate. **Arguments,** on the other hand, do advocate opinions; information may be used to explain an idea, to justify it, or to persuade others to accept that idea. Arguments are not supposed to be neutral but take a position and express a bias. Let's review their differences in these two examples:

Changing Our National Anthem

1. Rep. Andrew Jacobs, D-Ind., has introduced a bill that would change the national anthem to "America the Beautiful." He says that both musicians and the general public agree that "The Star-Spangled Banner" is just too difficult to sing correctly. However, although everyone might agree with him on this score, winning public support for the change might not be so easy. According to a recent telephone poll conducted by *Time* magazine, 67 percent were against this replacement.

2. I am in favor of replacing "The Star-Spangled Banner" with "America the Beautiful." Our present anthem, with its incredible range of octaves, makes it difficult even for an opera singer to perform. As a result, most of us can only hum along. Moreover, the content of the lyrics is antiquated, hard to remember, and warmongering. "America the Beautiful" spares us all these problems.

Discussion Break Question

1. The idea of changing our national anthem is a controversial proposal. Why is the first example a report on the subject and not an argument?

2. The second example is an argument and not a report. How is it significantly different? What makes it an argument?

A report can tell a story, as in the first example, "Changing Our National Anthem"; it can offer findings, interview supporters and detractors; and it can offer a hypothesis to predict a final outcome. Nevertheless, a report leaves the final conclusions up to the reader. Even when a report is made concerning a controversial subject, pro and con positions may be quoted, but the report itself remains objective.

> Today a House Representative introduced a bill that would change the national anthem to "America the Beautiful." He argued that both musicians and the general public agree that "The Star Spangled Banner" is just too difficult to sing. However, one of his esteemed colleagues opposed the bill, saying: "You'll never get that idea off the ground. We have enough trouble hanging

onto our traditions, and for better or worse, "The Star Spangled Banner" holds too many memories for us to part with no matter how hard it is to sing."

Another difficulty we face in making the separation between arguments and reports lies in the fact that *arguments are sometimes disguised as reports*. This practice is particularly prevalent in many of the so-called news magazines which offer news reports that are actually opinion pieces because of their slanted language, selection and emphasis of information. Here is a more light-hearted example of a report with a biased perspective:

Oh, Say Can You Sing It?

> To put audiences out of their pregame misery, many stadiums resort to canned versions of error-free performances of "The Star-Spangled Banner." . . . But a taped version takes away the thrill of victory and the agony of defeat inherent in every live performance, as well as the singers' inalienable right to get it wrong. (*Time*, February 12, 1990, p. 27.)

Class Discussion

Identify the following as either reports or arguments:

1. "The rate of population growth is slowing down, but the total numbers continue to rise. Each year, we add 80 million, the equivalent of the population of Germany, to the world total. In 2000, there will be more than six billion people in the world. During the 2060's, there may be 20 million." (*The Macmillan Atlas of the Future*, p. 24.)

2. "Conservation to some people once implied sacrifice, deprivation and lower living standards. Now even many of them recognize that *conserving energy is the cheapest, safest, cleanest and fastest way to avoid future energy crises*." (Sen. Alan Cranston, D-Calif., newsletter to constituents, November 1984)

3. "Too often the American economic system is looked upon as being a kind of battlefield between two opposing sides—consumers and the business/industrial community. This is a misguided but widely held viewpoint. *It is wrong to believe that consumers are at the mercy of business and industry . . . what is good for business is good for the consumer*." (Robert Bearce, "Free Enterprise," *Your Heritage News*, May 1984)

4. "California officials are poised this week to order a controversial $1 billion reformulation of gasoline that bans a clean-fuel additive that has contaminated water supplies, yet aims to ensure that smog does not worsen in return. The proposal before the Air Resources Board, which would increase the cost of gasoline by an estimated 6 cents a gallon, has drawn the opposition of most oil companies. . . . The octane booster MTBE has been added to California gasoline in large

volumes since the mid-1990's as part of a mandate to produce cleaner-burning gasoline that substantially cleans up auto exhaust. Reformulated gasoline has done more to reduce smog than any other regulation in recent decades, air quality official say. MTBE, though, rapidly leaded from underground water supplies, forcing some wells to be shut down. . . . MTBE has been linked to cancer in animal studies and carries a strong odor and taste." (*Los Angeles Times*, 12/6/99)

5. *Making Suicide Pay* "There is finally good news for Mr. Milo Stevens, the 26-year-old incompetent who botched a suicide attempt in 1977 during which he launched himself into the path of a New York Transit Authority subway train. He has won a $650,000 negligence settlement and is still free to try again." (*American Spectator*, March 1984)

HOW IS THE ARGUMENT STRUCTURED IN TERMS OF REASONS AND CONCLUSIONS?

A quick method for analyzing an argument is to disassemble its structure, first identifying its conclusion, and then separating that statement from the reasons offered to support it.

In the chapters that follow, you will be learning more about standards and forms for inductive and deductive reasoning. You will learn that with induction, arguments are structured in this manner:

Data

Data

Data

Data

Conclusion that interprets the data (a hypothesis)

In deduction we think with the syllogism:

Major Premise

Minor Premise

Conclusion

Arguments use both inductive and deductive reasoning. Simplified models such as these reveal their structure. We will learn more about how these models help us understand the rules of reasoning in the next chapter. For now we only want to focus on the two essential aspects of an argument: (1) what point is being made and (2) how this point is supported. If we can identify these two elements quickly in an argument, we can size up its structure. Thus, when reading the chapter's opening arguments on

Conclusion: A clear statement of what an argument intends to prove. This statement serves as the argument's thesis, final opinion, or judgment. It clearly shows the author's position on an issue.

Reason: Statements offered to explain, justify, or support the conclusion of an argument. Reasons can take the form of statements of facts, statistics, evidence, or reasoning. Any number of reasons can be offered to support one conclusion.

gun control, you may have sensed that some of them were better reasoned than others, but you may not have been really sure how to explain why or why not. Seeing arguments in terms of their structure can help us begin to do that. It also helps us write better arguments as well.

The next few pages offer a rapid method for recognizing these two elements in arguments; this method explains arguments as structures consisting of *reasons and conclusions*.

Both inductive and deductive arguments consist of both conclusions and reasons. As you will discover in the following chapters, the term *reasons* can be used to include both the premises of deduction and the factual evidence of induction and the term *conclusion* include inductive hypotheses as well as deductive conclusions. In both cases, separating conclusions from their reasons is not always easy. Yet we have to make this separation in order to determine what conclusion we are being asked to accept, and whether or not sufficient and adequate reasons given in its support. This portion of the chapter will offer exercises for practice in identifying and analyzing arguments in terms of their reasons and conclusions.

Identifying the Conclusion of an Argument

The key to understanding any written argument is to first search for its conclusion. Although the word conclusion is generally understood as a final summary statement in an argument, the conclusion functions more like the thesis of a composition, which sometimes appears first. In the formal reasoning of induction and deduction, a conclusion is the *last* step in a reasoning process:

Inductive

Yesterday I was happy singing.

Last week I was happy singing.

Every time in my life I sing, I feel happy.

Conclusion: Singing makes me happy.

Deductive

Singing makes me happy.

I am singing.
_____

Conclusion: I am happy.

In an argument, a conclusion is the bottom line of a decision, while the reasons are the evidence and thoughts that support this decision. Yet the problem remains that although we know our own conclusions, it is not always that easy to find them in the written arguments of others, especially since statements of reasons can look like very much like conclusions:

> Over the past two years, actions by local governments against homeless people have risen sharply. [reason] A 16-city study released last week by the National Law Center on Homelessness & Poverty found that cities are increasingly passing and enforcing laws that criminalize conduct associated with homelessness, such as sleeping, begging, and even sitting in public places. [reason] But passing laws against the homeless will not end homelessness. [conclusion] (Column Left/ Maria Foscarinis, Jim Scheibel, *Los Angeles Times*, 12/16/93)

Here the first statement is a conclusion supported by the second sentence. Yet, in this context, both of the first two sentences serve as reasons to support the final sentence, which is the author's thesis, or the argument's conclusion.

One secret for recognizing conclusions is to look for the signals of the so-called inference indicator words that precede conclusions.

Here are some examples of the way in which these words signal the conclusions of arguments:

1. *The truth of the matter is* that homelessness is the foe, not the homeless.

2. *In my opinion* homeless people must follow the rules just like anyone else.

3. *It all goes to show* we have to establish a bottom line of dignity and subsistence for all.

4. *Therefore* it's time we put an end to the problem of homelessness.

Identifying Reasons

Reasons are statements of opinion, propositions, premises, or statements of evidence offered to explain, justify, or support conclusions.

1. I am not in favor of accepting unsanitary and unregulated street camps for homeless people. [conclusion] Homelessness is not a

> **Conclusion indicator words** include: *therefore, so, in fact, the truth of the matter is, in short, it follows that, shows that, indicates that, suggests that, proves that, we may deduce that, points to the conclusion that, in my opinion,* and *the most obvious explanation is.*
>
> **Reason indicator words** include *because, first . . . second, since, for, for one thing, in view of the fact that, for the reason that, is supported by, for example, also.*

healthy choice. [reason] It's important to reinforce their own desires to get off the streets and rejoin society. [reason]

2. Instead of attacking homeless people, cities should attack homelessness. [conclusion] Grocery carts can be donated instead of repossessed by police. [reason] Day jobs can be provided instead of making begging a misdemeanor. [reason]

As is the case with conclusions, reasons are easier to identify when we supply them ourselves than when we read or hear them in someone else's argument. Yet, we need to identify the reasons in order to decide if they provide adequate and sufficient support for the conclusion. In the first argument given above, if only one reason had been offered, the support would have been insufficient. Both reasons together make a stronger argument, although both will need more expansion and development to be convincing, as would occur in a longer complete argument.

The task of analysis then begins by flushing out the reasons, which means looking for the conclusion first. In a short argument, once we identify the conclusion, the reasons are simply what remain.

Another technique for identifying reasons is to look for the so-called inference indicator words that often introduce reasons.

Here is an example of how such indicator words signal statements serving as reasons:

"I am in favor of sending the homeless to live in state-operated farm communities [conclusion] *first because* it would provide them with a healthier lifestyle than living on the streets [reason] *and secondly* farming would allow them to raise their own food and give them something constructive to do."

Exercises

Identifying Reasons and Conclusions

In the following statements, underline the conclusions and number the reasons:

_____ 1. Students who want well-paying careers upon graduation should train themselves to be computer programmers. Most cities are full of advertisements for computer programmers.

_____ 2. By the study of different religions we find that in essence they are one. All are concerned with revelations or breakthrough experiences that can redirect lives and empower them toward good.

_____ 3. I am not pro-abortion at all. I think that people nowadays use abortion as an easy form of birth control. It's also against my religion.

_____ 4. Guns kill people; that's why handguns should be banned.

_____ 5. Deep fat frying can greatly increase the calories of foods such as fish, chicken, and potatoes. Therefore, it is better to bake, boil, or steam foods.

_____ 6. "It is important that individual citizens equip themselves with a baloney detection kit to determine whether politicians, scientists, or religious leaders are lying—it's an important part of becoming a citizen of the world." (Carl Sagan)

_____ 7. America should put a freeze on immigration. Its first duty is to take better care of its own disadvantaged, poor, and unemployed.

_____ 8. America boasts about its wealth and prosperity as the world's most competitive economy. Yet its citizens are told there is not enough money for health care, environmental protection, for parks, safety nets for the poor and elderly, or public funding for the arts. Isn't there something wrong with this picture?

_____ 9. "If nothing happened, if nothing changed, time would stop. For time is nothing but change. It is change that we perceive occurring all around us, not time. In fact, time doesn't exist." (Julian Barbour, British physicist.)

_____ 10. I don't drink because alcohol gives me a brief high followed by a longer depression.

More on Distinguishing Reasons from Conclusions

Implied Conclusions. Now that we have learned how to dismantle arguments and separate reasons from conclusions, we are ready to confront a few final complexities. To begin with, *sometimes the conclusion is not stated at all but merely implied*. This was the case in many of the arguments presented in the opening of this chapter. Let's take this one by John Lott:

> I find that just as criminals can be deterred by higher arrest or conviction rates, they can also be deterred by the fact that would-be victims might be able to defend themselves with a gun. Criminals are less likely to commit a crime if the probability is that a victim is going to be able to defend themselves increases.

Here the most implied conclusion is basically: "I am opposed to more gun control legislation." In some arguments, however, the missing conclusion may be more difficult to formulate.

> It has been claimed that 80–90% of all cancers may be caused by environmental pollutants. The incidence of cancer is increasing now and will continue to increase. Governments spend millions of dollars researching causes of cancer, leukemia, and inherited disease, but simultaneously spend billions of dollars in [the nuclear power] industry that will directly propagate these diseases. (Helen Caldicott, MD, "Medical Implications of Nucelar Power." Helen Caldicott website.)

In this quotation, Dr. Caldicott only provides reasons which she claims to be facts. Yet her conclusion, which is implied, could take many forms, such as:

- Citizens should educate themselves about the medical dangers of nuclear power.
- Governments cannot be trusted to put the health of its citizens before those of industry.
- Citizens should demand that their governments stop supporting nuclear power and instead do all they can to prevent the environmental causes of cancer.

Conclusions in a Series

Sometimes a series of conclusions can be offered as reasons for an implied conclusion. In the following quotation, the speaker is offering a parody of the reasons given in the Preamble to the Constitution for the creation of that Constitution. These conclusions serve as his argument's reasons.

> The arms race does not form a more perfect union. The arms race does not insure domestic tranquility. The arms race does not provide for the common

defense. The arms race does not promote the general welfare. And finally, the arms race does not secure the blessings of liberty to ourselves and to our posterity. (Bishop Walter F. Sullivan, testimony before special congressional ad hoc hearings on the full implications of the military budget, January 1982.)

Conclusion at the Beginning

Conclusions do not always appear at the end of an argument: sometimes they appear in the beginning, as in newspaper headlines.

> *Mystery Traffic Jams*
>
> It's one of the great conundrums of commuting—you're sailing along a freeway at 50 miles per hour, when suddenly the brake lights go on in front of you and in seconds, you're down to stop-and-go. Creep, crawl. Creep, crawl. After a while, the traffic jam loosens, and you are back up to 40 or 50. (*San Francisco Chronicle.* 12/6/99, p. A17.)

Conclusion in the Middle

Sometimes a conclusion appears in the middle of a series of statements.

> Well drivers are not the only ones who wonder about this. In fact there are hundreds of people who get paid to study traffic jams. . . . *"It's the mystery traffic jam,"* [conclusion] says an airborne TV station traffic reporter . . . who spent the past 10 years watching the ebb and flow . . . from his lofty perch. (*San Francisco Chronicle*, 12/6/99, p. A17.)

As we stated earlier, when we want to analyze arguments, the first step is to identify the conclusion. Obviously, we need to determine clearly *exactly what the author is claiming to prove* before becoming involved in a reaction of agreement or disagreement. By identifying the conclusion, we know the author's exact position. We may agree or disagree with this position—but first we must know what it is. If we should mistake one of the reasons for the conclusion, we may find ourselves going off on a wrong track in our analysis and rebuttal. But once we have identified the conclusion, we can easily determine the reasons and isolate them for examination and evaluation.

The final advantage of learning how to identify conclusions and reasons is that it saves us the time of wrestling with poor arguments. When we have the skill to quickly survey and assess an argument's structure, then we can decide whether or not this argument is worth our serious consideration. Moreover, when we are writing our own arguments, we will know how to build them on a clear and aware foundation and thus demonstrate a visible structure of conscious thought.

Exercise

More Practice in Identifying Reasons and Conclusions

Analyze the following arguments by underlining the conclusions, or by supplying the conclusion in writing if it is only implied. Note that sometimes a conclusion may be part of a sentence, or the conclusion may be offered alone without any reasons attached.

_____ 1. Frequent snacks of high-energy food are not harmful to backpackers. Indeed, hikers are found to have more energy and less weariness if they snack every hour.

_____ 2. Broadcast television is not appropriate in the courtroom. The relentless pressure of the media threatens the balance between the First Amendment's press freedom and the Sixth Amendment's fair trial rights.

_____ 3. "Whereas birth is a cause for celebration, death has become a dreaded and unspeakable issue to be avoided by every means possible in our modern society. Perhaps it is that death reminds us of our human vulnerability in spite of all our technological advances." (Elisabeth Kübler-Ross)

_____ 4. "Do not stop thinking of life as an adventure. You have no security unless you live bravely, excitingly, imaginatively; unless you choose a challenge rather than competence." (Eleanor Roosevelt.)

_____ 5. There's nothing like the taste of fresh, hot brownies. Bake your own the easy way with Brownlee's Brownie Mix! (advertisement)

_____ 6. No doctor should have the right to allow a patient to die. No doctor is God.

_____ 7. Videos are a good way to entertain children. You can control what they watch, and there are many worthwhile films to choose from.

_____ 8. Since the 1920s, sperm counts have declined among American men. The underlying causes are uncertain, but the factors of stress and toxic chemicals are being considered.

_____ 9. If only 1 percent of the car owners in America did not use their cars for one day a week, they would save 42 million gallons of gas a year and keep 840 million pounds of CO_2 out of the atmosphere.

_____ 10. Because of their greater use of prescription drugs, women turn up in hospital emergency rooms with drug problems more frequently than men. (FDA consumer report)

Exercise

More Practice with Longer Arguments

Underline the conclusions and number the reasons given in the following arguments:

_____ 1. "People think non-violence is really weak and non-militant. These are misconceptions that people have because they don't understand what non-violence means. Non-violence takes more guts, if I can put it bluntly, than violence. . . . We are convinced that non-violence is more powerful than violence. We are convinced that non-violence supports you if you have a just and moral cause. If you use violence, you have to sell part of yourself for that violence. Then you are no longer a master of your own struggle. " (Cesar E. Chavez)

_____ 2. "An enigma presents itself which in all ages has agitated inquiring minds. How can it be that mathematics, being after all a product of human thought which is independent of experience, is so admirably appropriate to the objects of reality? Is human reason, then, without experience, merely by taking thought, able to fathom the properties of real things? In my opinion, the answer to this question is briefly, this: as far as the propositions of mathematics refer to reality, they are not certain; and as far as they are certain, they do not refer to reality." (Albert Einstein)

_____ 3. "This book is about a pervasive warlike atmosphere that makes us approach public dialogue . . . as though it were a fight. It is a tendency in Western culture in general, and in the United States in particular, that has a long history . . . It has served us well in many ways but in recent years has become so exaggerated that it is getting in the way of solving our problems. Our spirits are corroded by living in an atmosphere of unrelenting contention—an argument culture." (Deborah Tannen, Introduction to *The Argument Culture*, Random House, 1998, p. 3.)

_____ 4. "Imagine a wondrous new machine, strong and supple, a machine that reaps as it destroys. It is huge and mobile, something like the machines of modern agriculture, but vastly more complicated and powerful. Now imagine there are skilled hands on board, but no one is at the wheel . . . It is sustained by its own forward motion, guided mainly by its own appetites. . . . This machine is the subject of this book: modern capitalism driven by the imperatives of the global industrial revolution. The metaphor is imperfect, but it offers a simplified way to visualize what is dauntingly complex and abstract and impossibly diffuse—the drama of a free-running economic system that is re-ordering the world. (William Greider, *One World, Ready or Not, Touchstsone,* 1997, p. 11)

CORE DISCOVERY WRITING APPLICATION

Writing a Short Persuasive Argument: A Letter of Complaint

This assignment is about claiming your own power. It is a practical opportunity to stand up for something you believe in, to defend yourself or others against some injustice, and to initiate or restore communication with someone. This assignment will take the simple form of writing an effective argument in a short letter of complaint. In this letter, you will only need to describe what you consider to be an injustice and then communicate clearly what you want.

The Steps

1. Address the letter to a specific individual: to a friend, a parent, an elected official, a landlady, or a newspaper editor. In short, address it to someone who has some power to do something about the situation that concerns you. It may take some research to determine who this person is, but that is a key part of the assignment.

2. As you outline your letter, use neutral, descriptive, and non-blaming language to explain

   • what the situation is;
   • what is unfair about it;
   • what you want from the other person now.

   Your final paragraph should serve to keep the two of you connected by asking for reactions, a call, an appointment, or an agreement within a time frame that you suggest. (For instance, you might conclude by saying "I would like very much to hear what you have to say in response, and I would welcome hearing from you by phone or letter. If I have not heard from you within a week, then I will call you.")

3. Use reasoning and evidence to support your case. Make your conclusions straightforward and simple. Be clear about what you want but also remain courteous and respectful.

4. The length of your letter should be one to two pages typed; use a business letter format.

Writing Preparation

In choosing your topic, select a situation that feels genuinely unjust and unfinished to you, one that you have not been able to handle in a way that you would like. The more emotion you feel on the subject, the greater the challenge will be to formulate an effective, well-reasoned argument. When we feel very angry, sad, or apathetic, it is difficult to think clearly or make ourselves heard. Yet, writing and revising to work through your emotions can summon the clarity and power needed to present your case effectively. If at the beginning you feel overwhelmed by feelings, write them out or hit some pillows until you blow off steam. When you feel more collected, you can compose your argument. After you have finished your first draft, reread it, asking yourself whether your purpose was to make the other party feel ashamed, guilty, or wrong. Blaming the other person may make you feel better temporarily, but will not help you get what you really want. If we try to make people feel guilty, they will resist hearing what you have to say and not want to cooperate. Instead use neutral descriptive language; report what happened with objectivity. Be quite specific about how you see the problem and what you want the other person to do for you. Remain respectful both of yourself and the person you are addressing. Do not make demands or give ultimatums, but make requests that the other party can meet.

Peer Review

To follow up on this exercise in class, exchange your letter or essay with a partner and do the following:

1. Underline the conclusion and circle the reasons.
2. Answer these questions on a sheet to attach to your partner's work:
    (a) Which reasons clearly support, justify, or explain the conclusion? Which do not?
    (b) Are more reasons needed? Explain.
3. If any portion is not clear to you, circle it and ask your partner to explain it to you.

When you receive your work back, consider the comments. If you cannot agree with the critique, seek another partner and go through the same process verbally. If you find the criticisms helpful, revise your work accordingly.

Scoring for Letter of Complaint

1. Letter is addressed to a specific person who has the power to do something about the situation. 10 points

2. Organization is simple and clear, describes the situation, the complaint, and is requesting a specific action. 10 points

3. Request made that is clear and possible to fulfill. 10 points

4. Conclusion is clear; sufficient and adequate reasons are given. 10 points

5. Topic chosen involves challenge of self-control. (Not a routine letter as returning a defective product.) 20 points

6. Language does not blame, make guilty, or cause defensiveness. 10 points

7. A final connecting statement is made, requesting, but not demanding, a response within a stated period of time. 10 points

8. No distracting errors of punctuation, sentence structure, spelling. 20 points

WHAT ARE THE STRENGTHS AND WEAKNESSES OF THIS ARGUMENT?

To make a list of standards for judging the strengths and weaknesses of an argument would mean reviewing most of the material covered in the past several chapters of this text. These six questions summarize such standards:

1. Are the reasons adequate to support the conclusion?

2. Are there any hidden assumptions in this argument?

3. Are any central words ambiguous or slanted to incite prejudice?

4. Are there fallacies in its reasoning? (You will learn how to use this question in the next chapters.)

5. Is any important information or evidence omitted?

6. Is any information false, contradictory, or irreconcilable?

All but the final three questions have already been discussed in this text. Fallacies will be explained in the next chapters. What follows now is an explanation of the last two questions.

Detecting Missing Information

Crucial information can be purposely or inadvertently omitted in an argument or a report. A critical thinker pays attention to what is missing.

Detecting missing information is not so difficult when we are familiar with the basic facts about a subject. In the Appendix of this text, you are offered a choice of assignments involving argument analysis. As you complete the research required by this assignment, you will gradually accumulate a sense of all the facts that this controversy entails. As this knowledge increases, so will your ability to judge how different arguments use this information: which information is given the most emphasis, which is minimized, and which is omitted altogether.

Detecting missing information in arguments on unfamiliar subjects, however, is not so easy. Here we have to depend on our ability to observe, read carefully, and ask questions. Looking for the most important missing elements under three categories—missing definitions, missing reasons and conclusions, and missing information—can be helpful.

These categories, which also function as standards, have already been discussed in this text. The importance of definitions was stressed in the second chapter, where you learned how their absence confuses argumentation and general understanding. In this chapter, you have learned how to look systematically for reasons and conclusions. In your work on inferences, you encountered the problems caused by pertinent missing information. Nevertheless, it takes active concentration and thinking to detect the absence of crucial information. Oddly enough, such awareness begins by just noticing when we are confused. Our first reaction might be to blame ourselves; however, sometimes the confusion is due to missing information. Consider, for instance, the following advertisement:

> *Our highest rate for five years. Guaranteed.* Now for a limited time only you can lock into our highest rate for up to five years with an Iowa Federal five-year C.D. If you're retired, think about what this could mean. You won't have to worry about dropping interest rates for a long time. And it's FSLIC insured. Completely safe.

If you don't feel tempted to rush right down to invest, you might realize that the actual interest rate is never mentioned. And here you are being asked to "lock into" it for a period of five years! Thus, it may be true after all that you won't have to worry about dropping interest rates: you may spend more time regretting missing the higher ones. To forget to read carefully for missing information may result in later being unhappily reminded of the adage "Let the buyer beware."

Class Discussion

What questions would you ask of the writers or speakers who said the following?

1. *Weight problem?* You've tried every kind of diet, exercise, pills and if you do lose a pound or two, it's back in no time. Everybody offers their advice, which is even more frustrating. Your weight problem is taking over your life. At our Health Spa, health specialists will work to take your weight off for good. Call us. Toll free. Georgetown Hospital Health Spa.

2. You are invited to my twenty-first birthday party. Prizes will be given for those who arrive Friday evening exactly at 7:07 P.M. in the Sigma Delta Dormitory lounge.

3. He hit me first.

4. Oh, honey, by the way, my former boyfriend came into town today and gave me a call.

5. I have to go out now and take care of some business.

6. The government should subsidize tobacco growers more than it does. If American tobacco growers are unable to meet production costs, they will be forced to quit growing tobacco, and we will be entirely dependent on foreign sources. Besides, tobacco farmers are making lower profits today than they were ten years ago.

7. Our religion forbids sexual misconduct.

8. *Nuclear Power Is Cheaper Energy for Tomorrow*
   "The price of electricity from fossil fuel plants will always depend heavily on the cost of fuel, which is unpredictable. The cost of nuclear fuel is more stable; its supply is within our control; and there's plenty of it. As a nuclear plant's construction costs are paid for, its lower fuel costs *hold down* the price of the electricity. Eventually, the lower cost of fuel more than makes up for the higher cost of construction." (advertisement, U.S. Committee for Energy Awareness)

Detecting False or Contradictory Information

A final topic in this chapter concerns how to approach information or claims that you might suspect to be false. As critical readers, we cannot hold court hearings to prove lies, but we can remember to watch for any discrepancies or contradictions that might suggest the presence of lies. *A sound argument that is both true and well reasoned does not contain contradictions.*

Of course, distinctions exist between contradictions based upon insufficient thinking (as discussed in "Inconsistencies and Contradictions" in Chapter 11) and contradictions denoting an imperfect structure of lies. However, for our purposes as critical thinkers, determining the difference is not usually the issue. What matters is to remember that any argument or claim that contains contradictions is unsound. At best, such an argument has to be placed on a kind of "mental hold," awaiting further evidence or study.

This same policy applies not only to discrepancies found in arguments but to inconsistencies between words and action, between evidence and denials, between different testimonies, between differing accounts of facts, between claims and consequences, and between what we are told and what we know to be true. In any case, no discrepancy ever appears with the label "discrepancy" marked clearly on it; its detection results only from alert perception and thinking.

READING

WOMAN AWARDED $25 MILLION IN SUIT AGAINST IMPLANT MAKER

A jury yesterday awarded $25 million in damages to a Houston woman who said she 1 developed an auto-immune disease from ruptured silicone-gel breast implants made by a subsidiary of Bristol-Myers Squibb Co.

In the biggest damage award against a manufacturer of silicone implants to date, 2 the Harris County jury ruled in favor of 45-year-old Pamela Jean Johnson in her suit against Medical Engineering Corp.

Previous cases have gone to trial in federal court. In April, a federal judge in San 3 Francisco upheld a $7.3 million damage award to a woman whose implant ruptured.

Johnson, who had sought $64 million in damages, charged that silicone leaked 4 from two sets of implants, attacked her immune system and caused various illnesses, forcing her to undergo a partial mastectomy.

Bristol-Myers Squibb, whose stock tumbled $3.875 to close at $67.375 on the 5 New York Stock Exchange after the ruling, said it will appeal the verdict.

Johnson smiled broadly and then broke into tears as Judge Don Wittig read the 6 verdict to a packed courtroom. The judge will issue a final ruling on the jury's verdict on January 11.

The trial, which began December 10, was the first in Texas for a product liability 7 case against a maker of silicone-gel breast implants.

Johnson's lawyer, John O'Quinn, told reporters that the verdict sent a message to 8 breast-implant manufacturers. "The message is you have to put safety first, ahead of profit. Human health is too important to market products that have not been proven to be safe," he said.

Similar lawsuits have been filed across the country by women who say they have **9** suffered illnesses stemming from breast implants that ruptured.

An estimated 2 million implants have been provided to 1 million to 1.3 million **10** women in the United States since they were introduced in the mid-1960s by Dow Corning Corp., a joint venture of Dow Chemical Co. and Corning Inc.

The implants were taken off the market in January after the Food and Drug Ad- **11** ministration called for a voluntary moratorium. The FDA has since limited their use to cases involving women with medical needs who take part in scientific studies. The action followed reports that the implants have caused arthritis-like diseases, debilitating skin conditions and possibly cancer.

Johnson received her first implants in 1976. They ruptured and were removed in **12** 1989. Another set of implants made by Medical Engineering was inserted but removed the same year when they ruptured. A third set, made by another company, was removed this year, according to her attorneys.

Johnson's attorneys charged that the Bristol-Myers subsidiary, which began mak- **13** ing silicone implants in 1972, told doctors that silicone gel would not leak from the devices even if the shell ruptured and that it would not harm human tissue.

The company's attorneys argued that the implants met all applicable federal reg- **14** ulations and that Johnson's illnesses were related to drugs she took, mainly for heart problems.

From *San Francisco Chronicle*, December 24, 1992. Used with permission of Reuters.

Study Questions

This article was written in 1992. In 1999 Dow Corning agreed to settle an amount of 3.2 billion dollars with 176,000 women who claimed they had been injured by silicone gel breast implants.

1. Assuming the information given in this article is accurate, list the contradictions you find in the actions and the statements of the FDA and Dow-Corning.
2. Were there any contradictions in the behavior of the defendant?
3. Do you think the women who sued the breast-implant manufacturers might have been more cautious about using these products if they had been trained in critical thinking skills?
4. Discuss any consumer or political situations you are aware of that involved injury law suits in which the defendants claimed they were injured because they accepted information later shown to contain discrepancies, contradictions, and falsehoods.

CHAPTER SUMMARY

• The critical reading of arguments is an active endeavor that requires involvement, interaction with questions, and evaluation.

2. The questions asked in the critical reading of arguments are

    (a) What viewpoint is the source of this argument?
    (b) What issue of controversy is being addressed here?
    (c) Is it an argument or a report?
    (d) How is the argument structured in terms of reasons and conclusions?
    (e) What are the argument's strengths and weaknesses?

3. The analysis of arguments in terms of their reasons and conclusions applies to both inductive and deductive arguments. Reasons include data, evidence, and premises, while conclusions include those deductively drawn as well as hypotheses.

4. The conclusion of an argument is the last step in a reasoning process. However, it may be stated at any time during an argument or not at all.

5. Reasons support conclusions. They may be generalizations that could function as conclusions in another context. Once the argument's main conclusion is uncovered, the reasons offered in support becomes clear.

6. Arguments state and defend a claim. Usually they also attempt to persuade. Arguments disguised as reports slant the facts and language toward a bias.

7. Reports that only relate events or state facts cannot be analyzed as though they were arguments.

8. An issue is a selected aspect of a topic of controversy upon which positions may be taken either pro or con. Issues are stated in neutral terms often beginning with the word *should* and ending with a question.

9. The following questions can serve as guidelines for analyzing the strengths and weaknesses of arguments:

    (a) Are the reasons adequate to support the conclusion?
    (b) Are there any hidden assumptions?
    (c) Are any central words ambiguous or slanted so as to incite prejudice?
    (d) Are there fallacies of reasoning?
    (e) Is any important information missing?
    (f) Is any information false or contradictory?

READINGS

WE CAN END THESE TRAGEDIES
Stop the Guns, Take Responsibility
Michael Bond

This is the first of two arguments pro and con on the issue of gun control. They both were written shortly after the shooting that occurred at Columbine High School in

Littleton, Colorado in April 1999. The author of this first argument is Michael Bond the former president of an international energy company, and a former member of the National Rifle Association. He lives in Littleton, Colorado. Read each argument carefully, then analyze each separately, following the questions that follow the readings.

The tragedy in Littleton Tuesday is so grotesque and unimaginable that no words are sufficient. There is no weeping, no sorrow, no anger that suffices. **1**

We cannot bring these precious children back. There can be no comfort for their parents. There is no way to comfort the dead. **2**

We can pray, hug each other, discuss the causes. But no amount of prayer saved these children. America has had plenty of "dialogue" about violence. We've had enough talk of "closure" after carnage. We've done enough "reaching out" to killers, the deranged, the pathogens of our culture. **3**

The only way not to perpetuate evil is to stop it. We know the instruments of the Columbine High School massacre, and of the school slaughters elsewhere that preceded it, and of those to come. With fanatic fervor, the gun manufacturers flood our streets with automatic weapons like those that killed my neighbors' children here in Littleton. Politicians and the gun lobby pass laws to sell armor-piercing bullets, the better to kill the policemen who risk their lives every day to protect us from each other. **4**

For months, the National Rifle Association and the Republican majority in the Colorado Legislature have been pushing three pro-gun bills. One allows anyone not already a felon to carry a concealed gun. The second voids nearly all local gun-control laws. A third prohibits suits against gun manufacturers. **5**

All three were on their way to passage and signature by the new Republican governor, Bill Owens. They have been temporarily shelved but will no doubt be resurrected. Even as the Columbine children were being gunned down in the school library, one bill's sponsor, Republican House Majority Leader Doug Dean, insanely argued that if teachers had been carrying concealed guns, this tragedy would have been avoided. The NRA will stage its national convention later this month in Denver. In the convention hospitality suites, where executives from Ruger, Colt, Remington and all the other merchants of death will pour the free liquor and plan how best to buy the next Congressman, the argument will be that guns didn't kill these children. I invite these men to walk the blood-soaked, brain-spattered halls of Columbine High. I invite them to explain their actions, and the capital gains behind them, to the parents of the dead and wounded. **6**

A few years ago a shooting in a high school, a single death, would have been unimaginable. Now we have had eight school slaughters in less than 40 months. There have been hundreds of lesser incidents—none of which would have been imaginable a generation ago. **7**

As a former NRA member, a gun owner and hunter, and as one who deeply fears for the future of his country, I suggest: **8**

- Ownership of handguns and assault rifles, except by law enforcement and the military, be prohibited.

- Advertisement of guns, as with other forms of killing such as tobacco, be prohibited in print and other media.
- Ownership of other guns (rifles and shotguns) be limited to those who have passed a licensing program and mental and criminal background tests, and who can show a need for ownership.
- Political contributions by gun manufacturers, their consultants, or other related parties be prohibited.
- All media, including the Internet, be controlled for the level of violence allowed. We spend billions to restrict trace chemicals in our children's foods but scarcely a penny to govern what goes into their minds.
- Parents be prosecuted for the acts of their children. In today's self-obsessed, emotionally illiterate America, this may be the only way parents can be induced to consider how their actions affect their children and the nation.

We can rid our country of this horror. We do not have to stand around like cattle   9
while our children are killed. We must begin by getting rid of guns.

Used with permission of *San Francisco Chronicle*, April 26, 1999.

TRAGEDY AND FARCE IN LITTLETON
Thomas Sowell

Thomas Sowell is a Senior Fellow at the Hoover Institution at Stanford University, a former professor of economics, and a newspaper syndicated columnist.

The shocking killings of school children in Littleton, Colo., has once more illustrated   1
Hegel's view that tragedy is often followed by farce. Immediately after the shooting, loudmouth talk show hosts and demagogic politicians have leaped front and center, proclaiming a need for more gun control.

Where do the gun controllers think the 200 million guns in this country are go-   2
ing to go if they pass more gun control laws? Will these vast numbers of firearms simply vanish into thin air? Will criminals turn in the tools of their trade to police?

Or does it matter what will actually happen? Is it enough for the gun controllers   3
that they will have "made a statement" and taken a stand on the side of the angels—regardless or what the consequences might be?

The most likely consequence of stronger gun control laws is the same as the con-   4
sequences of international disarmament agreements in the 1920s and 1930s: Those who are no threat to anybody will be disarmed shifting the balance of power in favor of those who remain armed and dangerous. It took a Second World War for us to learn that lesson internationally, but we have yet to learn it domestically.

There is no excuse for the widespread ignorance and demagoguery on gun con-   5
trol that hold sway in politics and the media, after a massive study by John Lott of the

University of Chicago has shown convincingly that armed citizens deter violent criminals. His study, "More Guns, Less Crime." shows that an increase in licensed gun ownership is almost invariably followed immediately by a decline in violent crime in the county where these licensing laws have been relaxed.

When an airplane crashes, costing hundreds of lives, does anyone suggest banning planes? When thousands die in automobile accidents, does anyone suggest banning cars? **6**

No one asks about how many lives have been saved by guns in the hands of law-abiding citizens defending themselves and their families against the violent criminals that liberal gun controllers allow to walk the streets. Lott's study is one of the few that even addresses that question. **7**

The very phrase "gun control" is a farce. Laws controlling guns have been on the books for years. The only meaningful question is whether those laws are to be tightened and how. What the so-called gun control advocates want is a sweeping ban on the legal possession of guns by law-abiding citizens. **8**

Typical of the demagoguery on this issue is the phrase "assault weapons"—a term that nobody has been able to define legally with any precision. Instead, ugly-looking weapons have been banned by name, while equally deadly ones that don't look so bad are still sold. **9**

All weapons are for assault. That is what makes them weapons, whether they are guns, bows and arrows or boomerangs. Because they are capable of assault, they are also capable of deterring assault, usually just by being pointed at a potential assailant. They are a lot better for protection than phoning 911 and waiting for the police to arrive. **10**

In short, guns save lives and guns take lives. If we are serious, then we can talk about how many lives are involved each way and what can we do to continue to deter violent criminals, while reducing the deaths caused by accidents or crime. **11**

Column appearing in *West County Times*, May 3, 1999. Used with permission of Thomas Sowell and Creators Syndicate.

Questions for Discussion or Written Analysis

Working alone or with a partner or group, write an outline that analyzes the argument of either reading that you select. Do this by answering each of these questions:

1. What is the debate question addressed by both arguments? Write down your statement of the debate question at the top of a page. Now begin your analysis by making two separate outlines that answer the six remaining questions.
2. What is the viewpoint of the writer? What are his qualifications and affiliations?
3. What is the final conclusion of the argument? Quote or summarize.
4. What reasons does the writer give in support of this final conclusion? Number and summarize each, using quotes as needed.
5. Do you find any key words that are ambiguous (not clearly defined) or words with connotations that convey hidden evaluations, bias, or prejudice? Quote and discuss each.
6. Is any essential information missing in the argument?
7. Discuss any information you find that seems to be false, inconsistent, or irreconcilable.

CHAPTER 10

Fallacies

What's a Faulty Argument?

Reprinted with permission of the Copley News Service, San Diego. Copyright 1985 San Diego Union.

If the senator depicted in the cartoon on this page were to use a mass mailing to convince his constituents of an absurdity, how do you think the argument would read? What signs suggest the defense of a lie? What clues reveal an unfair argument? How do you know when public consent is being "manufactured" or manipulated? We will consider some of these questions as we study these fallacies of reasoning.

You will find twenty fallacies discussed in this book. Each has a different name to illustrate a different reasoning error, an error that may be accidental or may be intentional. Each sidesteps the work of constructing a well-reasoned argument. Since remembering all of these fallacies at once can be difficult, they will be presented to you in two segments, beginning with this chapter. To further aid your understanding and recall, they have been classified into four major groups. Three of these groups, called the fallacies of trickery, are presented in this chapter. The fourth group, fallacies of inductive reasoning, appears at the end of Chapter 11.

Fallacy comes from the Latin word *fallacia*, which means deceit or trick.

A fallacy is a statement or argument that presents itself as soundly reasoned when it is not.

Discovery Exercise

Recognizing Fallacies

Environmental zealots threaten four industries in California—agriculture, mining, timber, and construction—and the people will no longer tolerate what the zealots are doing to the ability of Californians to make a living. The zealots can shut down the American economy. (Rep. William Dannemeyer R-Calif.)

1. Does this statement appeal to your own bias or not?
2. Is the argument fair and well reasoned?
3. What exactly is right or wrong about the argument?
4. If you are familiar with some fallacies, do any of the following apply: poisoning the well, slippery slope, bandwagon, slanted language, appeal to fear, hasty generalization, use of ambiguous wording?

FALLACIES OF TRICKERY

Since the times of the Greeks, types of fallacious reasoning have been catalogued and given names for study and identification. When we learn the names and characteristics of these fallacies, we gain three advantages:

- we learn more about the rules for good reasoning;
- we avoid using them ourselves;
- we are not influenced by arguments that contain them.

The effectiveness of fallacies lie in their pseudo-reasoning, their use of hidden appeals to our emotions, and their ability to distract our attention from their weaknesses. On the surface their argument may appear plausible, but a closer study reveals confusion or intentional manipulation. Fallacies fan the smoke of fear, pity, or prejudice; they distract from the issue, play with language, and assume what they should prove. In this chapter you will learn how to avoid using—or being influenced by—the following fallacies of trickery of language, emotions, and distraction:

Trickery with Language

- Vague Ambiguous Words
- Misleading Euphemisms
- Prejudicial Language

Trickery with Emotions

- Appeal to Fear
- Appeal to Pity
- Appeal to False Authority, Popular Wisdom, and Bandwagon
- Appeal to Prejudice: Personal Attack and Poisoning the Well

Trickery with Distraction

- Red Herring
- Pointing to Another Wrong
- Straw Man
- Circular Reasoning

FALLACIES INVOLVING TRICKERY WITH LANGUAGE

Three fallacies seek to persuade by relying on deceptive language. They are called the fallacies of word ambiguity, misleading euphemisms, and prejudicial language.

Fallacious arguments can be based on an inept use of words or a purposeful selection of words that are vague, ambiguous, and prejudicial in connotation. When the selection is intentional, such words can ward off questioning and hide the weaker aspects of an argument. Three varieties

CHART OF FALLACIES OF TRICKERY
COVERED IN THIS CHAPTER

Trickery with Language

1. **Word Ambiguity:** Seeks to gain an advantage in an argument by using vague or undefined words.
2. **Misleading Euphemisms:** Hides meaning or being evasive in an argument by creating words that make a less acceptable idea seem positive or neutral.
3. **Prejudicial Language:** Attempts to persuade through the use of loaded words that convey a bias.

Trickery with Emotions

4. **Appeal to Fear:** Seeks to persuade through arousing fear.
5. **Appeal to Pity:** Seeks to persuade through arousing pity.
6. **Appeal to False Authority:** Seeks to persuade by citing a fake or inappropriate authority.
7. **Appeal to Bandwagon:** Seeks to persuade by appealing to the wisdom of a popular momentum.
8. **Appeal to Prejudice:** 1.) **Personal Attack:** Attacks a person's character on matters irrelevant to the argument of another or to issues raised by that person. 2.) **Poisoning the Well:** Seeking to prejudice others against a person, group, or idea so that their arguments will not be heard on their own merits.

Trickery with Distraction

9. **Red Herring:** Instead of proving a claim, it diverts attention into other issues.
10. **Pointing to Another Wrong:** It distracts attention from an admitted wrong doing by claiming that similar actions went unnoticed and unpunished.
11. **Straw Man:** It misrepresents or caricatures an opponent's position; then refutes the false replica created: It also attacks a minor point in an argument, then claims this maneuver invalidates the whole argument.
12. **Circular Reasoning:** It assumes what it is supposed to prove by re-asserting a conclusion as though this claim needed no supporting reasons or by repeating the same conclusion in different words.

of fallacies of language that attempt persuasion through deceptive word use are called the fallacies of word ambiguity, misleading euphemisms, and prejudicial language.

Word Ambiguity

> **The fallacy of word ambiguity** occurs when a central word with several meanings is left vague or undefined. The reader is left to assume or guess what meaning is intended.

A good argument makes careful and conscious word choices. It wants to persuade, but to persuade fairly by making its language as clear as possible. A faulty argument tries to gain an unfair advantage by using words that might confuse others and lead them to agree with a claim they don't fully understand. The fallacy of ambiguity uses vague or ambiguous words for this purpose:

> "We should treat *drug* use as a private right that harms no one but the user."

Here, what is meant by *drug* is left undefined. The reader trained in critical thinking will stop and wonder if the author means hard drugs or just medications and stimulants. If such a question cannot be answered, then the argument is not worth more study. Consider some further examples:

> And where are all the jobs that welfare mothers are supposed to get? Even a burger joint wants you to work evenings and weekends, times when there is *virtually no* childcare.

Here, the words *virtually no* are ambiguous. Does this mean that childcare is scarce or that it is unreliable or unavailable? A better argument would mention the prohibitive costs of child-care for a single mother on a minimum wage. The writer may want to convey that single working mothers need more, and not less, assistance, but she makes her argument ineffective by not using her words with precision.

> School prayer will not help as long as students are taught immorality, e.g., basic condom training. Returning to teaching students *basic morality* will help. If public schools insist on teaching immorality, parents must have the choice to send their children to a school that teaches *fundamental morality*.

Here, the writer defines *immorality* as public education in the use of condoms. However, it is not clear what the writer means by "basic morality" or "fundamental morality." Does she mean to remain chaste from fear of pregnancy? That sex should be only for procreation in marriage? The Golden Rule? A thoughtful reader will not be able to proceed beyond these questions.

Class Discussion

The ambiguous words are in boldface in the material that follows. Discuss why they are ambiguous and how this affects the argument.

1. Writing in the February 15, 1993, *Forbes* magazine, Leslie Spender and *NR* Senior Editor Peter Brimelow came up with what is still, to the **great disgrace** of academic economists, the only **serious** estimate of affirmative action's cost to the economy: some $115 billion in **direct and indirect expenditures** in 1991. (Editor, *National Review*, March 1995)

2. A recent summary of over 200 studies, published in 1990, offers convincing evidence that the observation of violence, as seen in standard everyday television entertainment, does affect the **aggressive behavior** of the viewer. (Leonard D. Eron, Harvard School of Public Health, panel discussion, May 1992)

3. There is something intrinsically **anti-American** about the way Al Gore flagellates the U.S. over its environmental policies. (Rush Limbaugh)

Weasel words are words that appear to say one thing when in fact they say the opposite, or nothing at all. (Weasels are predators who steal into the nests of other animals, make small holes in their eggs, suck out the insides, and leave the hollow eggs standing.)

Advertisers often choose ambiguous words to lure buyers into projecting their own desires and hopes on advertising claims. For advertisers, the advantage of this approach is that they can later deny responsibility for the buyer's interpretations. Such ambiguities may take the form of such hollow words such as *helps*, as in "Helps prevent cavities," or *as much as*, as in "Saves as much as 1 gallon of gas." A few other familiar weasel words appear in the following ads:

1. Save on typewriters from a leading maker! SALE! SALE! $200! Made to sell for $495! (Here the word *sale* only tells you the store has something to sell. Perhaps it was overpriced in the first place.)

2. Women's coats—$54. A $75 value. (The word *value* is relative. Perhaps the store bought the coats especially for the sale and set the previous value arbitrarily.)

Cartoon by Kirk Anderson. Used with permission of Kirk Anderson.

3. These blouses have the *feel* of silk. (That an item has the *feel* of silk does not mean it is silk.)

4. Come see our sheepskin-look seat covers. (Remember, they are not saying that the items *are* sheepskin.)

Class Discussion

Identify the ambiguous words in the following sentences by underlining the words and stating how they function for persuasion:

1. All ingredients in this ice cream are natural and nutritious.

2. These pies are made from locally grown cherries and have that old-fashioned country taste.

3. Ace aspirin provides relief up to eight hours.

4. Ida Insect Spray helps fight mosquitoes.

5. Tony's Tonic helps you feel and look ten years younger.

6. You can save as much as 1 quart of oil a day.

7. Wear a jacket that has the feel of leather.

8. Cults enslave people.

9. The federal government has too much power.
10. You should be willing to do anything for love.

Misleading Use of Euphemisms

> **Euphemism** comes from the Greek word meaning good voice, or to use words of good omen. Euphemisms are inoffensive words used to maintain a level of social formality. All of us know what is meant when we hear *remains* for corpse or *bathroom* for toilet. **Misleading euphemisms,** however, do mislead us for they are deliberately created for the purpose of being evasive and manipulative.

Ordinary euphemisms allow us to avoid taboo subjects and maintain polite social interactions. Misleading euphemisms manipulate and deceive us; they are the staples of commercial and political propaganda. They can make the bad seem good and the good seem bad.

Misleading euphemisms perform the tasks of promoting and lying (also known by the euphemism of "public relations.") Such euphemisms camouflage actions, things, or events that could appear unacceptable in light of professed values. They intentionally distort truth and meaning. In George Orwell's novel *1984*, misleading euphemisms are grimly parodied in his creation of a state built on the slogans "War Is Peace," "Freedom Is Slavery," and "Ignorance Is Strength." Here the government ministries include the Ministry of Truth (which produces lies and propaganda), the Ministry of Love (which practices imprisonment, brainwashing, and torture), and the Ministry of Peace (which concerns itself with war).

The term "double-talk" is also used to describe misleading euphemisms, as when politicians speak of "disinformation" to describe lies planted in media releases, "contributions" for taxes, "investment" for spending, and "deficit reduction" for tax and spending increases. Public relations employees, both inside and outside the U.S. government, specialize in creating euphemisms. In the U.S. military, lists of official euphemisms are distributed to military officers for their use in relating to the public. Sometimes euphemisms serve as code words to sanitize military actions that might raise uncomfortable questions and offend our professed national values. Here are some examples or misleading euphemisms:

Misleading Euphemism	Conventional Term
Ziploc or body bags	plastic container for corpses
acceptable losses	number of our own soldiers expected to die in battle

Misleading Euphemism	Conventional Term
friendly fire	shooting our own soldiers by mistake
police action	unproclaimed act of war
unconventional warfare	combat methods violating Geneva Convention agreements
combat stress disorder	nervous breakdown of soldier from battle trauma
antipersonnel weapon	explosive with a casing designed to maim people in a large area
hot zone	area exposed to nuclear fallout or biological or chemical agents
rigged or amped out	describes soldier who has taken narcotics or amphetamines
black ops	officially unsanctioned activities such as kidnapping or assassinating enemy leaders

Class Discussion

1. In the novel *1984*, George Orwell predicts the development of a totalitarian government that will purposefully corrupt language in order to control thought. Do you feel that the use of political double-talk deceives Americans, or do you think these expressions are generally recognized with humor?

2. In the last decade a number of new words have been introduced into our language. Those who regard these words as ludicrous label them "politically correct." These new word substitutions proclaim the values of feminists, environmentalists, and the progressive left. Read the list and explain how they differ from the list of neutralized terms. Where are the euphemisms in this list?

Conventional Term	Politically Correct Term
paper	processed tree carcasses
eggs and milk	stolen nonhuman animal products
white skin	melanin impoverished
lumberjack	tree butcher
housework	unwaged labor
housewife	domestic incarceration survivor

> **The fallacy of prejudicial language** is an attempt to persuade through the choice of slanted or loaded words that convey a bias. The implication in such a tactic is that the words chosen only describe what is real and true.

Prejudical Language

In earlier chapters, we discussed slanted words and the way their word connotations convey positive or negative feelings. Let us now see how word connotations function as persuaders in the following exercise. Study the two following headlines:

- <u>Cultic America: A Tower of Babel</u>. They tend to be small, scattered and *strange*.
- Crying for the <u>Thugs</u>

1. What are the connotations of the underlined words, and what slant do they lend this information?

2. What associations do you have with the words cultic, Tower of Babel, and thugs?)

3. Compare the two headlines to the translations below. Do they give the same message?
   - New Religions in America: A Crisis of Separation. They tend to be small, scattered, and unfamiliar.
   - Haitian Leader Weeps During Funeral for His Police.

4. Read the following quotations and circle the words that could create a bias:
   (a) "Cultic America: A Tower of Babel"
       "If the cult watchers are to be believed, there are thousands of groups out there poised to snatch your body, control your mind, corrupt your soul. Witches' covens, satanic rituals, Krishna consciousness, fanatic fundamentalists, black and white supremacists, New Age cosmic crazies—few are armed but most are considered dangerous. They'll seduce you and fleece you, marry and bury you." (*Newsweek*, March 12, 1993)
   (b) "Crying for the Thugs"
       "Lieutenant General Raoul Cedras stood with top aides at a funeral yesterday in Port-au-Prince for 10 Haitian policemen and civilian security agents who were killed two weeks ago in a shootout with U.S. soldiers. . . . Cedras repeatedly wept during the service, burying his face in his hands." (*San Francisco Chronicle*, 10/6/94)

(c) "Activism Drowns Out Academia"

"Camping illegally in front of the chancellor's building, with six-star students engaging in a hunger strike, UC Berkeley Ethnic Studies students came across as such know-it-alls, it's surprising they think they need an education. If you thought ethnic studies was not a scholarly field, but a platform for angry kids with an ax to grind, you wouldn't walk away disappointed." (Debra J. Saunders, *San Francisco Chronicle*, 5/7/99)

(d) "America's dirty little war in El Salvador has so far been limited to thin transfusions of money and material as well as moral support for murderous regimes." (*Mother Jones*, June/July 1983)

(e) "During his career, Saddam Hussein has transformed himself into numerous expedient political persona, including a revolutionary, a party henchman, an Iraqi strongman, a devout Moslem, and a Pan-Arabish messiah. His mercurial ruthlessness, combined with his domestic terror tactics, his xenophobia, and his political acumen have enabled him to become the absolute ruler of Iraq." (*Congressional Quarterly*, 1991)

Some of the words you circled in these examples may contain evaluations that you agree with, but they do require acceptance of a bias. In these quoted excerpts, no supporting reasons are provided (although, to be fair, some reasons appear in the full arguments from which they are excerpted). Within these quotations, persuasion is attempted chiefly through evaluative word choices. The task for the critical reader is to separate word choice from word meaning and thus detach from the emotional power of word connotations. Having said all this, however, one has to allow that journalists will often use highly connotative words in order to grab their readers' attention. In this age of hype and hucksterism, when ideas need to be shouted in order to be heard, even writers who know how to construct sound arguments in neutral language may feel they have to turn the volume up to be heard.

Class Discussion

Which of these arguments rely primarily on slanted words in order to be persuasive?

1. "Is there anything more ridiculous in the news today than the protests against the World Trade Organization in Seattle? I doubt it. These anti-WTO-protesters—who are a Noah's ark of flat-Earth advocates, protectionist trade unions and yuppies looking for the 1960's fix—are protesting against the wrong target with the wrong tools." (Thomas L. Friedman, *N.Y. Times Service*, 12/2/99)

2. "Spud fans tell us that Spud Cigarettes has proved itself in the real smoking "tough spots" . . . where smoking is hardest and heaviest . . . because Spud's moist-cool, clean taste never fails. That's why so many are switching to Spud as a constant smoke. Have you discovered how Spud's mouth-happiness increases tobacco enjoyment?" (Advertisement in *The Literary Digest*, 5/6/1933)

3. "Wall Street money managers, investment bankers, and insurance companies are drooling over the prospect of trillions of dollars of Social Security revenue being funneled into the stocks and bonds markets and generating billions of dollars in fees, commissions and profits. *The Wall Street Journal* reported its anticipation of 'the biggest bonanza in the history of the mutual fund industry.' " (Bed Hudnall, Business Manager, Engineers & Scientists of California, Local 20, San Francisco.)

4. "Government and Greed Destroy the Forest"
   "Look at the balance sheet. Clearing the Amazon produces hardwoods which are essential for nothing. Dams flood the forest to generate electricity to make aluminum for throw-away cans. Iron ore is dug out of the ground to be sold at throw-away prices. Diseased cattle stroll about farting their greenhouse gases into the atmosphere to pander to a particular dietary preference in the cities. Rivers are polluted with deadly mercury to produce gold that is smuggled out through Uruguay to languish in the vaults of Swiss banks. The mass of the people of the Amazon are corralled into poverty, fearing for their lives. Indigenous people are persecuted to the verge of extinction. Can it really be for this that the greatest forest on earth is being made to disappear?" (David Ransom, *The New Internationalist*, May 1991)

FALLACIES INVOLVING TRICKERY
WITH EMOTIONS

> **Fallacies based on emotional trickery** appeal to fear, pity, popular wisdom, false authority, and prejudice.

A sure sign of a poor argument is one smothered in a sauce of evaluative words. Word connotations convey evaluations that can quickly trigger emotions and invite a conspiracy of bias. Once a reader is influenced by them, he or she may not even notice a lack of sound supportive reasons.

Fallacies of emotional trickery seek to persuade by exploiting our weaknesses instead of inviting conscious consideration and consent. They can be insidiously effective in attracting interest and clouding rational study of an issue. All of this does not mean that any argument that arouses emotion is fallacious. Usually we are not motivated to formulate arguments unless aroused by feelings. To be sane on many topics is to feel clear anger, indignation, or grief. However, a fallacious argument avoids or omits sound reasoning and depends primarily on arousing reactions such as fear, pity, greed, hatred, and malice.

Emotional Appeals to Fear and Pity

Appeals to fear are the staples of commercial advertising. The following examples may serve as familiar reminders:

1. "What your best friends won't tell you . . ."
2. (Picture of a frantic traveler who has lost her traveler's checks.) "Next time be safe with our fast call-in service."
3. (Picture of man in hospital bed in a state of shock after seeing his bill.) "Did you think one insurance coverage plan was enough?"
4. (Picture of burglars breaking into a house.) "Are you still postponing that alarm system?"

Class Discussion

The use of an appeal to anger has not been considered fallacious in the tradition of argumentation; apparently such an appeal is assumed to be legitimate since anger usually arouses people from complacency. Listed here are some appeals to fear, pity, and anger. Read the arguments and decide which you think are appropriate calls for fear, anger, or pity, and which are appeals based on exaggerations. Again, your judgments may depend on your personal values. Defend your answers.

1. "Berkeley, California has become a police state as police presence has increased from 12 cops to 40 to 60 on any given weekend night. Cops are everywhere, on foot, bicycle, motorcycle, undercover, and in both marked and unmarked cars. The police mobile substation, a menacing blue bus with smoked windows, cruises the area for added effect. Sinister jump squads, followed by a paddy wagon, keep tensions high by making quick arrests." (*Copwatch Report*, Fall 1992)

2. "Loretta Fortuna wants out. Sickened by odors wafting from the red toxic pools near her home, angered by the political battleground she's had to maneuver, grief-stricken by two miscarriages within a year and perpetually worried for the health of her two small sons, she

finally had enough. Fortuna has spent the past year waging a campaign on behalf of her family and neighbors to get a leaking waste dump near her home cleaned up. But now she has decided to move elsewhere, a disheartened casualty of a frustrating battle. The Gloucester Environmental Management Services landfill . . . is one site among 1,175 toxic nightmares nationwide waiting to be cleaned up." (Robert J. Mentzinger, *Public Citizen*, May/June 1990)

3. These are our beliefs. During your life you can accept them or not. If you do, you will be saved. Otherwise you will go to hell for eternity.

4. "'We are God in Here . . .' That's what the guards in an Argentine prison taunted Grace Guena with as they applied electrical shocks to her body while she lay handcuffed to the springs of a metal bed. Her cries were echoed by the screams of other victims and the laughter of their torturers." (Appeal letter from Amnesty International USA)

5. "Smokers know they are plague victims and suspect they may be carriers. So they puff on their butts behind a closed office door, and indulge their health-nut friends by abstaining from cigarettes during the dinner hour—which without a nicotine fix, seems to stretch on for days." (Richard Corliss, *Time*, April 11, 1994)

6. "Alarmed by a comet's violent collision last year with the planet Jupiter, scientists warned yesterday that speeding asteroids and comets could inflict far more damage on Earth than previously thought, perhaps even disrupting the climate and causing millions of deaths. . . . Among the ideas presented were the use of super-powerful spacecraft and well-timed nuclear explosives to pulverize potential invaders from outer space or to nudge them away from their Earth-bound orbits. . . . The meeting . . . is sponsored by the U.S. Department of Energy, NASA, and the Air Force Space Command." (*San Francisco Chronicle*, May 23, 1995)

7. "The consequences of the Democratic health care plans will be ruinous, tax increases, job losses, less money in your pocket to spend the way you want to spend it." (Political advertisement, 1994)

Appeal to False Authority

This is an argument whose chief or only support is a false or questionable authority. The argument is not upheld by sound reasons but by the alleged endorsements of individuals without credentials or expertise on the issue.

Appeal to False Authority

The appeal to false authority has five variations beginning with an appeal to a popular public figure:

- *Buzz Bonanza*, star of stage and screen, prefers Tasty Toothpaste.
- *The president of the United States* says that brushing your teeth once a week is enough.

Here Buzz Bonanza is clearly not a toothpaste expert. Yet, for those who adore him, such a discrepancy might be overlooked. Advertising psychology research has shown that if a consumer can be manipulated into equating a positive figure with their product, then the consumer will assume that owning the product will also mean owning the positive attributes of the figure. Thus we have so many product testimonials by film stars, athletes, and even former politicians. Admittedly, this ploy is both entertaining and highly effective.

An appeal to a false authority can also refer to authorities in the form of vague entities:

- *Doctors say* you should brush your teeth every day with Florident.
- *Experts agree* you should use an electric toothbrush.
- *Inside sources* at the White House say the president doesn't like to brush his teeth.

An argument can also place false authority in tradition, popular wisdom, and the bandwagon. Here are some examples of the appeal to the authority of tradition:

- If you want to be a real American, own a Ford and drink Coca-Cola.
- You have to go to law school. Every oldest child in this family for the past four generations has gone to law school.

False authority can also be claimed to reside in popular wisdom, or the infallible knowing of the masses:

> If you have any doubts about the status of American health care, just compare it with that in the other industrialized nations! *Ask anyone you know* from a foreign country where they would most like to be treated if they had a medical emergency. Ask them which country is the envy of the world when it comes to health care. (Rush Limbaugh)

> It is not fair to blame the U.S. government for not signing the international treaty to destroy all existing land mines. *Ask anyone in the world* about the U.S. record on human rights and about all it has done to alleviate human suffering.

Another variety of false authority is called the *bandwagon fallacy*. If a herd is headed in one direction, that must be the right direction. The bandwagon fallacy promises the exhilaration of joining in a march of irrepressible instinctive wisdom. It offers all the comfort of joining the crowd and coming over to the winning side. Here are some examples of bandwagon appeals:

(a) Don't vote for Proposition 9. The polls show it will lose 5 to 1.
(b) Everyone else does it; why can't I?
(c) Last year over 10 million people switched to Buckaroo Trucks!
(d) Buddy Springs! America's Beer!
(e) Join the Pepsi Generation!

In all these five appeals to false authority, you will notice the conclusions are unsupported by reasons. What appears instead is the pressure to trust bogus authorities or to trust the wisdom of conformity. While a good argument lays all its claims and proof on the table, an appeal to false authority suggests that one should not trust one's own reasoning but depend on some vague others who know better.

However—and this is most important to remember—the existence of the fallacy of false authority *does not mean that a good argument should avoid using and quoting authorities at all.* On the contrary, authorities with relevant expertise provide excellent support for reasons and are used routinely to lend them more credibility.

> The first comprehensive study of the geographic skills of America's youngsters shows they are "getting the message that they are part of a larger world," Education Secretary Richard Riley said yesterday. "We're not at the head of the class yet, but it's a good start," said National Geographic Society President Gilbert Grosvenor in releasing the results of National Assessment of Educational Progress tests. Nearly three-quarters of the 19,000 students tested in the first national study of geographic knowledge showed at least a basic understanding of the subject, the Education Department reported. (Associated Press, 10/18/99)

In this example you will notice that each claim is attributed to an authority. If you, as the reader, are in doubt about the qualifications of Richard Riley and Gilbert Grosvenor to offer opinions, at least you have been given enough clues for further research. However, when you decide to use authorities to support your own argument, admittedly it is not always easy to determine their suitability and reliability. So-called experts may have credentials, but you must also research their track records; furthermore, you might want to know whether other authorities agree or disagree with them. In summary, authority citation can offer impressive support for an argument, but assessing the qualifications and appropriate expertise of the authority requires experience and research.

An **authority** is someone who has expertise in a particular subject. Authority expertise depends on his or her credentials, accomplishments, reputation for competence and reliability, and peer recognition. *A confirming quotation from an appropriate, reputable, and unbiased authority can provide excellent support for claims made in an argument.*

Class Discussion

Explain how the following statements are different kinds of appeals to authority. Which are fallacious? Which legitimate?

1. My doctor says that I should take a nap every afternoon.
2. A ten-year study by leading scientists has found that Tuff toothpaste prevents decay in four out of five cases.
3. Buzz Bonanza, star of stage and screen, drives a Macho Motorcycle.
4. I read it in the newspapers.
5. Interviewer: "Do you feel national parks should be privatized?"
   Woman: "My husband says they should."
6. "Women have babies and men provide the support. If you don't like the way we're made you've got to take it up with God." (Phyllis Schlafly)
7. For over a quarter of a century our teachers have been committed to the idea that the best way to teach students is to withhold criticisms and build self-esteem. But both Alfred Binet, the father of intelligence testing, and Sigmund Freud, the father of psychoanalysis, described the development of self-criticism, which we learn from the criticisms of others, as the essence of intelligence.
8. "One out of every five Americans experience a mental disorder in any given year, and half of all Americans have such disorders at some time in their lives but most of them never seek treatment, the surgeon general of the United States says in a comprehensive new report." (Robert Pear, *New York Times*, 12/13/99)

Appeal to Prejudice: Personal Attack and Poisoning the Well

Prejudice is a complex feeling: a mixture of envy, fear, and resentment. A person who feels prejudice cannot maintain the openness necessary for clear reasoning. Arguments that seek to incite prejudice avoid the hard work of constructing a sound argument; the hope is that once the prejudice virus is transmitted, those infected will not even notice the argument's weaknesses. There are two basic fallacious appeals to prejudice. The first makes a direct attack. The second "poisons the well" or contaminates a whole environment so that it will be distrusted and avoided.

Personal Attack. This fallacious argument is familiar when political campaigns turn negative and opponents begin to trash one another. The fallacy of personal attack occurs when arguments are not considered on

---

The fallacy of personal attack (also known as the *ad hominem*) represents an argument that attacks a person's character instead of addressing what the person actually has to say. This tactic is unfair when the person's character is irrelevant to the substance of the argument.

The poisoning the well fallacy does not attack but contaminates. It incites prejudice against a person or group so that they will be distrusted, avoided, feared, or shunned.

---

their own merits, but their authors are attacked instead. Personal attacks distract with hand-grenade explosions; they leave smoke screens that hide the lack of a sound refutation. The fallacy of personal attacks may include frontal attacks, such as abusive name calling, or rear attacks, such as innuendo. Such arguments are fallacious because they distract attention into irrelevant issues.

- "I won't talk about what this female candidate has to say or refer to her by name except to say it rhymes with 'rich'" (Barbara Bush speaking of Geraldine Ferraro)
- "The late H.L. Hunt was one of the battiest billionaires Texas ever produced. The old trigamist (one better than a bigamist) used to crawl around his Dallas mansion spouting ultra-conservative drivel." (Molly Irvins, *Ft. Forth Star Telegram*)
- You're just a jerk! You can't tell me anything!

Poisoning the Well. This fallacy is another variety of personal attack. When any amount of poison is poured into a well, all its water becomes contaminated, so that no one dares drink from the well. Thus when a person, idea, or cause is discredited at the outset, people could be made to feel aversion, rather than neutrality and openness. This fallacy has four variations.

The first variety of poisoning the well uses a string of words with negative connotations:

- Of all the screwball, asinine, muddle-headed letters I have ever seen from this newspaper's readers, the one from Detroit advocating the legalization of drugs takes the cake.
- Every criminal, every gambler, every thug, every libertine, every girl ruiner, every home wrecker, every wife beater, every dope peddler,

every crooked politician is fighting the Klu Klux Klan. Think it over. What side are you on?

Poisoning the well can also take subtler forms when it uses innuendoes:

- This president, who has never worn a uniform, announced today that he would send our troops overseas.
- Senator Smith, known as the "waste-fill senator" because of the tons of propaganda he mails from his office, made a speech in favor of increasing immigration quotas before Congress today.

This latter example is a fallacious argument because even if Senator Smith deserves a bad reputation for his mailings, he might be able to make a well-informed, persuasive speech on immigration quotas. If it could be shown that he bought extravagant amounts of paper from paper mill lobbyists who exploited immigrant labor, such information might make this criticism relevant. But as this argument stands, his "waste-fill" reputation is beside the point. It only serves to incite prejudice against what he might have to say.

Poisoning the well can be directed not only against individuals but also against ideas or collective groups:

- The news media has been sounding the alarm lately, loudly decrying the terrorists, tax-evaders, and assorted huddled masses poised to overrun us. These racist and alarmist stories are in sync with the message from Washington. (Kelly Gettinger, *Progressive*, August 1993)

Poisoning the well can serve to discredit and thus ward off any argument a person or group might be prepared to offer:

- You are a man. I don't want to hear what you have to say. You can't understand what women feel.
- Bought politicians and PR firms will be trying to persuade you that handing our national parks over to private corporations is good for all of us. Don't let yourself be conned.

Class Discussion

Which of the following are examples of poisoning the well?

1. Those who object to irradiated foods are picky purists whose ideas run counter to common sense.

2. *"Three to Tango"* "Here is a sex soufflé that falls flat. . . . This is the kind of movie that TV stars do when they're on hiatus and trying to squeeze one in . . ." (Neve Campbell, *Rolling Stone*, 11/99)

3. "Today's teenage girls are aware of the outside world, and it makes them fearful. They are a generation that knows more but does less." (Jancee Dunn, *Rolling Stone*, 11/99)

4. "'Many companies charge drivers more than twice as much as other companies for identical insurance coverage . . .' That's the word from the California Department of Insurance following a new State survey on automobile insurance rates." (Ad from 20th Century Insurance)

FALLACIES USING THE TRICKERY OF DISTRACTION

The fallacies of red herring, pointing to another wrong, straw man, and circular reasoning use the ploy of distraction.

Four other fallacies—the red herring, pointing to another wrong, using a straw man, and circular reasoning—can be classified in many ways, but what they all have in common is a lack of support for their arguments. All use different tricks to diverting attention away from the weakness of their arguments. Some, like red herring and pointing to another wrong, distract attention from the issue raised to another issue. The straw man fallacy falsely represents the opponent's position, pretends this depiction is accurate, and then destroys the misrepresentation. Circular reasoning distracts through the illusion of support. Each of these fallacies can be difficult to identify because they can really succeed in distracting us. Yet they are fun to study.

Red Herring

> **The fallacy of red herring** does not offer reasons to support its conclusion but diverts attention to other issues that are irrelevant. The term *red herring* comes from a ruse used by prison escapees who would smear themselves with herring in order to throw the dogs off their own scents.

The red herring fallacy diverts our attention from the question at hand and throws us off track into irrelevancies. Four red herring tactics can be identified.

1. This first example shows a typical red herring sidetracking maneuver:

   Marijuana smoking is not all that harmful. I would feel safer in a car with a driver under the influence of marijuana than one under the influence of liquor any day.

Here, the claim that needs to be defended is "marijuana is not all that harmful." However, instead of offering support for this claim, the writer diverts our attention by comparing the relative safety of a driver under the influence of marijuana to one under the influence of alcohol. Such a comparison leads off and down a side trail into discussions of their relative effects on reflexes and perception. Meanwhile, the claim about marijuana not being all that harmful is forgotten or incorrectly assumed proven.

2. A red herring can be the most difficult of all fallacious arguments to detect because it can actually prove a claim but not the claim originally raised.

    Guns are not America's major problem, or even high on the list of our problems. Cars, cancer, accidents in the kitchen all kill far more people than guns do. It is not *guns* that we should be frightened of but the effects of poverty, lack of education, a judicial system that sends criminals and psychopaths back out into the streets. Guns are not a solution, but they are not the problem, either!

    In this case, the argument might prove that guns do not cause the majority of American fatalities. Further evidence could be provided to support his or her claim that the problems of gun violence are tied into a complex social system. But the argument sidetracks giving support for the claim that "guns are not America's major problem or even high on the list of our problems."

3. Another red herring tactic is to make one claim while pretending to support it with another claim, whereas neither claim actually has been supported.

    I cannot understand why the environmentalists feel it is harmful to cut down the redwood forests. This work provides a good living to loggers and their families.

    Here, no reasons are given for why it is not harmful to cut down the redwoods. Nor is the meaning of the word *harmful* clarified. Instead, the writer diverts our attention to other issues by introducing another ambiguous phrase "good living to the loggers." He could then lead us into debating whether the loggers have a right to maintain their livelihood while the profits and responsibility of the lumber company are also ignored; moreover, our attention goes to the writer's assumption that nothing is harmful as long as it provides an income for someone.

4. Finally, there is the more familiar bumper-sticker example of a fallacious red herring argument:

    Guns don't kill people. People do.

    In this case, the argument does not prove the claim that guns do not kill people. Instead it distracts attention into quibbling about whether or not people use guns and how people's ethics and habits affect their behavior. Moreover, this slogan also serves as a false dilemma argument, since the issue is not a matter of either people or guns, but of both necessarily operating together to kill other people.

Class Discussion

Study the following examples of red herring arguments. Write out (1) the issue and (2) the diversion.

1. TV can't be harmful to children, because it occupies their attention for hours and keeps them off the streets. (taken from S. Morris Engel's *With Good Reason*, St. Martin's Press, 1982)

2. Those who are so ferociously involved in Mothers Against Drunk Driving would better spend their time in working with A.A. to help alcoholics.

3. Why are you always nagging at me about the way I drive?

4. A policeman stops a car that is being driven by a dog. He cites the dog's owner who is sitting beside the dog in the front seat. The owner says: "Sure I let him drive, officer, but I never let him off the leash, even for a second."

Pointing to Another Wrong

> **The fallacy of pointing to another wrong** is also called two wrongs make a right. It distracts attention from a wrong-doing by claiming that similar actions went unnoticed, unjudged, or unpunished.

This fallacy is also called two wrongs make a right because it assumes that two wrongs cancel one another out. This weak defense can go unnoticed because it diverts attention into other issues, such as discussing whether or not the other instances are relevant or related. Pointing to another wrong can also divert attention from the issue by making attacks which would lure another into self defense.

Consider these examples of pointing to another wrong, and discuss, either with a class partner or in writing, how each argument lacks reasonable support.

1. Student to instructor: "Why are you getting after me for being late to class? You never say anything to that pretty woman who comes late to class every day."

2. Motorist to police officer: "Why are you giving me a ticket for going the wrong way on a one-way street? Didn't you see that red sedan I was following doing the same thing?"

3. So what if I don't separate the cans and newspapers out from the garbage for recycling. I don't have that much time. Neither do most other people.

4. The politically correct people will tell you that Columbus brought oppression, slavery, and genocide to the peaceful Indians. But Indians committed as many atrocities against the white people as well as against one another.

5. Why do you complain about cruelty to animals in scientific experiments? Look at the way animals are cruel to one another. Have you ever seen the way lions bite into the necks of zebras, rip open their insides, then eat their hearts and entrails?

Straw Man

> **The straw man fallacy** tries to persuade by misrepresenting another person's argument. A straw man is a fake human figure that can be constructed as easily as it can be destroyed. A person who commits this fallacy uses caricature, ridicule, and over-simplification to refute another argument. It may also attack and disprove an insignificant point of another's argument, and then claim that the whole argument has been completely refuted as a result.

The straw man fallacy is a false replica of an opposing argument. Once it is made out of straw, it then can be knocked over and scattered as easily as one could scatter a figure made of straw. This fallacy appears in three forms.

1. The straw man fallacy succeeds when those who hear the straw man argument forget that it misrepresents and distorts the argument opposed.

   • Those who are in favor of national health care want to give us army-style medicine. If the government starts running health care for us, we'll find ourselves waiting all day in barracks full of sick people, while the doctors are shuffling through piles of red tape in their offices and leaving for home by the time our turn arrives.

   • When you support picketing, you are supporting a conspiracy to commit extortion through disruption of business, intimidation, and slander. I have no sympathy for strikers who always have the option of going to work for someone else if they don't like the compensation or conditions offered by their employer. I feel they have no right to force the employer to change employment policy to suit them. Why does hiring people to do a specific job, for specific pay, force the employer to practically adopt the employee, catering to him or her from the cradle to the grave? It must be stopped and the extortionists jailed for long terms.

- I am bewildered by those who support the "three strikes and you are out" law. This tough position denies all possibility for change in people. With it, we turn our backs on these people, saying they can never get better. Thus, we buy into a cycle of hate and fear in a total rejection of love and compassion, locking ourselves up in our houses of fear just like we lock up the prisoners in our prisons.

2. The straw man fallacy might also discredit a trivial aspect of an idea, cause, or person, claiming that this part represents what is essential about the whole.

- I can't respect Hindus because they wear those red spots painted on their foreheads.

- He can't stand the Southern Germans; you know, all those "oom-pah pah" bands, the beer drinking, and all those thigh-slapping guys dancing in their leather shorts.

3. A straw man argument can also seek to discredit an idea on the basis of objections that are beside the point.

- Doctor: "You need to get more exercise. Why don't you walk to work?"
  Patient: "I can't walk to work—I work at home!"

- Father: "Why don't you wear your helmet when you ride your motorcycle? It's both unsafe and illegal to go without it."
  Son: "Dad, I can't do that. It's not cool."

- Boss: "What we need to get this business off the ground is for all the employees to meet together on a regular basis."
  Manager: "But we don't have a meeting room large enough for all of us!"

Circular Reasoning

The fallacy of circular reasoning is the assertion or repeated assertion of a conclusion without giving reasons in its support. It may imply that the conclusion is self-evident or rephrase the conclusion to sound like a reason.

The fallacious argument that is best known for neglecting to provide support for its conclusion is called circular reasoning. Circular reasoning creates an illusion of support by simply asserting its conclusion as though it were a reason, or by reasserting the same claim in different words. A translation of this new language will reveal that the argument is saying that "*A* is true because *A* is true."

- Kerosene is combustible; therefore it burns.

This fallacy also has another name: *begging the question*, which means to assume what one is supposed to prove, or to plea for acceptance, instead of earning acceptance through constructing a sound argument. However, it may be easier to remember this fallacy by the term *circular reasoning* because that it just what it does: it goes in circles. Here are some examples:

- Taxing inheritances is justified because people should pay a tax on money they have been given by their families.

Here, the first half of the sentence is repeated in different words in the second half, as though the second half were a supporting conclusion.

- Running is good for your health. If you want to be healthy, you should run.

Circular reasoning can offer inference indicator words like "therefore," which suggest an inference is being drawn from the first claim, when actually a valid inference is missing. Instead, we have two conclusions instead of a conclusion and a reason:

- Adultery and fornication are wrong. Therefore, it follows that contraception is wrong.

Here, the gap between the first claim and the second is huge. If we agree that adultery and fornication are wrong, why is contraception also wrong? To make a good argument, we have to provide links of explanation to show that one claim follows logically from the first.

Class Discussion

See if you can find the circular reasoning in these examples:

1. Movie stars are intelligent. If they weren't intelligent, they wouldn't be movie stars.
2. Concealed weapons should be discretionary. After all, people should have the right to conceal their guns if they wish.
3. To curse is immoral because it is wrong.

4.   Elect Donna Brown supervisor—she is a mother and realtor.

5.   The budget given the Pentagon by Congress again exceeded military requests by a few billion dollars. Isn't it obvious that when we have the best-funded defense in the world, we will have the best defense in the world?

6.   William Bennett: "Martin Luther King said what degrades humans is unjust, what uplifts them is just. Is there any doubt that TV talk shows degrade people?"

Talk Show Host: "I have 4 million viewers. Are you going to tell them that they can't watch my show any more?"

CHAPTER SUMMARY

1. Word ambiguity uses undefined and vague words in an argument, seeking to gain an advantage by using words that could be interpreted in more than one way.

2. Misleading euphemisms are words that hide meaning by clothing a less acceptable idea in positive or neutral connotations. The use of euphemisms is fallacious in an argument when the goal is to be evasive, to mislead, or to disarm awareness and objections.

3. Prejudicial language persuades through the use of loaded words that convey a bias while pretending to convey objective information.

4. Appeals to fear and pity seek to persuade through affecting emotions rather than through sound rational support for an argument.

5. Appeal to false authority seeks to influence others by citing phony or inappropriate authorities. This false authority might be a person, a tradition, or conventional wisdom. However, the appeal to an authentic and appropriate authority is not a fallacy; in fact, it can provide excellent support for claims.

6. Appeal to bandwagon is another example of the appeal to authority. In this case, the authority is the exhilarating momentum of the herd instinct.

7. Personal attack refutes another argument by attacking the opponent rather than addressing the argument itself. This fallacy can take the form of using abusive language or name calling.

8. Poisoning the well seeks to prejudice others against a person, group, or idea and prevent their positions from being heard. This technique seeks to remove the neutrality necessary for listening and to implant prejudice instead.

9. The red herring is a ploy of distraction. It makes a claim, then instead of following through with support, it minimizes the issue or diverts attention from it by bringing up other issues that are irrelevant. Those following this line of argument will soon find themselves off the track.

10. The straw man is an argument that misrepresents, oversimplifies, or caricatures an opponent's position; it creates a false replica, then destroys the replica, claiming it is a true representation. The straw man also invalidates by attacking a minor point as though the whole argument depended upon it.

11. Pointing to another wrong is also called two wrongs make a right. It says, "Don't look at me; he did it too!"

12. Circular reasoning is the assertion or repeated assertion of a conclusion as though the conclusion were a reason or as though it needed no supporting reasons. Circular reasoning assumes what it is supposed to prove.

CHAPTER QUIZ

Identify the following arguments either as *NF for not fallacious* or by the types of fallacious arguments indicated for each section. In some cases, you may find that more than one fallacy applies; choose the one you feel to be the most appropriate. Be prepared to defend your answers.

Part I
In this section, look for arguments that are *Misapplied Euphemisms, Band Wagon, Appeal to Fear*, and *Nonfallacious*.

_____ 1. It was announced today that our troops, who have been shelled for some weeks now in Lebanon, have made a *strategic transfer* to their ships offshore of that country.

_____ 2. In China, Europe, and Brazil, efforts are being made to control the population growth that adds one billion people to the planet every decade

_____ 3. "Africa, the birthplace of humankind, provides a disturbing clue to our future. As I fly across areas that were forests just years ago and see them becoming desert, I worry. Too many people crowd this continent, so poor they strip the land for food and fuelwood. The subject of my life's work and our closest living relatives, the chimpanzees and gorillas are slaughtered for food or captured for the live-animal trade. Pollution of air, land, and water abounds." (Jane Goodall, National Geographic Society)

_____ 4. Five million people have already seen this movie. Shouldn't you?

_____ 5. Why do I think the president's program is sound? Because the polls show that the vast majority supports it.

_____ 6. By a margin of two to one, shoppers prefer Brand X to any of the leading competitors. Reason enough to buy Brand X.

_____ 7. What if your bank fails and takes your life savings? Buy diamonds—the safe investment.

_____ 8. There is *virtually no tar* in these cigarettes.

_____ 9. It has been estimated that illegal aliens are costing our taxpayers in excess of $5 billion a year. Should our senior citizens be denied full health care benefits, should our children suffer overcrowded classrooms in order to subsidize the costs of illegal aliens?

_____ 10. There are plenty of people out there on the streets waiting to get your job. If you go on strike, you may find yourself out there with them.

_____ 11. The *natural* way to relieve muscular pain is through our vitamin ointment. It *relieves* pain from burns, stiff neck, backache, swelling, and so forth.

Part II

In the arguments before, decide if they are *Nonfallacious*, *Straw man*, *Poisoning the Well*, *Appeal to Pity*, and *Appeal to False Authority*.

_____ 12. American educators, in a recent survey, unanimously agreed that longer school days, more homework, and longer school years would only penalize children and not necessarily result in better learning.

_____ 13. The president of the United States says that the problem of illiteracy can be solved only by longer school days, more homework, and longer school years.

_____ 14. No use listening to those repressive environmentalists and economic zero-growthers who don't have anything under their thick skulls. They oppose any sane domestic policies that allow timber companies to do their jobs.

_____ 15. Elijah Jones was the tenth victim of police brutality this year. Arrested for murdering his two children in a fit of insanity due to the pressures of poverty, he had hoped, on release from a mental institution to make a new life for himself. But Sunday he was shot down mercilessly by the pigs when he ran from a police officer after robbing a liquor store.

_____ 16. Cigarettes are not addictive. I know this to be true because the Chairman of the R.J. Reynolds Tobacco Company testified before Congress that tobacco is not an addictive substance.

Part III

In this section look for arguments that are *Nonfallacious, Pointing to Another Wrong, Red Herring, Prejudicial Language,* and *Circular Reasoning.*

_____ 17. Using hidden notes on a test is not unethical; our professors wouldn't be where they are today if they hadn't done the same thing.

_____ 18. Maybe I do cheat on income tax, but so does everyone else.

_____ 19. When you support picketing, you support a conspiracy to commit extortion through disruption of business.

_____ 20. Some people would have us eliminate the use of all pesticides on fruits and vegetables. But both fruits and vegetables are essential for health and excellent sources of vitamins and minerals.

_____ 21. Why do you object to people smoking? What are you doing about the problems of smog pollution? Exhaust fumes are far more likely to give people lung cancer.

_____ 22. Capital punishment is justified for murder and rape because people should be put to death for violent and hateful acts.

_____ 23. Murder is morally wrong. Therefore it follows that abortion is wrong.

_____ 24. Senator X is trying to increase welfare benefits for single moms. Again he is trying to push one of his Socialist ideas down our throats. Socialism has been proven to be no good.

_____ 25. The U.S. government has no right to accuse us Chinese of human rights violations when the United States has the highest crime rate in the world.

_____ 26. A spokesman for a chemical industrial firm, when charged and fined for disposing of toxic wastes in the lakes of Illinois, protested, "Thousands of other industries are doing the same thing."

CHAPTER 11

Inductive Reasoning and Inductive Fallacies

How Do I Reason from Evidence?

"I forget . . . What are we making again?"

© 1984. Reprinted courtesy of Bill Hoest and *Parade Magazine*.

The kids in this cartoon are not following an architectural drawing or a definite mental plan but are working by trial and error. Creating as they go along, sometimes forgetting their original plan, their reasoning is haphazard and unsystematic.

Inductive reasoning is a method used to discover new information or to supply missing information. We could use it to guess what the kids are building. And the kids could use it to learn that nails alone will not keep the structure standing. When we use inductive reasoning, we observe, test, and check things out in some systematic fashion. Although it is an open-ended method of learning and discovering, it is not hit and miss, or trial and error, but has its own rules for arriving at the most reliable answers. This chapter serves as an introduction to the forms, methods, and rules of inductive reasoning.

Discovery Exercises

Defining Key Terms

Using at least two dictionaries, write down definitions of the following words:

1. induction
2. reasoning
3. empirical
4. scientific method
5. inductive reasoning

Answering a Survey on Test Performance

Write your answers to the following questions in preparation for discussion. Use a mindmap or cluster if you wish. Pay attention to the way in which you must reason in order to reply.

1. Think of a time when you made a high score on a challenging test. What are the steps to prepare yourself mentally, physically, and in actual study?
2. Think of a time when you did poorly on a challenging test. How did you prepare? What did you fail to do?
3. What conclusions can you draw on the basis of this comparison?

    Now discuss the following questions in class:

1. Explain how you were reasoning in order to answer these questions. Was this inductive reasoning?
2. How was this reasoning similar to, or different from, the way you worked mentally as you worked in the first exercises describing a fruit, vegetable, or tool?

LOOKING AT INDUCTIVE REASONING

Your study of this text began with descriptive exercises that required you to use the inductive thinking process. Now is the time to step back and consider the forms and rules of inductive reasoning.

Induction comes from the Latin *inducere* = to lead in. In logic, induction is to reason to a conclusion about all members of a class on the basis of an examination of a few members of a class. Induction reasons from the particular to the general.

In this last discovery exercise, as well as in the descriptive work you did at the beginning of this book, you used inductive reasoning. You observed, gathered data, then drew inferences about patterns, configurations, and meanings. You recorded your findings and reported them. This method of researching from personal observation is basic to the **empirical** or **scientific method**. It was the approach, you will remember, used by Samuel Scudder. In this chapter, we are going to look more abstractly at the nature and structure of inductive reasoning. You will also review the rules and standards used to guide scientific research that has been developed over many centuries.

Induction reasons from evidence about *some* members of a class in order to draw a conclusion about *all* members of that class. We use inductive reasoning to help us out in situations where an examination of all the data would be an impossible or impractical task. Samplings and extrapolation enable us to estimate how many voters nationwide favor a particular candidate, how many needles there are in a haystack, or how many stars there are in the universe. This chapter discusses a number of the methods that have traditionally been used to learn about the whole from a study of its parts. They include sensory observation, enumeration, analogical reasoning, pattern recognition, causal reasoning, and statistical reasoning.

REASONING FROM SENSORY OBSERVATION

Major scientific discoveries have resulted from accidents that just happened to be given close attention by someone who was both a curious skilled observer and inductive thinker.

The ability to observe and infer will always remain the primary skills of a scientist. (Indeed, such skills have always been indispensable for human survival.) Even a scientist who employs instruments such as a computer, microscope, or X-ray machine still depends primarily on personal skills of reasoning from sensory information. Moreover, some of the most dramatic discoveries in the history of science resulted from simple observing of the right thing at the right time. The book, *Serendipity*

Great Moments in Science

©1999 Stivers

1962: Bell Labs scientists discover that gravity does not function inside a ketchup bottle.

Used with permission of Mark Stivers.

> **Sensory observation** is the awareness of self and of the world through the basic senses of sight, touch, taste, smell, and hearing. Ancillary senses include a sense of time, weight, energy, pressure, motion, balance, direction, sexuality, feelings, emotions, pain, strength, weakness, solidity, lightness, darkness, color, fluidity, heat, cold, pitch, tonality, and vibration.

Accidental Discoveries in Science by Roysten M. Roberts tells many stories of accidental discoveries that led to such inventions as quinine, electric batteries, synthetic dyes, rayon, nylon, and antibiotics. Here is a summary of one of these stories:

> In 1903 the French chemist, Edouard Benedictus, dropped a glass flask one day on a hard floor and broke it. However, to the astonishment of the chemist, the flask did not shatter, but still retained most of its original shape. When he examined the flask he found that it contained a film coating inside, a residue remaining from a solution of collodion that the flask had contained. He made a note of this unusual phenomenon, but thought no more of it until several weeks later when he read stories in the newspapers about people

in automobile accidents who were badly hurt by flying windshield glass. It was then he remembered his experience with the glass flask, and just as quickly, he imagined that a special coating might be applied to a glass windshield to keep it from shattering. Not long thereafter, he succeeded in producing the world's first sheet of safety glass.

Class Discussion Question

1. Parallel stories of lucky scientific discoveries lie behind the inventions of penicillin, X-rays, Teflon, dynamite, and Post-Its. Describe how one of these discoveries, or any other you are familiar with, depended on both sensory observation and inductive reasoning.

REASONING FROM ENUMERATION

Induction can involve a simple counting of parts in order to draw conclusions about wholes.

Enumerate means (1) To count off or name one by one or (2) to determine a number from counting.

Induction uses enumeration in a range from simple counting to gathering statistics. The rules for good induction are concerned with how to draw the most likely and probable conclusions about wholes on the basis of a controlled sampling of parts.

This can of Chock Nuts contains exactly 485 peanuts.

This second can of Chock Nuts contains exactly 485 peanuts.

This third can of Chock Nuts contains exactly 485 peanuts.

(Therefore) all cans of Chock Nuts must contain exactly 485 peanuts.

You will notice that the conclusion drawn here uses the word "must" to suggest that the conclusion is at best a guess. It is an estimate of probability, a projection, or an **extrapolation**. If you open a fourth can and find 500 peanuts, then you will know that the conclusion was incorrect because the sampling was insufficient. Therefore, you would have to revise your experiment to count enough samples until a reliable average could be obtained.

Nevertheless, conclusions drawn from samplings can never be totally certain; at best they can only reflect probabilities. Yet probability estimates help out considerably in situations where we cannot obtain all the facts. If you have an old car that begins to have one or two major repair problems every six months, you can extrapolate a trend that may well continue until all parts are replaced. On the basis of this extrapolation, you may decide to buy a new car. However, you might wonder if that old clunker would have been the exception that held up forever.

ANALOGICAL REASONING

Inductive reasoning also draws conclusions from making comparisons in the form of analogies.

> **Analogy** means (1) to find a correspondence of similarity between things that seem different or (2) an inference that if two things are alike in some respects, they will be alike in other respects.

Inductive reasoning can also be based on analogies, which are a form of comparisons. All of us learn from making comparisons. Even a one-year-old can get the idea that if adults can stand upright and walk, then so can he or she. Analogies are used in the teaching of all subjects in order to make the unfamiliar more understandable by comparison with the familiar. In SAT tests, the ability to discern analogies is tested by the use of comparative ratios, such as TEACHER: CLASSROOM:: judge: courtroom. In the study of macroeconomics, a principle, such as how a government can control an economy, can be explained by comparison to the way a person can control the water level in a bathtub by judicious use of the faucet and the plug.

Analogical reasoning also serves as a mainstay of legal argumentation in countries such as Canada, England, and the United States, where the decisions depend on precedents. The requirement of precedents in law is that similar cases must be decided in a similar manner. Thus when an attorney argues a case, comparisons are made between the case in question and past rulings and decisions.

Finally, in the sciences, analogical reasoning has resulted in many discoveries and inventions. Here are two famous examples:

- Ben Franklin proved by a simple experiment that materials of different colors absorb heat differently. He put squares of cloth of different colors on some banks of snow and left them in the sun. In a few hours he noticed that a black piece had sunk into the snow the deepest, lighter-colored pieces less, and a white piece not at all.

From this Franklin reasoned that dark colors absorb the sun's heat more readily than the paler ones which reflect part of the sun's radiation. By analogous reasoning, he decided that people who live in tropical climates should wear white clothing.

- The invention of Velcro was based on a study of cockleburs. In the 1950's George deMestral began to wonder what made cockleburs stick to his jacket when he went on walks. When he took one under a microscope, he discovered that each seed bur was covered with hooks that had become embedded in the loops of his cloth jacket. Then he began to wonder if this pattern of hooks and loops could be put to some practical use. By analogous reasoning he came up with the concept of an alternative kind of fastener, which was eventually realized through manufacturing research.

DISCOVERING PATTERNS

Inductive reasoning looks for patterns, notes their characteristics, and draws conclusions about their nature and significance.

> **Pattern** is a design or form that is perceived. A pattern can involve shapes, images, ideas, words, signs, entities, sounds, or smells that suggest some recognizable configuration or rhythm.

In the inductive process, sensory observation is used to note details and forms, to compare similarities and differences, and thus to recognize designs. This was the case in the discovery of Velcro, where a microscope revealed the pattern of the seed bur that had hooked the loops of fabric. Gradually such a discernment of pattern leads to inferences about their correspondences, trends, and tendencies as well as to explanations or conclusions about their nature and meaning. All the accumulated evidence might be called the *parts* and the generalizations made about the *whole*. In medicine, the name given to the whole is called the *diagnosis*.

A child is brought to the doctor with the following symptoms: fever, cough, and eye inflammation. The doctor examines the patient and finds small red spots with white centers on the insides of her cheeks. The doctor begins to recognize a pattern of symptoms that could lead to a diagnosis of common measles. He knows that if a rash appears first on her neck and then on the rest of her body within three to five days, and if there is a diminution of the fever, then he can be sure of this diagnosis. However, the onset of other symptoms or the worsening of the patient's condition could suggest other possibilities.

Thus the process of examining a patient and arriving at a correct diagnosis (and with that a correct treatment) requires not only considerable knowledge, but skills in discerning patterns and forming dependable hypotheses about them.

REASONING FROM AND ABOUT CAUSES

We use inductive reasoning to determine the probable causes of events.

Cause From the Latin *causa* = reason, purpose. Cause means that which produces an effect, a result, a consequence; something that is responsible for an event; or a source of influence.

Induction is one form of reasoning that seeks to explain why certain things have occurred or might occur. Because our forebears wondered what caused our days to be divided between light and darkness, we gradually moved from the explanations of myths to the scientific explanations of astronomy and physics.

All humans show curiosity about causation because such knowledge makes life more predictable and thus more controllable. Every day newspapers supply us with facts and speculations concerning the causes of such events as natural disasters, crimes, and the rise and fall of the stock market. People want and need explanations of causality, although not all events can be satisfactorily explained.

Here is a simple example of such an event. In October 1985 a humpback whale, later affectionately called Humphrey, made an unprecedented visit to San Francisco Bay and from there to the Sacramento River Delta region, where he remained for twenty-four days. It took $50,000 and the combined efforts of many individuals to persuade him to return from the brackish water of the delta to the safety of his natural habitat in the ocean. The press offered many explanations about the cause of his visit and reluctance to leave. Their speculations included the following: (1) he was feeding on the wealth of fish he found there; (2) he was insane or suicidal; (3) he was confused and lost; (4) he was plagued by parasites and moving into fresh water to kill them; and (5) "he" was a "she" and pregnant, seeking a place for birthing.

"Miss California already, don't you Humphrey . . . ?" Used with permission of the *Minneapolis Star and Tribune.*

Class Discussion

Inductive reasoning, whether using sensory observation, enumeration, analogies, pattern recognition, or guesses about causation, has its own rules or standards for producing the most reliable or probable conclusions. Study the following examples that use inductive reasoning and explain why each one is well or poorly reasoned.

1. The leaves on our maple tree turn red in October.

   Some years it is cold in October, and some years it is warm through October. No matter what the temperature, our tree always turns in October.

   October makes the leaves of maple trees turn red.

2. I always get a cold after I go swimming.

   I only get a cold when I go swimming.

   The cause of my colds is swimming.

3. The last ten times I flipped this coin, it came up tails.

   The next time I flip it, it is certain to be tails.

4. I get nervous when I drink coffee.

   I get nervous when I drink tea.

   I get nervous when I drink cola.

   All drinks make me nervous.

5. Jules and Jim like the same dogs.

   Jules and Jim like the same foods.

   Jules and Jim must like the same people.

6. My lover promised to come see me at 8:00 P.M.

   I have waited until 4:00 A.M.

   He is not coming.

7. When I stopped smoking, I gained 10 pounds. Smoking keeps my weight down.

8. My wife and I know how beneficial fresh garlic can be to health, but we worried about the smell. Then we found a solution. We chop up pieces of garlic and put them inside a banana to share just before going to bed. Afterward I have never noticed any garlic on the breath. Even the next morning, there is no garlic smell. We believe we have discovered a cure for garlic breath.

9. I had a wart that was protruding and sore. I decided to try vitamin E. I applied the oil about two or three times a day, and in less than ten days the wart was gone. This proves that vitamin E cures warts.

REASONING WITH HYPOTHESES

A conclusion derived from inductive reasoning is never certain but only probable. The conclusion is less certain than the evidence itself.

> **Hypothesis** comes from the Greek word *hupothesis*, meaning a proposal, suggestion, or supposition. A hypothesis is the name given to a conclusion reached through inductive reasoning; a hypothesis is a trial idea, a proposal, or a theory.

A conclusion derived from inductive reasoning is called a *hypothesis*. You found a number of them in the story of Humphrey the whale. In the last example you just read about warts, the hypothesis was that vitamin E cures warts. The conclusions given in all the preceding examples, whether correctly reasoned or not, were hypotheses. Even if a valid hypothesis based on adequate evidence cannot be considered conclusive until it has been adequately tested over time. The discovery of even one exception, or counter example, challenges the truth of a hypothesis. Thus when we study inductive reasoning, we need to understand that since inductive generalizations have these limitations, special precautions have to be taken in order to reach the most probable hypothesis. Thus we learn the rules for gathering and examining evidence, for controlling variables, and for creating experiments that can be duplicated and thus tested by others. Moreover we have to be continually willing to modify and refine our hypotheses depending on the feedback we receive.

It takes time and testing to establish the truth of a hypothesis. Obviously Sir Isaac Newton's hypothesis that gravity explains an apple's perpendicular fall to the ground has not been improved upon. The discovery that a vaccination could prevent smallpox also proved to be true, although it took the interweaving of many hypotheses and many tests to establish its reliability. By 1979 vaccination had eradicated the disease worldwide.

The first hypothesis is not always the last; indeed, one hypothesis can serve to lead to another and another, or as imaginative guides for further research. Here are two examples of the way in which hypotheses can function as working assumptions:

- A patient developed a high fever and complained of pains in the kidney area; a kidney infection was first diagnosed by the doctor (first hypothesis). However, on a second visit, an examination of the patient's mouth and throat revealed enlarged and swollen tonsils (new evidence), and it seemed more likely at this point that the fever and kidney pains were due to the infected tonsils (new hypothesis).

- In the eighteenth century Europeans began to experiment with the nature of electricity. The similarity between lightning and electric sparks was observed, and it was conjectured that lightning was simply a big electric spark. Ben Franklin decided to test this hypothesis. Using analogous reasoning, he noticed that lightning and electric sparks were similar in color and in shape, that they traveled at about the same speed, and that both killed animals. Franklin published a proposal suggesting that a "sentry box" be built on a high tower with a man inside on an insulated platform who would draw sparks from passing clouds with a long pointed iron rod (test for a hypothesis). Before Franklin got around to trying out this experiment himself, it was conducted in France, and it was proved that clouds are electrified (proof of the hypothesis). Franklin then found a way to verify his hypothesis again, using his well-known kite experiment. He fixed a sharp-pointed wire to the top of a kite, then knotted a large iron key between the kite string and a length of ribbon used for insulation. When a storm cloud passed by, Franklin saw the fibers of the kite string stand on end and drew a spark from the key with his knuckle (second proof of the hypothesis in an experiment conducted under different conditions).

Class Discussion

Below are four examples of inductive reasoning that include hypotheses. Read and underline the hypothetical statements, and discuss whether you find adequate support for these hypotheses. What other hypotheses might better explain some of these situations? Note also if each example uses analogies, extrapolates and predicts from patterns, speculates about cause and effect, or gathers data and statistics.

1. A study of high school students in ten major U.S. cities showed that four out of every five were not coffee drinkers. It was conjectured that this statistic could be due to TV commercials showing only older people drinking coffee. A new advertising promotional scheme was devised to seek to change this ratio by showing teenagers enjoying coffee at athletic events, during class breaks, and on dates to see if it might change this ratio.

2. I have been wearing a wool knitted cap for the past ten years. People think it is strange, but it has kept me from having sore throats. Before I started wearing the cap, I had sore throats all the time. But since I started wearing it, I have not had any.

3. Japanese government officials and auto industry spokesmen said American drivers might be having trouble with their Japanese-made seat belts because their cars are too dirty. They reported finding animal hair in American cars, pieces of food, and soft drink drippings. In Japan, people do not drink or eat in their cars or even wear shoes. This explanation for the faulty seat belts (whose release button gradually became brittle and would not lock securely) came in response to reports that federal safety officials in the United States were planning to recall and repair defective seat belts in nine million cars. The Japanese manufacturers said that they had received no complaints in Japan about the 4.79 million vehicles on the road with the same seat belts. (Summarized from an article in the *San Francisco Chronicle*, May 23, 1995)

4. World bicycle production increased to more than 110 million units in 1994. The trend has been rising steadily since 1970. Bikes have been found to be speedier and more efficient than cars in grid locked U.S. cities for couriers, pizza deliverers, police, and paramedics. Developing countries, where bikes have long been popular, are also finding new uses for bikes, such as in San Salvador where they are used for trailer towing. The potential for their further growth is great. They

hold promise of becoming a valuable, environmentally friendly means of transportation. (Data summarized from *Vital Signs 1995*)

REASONING THROUGH STATISTICS AND PROBABILITY

Induction uses the sciences of statistics and probability to gather, organize, and interpret data and make predictions with this data.

Statistics The mathematics of the collection, organization, and interpretation of numerical data.

Probability In statistics the ratio of the number of actual occurrences of a specific event to the total number of occurrences.

Inductive reasoning can work with statistical samplings (a form of enumeration) and make predictions on the basis of an estimate of probabilities. For example, the payoffs for betting on the winners of horse races are determined by inductive reasoning. Suppose you read in the papers that today at Green Meadows racetrack the following horses will run with the odds as listed: Post Flag 9.90 to 1; Bru Ha Ha 3.40 to 1; Plane Fast 6.80 to 1; En-Durance 5.20 to 1. These odds are based on the Racing Association's estimates of each horse's chance of winning. Bettors who pick winners will be paid a multiple of the first number in each of these odds for each dollar bet.

The field of mathematics known as statistics is a science that seeks to make accurate predictions about a whole from a sampling of its parts. Probability and statistics have yielded some basic rules for evaluating the reliability of conclusions drawn by inductive reasoning from statistical samplings. For the purposes of our introduction to the subject, there are five basic rules:

1. The *greater* the size of the *sample* (or number of study subjects), the greater is the probability that that sample is representative of the whole of a *class* (or a group it is supposed to represent).

    The results of a survey of the coffee-drinking habits of students in one high school based on questioning only ten students would obviously not be as reliable as the results of a survey of the whole student body. However, samplings are made for the sake of convenience or necessity, and the same information can be extrapolated for a full population when some rules for size, margin of error, and random selection are followed. These rules are taught in the study of statistics. Yet, without knowing all these rules, you can still estimate that a survey of ten students could not speak for a whole high school, or one high school for all U.S. high schools.

2. The *more representative* the sample is of a class, the more likely it is that accurate conclusions will be drawn about the class from the sample.

   In a poll seeking a representative sampling of menopausal women in Illinois, the most representative respondents would probably be Illinois women between the ages of forty and sixty. Less likely to be representative would be women under the age of thirty. Moreover, a survey limited to women in their forties would also not be representative, nor would a survey of women in the city of Chicago only.

3. One *counterexample* can refute a generalization arrived at through inductive reasoning.

   If you complain that your friend *always* comes late and is *never* reliable, and then one day your friend arrives early, you have a counterexample that refutes your generalization.

4. If statistical evidence is offered, it should be offered in *sufficient detail* to permit verification. Sources or background material about the researchers should also be cited so others can determine their reputation and independence from vested interests in the study's outcome.

   In the following example, consider the vague references to "independent laboratory tests" as well as to the research data used to support the claims:

   FATOFF has been proven to cause weight loss. After years of research and expensive experimentation, an independent *laboratory* with *expertise* in biotechnology has finally uncovered a naturally occurring substance that can be taken orally in tablet form. Now it is being made available to millions of overweight men and women who are losing as much as 10 lbs. a month. It has taken over *15 years of research and over 200 medically documented studies* to produce FATOFF. But there is only one catch: FATOFF is expensive to produce.

5. When polls are taken, it is important to know not only whether a *reputable organization* or agency (such as Gallup, Roper, or Harris) took the poll but also the *exact formulation* of the question. Compare the following questions:

   (a) Do you favor a constitutional amendment that declares, "The English language shall be the official language of the United States"?

   (b) English is the language of the United States by custom, although not by law. In order to avoid the political upheavals over language that have torn apart Canada, Belgium, Sri Lanka (Ceylon),

India, and other nations, would you favor legislation designating English the official language of the United States?

The first question might elicit quite a different response than the second. When you hear or read about polls, be sure to see if the exact wording of the question is given so that you can analyze it for bias. Also, do not accept without question results from polls identified only vaguely as "a recent poll." If the pollster's name is given, consider whether it was an independent source or a source filtering information to represent its own political or commercial interests. You need to be able to determine whether the source was unbiased and whether the results are verifiable.

Class Discussion

The following examples offer statistical evidence. Rate the statistics given in each as *reliable* or *not reliable* and then state what rule or standard you used in making your judgment.

1. "According to the Center for Academic Integrity at Duke University, three quarters of college students confess to cheating at least once. And a *U.S. News* poll found 90 percent of college kids believe cheaters never pay the price. [*U.S. News* poll of 1,000 adults (including an over sample of 200 college students) conducted by Celinda Lake of Lake Snell Perry & Associates and Ed Goeas of the Tarrance Group. Oct. 18–23, 1999. Margin of error; plus or minus 3.5 percent.] (*U.S. News & World Report*, November 22, 1999)

2. "I would guess that the average office female makes 509 visits to the lavatory to a male's 230, and spends 10.7 minutes there to a male's 2.5. What management is going to put up with this 'primp time' featherbedding at equal pay?" (Edgar Berman, guest columnist, *USA Today*)

3. "It was May 1971 when Russell Bliss, a waste hauler, sprayed oil at Judy Piatt's stables in Moscow Mills, Mo., to help control the dust. A few days later hundreds of birds nesting in the stable's rafters fell to the ground and died. Soon, more than 20 of her cats went bald and died, as did 62 horses over the next three and a half years. Piatt herself developed headaches, chest pains and diarrhea, and one of her daughters started hemorrhaging. In 1974 the federal Centers for Disease Control in Atlanta identified the culprit as dioxin and traced it to Bliss's oil, which contained wastes from a defunct hexachlorophene plant that had paid him to dispose of it. Bliss, it turned out, had sprayed the waste-oil mixture on horse arenas, streets, parking lots and farms throughout the state, leaving what state Assistant Attorney General Edward F. Downey called 'a trail of sickness and death.'" (*Newsweek*, March 7, 1983)

DISCOVERY WRITING APPLICATION

Working from Facts to Inferences to Hypotheses

Follow these steps in this assignment:

1. Skim through books that list facts, such as *The Information Please Almanac, The Book of Lists, the People's Almanac, Statistical Abstracts of the United States.*

2. Find a group of related facts on one subject and write them down.

3. Draw all the inferences you can that would explain what these facts mean. Write them down as a list of potential conclusions.

4. From these select one conclusion that seems to you to be the most likely hypothesis to explain the facts' meaning.

5. Discuss this hypothesis and list what further facts you would need to determine whether or not it is true.

6. Make this a short essay assignment of one to two pages.

7. Title your paper with a question your hypothesis seeks to answer.

8. Make your thesis the answer to that question.

Student Writing Example

WHY ARE THERE FEWER INJURIES IN HOCKEY THAN IN OTHER TEAM SPORTS?

Shamma Boyarin

The Facts

Team sport injuries reported in U.S. hospitals in 1980*:

    463,000 injuries related to football
    442,900 injuries related to baseball
    421,000 injuries related to basketball
    94,200 injuries related to soccer
    36,400 injuries related to hockey

*Source: Susan Baker. *The Injury Fact Book*. Lexington, Mass.: Lexington Books, 1984.

Why Were Fewer Injuries Related to Hockey Reported?

Potential Conclusions or Hypothesis

1. Hockey is a less dangerous sport.
2. People who play hockey are tougher and less likely to go to the hospital with injuries.
3. Hockey is a less popular sport, so fewer people are injured.
4. Hockey is more safety conscious than other sports.

Discussion

On the basis of my knowledge of all five sports, I would say that
hockey is the most dangerous. And this factor of danger leads to
three practices that make hockey different from the other team
sports:

1. Hockey players, even nonprofessionals, are more likely to wear
   protective gear.
2. The rules of hockey are designed to prevent unnecessary injuries as much as possible. Referees enforce these rules more
   rigorously than in other sports.
3. Because it is a very tiring game, players are allowed to rest
   more often. A player with a minor injury can rest more and not
   aggravate the injury.

Because of these precautions, I do not think that the first two
hypotheses are likely. As for the third, hockey may be a less popular sport, and this may contribute to the smaller number of injuries,
but I don't think this can account for its dramatic difference from
the rest. I do not think that hockey is a less popular sport than soc-
cer, which reported nearly three times as many injuries. Therefore, I
select the final hypothesis as the most likely reason for fewer injuries in hockey, namely, hockey's players and officials are more
safety conscious.

Supporting Argument for the Thesis

I don't know how many people injured in hockey were in fact wearing protective gear, or how many of the injuries could have been
prevented by such gear, so I can't prove that protective gear prevented injuries. I also don't know how many games with injuries
were official games following strict rules. After all, a player injured
in a neighborhood game can step out whenever he feels like it.
Also the word related is vague. Does this include bystanders? Is a
baseball fan hit in the stands with a baseball included in "baseball-
related injuries"?

During the 1994 football game between Atlanta and San Francisco, two players started fighting. Their teams were penalized, but
they continued playing. If it had been a hockey game, both players
would have been thrown out of the whole game. Since hockey has
such a violent reputation, the referees are more strict with brawling
players. Finally, I can compare hockey to what I have read about injuries in football. Last year, Sports Illustrated ran an article on head
injuries in professional football. The magazine pointed out that many
injuries could be prevented by changing the rules a little, as well as
by putting an extra shell on players' helmets. They cited one player

who said that wearing such a shell did not hinder his performance. However, the NFL has not adopted these suggestions, which seems to indicate my theory is correct: there are fewer injuries in hockey because its players and officials are more safety conscious.

Used with permission of Shamma Boyarin.

Scoring for Working from Facts to Inferences to Hypotheses

1. Minimum of two pages. 10 points
2. Title includes questions your hypothesis seeks to answer. 10 points
3. Group of related facts listed taken from identified source. 10 points
4. Imaginative list of (more than three) inferences that could be drawn from these facts. 20 points
5. Further facts needed to determine reliability of hypotheses listed. 10 points
6. Adequate support for argument defending hypothesis. 30 points
7. No distracting errors of spelling, punctuation, sentence structure. 10 points

---

SUMMARY: INDUCTIVE REASONING

1. Inductive reasoning is the process of thinking that you used in describing a fruit, vegetable, or tool in Chapter 1 when you began by not knowing the identity of the covered object.
2. The inductive method is also called the empirical or scientific method. It appeared in the reading by Samuel Scudder.
3. Induction reasons from evidence about some members of a class in order to form a conclusion about all members of that class.
4. Induction can be done through sensory observation, enumeration, analogous reasoning, causal reasoning, and from pattern recognition.
5. A conclusion derived through inductive reasoning is called a hypothesis and is always less certain than the evidence itself.
6. Inductive reasoning is used as a method for obtaining information when it would be impossible to examine all the data available. This is done by taking statistical samplings or by making extrapolations.

INDUCTION

The first of May 1779, the troops under General John Sullivan commenced their march but did not arrive at Wyoming until the middle of June. . . .

The village was immediately set on fire, and the rich fields of corn were cut down and trodden underfoot. On the first of September, the army left the river, and struck across the wilderness. . . .

Once or twice the Indians threatened to make a stand for their homes, but soon fled in despair, and the army had its own way. The capital of the Senecas, a town consisting of sixty houses, surrounded by beautiful corn-fields and orchards, was burned to the ground and the harvest destroyed. . . . The fourth day it reached a beautiful region, then, almost wholly un-known to the white man. . . . As the weary columns slowly emerged from the dark forest and filed into this open space . . . they seemed suddenly to be transported into an Eden.

The tall, ripe grass bent before the wind—cornfield on cornfield, as far as eye could reach waved in the sun—orchards that had been growing for generations, were weighted down under a profusion of fruit—cattle grazed on the banks of a river, and all was luxuriance and beauty. . . . All about were scattered a hundred and twenty-eight houses—not miserable huts huddled together, but large airy buildings, situated in the most pleasant spots, surrounded by fruit trees, and exhibiting a civilization on the part of the Indians never before witnessed.

Soon after sunrise immense columns of smoke began to rise the length and breadth of the valley, and in a short time the whole settlement was wrapped in flame, from limit to limit; and before night those one hundred and twenty-eight houses were a heap of ashes. The grain had been gath-ered into them, and thus both were destroyed together. The orchards were cut down, the cornfields uprooted, and the cattle butchered and left to rot on the plain. A scene of desolation took the place of the scene of beauty, and the army camped that night in a desert.

The next day, having accomplished the object of their mission, Sullivan commenced a homeward march. . . . The thanks of Congress was pre-sented to Sullivan and his army for the manner in which they had fulfilled their arduous task.

Discussion Questions

1. Is this a neutral report? Is it an inductive argument?
2. What words suggest where the author's sympathy lies?
3. Does the author draw a conclusion about the significance of this event or does he leave it up to the reader?
4. Do you think he is using irony in the last sentence?

(Joel Tyler Headley, *Washington and His Generals*, 1859, an account of the 1779 tragedy of Cherry Valley and Wyoming in New York State when President George Washington ordered troops to secure the frontier against the Iroquois in case they should be in-fluenced by the English to attack Americans.)

7. The five basic rules for evaluating the reliability of hypotheses based on statistical samplings are as follows:
   (a) The greater the size of the sample, the greater is its probability of being representative of the whole of a class.
   (b) A sampling must be representative in order to lead to reliable results.
   (c) One counter example can refute a generalization arrived at through inductive reasoning.
   (d) Statistical evidence should be offered in sufficient detail for verification.
   (e) When evaluating the results of polls, it is important to examine both the polling agency and the polling question for bias.

QUIZ: INDUCTIVE REASONING

Rate the following statements as *true* or *false*. If you decide the statement is false, then revise the statement to make it a true one.

_____ 1. Inductive reasoning is also known as the scientific method.

_____ 2. You are out swimming in the ocean and you see some fish with prominent sharp teeth swimming around you. You know that some fish with sharp teeth are predatory. You take off without waiting around to see if they might harm you. Your decision is based on analogous reasoning.

_____ 3. You could use inductive reasoning to put together a picture puzzle if all the pieces were available, even if there were no box cover to show what the whole picture would look like when it was finished.

_____ 4. There is a contest to guess how many gumballs are in a jar. You can use inductive reasoning to figure this out.

_____ 5. Inductive reasoning could help you cook a new dish by carefully following instructions from a cookbook.

_____ 6. Inductive reasoning can extrapolate reliable predictions from only one or two examples of a phenomenon.

_____ 7. Counter examples can test or refute theories or generalizations.

_____ 8. A hypothesis is a theory that can lead to new facts and discoveries, but the hypothesis itself is not a certainty.

_____ 9. Statistical evidence is always reliable regardless of the attitudes of the people who research and present the information.

FALLACIES OF INDUCTIVE REASONING

In studying the material and completing the exercises in the first part of this chapter, you learned some standards for inductive reasoning and saw some examples of fallacious reasoning. Now we will study in more detail the chief fallacies that cause inductive reasoning to go wrong:

1. Hasty generalization
2. Either-or fallacy
3. Questionable statistic
4. Inconsistencies and contradictions
5. Loaded question
6. False analogy
7. False cause
8. Slippery slope

The Hasty Generalization

> **Hasty generalization** is the fallacy of over-generalizing, of drawing a conclusion about the whole from an insufficient sampling of its parts.

The hasty generalization is the fallacy that occurs most often in inductive reasoning. A hasty generalization is a conclusion reached prematurely without a fair and sufficient study of sufficient evidence. Often it expresses stereotypes.

1. All used car salesman are crooks. One of them sold me a lemon.
2. All old people are cheap. They never give me a fair tip when I park their cars.
3. No car mechanic can be trusted. They are only out to make a buck.
4. I waited half an hour for him to get dressed. All men are really more vain than women.
5. Chinese are tall, thin, and skinny.

In all these five cases, the samplings were too small to justify the conclusions drawn from them about the whole of all used car salesmen, and

---

CHART OF FALLACIES OF INDUCTIVE REASONING COVERED IN THIS CHAPTER

1. **Hasty Generalization:** A conclusion based on insufficient evidence.

2. **Either/Or Fallacy:** An argument that oversimplifies a situation, asserting that there are only two choices, when actually there are many.

3. **Questionable Statistic:** Citing statistics to back up an argument that is either unknowable or unsound.

4. **Inconsistencies and Contradictions:** Offering evidence that contradicts the conclusion or making claims that contradict one another.

5. **Loaded Question:** Using a biased question to obtain a predetermined answer.

6. **False Analogy:** Comparing two things that have some similarities but also significant differences that are ignored for the sake of the argument.

7. **False Cause:** Claiming a casual connection between events without reasonable evidence to support the claim.

8. **Slippery Slope:** An unwarranted claim that permitting one event to occur would lead to an inevitable and uncontrollable chain reaction.

---

so forth. Hasty generalizations are familiar to all of us; we tend to make them when we feel angry, or too impatient to deal with complexities. Hasty generalizations can also result from careless interpretations of the data:

- I read recently in a survey of U.S. medical students that it cost them, on the average, $20,000 a year to get through medical school. This means that only the wealthy can still make it into the medical profession.

This is a hasty generalization because it does not include information about the percentage who have scholarships or loans. Instead only the easiest assumption is offered to account for how the cost is covered.

How do we avoid hasty generalizations? First by being very careful in the use of the words *all*, *every*, *everyone*, and *no*. A single exception will disqualify any generalization preceded by one of these words, which are called *quantifiers*. Test to see if what you actually mean are the *qualifiers* such as *in this case, in some cases,* or *it appears* or *seems* or *suggests that.* A careful use of quantifiers and qualifiers can often make the difference between an accurate statement and a fallacious one. Let's see how the following generalization differs significantly from the one given above.

> This survey does not offer information about how medical students manage to pay for their high tuition. Some could be wealthy, while others might qualify for scholarships or loans. All that can be said is that a student who wants to attend medical school does have to consider the cost.

Class Discussion

Which of the following are hasty generalizations?

1. Most poor black people who live in cities are anti-Semitic. That's because their landlords are Jewish.

2. Every woman in the military that I ever met was a lesbian. They are all either lesbians or about to become lesbians.

3. Because Asian students are now becoming the majority ethnic group accepted for math and science studies into West Coast graduate schools, this suggests that Asians may be either genetically gifted in abstract thinking and/or culturally encouraged in it.

4. "Used car loans are typically more costly than loans on new ones. The average bank rate on a used car today is 9.2%—roughly 1 percentage point higher than for a new car according to Bankrate.com." (*Auto Arithmetic US News and World Report*, 11/22/99)

The Either-Or Fallacy, or False Dilemma

Either-or fallacy or **False dilemma** is a fallacious argument that oversimplifies a situation, maintaining that there are only two choices, when actually other alternatives exist.

An argument that presumes that there are only two ways of looking at a situation—or that only one of two choices can be made—when actually other alternatives do exist, is called the either-or fallacy, or false dilemma. Sometimes these false dilemmas appear in those frustrating questions on personality assessment tests:

1. When you see a friend coming toward you on the sidewalk, do you rush forward to greet the person or do you cross to the other side of the street?

2. Do you act impulsively rather than deliberately?

3. Do you have only a few friends or a large circle of friends?

More often, false dilemmas appear in poll questions: "Are you for or against the war on drugs? Such questions are convenient for tabulation purposes but do not allow for weighed discriminations that reflect actual opinion. You may be in favor of aggressive federal programs to prevent the import of cocaine, but not marijuana. Or you may prefer that more funding be given to programs of rehabilitation and prevention. When confronted with either-or questions, a thoughtful person is faced with another dilemma: that of refusing both choices or of compromising with an answer that plays into the questioner's assumption and bias.

The usual false dilemma argument oversimplifies a complex issue or seeks to intimidate:

- Live free or die.

- America. Love it or leave it.

- When you have a headache, all you can do is reach for aspirin.

- Are you with me or against me?

- When we outlaw guns, only outlaws will have guns.

- The Cougar convertible: you'll either own one or want one.

In each of these cases, the dilemma is built into the argument, simplifying the situation to fit premeditated terms or assumptions. Sometimes, as in these slogans and commercial appeals, the false dilemma serves as an intentional ploy to negate resistance; it tries to force others to agree to an oversimplification.

Here is such an example: "Mothers of young children can either have careers or stay at home. But they can't expect both to have careers and to raise happy children." This argument is based on many assumptions. The first is that the children are happier with the mother at home. Another is that the father's part is unimportant. Yet, many alternative possibilities exist that are not considered by the speaker. What if a mother has a business in her home? What if she is so successful in her career that she has to work only ten hours a week? What if she is a single parent who must work but who runs a janitorial service in which her children also work with her? A false dilemma assumes that there is only one choice, when imaginative thought could produce many more options.

Class Discussion

Analyze the false dilemmas just given and offer reasons for your agreement or disagreement with their designations as such.

Two out of three farmers approve of genetically engineered produce.

Used with permission of Mark Stivers.

The Questionable Statistic

> **The questionable statistic** is the fallacy of offering evidence in the form of statistics that are either unknowable, faulty, or misleading.

Inductive reasoning requires some knowledge of statistics and how statistics can be used or misused as evidence. As you learned earlier, to evaluate whether statistics are used fairly, you need to look for such things as the size of the sample, whether it was representative and random, whether a margin for error was considered, and what the margin was. These are only some of the basics involved in assessing the reliability of statistics. The fallacy of the questionable statistic refers to confusion or deception in the use of statistics, even to the point of citing figures that would be impossible to obtain.

Recall this use of statistics, quoted earlier:

- "I would guess that the average office female makes 509 visits to the lavatory to a male's 320, and spends 10.7 minutes there to a male's 2.5. What management is going to put up with this 'primp time' featherbedding at equal pay?"

In this case, the author is lightly mocking the use of statistics, implying that even if the actual figures are not this exact, everyone knows that his claims are true. But he does not offer either genuine statistics or evidence for his claim of the "primp time featherbedding" motive.

When statistical claims are false or deliberately misleading, they are not always easy to detect unless we have knowledge of the subject or of the laws of statistics. A sure warning sign is *unattributed figures* or figures given without a citation of their source, purpose, and methods of calculation.

- Why isn't alcohol illegal? It has the same rate of addiction (10 percent) as cocaine.

In this case, a critical thinker would want to know how *addiction* is being defined, how this figure was derived, who conducted the study, and whether this 10 percent figure was quoted out of context.

Here is another example, also uncited, with a flashing red light attached:

- Illegal aliens cost American citizens $5 billion a year.

First, the word *cost* is undefined; what expenses does this term cover? Second, "illegal aliens" refers to undocumented immigrants; therefore how were they counted, on what basis was their cost to the public estimated, and by whom? Whoever made this statement should not have made this claim at all unless she could have supplied this information as well as its source. Otherwise the reader is left wondering if the 5 billion figure is *an unknowable statistic*. Here is a clearer example of pure guesswork:

- If we legalize drugs, drugs would become much cheaper, at least one-fifth the cost. Then five times as many people would buy them. Then we would have five times as many addicts, and instead of 100,000 addicted babies born to addicted mothers each year, we would have a million.

The chief weakness of this argument is that it is based on the assumption that if drugs were legal, they would be less expensive. From there, the figure of "at least one-fifth the cost" seems to be drawn out of a hat. Next are repetitions of *five*, concluding with the dreadful statistic of one million addicted babies. The argument commits the fallacy of the unknowable statistic, not once but four times, seeking to establish as factual guesswork calculations for a hypothetical situation with too many variables and unknowns.

Sometimes it is more obvious that the statistics quoted could not have been gathered. Consider these examples:

- Two-thirds of all thefts are never detected.
- Two-thirds of all people have thoughts they would never admit to.
- Loss in federal taxes from those who barter instead of paying cash for goods is one billion dollars annually.

Class Discussion

What questions would you ask about the statistics used in the following statements?

1. Only 106 of an estimated 895 cases of rape that occurred in New England last year were reported.

2. "If it is elitist to say that 30 percent of the American people are dumb in the sense of uninstructed, then I'm an elitist. But it's true." (William F. Buckley Jr.)

3. It is a known fact that people use only 10 percent of their actual potential.

4. "If the *Roe* v. *Wade* decision remains in force until the beginning of the twenty-first century, our nation will be missing more than 40 million citizens, of whom approximately 8 million would have been men of military age." (from "It's 'Life for a Life'" quoted in "Notes from the Fringe," *Harper's* magazine, June 1985)

5. "Milk consumption is probably the number-one cause of heart disease. America's number-one killer. By the time the average American reaches the age of fifty-two, he or she will have consumed in milk and dairy products the equivalent cholesterol contained in one million slices of bacon. In 1994 the average U.S. citizen consumed 26 ounces of milk and dairy products per day. One 12-ounce glass of whole milk contains 300 calories and 16 grams of fat. Beer is taking a bad rap— protruding stomachs on overweight people should be called milk bellies, not beer bellies." *Milk: The Deadly Poison* by Robert Cohen, *Earth Island Journal*, winter 1997–98)

Contradictions and inconsistencies is the fallacy of making claims or offering evidence that contradict the conclusion.

Used with permission of David Sipress.

Contradictions and Inconsistencies

In this Sipress cartoon, the daughter surprises her mother by pointing out her use of two contradictory claims or premises. The daughter implies that one of the claims must be false. A similar example of reasoning from contradictory claims or **premises** follows:

> All men are equal; it is just that some are more equal than others.

The second cartoon by Stivers illustrates other kinds of contradictions. He shows us the incongruity between our fears of irradiated foods, yet our susceptibility to clever marketing. He also plays with the incongruity of having irradiated foods aggressively promoted given their usual low-profile marketing.

In political life we often hear and see contradictions, not only within statements, but between different articles or speeches, and sometimes between statements and actions. If you want to please as many people as possible, discrepancies often become the consequence. Here is an example of contradictions within statements:

> "Of course I cannot approve of hecklers disrupting my opponent's speeches. However, I would also say that in a democracy, they also have the right to be heard as much as the speaker."

Used with permission of Mark Stivers.

The example illustrates what is more commonly known as double-talk. Obviously, in a democracy no one can be heard if speakers are capriciously interrupted by others. This is also known as the fallacy of misapplied generalization: all people who want to speak should be allowed to speak in a democracy. Hecklers are people who want to speak. Therefore, hecklers should be permitted to (prevent others from speaking in order to) speak themselves.

Here is an example of a contradiction expressed in a television program interview:

> VETERAN: "We should not send American troops to Bosnia. No American life is ever worth being shed on foreign soil."
>
> INTERVIEWER: "But didn't you fight in World War II when American soldiers died both in Europe and Asia?"
>
> VETERAN: "Well, that war was fought because one man was trying to control the world. Hitler took over Europe and his allies controlled the East."

In this case, the veteran is not able to defend his claim that "No American life is ever worth being shed on foreign soil." He makes a generalization that allows for no exceptions. Then when the interviewer confronts him with the way in which his own military career contradicts this generalization, he assumes, rather than proves, that the motives of Hitler made World War II an exception.

Class Discussion

List the contradictions you find in the following examples.

1. I love mankind; it's just that I can't stand people.
2. "The Nuclear Regulatory Commission has imposed strict penalties for employees at nuclear plants found to be stoned from illicit drug use on the job; but no penalties were prescribed for workers discovered to be drunk at the nuclear controls. Asked about the more lenient approach to alcohol, an NRC spokesman said: 'The implications are less horrendous.' But a meltdown by any other name . . ." (David Freudberg, KCBS Radio, February 16, 1990)
3. I'd like to order one Big Mac, large fries, twenty pieces of chicken nuggets, two apple pies, one chocolate sundae, and a diet coke, please.
4. "Capital punishment is our society's recognition of the sanctity of human life." (Sen. Orrin Hatch, R-Utah)
5. "The more killing and homicides you have, the more havoc it prevents." (Richard M. Daley, former mayor of Chicago)

The Loaded Question

> **The loaded question** is the fallacy of using a biased question in order to obtain a predetermined result.

Loaded questions occur often in polls, as discussed earlier, in order to create a bias toward a certain answer: "Do you believe pornography should be brought into every home through television?" We are all familiar with the loaded questions "Have you stopped beating your wife?" and "Are you still a heavy drinker?" In such cases, the guilt is assumed and not proven. Any reply to the question traps the respondent into either an admission of guilt or a protest that could be interpreted as a guilty defense. Loaded questions are related to the fallacy of circular reasoning (begging the question), where conclusions are asserted without evidence or premises to support them.

Class Discussion

Which of the following are loaded questions and which are not?

1. Do you feel that a school voucher program should be permitted to dismantle U.S. public schools?
2. Where did you hide the murder weapon?
3. When are you going to stop asking me so many silly questions?
4. Are you going to be good and do what I say?
5. Would you eat British beef?
6. What do you think about the new brain research that says that emotional stability is more important than IQ in determining success in life?
7. Forty-three percent of U.S. grade school children are reading below grade level. Why? Is this because they are not learning phonics?
8. "What will you do on the day you discover our number one brand of arthritis medication?" (Ad with picture of a woman running along a beach.)

The False Analogy

> **The false analogy** is the fallacy of basing an argument on a comparison of two things that may have some similarities, but also significant differences that are ignored for the sake of the argument. (The Greek word *analogos* means according to ratio.)

As you learned earlier, an analogy is a form of reasoning in which two things are compared to one another. A good analogy often compares some abstract principle that is difficult to understand to a concrete familiar experience in order to make the abstract principle clearer. A good or sound analogy must compare two things or ideas that have major parallels in ratio. If one uses the analogy of a pump to explain the heart, the heart does not have to physically look like a metal pump with a handle, but it should at least function on the same principles. Here is an analogy taken from physics about the nature of subatomic particles: "If you wish to understand subatomic particles, think of them as empty space that is distorted, pinched up, concentrated into point-like ripples of energy." Here the appearance is the essential parallel that permits a visualization of something invisible to us.

In a false analogy essential parallels are missing that are either overlooked or willfully disregarded.

"Well, it's too bad that so many Indians had to die as America was settled by the white men. But you can't make an omelet without breaking a few eggs."

How do we decide whether an analogy is a true or a false one? A recommended technique is to first write out the equation that the analogy offers; then under two columns headed Similarities and Differences, compare the chief characteristics of each:

Claim "There is no convincing evidence to show that cigarette smoking is harmful. Too much of anything is harmful. Too much applesauce is harmful." (cigarette manufacturer)

Equation Too much cigarette smoking = too much applesauce

When we see the equation, we sense that something is not right here. For a further check, make a list of the similarities and differences between each. If the differences far outweigh the similarities, you have a false analogy.

Similarities	Differences
1. ingested into body	1. one ingested through lungs first and is not digestible
	2. one a food, other not a food
	3. one addictive, other not
	4. both don't affect body and consciousness in same way
	5. no evidence applesauce causes cancer, but evidence that cigarette smoking does

Discovery Exercise

Evaluating Analogies

Use the procedure just demonstrated to analyze the analogies that follow:

1. "There are no grounds for the claim that the incidence of lung cancer is higher in this county because of the presence of our oil refineries. Cancer can be caused by all kinds of things. People don't stop eating peanut butter because it causes cancer, do they?" (biologist working for an oil refinery)

2. Who is the endangered species? The spotted owl or the loggers of the Northwest?

3. We welcome immigrants because our country needs them the way old soil needs new seeds.

4. "Nature is cruel. It is our right to be cruel as well." (Adolf Hitler)

5. Vote for the incumbent. Don't change horses in midstream!

Class Discussion

Rate the following examples as either good analogies or false analogies and tell why:

1. Drug testing of employees could be an infringement of civil liberties but is necessary for the preservation of law and order. For the sake of survival, we often have to agree to the invasion of privacy and to limitations on free speech. Baggage and passengers must pass through metal detectors before boarding air-crafts. It is illegal to joke about explosives or guns when passing through security to board an air-plane.

2. "People and politicians, who really . . . don't know enough about the issue of acid rain have been brainwashed by the media and environ-mentalists into believing that we, in Ohio, are the primary cause of the decay. The biggest killers of human life in the U.S. are automo-biles, cigarettes and alcohol. Yet none of these products have been banned. Americans, and no Americans more than we in the coal fields, want to see a healthy and safe environment for all generations to come, but we just cannot accept legislation such as this without a scientific basis." (Rep. Douglas Applegate, D-Ohio, speaking against a House bill to require federally mandated emission limitations on the largest sources of sulphur dioxide)

3. "If you take a piece of meat and throw it in a pack of hungry dogs, they are going to kill each other over it. If you don't have any oppor-tunities available to you, and something that can make you easy money (selling crack cocaine) comes up, what are you going to do?" (Paris, Oakland rap artist)

4. Measuring a country's health by measuring its gross domestic prod-uct is rather like measuring a person's health by how much medical care he buys. Thus, a person who just had bypass surgery and can-cer radiation treatments would be considered healthy.

5. Reporter: "Should Americans be required to register their weapons as they register their cars?"

   Senator McCain: 'A gun and a car are not the same. How about treat-ing a gun like an elephant? They are not the same.'"(*Los Angeles Times*, 8/17/99)

> **False cause** is the fallacy of claiming a causal connection between events without reasonable and sufficient evidence to support the claim.

False Cause

Inductive reasoning is used to speculate about cause or to determine cause. The criminal justice system uses inductive reasoning to gather evidence to determine guilt or innocence. Faulty reasoning about causality can result in the arrest and conviction of an innocent person or the release of a guilty person. A trial presents evidence to the jury as support for causality in a crime.

False cause is a fallacious argument that insists on a causal connection between events that cannot reasonably be connected. False cause can also be an interpretation that is over-simplistic. Sometimes false cause reasoning can be ludicrous, as may be seen in the little Sufi teaching stories about Nasrudin, which were designed to teach good thinking habits:

> Nasrudin was throwing handfuls of crumbs around his house.
> "What are you doing?" someone asked him.
> "Keeping the tigers away."
> "But there are no tigers in these parts."
> "That's right. Effective, isn't it?"
> "When I was in the desert," said Nasrudin one day, "I caused an entire tribe of horrible and bloodthirsty Bedouins to run."
> "However did you do it?"
> "Easy. I just ran, and they ran after me."
> Two men were quarrelling outside Nasrudin's window at dead of night. Nasrudin got up, wrapped his only blanket around himself, and ran out to try to stop the noise. When he tried to reason with the drunks, one snatched his blanket and both ran away.
> "What were they arguing about?" asked his wife when he went in.
> "It must have been the blanket. When they got that, the fight broke up."

From Idries Shah, *The Exploits of the Incomparable Mulla Nasrudin.* New York: Dutton, 1972. Reprinted with permission of The Octagon Press, Ltd., London.

Blaming the wrong target is one kind of false cause. More frequent are those false causes that vastly oversimplify a situation, such as scapegoating. The term *scapegoating* refers to the ancient practice of offering ritual sacrifices for the appeasement of some god or some person or persons. Although we may now think sacrificing maidens on altars to the gods is barbaric, scapegoating rituals still abound in our personal, political, and social lives. In this Toles cartoon, we see the absurdity of blaming and punishing one person for TV violence.

Used with permission of the Universal Press Syndicate. © 1994 *The Buffalo News.*

Another version of false cause is known in Latin as *post hoc ergo propter hoc*, meaning "after this, therefore because of this." The post hoc fallacy reasons in a childlike way that because one event happened after another event, the second was caused by the first.

- First my cat ate a mouse, and then she had kittens. The mouse gave her the kittens.

- He committed the murder, but he couldn't help himself because he was under the influence of a sugar high after eating Twinkies.

Sometimes false cause arguments center around debates on the chicken-or-the-egg questions. The fictional character Nasrudin confuses us with his own confusion as he attributes his running away from the Bedouins the cause of their running after him. Here are two contrasting chicken-or-egg arguments:

- "The violence on the home screen follows the violence in our lives." (Del Reisman, president, Writers Guild of America)

- "Violence on TV is definitely a cause of the growing violence in our lives. It presents violence as an appropriate way to solve interpersonal problems, to get what you want out of life, avenge slights and insults and make up for perceived injustices." (Leonard D. Eron, professor of psychology)

Finally, all the examples of causal reasoning discussed here contain a traditional Western assumption that causality is linear, that one effect must result from one cause. More recently, science has begun to use *systems thinking* to study causality in a manner that is ecological, taking the widest perspective of context, of interrelated parts and cycles. Systems thinking is concerned with the way in which the wolf's predator role is actually essential to the health of the deer. Systems thinking reveals the folly of attempting to protect the deer by killing off the wolves, which leads in turn to an overpopulation of the deer, overgrazing, and eventually mass deer starvation. When we engage in systems thinking, we avoid the fallacious reasoning that results from the assumption that causality is always single and linear.

Class Discussion

False or questionable cause is a fallacy that is often found in political arguments. Analyze the following statements. Decide if you agree or disagree that they are examples of the fallacy of false cause and state why.

1. "As a white nation, we wish to survive in freedom in our own fatherland, and we demand to be governed by our own people. South Africa must retain the fatherland given us by God." (Andries P. Treurnicht, leader, far-right conservative party, South Africa; speech reported in *Los Angeles Times*, May 28, 1986)

2. The corruption of American youth has been caused by rock and roll music. Its rhythms and lyrics, together with the role models provided by its singers and musicians, have encouraged experimentation with drugs and promiscuity.

3. "Forests are disappearing fast from the world. Loss has been caused by logging, mining, the development of energy, farming, pollution. During the 1980's 8 percent of the world's tropical forest was lost. Another 10 percent of all the world's forests may be lost by 2050." (*Atlas of the Future*, 1998)

4. Americans buy Japanese cars, cameras, and stereos because they are unpatriotic. An ad campaign appealing to their patriotism could reverse this trend.

5. State-sponsored affirmative action, bilingual education, and multiculturalism are promoting dangerous levels of ethnic group tensions and conflicts.

> **Slippery slope** is the fallacy of arguing, without sufficient proof, that if one event is allowed to occur, a disastrous and uncontrollable chain reaction will result. The slippery slope appeals to fear and urges agreement on the basis of a situation that contains too many variables and unknowns

The Slippery Slope

The slippery slope is another fallacy that deals with causation. In this case the claim is made that permitting one event to occur would set off an uncontrollable chain reaction. In politics this is also called the domino theory: if one country falls, so will all the rest like a line of dominoes. This argument was often given as a reason that the United States should stay in Vietnam: if Vietnam fell to the communists, China would take over the rest of Asia.

The same argument was also cited for the U.S. presence in El Salvador: if El Salvador fell to the guerrillas, so would all of Central America and Mexico, thus jeopardizing the whole Western hemisphere. Although these were predictions of a possible scenario, as arguments they were fallacious in that they urged agreement on the basis of logic for a position that contained many variables and unknowns.

Here are three examples of arguments built on the fallacy of the slippery slope:

- If you offer people unemployment insurance, they will become lazy and expect the government to support them for life.

- Sex education in the schools leads to promiscuity, unwanted pregnancies, and cheating in marriages.

- "If you teach critical thinking in an Indian university, the young people would go home and question, then disobey their parents. Their families would quarrel and break up. Then they would question their bosses and everyone else. The next thing you know the whole country would fall apart." (comment made by a University of Bombay professor)

Class Discussion

Which of the following arguments are slippery slopes?

1. If I get Internet access, I'll start surfing the web, and the next thing you know, I will be up all night like the kids, drinking Pepsis and eating pop tarts, totally addicted to hopping around from site to another, wasting my time, ending up an unshaven geek and junkie.

2. "I cannot support the 'three strikes and you're out' law. This tough position denies all possibility of change in people. With it, we turn our backs on these people, saying they can never get better. Thus we buy into a cycle of hate and fear in a total rejection of love and compassion, locking ourselves up in our houses of fear just like we lock up the prisoners in our prisons." (Letter to editor, *San Francisco Chronicle*, 11/30/97)

3. "A widely acclaimed and disturbing study out of the University of Vermont has shown a 'decline in emotional aptitude among children across the board.' Rich and poor, East Coast or West Coast, inner city or suburb, children today are more vulnerable than ever to anger, depression, anxiety—a massive emotional malaise. The result is that boys who can't control their emotions later commit violent crime; girls who can't control emotion don't get violent, they get pregnant." (Daniel Goleman, author of *Emotional Intelligence*. New York: Bantam, 1995)

4. "Considering the legal union of same-sex couples would shatter the conventional definition of marriage, change the rules that govern behavior, endorse practices which are completely antithetical to the tenants of all the world's major religions, send conflicting signals about marriage and sexuality, particularly to the young, and obscure marriage's enormously consequential function—procreation and child-rearing." (William Bennett, "Leave Marriage Alone, *Newsweek*, 6/3/96)

SUMMARY:
FALLACIES OF INDUCTIVE REASONING

1. Hasty generalization is the fallacy of basing a conclusion on insufficient evidence.

2. The either-or fallacy, or false dilemma, is an argument that oversimplifies a situation, asserting that there are only two choices, when actually other alternatives exist.

3. The questionable statistic is the statistic that is either unknowable or unsound.

4. Inconsistency in evidence is the fallacy of offering evidence that contradicts the conclusion.

5. The loaded question is the use of a biased question that seeks to obtain a predetermined answer.

6. The false analogy is a comparison of two things that have some similarities but also significant differences that are ignored for the sake of the argument.

7. False cause is the fallacy of claiming there is a causal connection be-tween events without reasonable evidence to support the claim.

8. The slippery slope is the fallacy of claiming without sufficient proof that permitting one event to occur would lead to a chain reaction that could not be stopped. It ignores the many variables or unknowns in the situation.

QUIZ: FALLACIES OF INDUCTIVE REASONING

Part I

Identify the following ten arguments in this section by name, either as *NF* for *not fallacious*, or as Slippery Slope, False Cause, Questionable Statis-tic, Inconsistencies, and Contradictions.

_____ 1. All riders on the buses in a Boston suburb now pay for their rides with special credit cards. All buses are equipped with electronic scanners that record account number, route, time, and date. The American public is being conditioned for the complete Big Brother totalitarian surveillance of the future.

_____ 2. The French and the German objections to importing British beef are purely a matter of their stubborn national pride. There is no reason to fear this beef would infect any of their citizens with mad cow disease.

_____ 3. "Any regulations that dampen corporate profits in the oil and coal industries will backfire because environmental preserva-tion depends heavily on the health of the U.S. economy. The richer the U.S. is, the more it can help poorer countries with their pollution problems." (Public representative of a coalition for oil and coal users)

_____ 4. Some people hesitate to have children because of the expense and trouble. The trouble of having children is entirely sec-ondary to the blessing.

_____ 5. Legalizing marijuana would reduce the price by 50 percent.

_____ 6. The reason that I didn't stop for that light was that it was two o'clock in the morning.

_____ 7. If the baseball players start using drugs, then so will the man-agers, and the next thing you know all the games will be fixed and baseball will no longer be a real American sport.

_____ 8. You should never lie to your partner, although a little white lie never hurts.

_____ 9. "A CIA internal investigation found no evidence linking its employees, agents or operatives with the crack cocaine epidemic in the U.S. and no connection between the agency and three men at the center of that drug trade. The findings . . . dispute allegations made by the San Jose Mercury News in 1996 of a CIA link to cocaine trafficking in California. The CIA released the first of two volumes of conclusions reached by agency Inspector General Frederick Hitz, who led a 17-member team that reviewed 250,000 pages of documents and conducted 365 interviews." (Associated Press release, 1/30/98)

_____ 10. All people are equal but some deserve more privilege.

Part II
Identify the remaining ten arguments as Nonfallacious, Loaded Question, False Analogy, Hasty Generalization, Either-Or Fallacy.

_____ 11. "More than any other time in history, mankind faces a crossroads. One path leads to despair and utter hopelessness. The other, to total extinction. Let us pray we have the wisdom to choose correctly." (Woody Allen, "My Speech to the Graduates")

_____ 12. Son, listen, you talk like I do, you even like the same food I do. You're gonna become a musician like me. Don't fight it!

_____ 13. Are you still getting into the movies without paying?

_____ 14. Either you stay in school or you get a job. You can't do both!

_____ 15. One of the major causes for the rapid growth of the European population in the nineteenth century was the improvement of medical knowledge.

_____ 16. When you do laundry, you should separate light clothing from dark clothing and wash each separately, since light articles streak dark ones, and the dark items bleed on the light ones.

_____ 17. "Is two months' salary too much to spend for something that lasts forever?" (ad for diamonds)

_____ 18. I was turned down in two job interviews. I guess I just don't have what it takes.

_____ 19. Are you still fooling around with that guy?

_____ 20. Women, like rugs, need a good beating occasionally.

Detecting Fallacies in an Argument

So far, you have been examining fallacies in examples abstracted from the context in which they appear. The purpose of this assignment is to give you the opportunity to search for fallacies in an argument, to extract them, and to discuss the manner in which they affect the argument as a whole. This is a research assignment. *You will need to find a short argument: a good source for short arguments that often contain fallacies is letters to editors.* Comb newspapers and magazines for your choice, and photocopy it to accompany your analysis. Your parameters will be as follows:

1. *Topic*: Fallacies in an argument.
2. *Approach*: Critical analysis.
3. *Form*: Exposition and argumentation. Identify the fallacies involved and explain whether they affect or do not affect the soundness of the argument.
4. *Length*: Two typed pages, plus a one-page photocopy of the argument.

READING

"HE FIXES RADIOS BY THINKING!"

Richard P. Feynman

Richard Feynman (1918–1988) won the Nobel Prize in 1965 for his work in quantum electrodynamics. During World War II he was one of the Manhattan Project team who developed the atomic bomb. The excerpt is taken from his memoirs, Surely You're Joking, Mr. Feynman!, *which became a best-seller. Using a casual colloquial style, Feynman talks about a period in his boyhood in the late 1920's when he was around 12 years old and growing up in a small town outside of New York City. Throughout his life, Feynman found playful delight in using his mind to solve problems. As you read this simple story, notice how he was using the inductive method to solve a problem.*

One day I got a telephone call: "Mister, are you Richard Feynman?" 1
  "Yes." 2
  "This is a hotel. We have a radio that doesn't work, and would like it repaired. We 3
understand you might be able to do something about it."
  "Yes, we know that, but we'd like you to come over anyway." 4

It was a hotel that my aunt was running, but I didn't know that. I went over there **5**
with—they still tell the story—a big screwdriver in my back pocket. Well, I was small,
so *any* screwdriver looked big in my back pocket.

I went up to the radio and tried to fix it. I didn't know anything about it, but there **6**
was also a handyman at the hotel, and either he noticed, or I noticed, a loose knob
on the rheostat—to turn up the volume—so that it wasn't turning the shaft. He went
off and filed something, and I fixed it up so it worked.

The next radio I tried to fix didn't work at all. That was easy; it wasn't plugged in **7**
right. As the repair jobs got more and more complicated, I got better and better, and
more elaborate. I bought myself a milliammeter in New York and converted it into a
voltmeter that had different scales on it by using the right lengths (which I calculated)
of very fine copper wire. It wasn't very accurate, but it was good enough to tell whether
things were in the right ballpark at different connections in those radio sets.

The main reason people hired me was the Depression. they didn't have any **8**
money to fix their radios, and they'd hear about this kid who would do it for less. So
I'd climb on roofs to fix antennas, and all kinds of stuff. I got a series of lessons of
ever increasing difficulty. Ultimately I got some job like converting a DC set into an
AC set, and it was very hard to keep the hum from going through the system, and I
didn't build it quite right. I shouldn't have bitten that one off, but I didn't know.

One job was really sensational. I was working at the time for a printer, and a man **9**
who knew that printer knew I was trying to get jobs fixing radios, so he sent a fellow
around to the print shop to pick me up. The guy is obviously poor—his car is a complete wreck—and we go to his house which is in a cheap part of town. On the way,
I say, "What's the trouble with the radio?"

He says, "When I turn it on it makes a noise, and after a while the noise stops **10**
and everything's all right, but I don't like the noise at the beginning."

I think to myself: "What the hell! If he hasn't got any money, you'd think he could **11**
stand a little noise for a while."

And all the time, on the way to his house, he's saying things like, "Do you know **12**
anything about radios? How do you know about radios—you're just a little boy!"

He's putting me down the whole way, and I'm thinking, "So what's the matter **13**
with him? So it makes a little noise."

But when we got there I went over to the radio and turned it on. Little noise? *My* **14**
God! No wonder the poor guy couldn't stand it. The thing began to roar and wobble—
WUH BUH BUH BUH BUH—A *tremendous* amount of noise. Then it quieted down
and played correctly. So I started to think: "How can that happen?"

I start walking back and forth, thinking, and I realize that one way it can happen **15**
is that the tubes are heating up in the wrong order—that is, the amplifier's all hot, the
tubes are ready to go, and there's nothing feeding in, or there's some back circuit feeding in, or something wrong in the beginning part—the RF part—and therefore it's making a lot of noise, picking up something. And when the RF circuit's finally going, and
the grid voltages are adjusted, everything's all right.

So the guy says, "What are you doing? You come to fix the radio, but you're only **16**
walking back and forth!"

I say, "I'm thinking!" Then I said to myself, "All right, take the tubes out, and re-   **17**
verse the order completely in the set." (Many radio sets in those days used the same
tubes in different places—212's. I think they were, or 212-A's.) So I changed the tubes
around stepped to the front of the radio, turned the thing on, and it's as quiet as a
lamb; it waits until it heats up, and then plays perfectly—no noise.

When a person has been negative to you, and then you do something like that,   **18**
they're usually a hundred percent the other way, kind of to compensate. He got me
other jobs, and kept telling everybody what a tremendous genius I was, saying, "He
fixes radios by *thinking!*" The whole idea of thinking, to fix a radio—a little boy stops
and thinks, and figures out how to do it—he never thought that was possible.

Discussion Questions

1. How does Feynman use inferences to search for a cause for the problem?
2. How does he use enumeration?
3. How does he formulate and test his hypothesis?
4. How is the hypothesis confirmed?

CHAPTER 12

Deductive Reasoning

How Do I Reason from Premises?

Used with permission of John Jonik.

When we use our eyes, we can see the contradiction between the situation and the deductive reasoning used by the insurance agent. The agent's logic is based on a false hidden assumption.

What is that assumption?

The study of deductive reasoning, called logic, shows us how to take such a statement and break down its thought structure; when we can do that, we can begin to see its strengths and weaknesses.

This chapter will explain the fundamental standards that govern deductive reasoning. It will introduce you to logic's basic vocabulary and explain the interplay of deduction and induction in our thinking. However, this chapter only attempts to serve as a preliminary to the complex subject of logic; hopefully it will encourage you to learn more by taking a college logic course.

Discovery Exercises

What Is Deductive Reasoning?

Using at least two dictionaries, look up the terms *deduction*, *deductive logic*, and *reasoning*. Then write out in your own words a definition of deductive reasoning.

Evaluating Deductive Arguments

Study the following short deductive arguments. Which of these seem to you to be based on good reasoning and which do not? Explain the basis for your decision in each case.

1. America believes all people should be free. Therefore, whenever America intervenes in the politics of other countries, it is in order to make them free.

2. God made men to serve women. Therefore, men should obey their women.

3. Warts are caused by touching toads. This child has a wart on her finger. This child has touched a toad.

4. "The Supreme Court's Miranda ruling (giving defendants the right to have a lawyer present during questioning) is wrong and only helps guilty defendants. Suspects who are innocent of a crime should be able to have a lawyer present before police questioning. But the thing is you don't have many suspects who are innocent of a crime. That's contradictory. If a person is innocent of a crime, then he is not a suspect." (Attorney General Edwin Meese, quoted in the *Oakland Tribune*, October 6, 1985)

5. If she had been the last person to leave the house, she would have locked the door. However, the door was unlocked. Therefore, she was not the last person to leave the house.

6. If the temperature goes below freezing, the orange crop will be lost. The temperature went below freezing. The orange crop will be lost.

Now write down your answers to the following questions in preparation for class discussion:

1. Which of the preceding arguments contain statements that are false?
2. In the examples with the false statements, are the inferences nevertheless reasonable?
3. Are there any that may contain true statements but seem illogical in their reasoning?
4. Are there any that contain statements that are true and seem well reasoned?
5. Can you infer any rules for deductive reasoning from what you have learned here?

ABOUT DEDUCTIVE REASONING

Deduction is taught through the study of formal logic, or the science of good reasoning.

> **Deduct** is from the Latin *deducere*, to lead away. In deductive reasoning we infer, or lead away, from a general principle in order to apply that principle to a specific instance.
>
> **Logic** is the science of good reasoning. Both **inductive logic** and **deductive logic** are concerned with the rules for correct reasoning.

We learn *deduction* through the study of formal logic. It is called *formal* because its main concern is with creating *forms* that serve as models to demonstrate both correct and incorrect reasoning. Unlike induction, where an inference is drawn from an accumulation of evidence, deduction is a process that reasons from a series of carefully worded statements. These statements are about relationships between classes, characteristics, and individuals. The first statement is typically about all or some members of a class. You will notice that these statements seem obvious, even childlike, in their simplicity:

All humans are mammals.

Jane is a human.

Jane is a mammal.

All horses are herbivorous.

This animal is a horse.

This animal is herbivorous.

All cats are night animals.

This creature is a cat.

This creature is a night animal.

In these examples, the first statement is about all members of a class; here the classes were

- humans
- horses
- cats

The second statement identifies something or someone as belonging to that class:

- Jane is a human.
- This animal is a horse.
- This creature is a cat.

At this point, the two statements lead to an inference that becomes the conclusion:

- Jane is a mammal.
- This animal is herbivorous.
- This creature is a night animal.

Here you will notice that the conclusion is inevitable. The only inference one could possibly draw from the two statements "all humans are mammals" and "Jane is a human" is that Jane is a mammal. Compared to the inductive hypothesis, which always remains open, the deductive conclusion is unavoidable. The only objective of deductive reasoning is drawn from a correct inference from a group of claims. And that inference is a final conclusion.

Nevertheless, deduction often begins with a generalization that has been derived from inductive reasoning. Such is the generalization "All horses are herbivorous." This is a conclusion based on inductive observations repeatedly confirmed.

Deduction also works with generalizations not necessarily derived from inductive reasoning. For instance, it can begin with a belief:

Horses are not humans.

Indeed, deduction starts with any statement that makes a claim. And a claim, which is an assertion about something, can be worked with logically, regardless of whether the claim is true or not. This is possible because deduction's main concern is not with sorting out evidence and searching for truth; its main concern is studying implications. The focus of deduction is on logic, or the rules of reasoning. Nevertheless, the truth of a statement is important in logic, and the objective of deductive reasoning is to arrive at conclusions that are true.

To summarize, the purpose of deductive logic is to help us reason well with the information we have already acquired. It offers us models, guidelines, and rules for correct reasoning that can lead us to draw reliable conclusions from that information. Thus *logic*, by definition, is the science of reasoning or the science of inference.

One major barrier to understanding logic is its technical vocabulary. This vocabulary is needed to identify the components of deductive arguments and to convey its rules for correct usage. However, for the student, the task of mastering this terminology can seem formidable at first. Therefore this chapter will divide the study of this terminology into two segments: the basic vocabulary and the more advanced terminology that describes the rules for valid reasoning in terms of the formal fallacies.

THE BASIC VOCABULARY OF LOGIC

The following are key terms needed to understand the basics of logic: *argument, reasoning, syllogism, premise* (major and minor), *conclusion, validity, soundness*. They will be defined and explained one at a time.

Argument

Arguments appear in both deductive and inductive forms. As we have seen before, deductive arguments involve one or more claims (also called *premises*) that lead to a conclusion:

All people who flirt are showing interest in someone.
She is flirting with me.

She is showing interest in me.

Inductive arguments also establish claims through reasoning based on experiences, analogies, samples, and general evidence. Compare the following example to the preceding deductive argument:

> **Argument**: a set of claims in the form of reasons offered to support a conclusion.
>
> **Reasoning** is to draw conclusions, judgments, or inferences from facts or premises.

This woman seeks me out whenever she sees me having my lunch on the lawn. She comes over and sits next to me. She asks for a sip of my coffee.

She teases me and makes me laugh a lot.

She is interested in me.

Reasoning

Both arguments use reasoning to arrive at a conclusion. *Reasoning* draws conclusions, judgments, or inferences from facts or premises. Deductive arguments start with one or more premises and then investigate what conclusions necessarily follow from them.

If I flirt back, she will encourage me further.

I will flirt back.

She will encourage me further.

Sometimes these premises appear in long chains of reasoning:

(1) If I am nice to her, she'll think I'm flirting.

(2) And if she thinks I'm flirting, she'll come on to me.

(3) And if she comes on to me, I'll have to reject her.

(4) And if I reject her, she'll be hurt.

(5) I don't want her to be hurt.

Therefore, I won't be nice to her.

Syllogism

Logic arranges deductive arguments in standardized forms that make the structure of the argument clearly visible for study and review. These forms are called *syllogisms*. We do not speak in syllogisms, which sound awkward and redundant, but they are useful constructs for testing the

> **Syllogism** is a standardized form that makes the structure of a deductive argument visible. A syllogism consists of two premises and a conclusion. From the Greek *syllogismos*, a reckoning together.

reliability of a deduction according to the rules of logic. We have already considered a number of syllogisms, beginning with

All humans are mammals.

Jane is a human.
_____

Jane is a mammal.

Premises and Conclusion

> **Premises** are the claims made in an argument that provide the reasons for believing in the conclusion. In a syllogism, they usually appear as two statements that precede the conclusion. Premise comes from the Latin *praemittere*, to set in front.

A syllogism usually contains two premises and a conclusion. The first statement is called the *major premise* and the second is called the *minor premise*.

Major premise: No flirts are cross and mean.

Minor premise: This man is cross and mean.
_____

Conclusion: This man is not a flirt.

In deduction, the reasoning "leads away" from a generalization about a class to identify a specific member belonging to that class—or it can lead to a generalization about another class. In the preceding deductive argument, the major premise states a generalization about the class of flirts: none is cross and mean. The minor premise asserts that a specific individual does not belong to that class: *because* he is cross and mean, he *must* not be a flirt. Between the word *because* and the word *must* lie the inference and the logic. Such reasoning can be checked for reliability by outlining the argument in the strict form of the syllogism.

Validity

The standards used for testing reliability are based on some specific rules that determine an argument's *validity* and *soundness*. Validity has to do with reasoning and soundness with both reasoning and truth. A deductive

---

A **valid** argument is one in which the conclusion has been correctly inferred from its premises. Valid comes from the Latin *valere*, to be strong.

Deductive logic is concerned with the rules for determining when an argument is valid.

Sound A sound argument is one *in which the reasoning is valid and the premises are both true*. The word "sound" comes from an Old English word, *gesund*, which means healthy.

---

argument is said to be valid when the inference follows correctly from the premises:

> All fathers are males.
>
> Jose is a father.
> _____
> **Jose is a male.**

Here, because Jose is a member of the class of fathers, and all members of that class are males, it follows logically that Jose must be a male. Moreover, even if we only *assume* these premises are true, it is entirely reasonable to infer that he is a male. We do not have to ponder the matter any further.

On the other hand, invalid reasoning might proceed like this:

> All fathers are males.
>
> Jose is a male.
> _____
> **Jose is a father.**

In this argument, the first two premises do not imply this conclusion. The conclusion may be true or it may not be true. But we cannot make that determination on the basis of this line of reasoning. Even if we are certain that all fathers are males and that Jose is a male, we still cannot infer from these premises alone that Jose is a father. The conclusion could be false. Therefore, this argument is invalid. (More examples of validity and invalidity follow on pages 357–359.)

Soundness

Standards for judging arguments refer not only to correct reasoning but also to the truth of the premises. These standards are conveyed by the use of the word *sound*. Now, a deductive argument is sound if the premises are true and the argument is valid. A sound argument is one that uses

---

An argument can be valid even though the premises are not true.

The rule for determining soundness is that if the premises are both true and the argument is valid, the conclusion cannot be false.

---

true premises and correct reasoning to arrive at a conclusion that cannot be false. By this definition, this argument is sound because its premises are true and its reasoning valid:

All fathers are males.

Jose is a father.

Jose is a male.

However, the argument given below is not sound because, although it contains true premises the reasoning is invalid, leading to a conclusion that could be false.

All fathers are males.

Jose is a male.

Jose is a father.

So far, so good. Yet there are some other complexities. An argument can be valid *even though the premises are not true*:

All men are fathers.

All fathers are married.

All men are married.

In this case, if all men are fathers and all fathers are married, then it would follow that all men are married. Yet common sense tells us that both the premises and the conclusion are false. Here is another such example:

All fathers are baseball fans.

All baseball fans like beer.

All fathers like beer.

Thus, the logician makes a distinction between the truth or falseness of statements in an argument and the validity of the entire argument. The term *sound* is used to signify that an argument is valid and the premises are true. The rule for determining soundness is that if the premises are both true and the argument is valid, the conclusion cannot be false.

To summarize, deductive arguments can be structured into a unit for the purposes of simplicity, clarity, and analysis according to standards for good reasoning. Now with this understanding of the basic vocabulary of logic, we can now consider in greater detail the unit of deductive argumentation—the syllogism.

STANDARDIZED FORMS IN SYLLOGISMS

Syllogisms have been discussed as a standardized form that makes the structure of a deductive argument visible. A syllogism presents claims concerning a relationship between the terms (classes or individuals) given in the premises and the conclusion. A standardized language, which makes these relationships clearer, has also been developed for phrasing the premises within the syllogism. Here are six examples of the standardized phrase forms used for expressing premises:

1. All _____ are _____.
2. All _____ are not _____.
3. No _____ are _____.
4. Some _____ are _____.
5. Some _____ are not ____.
6. If _____, then _____.

You will notice that in the first four forms, each of the blanks offers space for an adjective or noun phrase and each is connected by forms of the verb *to be* expressed in the present tense. This simplification allows a reduction of everyday language into verbal equations, thus making the task of argument analysis much easier. Now let's see how natural language has to be translated into this kind of standardized language for use in syllogisms. Compare the following translations:

Natural Language	Standardized Language
1. Ice cream always tastes sweet.	1. All ice cream food is sweet food.
2. Cats never take baths.	2. No cats are animals that take baths.
3. Some airlines have lower fares.	3. Some airlines are lower-fare transport.
4. f she is over seventy, she must be retired.	4. If she is a person over seventy, then she is a retired person.

Discovery Exercise

Practice in Constructing Syllogisms*

1. Rephrase each of the following sentences into a standard major premise. Then see if you can add a minor premise and a conclusion.

   (a) All horses have exactly four legs.

   (b) Everybody's got needs.

   (c) All coal miners are poor.

   (d) Many eighteen-year-olds are college students.

   (e) No eight-year-old is a college student.

   (f) Lead is poisonous.

   (g) If he's late, he'll be sorry.

2. Fill in the blanks in the following sentences so that all the syllogisms are valid:

   (a) All horses are mammals.

       All _____ are animals.

       All horses are animals.

   (b) All horses are living things.

       All living things are things that reproduce.

       All _____ are things that reproduce.

   (c) No sheep are creatures that sleep in beds.

       This creature is sleeping in a bed.

       Therefore, this creature is _____.

   (d) If today is Tuesday, this must be Belgium.

       This is _____.

       This must be _____.

3. Choose the correct answer in each of the following cases:

   (a) All beers are liquids.

       It therefore follows that:

       (1) All liquids are beers.

       (2) No liquids are beers.

       (3) Neither (1) nor (2).

   (b) Florida is next to Georgia.

       Georgia is next to South Carolina.

       (1) Florida is next to South Carolina.

*For the style and method used in these exercises, I am indebted to Matthew Lipman's *Philosophical Inquiry: An Instructional Manual to Accompany Harry Stottlemeier's Discovery*, 2nd ed. Published by the Institute for the Advancement of Philosophy for Children, Upper Montclair, N.J., 1979.

(2) South Carolina is next to Florida.

(3) Neither (1) nor (2).

(c) Ruth is shorter than Margaret.

Margaret is shorter than Rosie.

It therefore follows that

(1) Ruth is shorter than Rosie.

(2) Margaret is shorter than Ruth.

(3) Ruth is taller than Rosie.

WHAT SYLLOGISMS DO

The logician accomplishes a number of purposes by standardizing the phrasing of arguments in syllogism:

(1) to clarify the claims of the premises;

(2) to discover and expose any hidden premises;

(3) to find out if one thought follows logically from another.

Each of these objectives will be discussed in turn.

What Is Said and Is It True?

Of course he is cheating on his wife. Doesn't he always come home late?

You will sense that something is wrong with this statement, but where do you begin? Here is where a syllogism helps out, since a translation into a syllogism exposes an argument's structure:

All wife cheaters are people who always come home late.

He is a person who always comes home late.

He is a wife cheater.

Here the syllogism reveals a stereotype or hasty generalization in a *hidden major premise*. The words *all* and *always* make the claim in this hidden premise false. We could easily point out exceptions, such as "wife cheaters" who are punctual or loyal mates who work late. But in addition, *wife cheater* is an ambiguous term. What actions constitute wife cheating? The second premise also contains the vague terms *always* and *late*, which could be exaggerations. What does *late* mean? One minute or four hours? Does this mean *late* according to one person's expectations or according to a mutual agreement? Then there is the vague term *always*. If the person accused came home early only once, the generalization would not hold. Thus, although the reasoning may be valid, the argument's use of vague terms and false generalizations makes it unsound.

Now, let's consider another example.

Our guest is Japanese. We had better cook rice rather than potatoes for dinner.

Here is the syllogism that such reasoning is based upon.

No Japanese is a potato eater.

Our guest is Japanese.

Our guest is not a potato eater.

The syllogism shows the reasoning is valid, but again the major premise, which had been hidden, is revealed as containing too broad a generalization to be true. For this reasoning, the conclusion is uncertain. Therefore, the argument is unsound.

Here is another example. You may have seen this claim on billboards:

Milk is good for everybody.

Because the billboard supplements this claim with attractive happy people, you may well conclude that you should remember to drink more milk. However, a syllogism will reveal some hidden aspects in this claim worth studying. First there is the ambiguity of the word *good*. *Good* has at least two meanings in this context: healthy and tasty. But a syllogism cannot function with words that have double meanings. In poetry, double meanings are effective. But in arguments, double meanings can be manipulative: they encourage assumptions and escape accountability. If the milk cooperative that paid for the ad was sued, its attorney could claim in court that the company was not claiming that its product was healthy, but only tasty.

Nevertheless, suppose you assume that *good* means healthy in this case. You would write out the syllogism thus:

People who drink milk are people made healthy.

I am a person who drinks milk.

I am made healthy.

Thus if you assume that the premises are true, the reasoning is valid. But when you want to know whether the argument is sound, you must ask questions to test the truth of the generalization in the major premise. Are there exceptions that would challenge its universality? What if my brother is allergic to milk? What about nutritionists who say that cow's milk is good only for cows? Again, as this syllogism shows, we have a false generalization, leading to an uncertain conclusion and therefore the whole is an unsound argument.

Is There a Hidden Premise?

A major advantage of using syllogisms is that they reveal hidden premises—as you found in the major premises of the preceding examples. Consider the following examples where questionable hidden premises appear in both the minor premises and conclusions. Note how the form of the syllogisms requires that they be exposed.

1. Senator Jones is a Democrat. Expect him to tax and spend.

    All Democrats are taxers and spenders. (hidden premise)
    Senator Jones is a Democrat.
    _____

    Senator Jones is a taxer and spender.

2. Do I think he's sexy? Well, he drives a truck, doesn't he?

    All those who drive trucks are sexy. (hidden premise)
    He drives a truck.
    _____

    He is sexy. (implied conclusion)

    In the second example, both the major premise and the conclusion are hidden or implied. This often happens in advertising slogans:

    The burgers are bigger at Burger John's!

    As a syllogism, this reads as follows:

    Bigger burgers are better burgers. (hidden premise)
    Burger John's burgers are bigger.
    _____

    Burger John's burgers are better. (hidden conclusion)

    You should buy Burger John's burgers. (additional hidden conclusion)

Is the Reasoning Correct?

Here the logician is concerned with validity or correct reasoning. Here is an argument that is obviously valid:

    She is either married or single.
    She is married.
    _____

    Therefore, she is not single.

    The inference expressed in the conclusion automatically follows: she cannot be both married and single at the same time. Therefore if she is married, she cannot be single. The syllogism makes the validity of the reasoning transparent.

Now let's consider first a more difficult example, one that appeared in a discovery exercise that opened this chapter.

> Suspects who are innocent of a crime should be able to have a lawyer present before police questioning. But the thing is you don't have many suspects who are innocent of a crime . . . If a person is innocent of a crime, then he is not a suspect.

Here is a translation of that statement into a syllogism:

All innocents are not suspects.

You are a suspect.

You are not innocent.

In this case the reasoning is valid if you assume that both of the premises are true. It follows logically that if the categories of innocents and suspects are mutually exclusive, then if you belong in the category of suspects, you cannot belong in the category of innocents. However, the argument is not sound, since the major premise "All innocents are not suspects" is not true even though the minor premise "You are a suspect" might be. Now let's take this argument a step further.

If you are a suspect, then you are questioned by the police.

You were questioned by the police.

You are a suspect.

Here, even if both the major and minor premises were true, the conclusions could still be false. Suspects are not the only category of individuals questioned by the police. Police also question witnesses and bystanders. (Moreover, the implication of this line of reasoning is that if you are a suspect, you are guilty. But policemen do not make judgments about guilt or innocence; this is the function of a judge and jury.) However, simply on the basis of what is stated, the argument is invalid because the conclusion "You are a suspect" is not implied by its premises. Suspects are not necessarily always questioned by the police and not all people questioned by the police are suspects. The illogic of the reasoning here can be recognized intuitively, but the syllogism exposes the way in which it is illogical.

Logicians have a number of rules for helping them determine whether or not an argument is valid. However, understanding these rules requires knowledge of further technical terms, which will be discussed in the next section of this chapter.

Exercise

Reviewing the Vocabulary of Logic

Work with a classmate to write down the definitions you can remember of the following words: *logic, reasoning, deductive* and *inductive reasoning, premise* (major and minor), *conclusion, argument, syllogism, true statement, valid argument, sound argument, hidden premise, hidden conclusion*. When you have finished, compare your definitions with the chapter summary on pages 371–372. If there is a discrepancy, or if any of the definitions are still unclear to you, review the text discussion until you can explain the term to your partner.

THE FORMAL FALLACIES

> **A formal fallacy** is an error that may be detected in the **form,** or the structure, of a deductive argument. **An informal fallacy** is an error that can only be detected through an analysis of the **content** of the argument.

In the two preceding chapters, we learned to identify twenty informal fallacies, or arguments that contained false or deceptive or manipulative statements, all of which involved errors in the *content*, or the thoughts and views expressed. These informal fallacies occur in both inductive and deductive reasoning. The term "informal" is used to distinguish them from the formal fallacies, or errors in the *forms* of deductive reasoning. These errors, however, only become apparent to us when we have a knowledge of the rules for constructing them correctly within the syllogism. Moreover, in order to understand these rules, we need to extend our technical vocabulary.

A few of the most common formal fallacies are demonstrated in the following pages. They will first be presented to you in the form of Discovery Exercises without the use of any technical terminology. Here you will be given an opportunity to study models of valid and invalid reasoning to see if you can discover the rules for yourself. Then, afterwards, you should be better prepared to understand the technical terms used to explain these rules that will be defined in a following section of this chapter.

Discovery Exercises

Looking at Some Formal Fallacies

The following are four sets of valid and invalid arguments. To the right of, or below them, are diagrams that show the relationship described by the syllogism. The asterisk (*) in these diagrams shows that at least one case or example can be found in the area where the asterisk appears. Study each set and see if you can explain to a class partner why some syllogisms are valid whereas others are not. When you have finished all four sets, go on to the next exercise, where you will match these models to other syllogisms.

Set 1

A. Valid argument

All rock stars are musicians.

Ricky Martin is a rock star.

———————————————

Ricky Martin is a musician.

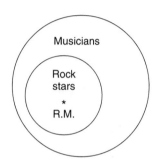

B. Invalid argument

All rock stars are musicians.

Ricky Martin is a Puerto Rican.

———————————————

Ricky Martin is a musician.

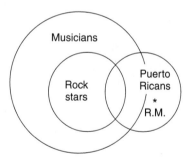

C. Invalid argument

All rock stars are musicians.

Ricky Martin is a musician.

———————————————

Ricky Martin is a rock star.

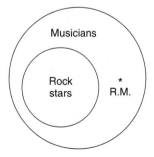

Set 2

A. Valid argument

No rock star is an amateur.

Mariah Carey is a rock star.

Mariah Carey is not an amateur.

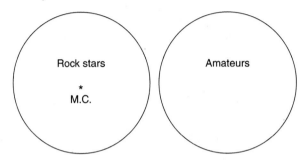

B. Invalid argument

No rock star is an amateur.

Louis Armstrong is not a rock star.

Louis Armstrong is an amateur.

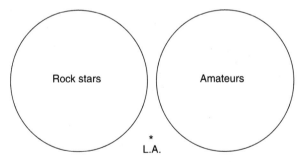

Set 3

A. Valid argument

All rock stars are musicians.

Some women are rock stars.

Some women are musicians.

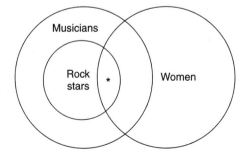

B. Invalid argument

All rock stars are musicians.

Some women are rock stars.

_____

All women are musicians.

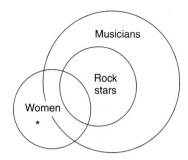

Set 4

A. Valid argument

If Ricky Martin is a rock star, then he is a musician.

Ricky Martin is a rock star.

_____

Ricky Martin is a musician.

B. Invalid argument

If Jay-Z is a rock star, then he is a musician.

Jay-Z is not a rock star.

_____

Jay-Z is not a musician.

C. Invalid argument

If Jay-Z is a rock star, then he is a musician.

Jay-Z is a musician.

_____

Jay-Z is a rock star.

Identifying Formal Fallacies by Type

To check how well you understand the various types of fallacies illustrated in the preceding exercise, see if you can match the invalid arguments that follow to the same type of argument in the preceding sets. After you have assigned them the numbers of their corresponding models, consult the answers supplied at the end of this exercise.

1. If I ever finish writing this autobiography, I shall die.

   I will not finish writing this autobiography.

   _____

   I will not die.

2. If he is a right-winger, then he is a Republican.
   He is a Republican.

   He is a right-winger.

3. No person is perfect.
   Our pet is not a person.

   Our pet is perfect.

4. All Democrats are big spenders.
   Some women are Democrats.

   All women are big spenders.

5. All women are big spenders.
   Peggy is a stockbroker.

   Peggy is a big spender.

6. All communists are atheists.
   Oscar is an atheist.

   Oscar is a communist.

Answers

1. 4B   2. 4C   3. 2B   4. 3B   5. 1B   6. 1C

TECHNICAL NAMES FOR THE FALLACIES
WITH THEIR RULES

By completing the Discovery Exercises, you have probably begun to get a feel for the different types of fallacies that are possible in syllogisms, and the reason they render arguments invalid. We want to look now at the names of some common formal fallacies, as they were illustrated in the Discovery Exercises. At the same time, we will learn the rules that govern them. The five formal fallacies we will consider here are the following:

- The fallacy of four terms
- The fallacy of the undistributed middle term
- The fallacy of faulty exclusions

- The fallacy of illicit distribution
- The invalid hypothetical syllogism

The Fallacy of Four Terms

A **term** refers to nouns or classes used in the premises or the conclusion.

A syllogism must have exactly three terms, each used twice.

Item 1B in the first Discovery Exercise exemplified the fallacy of four terms:

All rock stars (middle term) are musicians (major term).

Ricky Martin (minor term) is a Puerto Rican (fourth term).

Ricky Martin (minor term)[subject] is a musician (major term) [predicate].

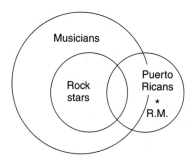

Here the word *term* refers to nouns or classes used in the premises and the conclusion, all of which are *propositions*. The fallacy of four terms violates this rule: *a syllogism must have exactly three terms, each used twice.*

This invalid syllogism has a fourth term—Puerto Rican—and only the term *musician* is used twice. Syllogisms must have the following:

- a *major term*, appearing in the predicate of the conclusion,
- a *minor term*, appearing as the subject of the conclusion, and
- a *middle term* that links the major and minor terms in the premises but does not appear in the conclusion.

The proposition that states Ricky Martin is a Puerto Rican does not show his relationship to the class of rock stars. Therefore, the first premise that all rock stars are musicians is not shown to be applicable to him, and thus the conclusion that he is a musician cannot be inferred from the information given.

In the diagram (called an Euler diagram) the asterisk (*) marks the minor term. (In this case, R.M. for Ricky Martin.) In the case of invalid arguments, the asterisk here shows us that R.M. could be outside the class of those Puerto Ricans who are also musicians and rock stars. Thus the conclusion may be false here even though the premises are true. Ricky Martin may be a Puerto Rican, but he is not necessarily for that reason a rock star and a *musician.*

The Fallacy of the Undistributed Middle Term

> **The middle term must be distributed at least once**.
>
> **A term is distributed when the term refers to every member of a class denoted by the term**.

The fallacy of the undistributed middle term was illustrated by invalid argument 1C earlier:

All rock stars (major term) are musicians (middle term).

Ricky Martin (minor term) is a musician.

_____

Ricky Martin is a rock star.

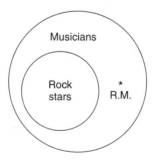

The rule that applies to the fallacy of the undistributed middle term is: *the middle term must be distributed at least once.*

Now what does the expression "distributed" mean in this context? In logic, a term is distributed when the term refers to every member of a class denoted by the term.

In our example the major term (rock stars) is distributed but the middle term (musicians) is not. Not all members of the class referred to by "musicians" are not covered by some assertion. If one says, "All rock stars are musicians," or "No rock stars are musicians," the term *rock stars* is distributed; one knows in both cases that *all rock stars* are either included or excluded from the larger category of musicians. However, one does not know this much about the term musicians itself.

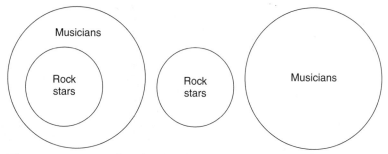

There are many other kinds of musicians besides rock stars. Therefore, although the premise states that Ricky Martin is a musician, he could be in the subclass of musicians who are not rock stars. We cannot reason on the basis of this information alone that Ricky Martin is a rock star. This is more apparent if we substitute for his name the name of a musician who is clearly not in actuality a rock star, but a rap artist.

All rock stars are musicians.

Missy Elliott is a musician.

Missy Elliott is a rock star.

The Fallacy of Faulty Exclusions

The fallacy of faulty exclusions was exemplified by invalid argument 2B:

No rock star is an amateur.

Louis Armstrong is not a rock star.

Louis Armstrong is an amateur.

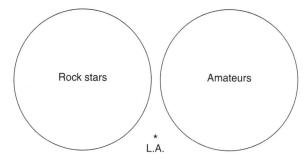

> **A syllogism must have either no exclusion or two exclusions, one of which must appear in the conclusion.**
>
> **Any term distributed in the conclusion must be distributed in the premise in which it appears.**

This is the rule violated by this fallacy: *a syllogism must have either no exclusion or two exclusions, one of which must appear in the conclusion*. In the invalid argument, we have two exclusions in the premises but none in the conclusion.

Exclusions are terms that are not included in a class; *inclusions* are terms that are part of another class. In the valid argument that follows, the term *rock stars* is excluded from the class of amateurs, and in the conclusion Mariah Carey is excluded from the class of amateurs. The syllogism thus follows the rule.

No rock star is an amateur.

Mariah Carey is a rock star.

_____

Mariah Carey is not an amateur.

In contrast, the reasoning in the opening invalid argument is obviously false. If no rock star is an amateur, then any person who is not a rock star may be, or may not be, an amateur.

The Fallacy of Illicit Distribution

The fallacy of illicit distribution was exemplified by invalid argument 3B:

All rock stars are musicians.

Some women are rock stars.

_____

All women are musicians.

This is the rule violated by this fallacy: *any term distributed in the conclusion must be distributed in the premise in which it appears*. In our invalid argument, *women* is distributed in the conclusion, but not in the premise in which it appears.

Illicit distribution means that a term cannot claim to represent part of a class in one of the premises and then the entire class in the conclusion. In our example, we know from the minor premise that *some women are rock stars*, but although we know all rock stars are included in the class of musicians, we cannot conclude from this line of reasoning that all women are.

The Invalid Hypothetical Syllogism

> **The minor premise must affirm the antecedent** (what comes before) or **deny the consequent** (what comes after).

The invalid hypothetical syllogism was exemplified by invalid arguments 4B and 4C:

If Jay-Z is a rock star, then he is a musician.

Jay-Z is not a rock star.

Jay-Z is not a musician.

If Jay-Z is a rock star, then he is a musician.

Jay-Z is a musician.

Jay-Z is a rock star.

This is the rule violated by this fallacy: *the minor premise must affirm the antecedent or deny the consequent*. In the first example, the minor premise denies the *antecedent*; in the second, the minor premise affirms the *consequent*.

Here the antecedent is the statement "If Jay-Z is a rock star," which comes before the consequent, or "he is a musician." The rule says that the minor premise (or second premise) either must claim that the antecedent is true or has occurred or must assert that the consequent is false. If, on the other hand, the minor premise denies the antecedent or affirms the consequent, then it offers information beyond the scope of the major premise. If we say Jay-Z is not a rock star, and therefore is not a musician, we are mocking the syllogism. The same is true if we claim that he is a musician and therefore a rock star.

Reviewing the Vocabulary of Formal Fallacies

If you wish to study this subject more closely, review the definitions of the following words by writing down what you can remember of them: *major, middle,* and *minor terms, major premise, minor premise, exclusion, inclusion, distributed, illicit distribution, affirm, deny, antecedent, consequent.* Check your definitions against the text.

Class Discussion

Write down your answers to the following questions, in preparation for a class discussion.

1. The following syllogisms illustrate the fallacy of four terms. Identify the fourth term for each.

    (a) All artists are art lovers.

    Raymond is a painter.
    _____

    Raymond is an art lover.

    (b) An expert swimmer could cross the channel.

    Nadine is a swimmer.
    _____

    Nadine could cross the channel.

2. These syllogisms have faulty exclusions. Explain how this happens in each case.

    (a) A good pianist would not make that mistake.

    Loretta is not a good pianist.
    _____

    Loretta would not make that mistake.

    (b) Gold investors are not wise.

    Mr. Hill is not wise.
    _____

    Mr. Hill is a gold investor.

3. These syllogisms have undistributed middle terms. Explain why.

    (a) Some baseball players are drug-takers.

    Peter is a baseball player.
    _____

    Peter is a drug-taker.

    (b) All Woody Allen's films are funny.

    Never Been Kissed is funny.
    _____

    Never Been Kissed **is by Woody Allen.**

4. This syllogism illustrates illicit distribution. Explain why.
    (a) All who go on picnics are happy.

    Many children go on picnics.
    _____

    All children are happy.

5. The following are invalid hypothetical syllogisms. Explain why.
   (a) If he studied, he passed; but because he didn't study, he didn't pass.
   (b) If she studied, she passed. She did pass. Therefore she studied.

SUMMARY: THE INTERPLAY OF INDUCTIVE AND DEDUCTIVE REASONING

Whether we are aware of it or not, our thinking moves back and forth between inductive and deductive reasoning all the time.

Inductive and deductive thinking are not isolated modes. They interweave in our minds constantly throughout the day as we confront both serious problems, such as environmental degradation, and mundane ones, such as daily transportation. Let's consider the latter for illustration purposes. Suppose you have an apartment in the Boston suburb of Needham and commute to Boston University downtown. You have a car, but you prefer to commute by the T train. You made this decision by reasoning deductively:

All public trains are faster than car transport.

I want faster-than-car transport.

I will take public trains.

Suppose this reasoning stands you in good stead for some months. However, one morning you arrive at the station to find an unusually large crowd of people waiting there. You wonder what this means. Are there fewer trains today? Has there been an accident? Will we all be delayed? You form hypotheses through inductive reasoning. You seek to test each hypothesis by searching for more information from those waiting. But all they can tell you is that their expected train has been delayed. Therefore you reason deductively:

Delayed trains are unpredictable in schedule.

This train is delayed.

This train is unpredictable in schedule.

Then you reason inductively again in order to decide whether to wait or go home and get your car. You weigh the unknown factor of when the train will arrive against the time it might take to go home, get your car, and drive through heavy traffic. You decide that, although the delayed train *may* make you late, driving your car will *certainly* make you late.

CHART OF COMPARING INDUCTIVE AND DEDUCTIVE REASONING

Inductive Reasoning	Deductive Reasoning
Specific to general (usually, not always).	General to specific (usually, not always).
Purpose is to reach a conclusion for testing and application.	Purpose is to reach a conclusion that cannot be false.
Discovers new laws.	Applies known laws to specific circumstances.
Thinking guided by theories, observation, research, investigation. Data are collected and analyzed. Sudden insights and unexpected discoveries can occur.	Thinking makes inferences about the relationship of claims.
Tests verify measure of truth in terms of reliability, accuracy, applicability, and their ability to be replicated.	Truth of premises is assumed or determined by reasoning.
Conclusion is a *hypothesis* or statement of probability.	Conclusion is final.
Indicator words that show this is a hypothesis: *probably, improbable, plausible, implausible, likely, unlikely, reasonable.*	Indicator words that show this is a conclusion: *necessarily, certainly, absolutely, definitely.*
Even if the premises are true, the conclusion is only probable and could even be false. More data or major changes could call for further testing.	If the premises are true, or assumed to be true, and the reasoning valid, the conclusion cannot be false.

And so, on the basis of your estimate of time and probability, you choose to wait in the station. Since you made this decision carefully, you will not get upset if the train is delayed for yet another half hour. And you can be glad you did not impulsively run home to get your car without thinking the matter through, only to feel your blood pressure go up when you found yourself stuck in traffic with the train passing you by. You made a conscious decision to take the consequences with responsibility.

In college we study deduction and induction separately both for convenience and because of their different structures and standards. But whether we are aware of that or not, in our thinking we move back and forth between the two modes all the time. Yet, taking conscious notice of how our thinking moves between the deductive and inductive mode has considerable advantages; we then can purposely direct our thinking to the mode that is more appropriate. This awareness also allows us to use the different standards of the two modes to evaluate what we are doing. Thus, we have a greater probability of arriving at better decisions. And even if we are disappointed with the results of our decisions, at least we know that we made a conscious choice that we can learn from.

WRITING APPLICATION

Writing a Deductive Argument

Write a deductive argument within the following parameters:

1. *Topic*: Application of an aphorism, or wise saying, to life.
2. *Approach*:
    (a) Explain the aphorism.
    (b) Define its terms.
    (c) Illustrate it.
    (d) Choose to agree, disagree, or both.
3. *Form*: Exposition and argumentation—explain, justify, and persuade through logic, reasoning, and example.
4. *Length*: Concise two pages.
5. *Subject*: Choose your own aphorism or select one of the following:
    (a) "The most savage controversies are about those matters as to which there is no evidence either way." (Bertrand Russell)
    (b) "Man is a social animal who dislikes his fellow men." (Delacroix)
    (c) "Competition brings out the best in products and the worst in people." (David Sarnoff)
    (d) "Failure is when you stop trying."
    (e) "People get the kind of government they deserve."
    (f) "Prejudice is never easy unless it can pass itself off as reason." (William Hazlitt)
    (g) "Life was meant to be lived, and curiosity must be kept alive. One must never, for whatever reason, turn his back on life." (Eleanor Roosevelt)

BUILDING ARGUMENTS

DEDUCTION

Great Spirit, my Grandfather, you have said to me when I was still young and could hope, that in difficulty I could send a voice four times, once for each quarter of the earth, and you would hear me.

Today I send a voice for a people in despair.

To the center of the world you have taken me and showed the goodness and the beauty and the strangeness of the greening earth, the only mother, and there the spirit-shapes of things, as they should be, you have shown me, and I have seen. At the center of the sacred hoop you have said that I should make the tree to bloom.

With tears running, O Great Spirit, my Grandfather—with running eyes I must say now that the tree has never bloomed. A pitiful old man, you see me here, and I have fallen away and done nothing. Here at the center of the world, where you took me when I was young and taught me; here, old I stand and the tree is withered, my Grandfather.

Again, and maybe the last time on earth, I recall the great vision you sent me. It may be that some little root of the sacred tree still lives. Nourish it, then, that it may leaf and bloom and fill with singing birds. Hear me, not for myself but for my people; I am old. Hear me, that they may once more go back into the sacred hoop and find the good road and the shielding tree.

(Black Elk, shaman of the Oglala Sioux, 1912)

Exercise

1. Can a prayer or prophecy be a deductive argument?
2. Write out the syllogism behind the reasoning of the first statement (major premise, minor premise, and conclusion). Also write out the syllogism behind the narrator's reasoning about the sacred hoop.
3. Write a deductive argument in which you make a claim about Black Elk's prayer. Support it with premises and draw a conclusion.

Speeches of the Native Americans offered in this series were taken from Virginia Irving Armstrong, *I Have Spoken.* Athens, Ohio: Swallow Press/Ohio University Press, 1989.

CHAPTER SUMMARY

1. Deductive reasoning is the process of starting with one or more statements called premises and investigating what conclusions necessarily follow from these premises.

2. Deduction is the subject of formal logic, whose main concern is with creating forms that demonstrate reasoning.

3. Logic has its own technical vocabulary. The following is a summary of the definitions of key terms:

Argument	A conclusion supported by reasons.
Claim	A true or false assertion about something.
Conclusion	The last step in a reasoning process. It is a judgment based on evidence and reasoning, an inference derived from the premises of an argument.
Hidden Premise or Conclusion	A premise or conclusion that is not stated but implied in an argument. When the argument is cast in a syllogism, the missing premise or conclusion is expressed.
Hypothesis	A theory, explanation, or tentative conclusion derived through inductive reasoning based on a limited view of facts or events.
Inductive Reasoning	The process of noting particular facts and drawing a conclusion about them.
Logic	The science of reasoning; also called the science of inference.
Premises	Statements, evidence, or assumptions offered to support a position.
Propositions	Claims, statements, or assertions used in an argument. They can be either premises or conclusions and either true or false statements.
Reasoning	The act or process of arriving at conclusions, judgments, or inferences from facts or premises.
Sound	A sound argument is one in which all the premises are true and the reasoning is valid.
Syllogism	The formalized structure of a deductive argument, usually written, in which the conclusion is supported by two premises.
True	Corresponding to reality.

Valid   A valid argument is one in which the reasoning
                      follows correctly from the premises to the conclu-
                      sion. An argument can be valid without the prem-
                      ises or conclusion being true.

4. The standardized language of syllogisms allows a reduction of every-
    day language into verbal equations.

5. Syllogisms allow logicians to determine what is being said, to iden-
    tify hidden premises, and to find out if the argument makes sense.

6. Deductive and inductive reasoning are not isolated pursuits but are
    mentally interwoven both in major and mundane problem solving.

7. It is possible to infer the rules of valid and invalid reasoning from the
    study of models.

8. A study of formal fallacies involves an understanding of such words
    as *major, middle,* and *minor terms; exclusion, inclusion, distributed, il-
    licit distribution, affirm, deny, antecedent, consequent;* and *major and
    minor premise.*

CHAPTER QUIZ

Rate the following statements as *true* or *false*. If you decide the statement
is false, revise it in the simplest manner to make it read true.

_____ 1. A premise is a reason given to support a conclusion.

_____ 2. Syllogisms are used in logic because logicians like to make
           their knowledge arcane, or hidden and secret.

_____ 3. Logic is less concerned with truth than with whether one state-
           ment follows reasonably from another.

_____ 4. Reasoning occurs only in deduction—not in induction.

_____ 5. A generalization reached through induction can become a
           premise used in a deductive syllogism.

_____ 6. "All homeowners are taxpayers. He is a property owner. There-
           fore, he is a taxpayer." This is a valid argument.

_____ 7. "Bloodletting reduces fever. This patient has fever. This patient
           needs bloodletting." This syllogism shows valid reasoning al-
           though both premises may not be true.

_____ 8. "White-skinned people are superior to dark-skinned people.
           Therefore, it is the manifest destiny of white-skinned people
           to rule dark-skinned people." No country would ever accept
           such fallacious reasoning as this.

State whether the reasoning in each of the following syllogisms is correct or incorrect:

_____ 9. "If the two parties agree, then there is no strike.
The two parties agree.

Therefore, there is no strike.

_____ 10. "If the two parties agree, then there is no strike.
There is no strike.

Therefore, the two parties agree.

_____ 11. "If the two parties agree, then there is no strike.
The two parties do not agree.

Therefore, there is a strike.

_____ 12. "If the two parties agree, then there is no strike.
There is a strike.

Therefore, the two parties do not agree.

After you have decided, compare your answers to those given here. Explain why these answers are correct.

9. correct 10. incorrect 11. incorrect 12. correct

READINGS

THE DECLARATION OF INDEPENDENCE
Thomas Jefferson

Based on a clear line of deductive reasoning, this great historical document written in 1776 is also an enduring work of literature. Jefferson begins by stating some "self-evident truths," or axioms, which set off a revolution and formed the ideological basis for the laws of a new government. This document can be studied as a structure of reasoning in four parts. Given below are the first and last parts. Notice as you read how they function as the major premise and conclusion of an argument.

When in the Course of human events, it becomes necessary for one people to dis- 1
solve the political bands which have connected them with another, and to assume among the powers of the earth, the separate and equal station to which the Laws of Nature and of Nature's God entitle them, a decent respect to the opinions of mankind requires that they should declare the causes which impel them to the separation.

We hold these truths to be self-evident, that all men are created equal, that they 2
are endowed by their Creator with certain unalienable Rights, that among these are

Life, Liberty and the pursuit of Happiness. That to secure these rights, Governments are instituted among Men, deriving their just powers from the consent of the governed. That whenever any Form of Government becomes destructive of these ends it is the Right of the People to alter or to abolish it, and to institute new Government, laying its foundation on such principles and organizing its powers in such form, as to them shall seem most likely to effect their Safety and Happiness. Prudence, indeed, will dictate that Governments long established should not be changed for light and transient causes; and accordingly all experience has shown, that mankind are more disposed to suffer, while evils are sufferable, than to right themselves by abolishing the forms to which they are accustomed. But when a long train of abuses and usurpations, pursuing invariably the same Object evinces a design to reduce them under absolute Despotism, it is their right, it is their duty, to throw off such Government, and to provide new Guards for their future security. Such has been the patient sufferance of these Colonies; and such is now the necessity which constrains them to alter their former Systems of Government. The history of the present King of Great Britain is a history of repeated injuries and usurpations, all having in direct object the establishment of an absolute Tyranny over these States. To prove this, let Facts be submitted to a candid world . . .

We, therefore, the Representatives of the United States of America, in General **3** Congress, Assembled, appealing to the Supreme Judge of the world for the rectitude of our intentions, do, in the Name, and by Authority of the good People of these Colonies, solemnly publish and declare, That these United Colonies are, and of Right ought to be Free and Independent States; that they are absolved from all Allegiance to the British Crown, and that all political connection between them and the State of Great Britain, is and ought to be totally dissolved; and that as Free and Independent States, they have full Power to levy War, conclude Peace, contract Alliances, establish Commerce, and to do all other Acts and Things which Independent States may of right do. And for the support of this Declaration, with a firm reliance on the protection of divine Providence, we mutually pledge to each other our Lives, our Fortunes and our sacred Honor.

Study Questions

1. In the first sentence it is stated that people are entitled by "the Laws of Nature and of Nature's God" to separate and equal stations. What does this mean? Is there any evidence offered to back this claim?
2. Outline the deductive reasoning offered in the second paragraph. Which truths does Jefferson claim to be self-evident? What is the purpose of governments? From where do they derive their power?
3. How does Jefferson anticipate the argument that this kind of reasoning would allow people to overthrow governments "for light and transient causes"?
4. In the last paragraph, in the name of what authorities does he make the declaration?
5. Compare this document, and the reasoning used therein, with two of its offspring, *The Seneca Falls Declaration* written by Elizabeth Cady Stanton (1848)

and *The Universal Declaration of Human Rights* (1948) which was, in large part, authored by Eleanor Roosevelt.

LETTER FROM A BIRMINGHAM JAIL

Martin Luther King, Jr.

This letter was written by Martin Luther King, Jr., in 1963 after his arrest at a sit-in to protest segregation of eating facilities. His actions resulted in a turning point for the civil rights movement in that, in the same year, the Supreme Court ruled that Birmingham's segregation laws were unconstitutional. Notice how in this short excerpt he draws major premises from statements made by authorities and then reasons from these premises.

I would agree with St. Augustine that "an unjust law is no law at all." . . . How does one determine whether a law is just or unjust? A just law is a man-made code that is out of harmony with the moral law. To put it in the terms of St. Thomas Aquinas: an unjust law is a human law that is not rooted in eternal law and natural law. Any law that uplifts human personality is just. Any law that degrades human personality is unjust. All segregation statutes are unjust because segregation distorts the soul and damages the personality. It gives the segregator a false sense of superiority and the segregated a false sense of inferiority. Segregation, to use the terminology of the Jewish philosopher Martin Buber, substitutes an "I-it" relationship for an "I-thou" relationship and ends up relegating persons to the status of things. Hence segregation is not only politically, economically, and sociologically unsound, it is morally wrong and sinful. Paul Tillich has said that sin is separation. Is not segregation an existential expression of man's tragic separation, his awful estrangement, his terrible sinfulness? Thus it is that I can urge men to obey the 1954 decision of the Supreme Court, for it is morally right, and I can urge them to disobey segregation ordinances, for they are morally wrong.

Questions

1. State King's argument in the form of a syllogism.
2. Why do you suppose King chose to refer to the authorities of (Catholic) church philosophers (St. Augustine and St. Thomas Aquinas) as well as a Jewish and Protestant theologian such as Martin Buber and Paul Tillich?
3. Which terms does he define and why?
4. What conclusions does he draw from his premises?
5. Explain how the sound logic of his reasoning makes his argument so compelling.

OBJECTIVES REVIEW OF PART III

After you have finished Part III, you will understand:

Why arguments are supported claims.

How reasons differ from conclusions.

What questions to ask in analyzing arguments.

Why fallacies make arguments deceptive.

Definitions and examples of twenty informal fallacies and five formal fallacies.

The forms and standards of inductive and deductive thinking.

The concepts of empirical reasoning, scientific method, hypothesis, probability, and causal reasoning.

The basic vocabulary of logic.

The functions of the syllogism.

The differences between deductive and inductive reasoning.

How inductive and deductive reasoning interplay in our thinking.

And you will have practice in developing these skills:

Identifying conclusions and separating them from reasons.

Identifying reports and separating them from arguments.

Articulating the question at issue.

Analyzing arguments.

Writing a persuasive argument under the pressure of strong feelings.

Researching and preparing your take-home final.

Evaluating deductive arguments for validity and soundness.

Identifying hidden premises.

Applying different standards to inductive and deductive reasoning.

APPENDIX

The Research Paper

RESEARCH PAPER ASSIGNMENTS IN THIS TEXT

If you have been assigned a research paper due at the end of the semester, you should begin your research by the time you finish Chapter 9 on Arguments. Instructions are provided in this Appendix for two research writing assignments. Each assignment will challenge you to integrate all the critical thinking skills you have learned and apply them to writing about a controversial issue of your own choice. You may be asked to do only the first assignment, an outline analysis of two arguments, or you may be required to write a longer argumentative essay.

This section includes instructions for these two assignments together with suggestions for scheduling and researching. To give you a visual model to follow, a portion of one student sample writing also appears in this section. This sample offers an analysis of one of the two arguments on gun control, which appear in the reading section at the end of Chapter 9.

TWO RESEARCH WRITING APPLICATIONS

FIRST RESEARCH OPTION: ANALYSIS OF TWO ARGUMENTS PRO AND CON ON A RECENT CONTROVERSIAL ISSUE

This assignment can also serve as a final take-home exam since its purpose is to allow you to demonstrate all the knowledge and skills you learned while studying this book. Nevertheless you should begin to prepare for it at least a month before the end of your semester and before you finish reading the text. Indeed, having this assignment as a goal will help you understand the last three chapters even better. Listed below are the skills that this assignment requires. They include being able to do the following:

- Isolate a recent controversial issue.
- Research to find two arguments from two different sources representing two different viewpoints on one debate question related to that same issue.

- Identify the political or social orientation of a viewpoint.
- Select a complete argument, either in full or extracted from a larger article, in order to analyze its structure, strengths, and weaknesses according to standards learned in this text.
- Compare, evaluate, and summarize both arguments, then choose the better argument on the basis of critical thinking standards.
- Follow instructions and communicate your findings clearly.

Instructions for the Argument Analysis Assignment

This assignment is not an essay assignment but an outline analysis of two arguments. A student sample of half of this assignment appears in the latter part of this appendix. Read these instructions first. Then skim through the student sample to see how it serves as a visual model of the outline format you will be using. Finally, return to read the remainder of the guidelines offered here.

Outline Form Used in this Assignment

Offer your complete analysis of each argument one by one. Use the outline topic form that appears below, and follow through all these steps with each argument. A photocopy of each argument you selected to analyze should appear at the end of each outline.

PART I: TITLE PAGE: Write the debate question on the title page followed by your name, the date, your course number, and a short table of contents.

PART II: HEADINGS: At the top of your first page fill in the following information:

1. **The debate question:**
2. **Title:** (of the article or argument, magazine or newspaper)
3. **Date of publication:**
4. **Form:** Argument Pro or Con (This is to test your ability to distinguish an argument from a report.)
5. **Viewpoint:** Label the viewpoint politically or socially.

PART III: BASIC STRUCTURE OF THE ARGUMENT

6. **Conclusion:** State the argument's conclusion using your own words or short quotes
7. **Reasons:** List all the reasons given in the argument to support this conclusion. (Do this in your own words or with short quotes.)

PART IV: CRITIQUE QUESTIONS Review the argument according to the following items. Discuss each fully and systematically. Remember this is not just an exercise in finding flaws; you may find much in the argument to commend.

8. Argument structure: How is the argument structured? Briefly describe and evaluate the way it is put together without getting into too many details. Generalize about its special features and mention how the conclusion and the reasons are presented.

9. Ambiguous or prejudicial words: Are any central words in the argument ambiguous or prejudicial?

10. Fallacies: Does the argument contain any fallacies? If so, identify each fallacy and discuss how each one appears with specific examples.

11. Hidden assumptions: Does the argument make any hidden assumptions? What are they and how do they affect the argument?

12. Missing information: Is any important information missing?

13. Contradictory or false information: Is any information false, irreconcilable, or contradictory?

PART V: FINAL SUMMARY COMPARING THE TWO ARGUMENTS On a final page, summarize the two arguments. Which viewpoint do you find the more persuasive and why? Remember you are not being asked to defend your own viewpoint on this issue but only to show why you find one to be the more persuasive argument.

Total Format

Follow your instructor's directions for presenting your work. You might use a simple notebook, which will consist of from four to six pages of analysis in addition to the photocopied arguments, a title page, and table of contents page, making about ten pages in all. Make clear photocopies of each argument before you attach them to your paper. Take pride in giving your work a professional appearance.

Research Preparation

Choose one topic of recent controversy that interests you. Stimulate your thinking by following the daily news, by browsing in the library or on the Internet, and by studying magazines and newspapers representing different points of view. Remember you are looking for a subject of current controversy—one that will demand more thinking—than a topic that has been around long enough to accumulate a lot of familiar opinions. Let's suppose for instance, that you pick up a recent magazine called *Natural*

Health and notice an article inside on the subject of irradiated foods. You might be surprised to read that Congress is considering a bill that would no longer require irradiated foods to bear prominent labels. Your curiosity might motivate you to find out more about this whole subject. You might first go onto the Internet and type in "irradiated foods" in search engines such as Goggle or Alta Vista. After reading a few recent articles on the subject, both reports and arguments, you might then try a multiple search option such as GoGettem Web Search, which could bring up hundreds of articles to choose from. Should irradiated foods be a current hot news item, you could also go to a library to read such newspapers as *The Washington Post, The New York Times,* and *The Los Angeles Times.* You can also find online web sites for these newspapers where you can search for articles written on irradiated foods during the past year; you could also use their archive for articles published in years past. After making an initial survey of the topic, you could then begin to print out a collection of the best reports and arguments for your research file. Before long you should feel reasonably informed on the topic. The test would depend on whether you know the following:

- What are the main issues or unresolved problems related to irradiated foods?
- What are the arguments pro and con on each issue?
- What are the debate questions being addressed?
- What groups, individuals, or organizations are representing each position?

Suppose the issue of the *safety* of irradiated foods is what interests you most. However, you may decide not to work with this issue, since it would involve technical opinions and speculations. You may then decide to search for pro and con arguments on the *labeling* of irradiated foods; however, as it turns out, you can only find one suitable argument. On the other hand, you have found two good pro and con arguments on the issue of the *need* for irradiated foods. At this point, you decide to select this issue for your research paper. Therefore you formulate the debate question that both of your arguments address: "Do we really need irradiated foods?"

Debate questions are sometimes stated within arguments; sometimes they appear in their headings above pro and con arguments that appear on editorial pages of newspapers. They are spelled out in publications like *Speeches of the Day* or *The Congressional Digest.* Nevertheless, in most cases, you will need to study your argument selections carefully in order to recognize the debate question they are commonly addressing. Here you may need the assistance of the instructor. Before proceeding, you need confirmation that you have formulated your debate question correctly.

(If you want to learn a great deal more about preparing and writing the research paper, refer to the list of handbooks listed on page 383.)

Arguments Not Reports

A second confirmation that you will need concerns your selection of an argument rather than a report. *No matter how much work you do on this assignment, you will not succeed if try to work with reports rather than arguments.* Reports sometimes give short quotes of pro and con arguments; however, what you need are two single coherent arguments written each by one person expressing one person's point of view. If you doubt whether you have an argument or a report, be sure to get your instructor's opinion before beginning this assignment.

Length and Viewpoints of Arguments Selected

Your argument selections should be short, not more than twelve paragraphs. If you want to excerpt your argument from a longer article, photocopy the whole article and attach it to your final paper with a border around the section you choose to analyze. (However, make sure the section you choose is a complete argument in itself.) Newspaper editorials and letters to the editor can also serve as short arguments. If you are working on a political topic, find two different views, such as liberal and conservative, from two different published sources. If you choose a sociological issue, such as physician-assisted suicide, find two different perspectives such as a physician's view, a minister's view, and/or a relative's view.

Scoring for Analysis of Two Arguments

1. Two different arguments (not reports) from two different authors addressing the same issue and taken from two different publications. 20 points

2. Follows the format required; photocopies are attached. 10 points

3. Conclusion and reasons correctly identified; all reasons are listed. 20 points

4. Accurate and insightful critique that addresses: 42 points (7 points each)

Analysis of argument structure
Ambiguous and prejudicial words
Fallacies of reasoning
Hidden assumptions
Missing information and/or false information
Any other pertinent characteristics

5. Final summary that compares the two and chooses the better argument. 8 points

---

SECOND RESEARCH WRITING OPTION:
AN ARGUMENTATIVE ESSAY
WRITING AN ARGUMENTATIVE
RESEARCH ESSAY

Here is an opportunity for you to express and defend your own view in depth on one current controversial issue. You can prepare by completing the previous assignment or by taking up a different issue that you researched independently. This will be a research paper from ten to thirty pages in length, depending on your instructor's specifications.

Preparation Instructions

Prepare to write an argumentative essay by following these steps:

1. Write out fully your own viewpoint on the issue that you have researched for several weeks, either for the previous assignment, or in consultation with your instructor. Write freely without self-censorship for as many pages as it takes to exhaust what you have to say.

2. Now shape your principal claim into a thesis, taking care to choose your key terms carefully. Use clustering as needed.

3. Leaving wide spaces between each statement, outline your support for this thesis in terms of claims and/or evidence.

4. Consult your research file and notes to see what information you have that might be pertinent to use for illustration and support. Take notes on what further research you may need to complete now and as you go along. Make notes on your outline concerning where you need supporting information or quotations. As you organize the data in your research file, remember that you will be quoting or referring to sources in the MLA style of documentation. Use a reference handbook recommended by your instructor for information about the MLA style or consult one of the reference manuals suggested on page 383 of this Appendix. You will need to prepare a "Works Cited" list as well as a bibliography. Therefore as you do your research be sure to record all the citation data you will need in order to save yourself a frantic search the night before your paper is due. You might also want to consult a handbook for more research suggestions or to review the skills of proper summarizing, quoting, and paraphrasing in order not to plagiarize your sources.

5. As you write and revise your outline, note where you need to acquire more evidence or examples and where you already have enough material to write the number of required pages.

6. Keep your outline before you as you write. Tack it up on the wall. Read and reread it to make sure that each part of the essay relates to your thesis. Revise it as needed.

Writing the First Draft

7. Now start to flesh out the skeleton of your outline. Introduce your subject, stating the issue in your first paragraph. Explain why this issue interests you and why it should be of interest to the reader. You might summarize some of the different positions taken on this issue. Then state your position—your thesis or principal claim. Also provide any definitions necessary to explain how you are using your terms.

8. As you write, seek to be as clear as possible. Guide your readers so that they can know exactly what you are doing at each step as you pursue your argument. Read your work aloud to friends to discover what they need to hear to understand you.

9. In the second paragraph or paragraphs give an argument to defend your principal claim, clearly stating your premises and conclusion as well as your evidence.

10. In the paragraph that follows, state any major objection or objections that others might have to your argument. You can counter these with further arguments or evidence.

11. If you think of further criticisms that might be made of your counter argument, reply to these.

12. As you continue to write your draft, decide at some point whether you can fully support your original thesis or whether you might need to modify it. If this should occur, go back to your outline and revise accordingly.

Final Touches

13. When you have finished your final draft, find another good listener. Notice where you are not understood or where, in explaining, you find that you need to say more in writing.

14. Rewrite your work as necessary to improve coherency and correct errors.

Suggested Handbooks for Guidance in Research Writing

1. Hacker, Diana. *A Writer's Reference*, 4th Edition. Boston: Bedford/St. Martin's, 1999.

2. Horner, Webb & Miller. *The Harbrace College Handbook,* 13th Edition. Harcourt College Publishers, 1998.

3. LaGuardia, Dolores, and Hans P. Guth. *The Access Handbook.* Boston: Allyn and Bacon, 2000.

4. Lester, James D. *Writing Research Papers. A Complete Guide,* 9th Edition. New York: Addison-Wesley, 1999.

5. Ruszkiewicz, Hairston, and Seward. SF Writer. New York: Longman, 1999.

Scoring Sheet for Argumentative Essay

1. Thesis is clearly stated with all key terms defined. 10 points

2. Support is adequate and complete in defense of the thesis. 30 points

3. Paper shows the author is well informed on the issue selected. 20 points

4. All citations and bibliography are correctly presented in MLA form. 10 points

5. The argument is persuasive. 10 points

6. Writer is able to summarize, to use quotations, or paraphrase as needed. 10 points

7. No distracting errors in spelling, mechanics, and sentence structure. 10 points

---

STUDENT MODEL PAPER

ANALYSIS OF TWO ARGUMENTS ON THE ISSUE: "DOES THE TRAGEDY AT LITTLETON CALL FOR STRICTER GUN CONTROL?"

Elvira Orozco
Contra Costa College
May 15, 1999

TABLE OF CONTENTS

> *Author's note to the reader: This page shows you a format to use. Part II Argument B with its critique, and Part III the concluding summary, are not included here. Both of the arguments analyzed by Elvira Orozco appear as readings at the end of Chapter 9 on Arguments.*

Argument A: Pro on the Issue

Title: "We Can End These Tragedies: Stop the Guns, Take Responsibility."
Source: *San Francisco Chronicle*
Date: April 26, 1999
Form: Argument
Viewpoint: Michael Bond offers a left liberal perspective on gun control. His credentials suggest that he may have been more conservative in the past when he was a member of the National Rifle Association and a president of an international energy company. In addition, he speaks as a citizen of Littleton, Colorado.

Argument Analysis

Conclusion

"We can rid our country of this horror. . . . We must begin by getting rid of guns."

Reasons

- We can't bring back the dead children from Littleton but we can get rid of guns.
- Guns are "the instruments of the Columbine massacre, and of the school slaughters elsewhere that preceded it, and of those to come."
- Gun manufacturers are flooding the streets with guns.

- Politicians are influenced by gun lobbyists to pass laws that allow "the sale of armor-piercing bullets" such as those that kill our policemen.
- The NRA and the Republican majority in the Colorado legislature have been "pushing" three pro-gun bills.
- Republican House Majority Leader Doug Dean "insanely argued that if teachers had been carrying concealed guns, this tragedy would have been avoided."
- In the approaching NRA national convention in Denver, gun manufacturers will bribe congressmen and persuade them "that guns didn't kill these children."
- "We have had eight school slaughters in less than 40 months. There have been hundreds of lesser incidents—none of which would have been imaginable a generation ago."
- "As a former NRA member, a gun owner and hunter, and one who deeply fears for the future of this country, I suggest:"
- Prohibition of handgun and assault rifle ownership except by police and military.
- Advertisement of guns (and tobacco) should be prohibited.
- Ownership of other guns (rifles and shotguns) should be limited on basis of licensing and tests.
- Political contributions by gun manufacturers should be prohibited.
- The level of violence depicted in the media should be controlled.
- Parents should be prosecuted for the acts of their children.

Critique of the Argument

Brief Description of the Argument's Structure

The argument is divided into three parts. In opening his argument, Michael Bond gives poetic expression to grief and outrage concerning the Columbine High School tragedy. In the first three paragraphs he reinforces the point that there is no way to make up for this tragedy. In the fourth paragraph he states his theme (and conclusion) that remains consistent throughout the remainder of the argument, namely, all we can do is to get rid of the guns to prevent such tragedies from occurring in the future. Then begins the second part of his argument where he offers many reasons to convince the reader that drastic action is needed for stricter gun control. In the final part of his argument he makes 6 recommendations for preventing future gun violence, and he concludes with a clear and concise re-statement of his thesis. The frame of his viewpoint as a Littleton citizen and former NRA member, writing shortly after the tragedy, also lends his argument considerable credibility.

Ambiguous and Prejudicial Words

There are times when the writer depends on prejudicial words rather than reasons. In the third paragraph, he dismisses any idea of reconciliation: "We have had enough 'reaching out' to killers, deranged, the pathogens of our culture." In the same paragraph he speaks of "school slaughters," "fanatic fervor," of automatic weapons "flooding" our streets, of "armor-piercing bullets" killing policemen. He evaluates Doug

Dean's argument as "insane." He uses his imagination: ". . . executives from Ruger, Colt, Remington and all the other merchants of death will pour the free liquor and plan how to buy the next Congressman." He invites them "to walk the blood-soaked, brain-splattered halls of Columbine High." Some might say that he is simply trying to arouse his audience out of their complacency, yet his method is indirect, and thus not entirely fair. Ambiguous words are less evident in the argument. One has to read his closing suggestions carefully to wonder what he means when he asks that "the level" of violence be "controlled." He also speaks vaguely of today's "self-obsessed, emotionally illiterate America."

Fallacies

Appeal to Fear and Pity

The author employs the appeal to fear and pity several times in the argument. One could say he appeals to our pity in order to gain our attention in the first paragraph: "The tragedy in Littleton is grotesque and unimaginable. There is no weeping, no sorrow, no anger that suffices. We cannot bring these precious children back. There is no way to comfort the dead." However, some might argue that he is merely stating the facts which deserve our pity, or at least our serious concern. It is clearer that he is appealing to fear when he says "With fanatic fervor, the gun manufacturers flood our streets with automatic weapons like those that killed my neighbor's children here in Littleton." It is a fact that violence from automatic weapons is growing in our society, and there is just cause for fear about this situation, but he depends here on emotional appeal when he could offer statistics. He also adds to our fears by the way in which he describes the pro-gun laws pending in the Colorado legislature. However, some might say such fear is warranted.

Poisoning the Well

Paragraphs 3, 7, and 15 contain this fallacy. In paragraph 3, he writes "We've done enough 'reaching out' to killers, the deranged, the pathogens of our culture." He is impatient with those who want dialogue rather than action. Then, in paragraph 7 he describes how "In convention hospitality suites, executives from Ruger, Colt, Remington and all other merchants of death will pour free liquor and plan how to buy the next congressman. The argument will be that guns didn't kill these children." Here he seeks to incite prejudice against the gun-manufacturers and prevent them from being heard. Finally, in paragraph 15, he seems to write us all off as "self-obsessed, emotionally illiterate America."

Hasty Generalization

As I just mentioned before, in paragraph 15 he over-generalizes about this society as "self-obsessed, emotionally illiterate." He offers a hasty conclusion without evidence. Are we all self-obsessed and emotionally illiterate? The same may be said of his concluding statement "We don't have to stand around like cattle while our children are killed." While this comparison might be emotionally effective, it is not an entirely true statement.

Hidden Assumptions

First, in paragraph 3, the author claims that this society has had plenty of "dialogue" about violence, has talked too much of "closure after carnage" and "reaching out" to killers. The hidden assumption is that we have been too lenient and understanding and have not taken any concrete steps to stop violence and tragedies like Littleton. Secondly, he assumes, rather than proves, that gun sellers and the gun trade are responsible for the violent crimes and tragedies that are happening in our schools. Thirdly, he assumes that Republican politicians are pro-guns. Fourth he assumes all politicians are corrupted. Fifth, he assumes gun-sellers and corrupt politicians jeopardize the lives of innocent people. All these five hidden assumptions may induce the reader to accept his thesis too readily without realizing that he has not furnished proof for these hidden claims.

Missing Information

The author does not present any statistics about gun crimes, which might have strengthened his argument. In addition, he might have provided a few more details about the pro-gun bills. Another missing element that would have strengthened his argument would have been some description of what he personally witnessed at Columbine High or in the Littleton community. He might also have explained why he resigned from the NRA.

Contradictory Information

There seems to be a contradiction in his recommendations for "getting rid of the guns." He wants a complete ban on ownership of handguns and assault rifles, except by the military and police, and yet he would allow rifles and shotguns to be owned provided some rigorous safeguards are met. He does not explain his reasoning, but seems to assume that rifles and shotguns would not be used as readily against people.

INDEX